# R·O·M·A·N C·O·R·I·N·T·H

# R·O·M·A·N C·O·R·I·N·T·H

## AN ALTERNATIVE MODEL FOR THE CLASSICAL CITY

## Donald Engels

The University of Chicago
• Chicago and London •

**Donald Engels** is associate professor of history at the University of Arkansas at Fayette-ville. He is the author of *Alexander the Great and the Logistics of the Macedonian Army.*

The University of Chicago Press, Chicago 60637
The University of Chicago Press, Ltd., London
© 1990 by The University of Chicago
All rights reserved. Published 1990
Printed in the United States of America

99 98 97 96 95 94 93 92 91 90    5 4 3 2 1

Library of Congress Cataloging in Publication Data

Engels, Donald W.
   Roman Corinth: an alternative model for the classical city /
Donald Engels.
       p.    cm.
   Includes bibliographical references.
   1. Corinth (Greece)—Economic conditions.   2. Corinth (Greece)—
Social conditions.   3. Cities and towns, Ancient.   I. Title.
HC37.E54   1990                                        89-27004
307.76′0938′7—dc20                                     CIP
ISBN 0-226-20870-2 (alk. paper)

What are you? A human being. If you see yourself as something separate, it is natural for you to want to live to old age, to be rich, and to enjoy health. But if you regard yourself as human and as part of some whole, for the sake of that whole you may have to suffer illness, make a voyage and run risks, be in want, and even die before your time. Why then are you vexed? Do you not know that as the foot, if detached, will be longer be a foot, so you too, if detached, will no longer be a part of humanity? For what is a human being? A part of a city; first that of the gods and men and then, that city which is very close to it, the city that is a miniature of the universal one.

Epictetus, Discourses 2.5.25–26

# Contents

*A gallery of photographs follows page 42*

# Acknowledgments

Many people have helped me during the research and writing of this work. James Wiseman first took me to Corinth as an archaeological trainee in 1970. I have benefited from discussions with Charles K. Williams at the site in 1979. I am grateful to the American Philosophical Society for a grant that helped pay for my trip to Corinth in that year.

Since then, I have received much help, advice, and encouragement from numerous individuals, especially Ernst Badian, Michael Jameson, Kurt Raaflaub, and Chester Starr. A special word of thanks to Allan Janik for his encouragement, and help in clarifying and focusing theoretical matters. Special thanks are also due to Theodore F. Brunner of the *Thesaurus Linguae Graecae* for tracking down all Greek references to Corinth.

Above all, I would like to express my gratitude to the two anonymous readers for the University of Chicago Press. Many of their suggestions for improvement have been encorporated into the text. The work is now much stronger than it would have been without their help. I am also grateful to the late Arnaldo Momigliano for his helpful comments, and to my colleagues at the University of Arkansas for providing a rational and democratic environment in which to complete the work.

*Fayetteville, Arkansas*
February 1989

# Introduction:
# The Study of Classical Cities

For many modern readers, Corinth was one of the more interesting places to be in the Roman world. After Rome itself, Athens, Jerusalem, and perhaps Antioch, we know more of human interest that occurred there than for almost any other Roman city. For this, we must thank our sources: Strabo, Plutarch, Pausanias, Apuleius, and, above all, Saint Paul. In criticizing, cajoling, exhorting, and in loving them, Paul's letters to his Corinthian congregation have left a vivid impression of an ancient urban population— its values, beliefs, fears, and hopes—that is unmatched for any other city except Rome.

This work began as a social and economic history of Roman Corinth. While writing it, I began to think about the relationship between classical culture and classical cities. Specifically, I wondered how classical political institutions and value systems influenced the political economy of the city. It became apparent to me that the present model of the "consumer city" is inadequate, not only for Corinth, but for virtually all classical cities. According to this view, which dominates present thinking about classical cities, their economies were dependent on the rents and taxes collected from peasants in the countryside belonging to the city. Also, according to the recent revival of this idea, classical cities were partially agro-towns, supported by the agricultural production of urban residents who commuted back and forth to their fields.

The related concept of primitivism has also dominated recent studies of the ancient economy, and this has affected our understanding of classical cities. According to this notion, the classical world was innocent of many market values and institutions. Classical peasants lived at the margin of human existence and had little or nothing left over after they paid their taxes, rents, and maintenance. Therefore, classical cities could not have been supported by the voluntary exchange of peasant surplus for urban goods and services, since the peasant had little or no surplus at his disposal and no knowledge of a market.

In subsequent pages, I will try to demonstrate why the primitivist, consumer-city paradigm is inadequate and develop a new model—the service city—that was indeed supported by the voluntary exchange of peasant

1

surpluses for urban goods and services. I will show that ancient peasants had approximately twice the surplus available to them for such exchanges than is now supposed. Large cities, such as Corinth, located on major trade routes were also supported by the goods and services they provided to travelers, traders, and tourists. This alternative model is not offered as a final answer to the problem of the political economies of classical cities, but merely as a competing view.[1] I hope that the present work will stimulate a debate about the two models that will lead to a fuller understanding of classical cities.

The study of classical cities is beset by many conceptual problems, and these must be addressed before we begin our study of Corinth. In the field of ancient history, M. I. Finley has done more than anyone else to help resolve the epistemological issues concerning Greek and Roman social and economic organization. The methodological problems confronting any attempt to understand classical cities are so profound that Finley had even suggested the abandonment of the study of individual towns: "In the end, I believe that the history of *individual* ancient towns is a *cul de sac,* given the limits of the available (and potential) documentation, [and] the unalterable condition of the study of ancient history."[2]

Despite the immense research concerning the nature of cities in other ancient cultures, studies about the nature of classical cities have been comparatively rare. Since Gordon Childe discovered the "urban revolution" there has been a growing and sophisticated literature about the beginnings of urbanism in Mesoamerica, Mesopotamia, and ancient China. Since the early nineteenth century, another vast quantity of research has been devoted to "the rise of towns" in the Middle Ages. However, Finley believed, the intervening classical period appears as a vacuum or prohibited space:

> There is considerable publication about what is sometimes grandiloquently called "ancient town planning," . . . but a town is more than the mere arithmetical total of layout and drains and inhabitants, and it is remarkable that the ancient city *qua* city has aroused so little interest. Had it not "disappeared" at the end of antiquity, it would not have to "rise" again; that simple logic alone should have forced attention on it.[3]

Finley thought that one of the reasons why little has been done to understand the nature of classical cities since Max Weber wrote *De Stadt* over sixty years ago, is that important questions have not been asked. Historians and sociologists have not established adequate criteria to differentiate ancient cities from cities in other eras, and to differentiate among various types of ancient cities.[4]

There are, to be sure, a growing number of "histories" of individual towns, Greek and Roman, from the archaic age to the end of antiquity. With scarcely an exception, however, they lack a conceptual focus or scheme: everything known about the place under examination appears to have equal claim—architecture, religion and philosophy, trade and coinage, administration and "international relations." The city *qua* city is flooded out. The approach is usually descriptive and positivistic, "collecting evidence and interrogating it with an open mind": the unexpressed assumptions about the economy are usually "modernizing." . . . If my evaluation of the current situation is a bleak one, that is not because I dislike the questions that are being asked but because I usually fail to discover any questions at all, other than antiquarian ones—how big? how many? what monuments?[5]

The reasons for many of Finley's criticisms lie in the strong empirical tradition that has dominated much of Anglo-Saxon scholarship in the classics. This empiricism—the collecting of evidence with only a limited theoretical framework—has informed the study of classical literature, history, and archaeology. Although the scholarly traditions of France, Germany, and Italy have a more theoretical basis, they have somewhat uncritically accepted the consumer-city view, first expressed in its modern form by Max Weber and Werner Sombart in the 1920s.[6]

The recent concern with theory in ancient history owes most to Finley, who revived the consumer-city idea for classical cities in various works of the 1970s. He also introduced the concept of primitivism. Finley's ideas have had a widespread influence outside the Anglo-Saxon tradition as we will see in the conclusion of this volume.

In my opinion, Finley probably suggested the primitivist, consumer-city paradigm to stimulate a debate about the nature of the classical political economy, but unfortunately, this has not occurred. This paradigm has become so dominant that it has inhibited the development of possible alternatives to an extent that probably would have annoyed Finley himself. His preeminent position in our field has helped establish the idea as received gospel, something to be accepted without question or analysis. The relative lack of a theoretical perspective, especially in the Anglo-Saxon tradition, has insured that the paradigm would sweep all before it with little resistance. Other reasons for the widespread acceptance of the idea will be discussed in the conclusion. In this work I will confront these ideas with an alternative model of the classical city.

We must take heart however from Greece itself, the homeland of the concept of "idea" and "theory." We must also acknowledge, that unlike empirical research, conceptual thought will never achieve exactness or perfection. Nevertheless, the lack of perfection has not prevented a vast conceptual literature from developing concerning ancient cities throughout the Old and New Worlds; a literature in which the classical period has not been well represented.[7]

In an often-quoted dictum about geology in the 1830s, Charles Darwin wrote:

> There was once much talk that Geologists ought only to observe and not theorize; and well I remember someone saying that at this rate a man might as well go into a gravel-pit and count the pebbles and describe their colors. How odd it is that anyone should not see that all observation must be for or against some view if it is to be of any service.[8]

That the collection of evidence should occur not for its own sake, but to answer problems, has been the hallmark of the Western intellectual tradition since Thales.

Astronomers believe that only 5 to 10 percent of the known universe is capable of being measured and studied. The remaining 90 to 95 percent of the matter of the universe may never be analyzed, regardless of the future development of instrumentation.[9] Nevertheless, this lack of perfection has not put an end to intellectual progress in astronomy. Furthermore, paleontologists have only the tiniest fraction of the fossil evidence at their disposal, and the fossil evidence represents only the smallest part of past living matter on the planet. Yet, this has not prevented the development of many fruitful theories concerning evolutionary biology.

On the other hand, it needs to be stressed that the type of analysis envisioned by Finley requires that a massive amount of empirical research be conducted first. The present work would have been quite impossible without the patient and dedicated labors of generations of archaeologists and historians working on Corinth. Furthermore, it seems necessary that individual cities be studied before ideal types can be discovered.

A further obstacle to understanding the nature of classical cities has been the separation between social and religious values and economic analysis. This has led to a sharp dichotomy in some recent interpretations that employ the primitivist, consumer-city paradigm. We find superimposed on broadly based, and even democratic political values and institutions a consumer-city type of political economy that was more characteristic of the despotic late Empire and early Dark Ages (ca. A.D. 285–600) than the classical era (ca. 500 B.C.–A.D. 200). Before we begin our study of Corinth, it is necessary to examine some classical ideas concerning the city.

## The Classical Concept of the City

To understand our assumptions about cities, we must first understand the attitudes towards mankind implicit in them. The notion of the consumer city makes many assumptions about the nature of the relationships between town and country in the classical era. These assumptions are not only political and economic, but also moral.

According to this notion, cities exploit and oppress the country dwellers through excessive taxation and rents, leaving them almost nothing for themselves.[10] On this view, the city dwellers were basically evil, dominated by greed and the desire to expand their power as far as possible over their rural compatriots. One remarkable feature of the consumer-city theory is that it seems to ignore the evidence of what the classical world wrote about its cities. Plato, Aristotle, Cicero, and numerous others made many shrewd observations concerning classical city-states. In these and other authors, there is no sharp political, economic, or religious division between town and country.[11] In classical Greek and Republican Roman cities, country dwellers had full political and judicial equality with urban dwellers, and although the latter may have called the former "bumpkins" or "hayseeds," all regarded the city as the focus of their culture. Only under tyrannies, when the tyrant lived in the acropolis, surrounded by his armed bodyguard, oppressing the peasantry with arbitrary rule and land taxes, can the city be said to have oppressed the country. Nevertheless, tyrannies were a temporary phenomenon and imparted no lasting stigma of evil on the city.

The classical city was firmly based upon the classical conception of mankind. Since Homer, man was thought to be kin to the gods and to share reason with them. The culmination of this classical view is perhaps best seen in the principles of stoicism.

This system of philosophy dominated the thought and action of much of the Roman aristocracy during the Empire, and is therefore vital for the understanding of cities during this era. Stoicism perceived the world as governed by a universal God who is also Reason (*Logos*). All mankind shares reason, and, therefore, we all share God: "Do you know that you are God's temple and that God's spirit dwells in you?"[12] This is a Stoic concept that Paul used to help his Corinthian congregation understand the new Christian God. God's activities in the world are governed by reason and operate through natural laws. It was the stoic's duty—taken very seriously by the Roman elite—to make the laws of his community correspond as closely as possible to the laws of nature, which were God's laws. Stoics therefore took an active role in the public, communal affairs. The fruits of their labors can be found, not only in the corpus of Roman law, but also in the governing policies of cities during the Roman Empire.

The principles of stoicism were perhaps best expressed by Cicero in his *De Legibus:*

But what is more divine, I will not say in man only, but in all heaven and earth, than reason? And reason, when it is full grown and perfected, is rightly called wisdom. Therefore, since there is nothing better than reason, and since it exists both in man and God, the first common possession of man and God is reason. But those who have reason in common must also have right reason in common. And since right reason is Law, we must believe that men have Law also in common with the gods. Further, those who share Law must also share Justice; and those who share these are to be regarded as members of the same common-wealth. If indeed they obey the same authorities and powers, this is true in a far greater degree; but as a matter of fact they do obey this celestial system, the divine mind, and the God of transcendent power. Hence, we must now conceive of this whole universe as one commonwealth of which both gods and men are members . . . Hence, we are justified in saying that there is a blood relationship between ourselves and the celestial beings; or we may call it a common ancestry or origin.[13]

Cicero and other stoics based many of their views concerning the nature of mankind on the common characteristics that the law codes of many different peoples shared. The Romans called this universal law the *ius gentium,* the law of all nations, and it formed the basis for much Roman law. The Romans saw (as did their Hellenistic Greek predecessors) that all civilized human communities shared basic concepts of right and wrong and incorporated these concepts into their laws. The stoics believed that the *ius gentium* is the reflection of the natural law of God when it operates in human communities. In his discussion of justice, Cicero notes that all men, even criminals, recognize the difference between right and wrong:

But if it were a penalty and not Nature that ought to keep men from injustice, what anxiety would there be to trouble the wicked when the danger of punishment was removed? But in fact there has never been a villain so brazen as to deny that he had committed a crime, or else invent some story of just anger to excuse its commission, and seek justification for his crime in some natural principle of right. Now if even the wicked dare to appeal to such principles, how jealously should they be guarded by the good![14]

Although nations may pass bad laws, they too will be recognized as being wrong:

But if Justice is conformity to written laws and national customs, and if, as the same persons claim, everything is to be tested by the standard of utility, then anyone who thinks it will be profitable to him will, if he is able, disregard and violate the laws. It follows that Justice does not exist at all, if it does not exist in Nature, and if that form of it which is based on utility can be overthrown by that very utility itself. And, if Nature is not to be considered the foundation of Justice, that will mean the destruction of the virtues on which human society depends. For where then will there be a place for generosity, or love of country, or loyalty, or the inclination to be of service to others or to show gratitude for favors received? For these virtues originate in our natural inclination to love our fellow men, and this is the foundation of Justice. . . .

But in fact we can perceive the difference between good laws and bad by referring them to no other standard than Nature. . . . For since an intelligence common to us all makes things known to us and formulates them in our minds, honorable actions are ascribed by us to virtue, and dishonorable actions to vice.[15]

These stoic ideals had important consequences for cities. They not only informed the law codes, but also the public policies that made classical cities unique. Supplies of clean water, often brought in from distances at great expense, paved streets, sewage disposal, public art, public baths, and numerous other public facilities, all reflect, however imperfectly, the stoic ideals of public service and rational planning that embodied the will of God himself.

Classical man did not see his cities as centers of evil because he did not see himself as evil. Fortunately for Western democratic societies, these attitudes towards the basic reasonableness and decency of humanity were revived by the Renaissance and Enlightenment, and formed the conceptual bases for our governments. Only when people so regard themselves is self-government, the ability to make laws, the presumption of innocence, and service on juries possible.

# 1
# The City-State of Corinth

> Where is your wondrous beauty, Dorian Corinth?
> Where is your crown of towers, your ancient wealth
> the temples of the gods, your homes? Where are the
>     matrons
> of Sisyphus, and where are the people that once were
>     myriads?
> Lamented land, no trace of you is left,
> war seized and consumed your every part.
> Only we Nereids, the daughters of Oceanus, are left
> to mourn your passing, like halcyon days.
>     ANTIPATER OF SIDON, *Anthologia Palatina* 9.151

From a small beginning, Corinth grew to become the largest city in Greece by the Second century A.D. It was both an intellectual and cultural center, as well as a vital link in the commercial network of the eastern Mediterranean. The city's large population of Roman and Italian immigrants made it an ideal capital for the senatorial province of Achaea. Corinth was also the focus of the missionary activity of Saint Paul, and thanks to his letters and the account in Acts, we possess a greater knowledge of its church and converts than for any other early Christian community. For these reasons alone, Roman Corinth merits its own history.

This chapter will be devoted to the geography and history of the city state of Roman Corinth, as well as the political institutions of the city. Inasmuch as the separation between political and economic analysis found in some social and economic histories has inhibited our understanding of the ancient political economy, it is hoped that the discussion of political institutions in this chapter may help us better understand the city's economy that will be examined in chapters 2 and 3.

## The Geography of the Corinthia

Corinth, like all other Greco-Roman city-states (called a *polis* in Greek and *civitas* in Latin) was divided into two parts: the city proper (*asty* or *urbs*), and the countryside which belonged to it, with its towns and villages (the *chora* or *territorium*). It is important to keep these terms distinct because they are of critical importance in analyzing the city state's economy. When reference is made to the city-state of Corinth (the city proper and its

8

countryside), the name Corinth will be used, when the countryside alone is being discussed, the name Corinthia will be applied, and when the city proper is being discussed, the terms "city" or "city of Corinth" will be used.

The city-state of Corinth was bounded by Megara on the north, Sikyon to the west, and Cleonae, Argos, and Epidauros on the south. To the east is the Saronic Gulf. From the earliest times, Corinth owed much of its economic strength to its control of the Isthmus of Corinth and its strategic position in the transit trade between the eastern and central Mediterranean.

The region north of the Isthmus is called Perachora, and is dominated by the Geranian Range (highest elevation 1,351 meters) dividing Corinth from Megara. These mountains consist of a complex structure of Pliocene, Miocene, Cretaceous, and Triassic limestones, with later igneous intrusions.[1] Within the mountains themselves are some small upland valleys and plateaus at Schinos, Perachora, and Bissia. As one travels southwest along the Saronic Gulf, the Geranian Mountains fade into the narrow alluvial coastal plain. To the south is the barren plateau of the Isthmus. Travel is difficult in the Perachora; the route along the Saronic Gulf to Megara, although quite practicable along the coastal plain near the Isthmus, gradually narrows to the northeast, as the Geranian mountains plunge precipitously into the sea. Here lay the notorious Scironian Road (named after the thief Sciron), a narrow footpath infested with robbers, winding perilously along the sea cliffs.[2] A more frequently used route went through the 600-meter-high pass between Mounts Makri Playi and Lysi. Although this pass is mountainous, it was less dangerous than the Scironian road. A third route from Megara follows the Gulf of Corinth southwestwards, ascends the small upland plateau of Bissia, and continues west through Perachora. Here, one could choose to continue west to the sanctuary of Hera at the tip of the Perachora peninsula, or proceed southeast along the coastal road skirting the southern outlier of the Geranian Range.

The most important inland settlement of the Perachora was at Asprokambos (its ancient name is unknown) and perhaps it was a small regional marketing center. Along the Saronic Gulf lay the important port of Crommyon and the smaller port of Sidous. The ancient temple of Hera at the western tip of Perachora still remained in use during the Roman era.

The central region of the Corinthia contains only three significant elevations, the fingerlike Mount Onium stretching from the Saronic Gulf south of Cenchreae westwards for some eight kilometers (highest elevation 584 meters), the height of Acrocorinth itself (574 meters), and another small mountain, 5 kilometers south of Acrocorinth (701 meters). The citadel of Acrocorinth, standing in relative isolation near the center of the region, truly dominates the Corinthia. From its peak one can see virtually the entire territory of the ancient city.

Underlying much of the central region is a vast deposit of marl, dating
to the Pliocene era when the area was at the bottom of a large lake.[3] Along
the cutting for the modern Corinthian canal, the depth of this deposit can
be traced for 83 meters, and it undoubtedly extends much deeper, perhaps
for another 100 meters. The marl consists largely of whitish clay, and
through a complex sequence of faulting, uplifting, and sloping, part of it
lies exposed along the edges of the Pleistocene terrace upon which the
ancient city rested. This huge deposit was important for the ancient Corinthians for two reasons. First, it gave them an inexhaustible supply of clay
for the manufacture of pottery, roof tiles, and terracotta objects. Second,
large quantities of water trapped by the impenetrable marl deposits flowed
northwards underground and gushed out from several natural springs along
the terraces underlying the city. The greatest of these springs, Peirene, has
an average flow rate of 18 cubic meters per hour, enough in itself to supply
the needs of a large city.

Overlying the marl deposits are later, Pleistocene formations, one of
which was of particular importance for the Corinthians: a lightweight sandstone with which much of the classical city was built.[4] This building-stone
was popular, not only among the Corinthians, but also among their neighbors, as its use to construct parts of the sanctuaries at Delphi and Epidaurus
testifies.[5] The stratum of this lightweight stone is also exposed along the
edges of uplifted or eroded terraces, especially west of the Isthmian sanctuary to the region of the city of Corinth itself. There are numerous traces
of ancient quarrying activity all along these exposed outcrops.[6] Acrocorinth (mainly composed of Mesozoic limestone and conglomerate) also supplies a hard, white, crystalline limestone which, although too hard and
brittle to use for building construction, was ideal for paving the Lechaion
Road during the Roman era. The Pliocene marl deposits and the later Pleistocene sandstone and conglomerate formations are known collectively as
the neogen.

The soils of the central region of the Corinthia are mainly derived from
the decomposition of the underlying neogen which produces a type of soil
called rendzina. This loam soil has a silty texture and contains varying
proportions of sand, marl, and limestone, depending on the nature of the
local, underlying neogen.[7] It retains water quite well, particularly through
the dry summer, and can chemically convert humus and other organic debris into nitrogen for plants. Hence, this type of soil was ideally adapted
for ancient agriculture in an arid region such as the Corinthia and was well
suited for the ancient ard-type plough which merely scratched the surface
of the tilth.

Unlike the Argive plain, almost none of the soil of the Corinthia is alluvial.[8] One narrow band of alluvium (averaging about 200 meters wide)
runs along the coast of the Corinthian Gulf from the Nemea River to the

area of Lutraki. Other small deposits of alluvium are found along the coast of the Saronic Gulf from Crommyon to the canal region, in narrow valleys of the Longopotomos and Xerias Rivers, and in small, isolated upland valleys of the mountains along the Epidaurian and Argive frontier.

The coastal plain north of the city, some 5 kilometers wide and 15 kilometers long is of rendzina and not alluvium. Today, thanks to water brought by an aqueduct from Lake Stymphalus, the plain can be irrigated in the spring, and hence, although its soil is similar to that of the rest of the central area, it can produce in far greater abundance. Citrus fruits, apricots, and other crops are grown, and today, the Corinthia is a major producer of wine, table grapes, and raisins (the word currant is a corruption of the word Corinth through French). There is abundant evidence that this coastal plain was among the most productive regions in Roman Greece. Macedonius refers to rich Corinthian harvests, and Cicero to "that most fruitful and excellent land of the Corinthia which was added to the revenues of the Roman people by the successful campaign of Lucius Mummius."[9] These two passages probably refer to the coastal plain, since it is the only land of the Corinthia that can be irrigated to some extent from the runoff of Corinth's springs. The coastal plain between Corinth and Sikyon was proverbially productive, as numerous anecdotes from the Roman and Byzantine eras testify, not because of any superior natural fertility, but because of the efforts of Corinthian farmers, who were not slow to see the benefits of intensive agriculture practiced near the city. One story concerned a man, "who inquired of the Delphic Oracle: 'How may I get rich, son of Zeus and Leto?' The god mockingly replied: 'By acquiring what lies between Corinth and Sikyon.' "[10] A wine press and what is perhaps an olive oil settling tank have been found in a Roman farm west of the city, near the plain.[11]

Human settlement in the Corinthia has always been concentrated in the central plain. In addition to the city of Corinth itself, with its two ports, Lechion and Cenchreae, the region was the location of several large towns, such as Tenea and Ayios Charalambos (Assae?), and the great sanctuary of Isthmia. Within a short radius of the city are several villas, which no doubt supplied the urban market with specialized agricultural products.

The southern region of the Corinthia consists of sparse and rugged mountains of Jurassic and Triassic limestones, with small pockets of alluvium in the upland valleys of Angelokastro and Kephalari. Some of these mountains are still forested, and are exploited for wood, pitch, and resin. The three intermittent rivers of the Corinthia—the Nemea, the Longopotomos, and the Xerias (Solomos or Leukon)—all have their origins in these mountains. The Nemea, in its lower course, formed the boundary between the Sikyonia and the Corinthia, and has it origins in the mountains to the south of the Nemean Plain. From there is flows north past Mount Apesas, which dominated Corinth's western border, and empties into the

Corinthian Gulf. The Longopotomos drains the plain belonging to Corinth's other western neighbor, Cleonae, and, after receiving many small tributaries, empties into the Gulf near Assae. The most extensive river system is the Xerias. Rising in the mountains along the Epidaurian border, it drains the fertile plain of Tenea, and passes between the Onium Range and Acrocorinth before emptying into the sea near New Corinth. In addition to these larger streams there are many seasonal freshets and mountain torrents. All the major roads south to the Argolid and Epidauria follow the valleys of these streams.

The sparse rainfall of the region explains why none of Corinth's streams are perennial. The Corinthia receives only about 400 millimeters per year (16 inches) and in the rest of Greece, only Attica, the Eastern Argolid, and the Aegean Islands receive less. Water has always been a precious commodity here, and not only the streams but even the wells of the region run dry in the summer months.[12] Only the prodigious natural springs of the city, and a few smaller springs in outlying locations, flow all year around.

In the remainder of this work, I will focus on the city of Corinth itself. Reflecting the city's major functions as a provider of urban goods and services to a wide market, the city's center was dominated by temples and especially the massive commercial and service facilities–the shops and stoas. The reader will find a full discussion of its monuments and physical layout in chapter 2, and in plans 1 and 2.

The city of Corinth was called the Aphrodite of Roman cities by Aelius Aristeides in the late second century,[13] and it must have presented a magnificent appearance to visitors. A tourist disembarking at Lechaion in that era would see the great lighthouse, and a sanctuary of Poseidon, the god of the sea, with its bronze statue. The man-made harbor—one of the largest in the Roman world—would be crowded with vessels from all over the Mediterranean. Its quays and warehouses would be packed with goods coming from as far as India, China, and even Indonesia: spices, silks, precious stones, exotic woods, marble blocks of every color in the rainbow from Anatolia, North Africa, Italy, and producing areas of Greece, amphoras filled with wines, olive oils, and other vegetable oils, copper and tin ingots for the city's bronze foundries, and blocks of Corinth's own building stone for export. He would see travelers, merchants, and tourists such as himself from Alexandria, Sardinia, North Africa, Italy, Syria, Judaea, Anatolia, and from all parts of Greece. Many came to see the sights, some came from afar as religious pilgrims to visit the hallowed ground of Old Greece. Others came as participants and spectators in the Isthmian games. Some came to stop over on their journeys that would take them further east or west.

Looking north, our visitor would see, beneath the protecting height of Acrocorinth, the vast panorama of the city spread out in all directions down to the harbor itself; a sharp eye could just make out the famous temple of Aphrodite on its summit.

Walking north along the Lechaion Road towards the city he passed through the mercantile suburb, beneath colonnaded sidewalks that protected from the sun and weather. Ascending the terraces upon which the central city was located, he would see the Asklepieion, with its temple, colonnades, and bathhouses, and the Old Gymnasium on his right. Nearby, he might have stopped to refresh himself at the beautiful Fountain of Lerna (Fountain of the Lamps). Here he could wash away the salt spray in the basins of the fountain house, and even take a swim in its large swimming pool. He knew that wherever he drank water or bathed, the water could be clean and safe. The supplies were continually replenished by the flow of water coming directly from their sources in the numerous springs around the city.

Continuing his journey up the Lechaion Road, he would see an impressive public bath on his left and another smaller one on his right, surrounded by elegant homes. Moving closer to the Forum—the civic and economic center of the city—large market buildings, basilicas, and the law courts, would line the colonnaded street. On his left would be the Baths of Eurycles, public latrines, and the Peribolos of Apollo with its famous works of art, and next, the great Fountain of Peirene, recently refurbished by the Attic benefactor Herodes Atticus, with its draw basins and swimming pool. The prodigious flow rate of the fountain was enough in itself to supply the needs of a great city. Approaching the Forum, he would pass beneath the majestic triumphal arch surmounted by two gilded, horse-drawn chariots, one driven by Helios and the other by his ill-fated son, Phaëthon.

The forum itself was a vast, open space thronged with merchants, street-hawkers, travelers, and local residents. Varicolored tents covered the market stalls. Surveying the scene, he would see important works of public art: paintings, marble sculpture,and works of bronze by renowned artists. The Forum was the religious as well as commercial core of the city, and contained numerous shrines, sanctuaries, and temples, the greatest of which was the Archaic Temple, perhaps dedicated to Corinth's founding dynasty, the Gens Julia. Surrounding the Forum were the temples, shops, stoas, and the administrative offices in the imposing South Stoa. Perhaps the governor was present at a public hearing at his tribunal near the center of the Forum.

What would strike our visitor most was the dazzling colors, white marbles and marble stuccos, and the astonishing variety of polychrome marble revetment with which many of the buildings were covered: blues, violets, greens, reds, and yellows in every conceivable combination. By now he would have been convinced that he had indeed entered the Aphrodite of cities, the promenade of Hellas, the shining light of Greece.

## The Last Days of the Greek City

Hellenistic Greece, although now overshadowed politically and economically by the great powers of Macedonia, Syria, and Egypt, retained its role as the cultural and religious center of the Greek-speaking world, a world whose boundaries now extended as far east as the Indus River. The commercial centers of Greece still retained their prosperity during this era, especially Rhodes, Ephesus, the island of Delos after 167 B.C., and Corinth itself. In fact, Corinth was well on its way to surpassing Athens in importance by the second century B.C. Cicero observed that so many Corinthians were engaged in commerce during the second century that they neglected agriculture altogether.[14]

During the third century B.C., southern Greece was the scene of a political struggle between Macedonia and the newly formed Achaean League. In 243 B.C., when Aratus of Sikyon captured the city from its Macedonian garrison, Corinth became a member of the League, a federation of Greek states formed to resist Macedonian expansion. It returned to Macedonian control, however, after the Battle of Sellasia in 222 B.C. (when the Spartans under their king, Cleomenes, were defeated by a Macedonian army under Antigonus Doson) and the city resumed its role as one of the Three Fetters of Greece, through which the Macedonians maintained their control of the country. After the Roman victory over the Macedonians at Cynocephalae in 197 B.C., Corinth again returned to the Achaean League. In the succeeding year, the Roman victor, Flamininus, made his famous proclamation of *libertas* to the Greeks from the stadium at Isthmia.

However, to the Greeks, freedom (*eleutheria*) meant complete political autonomy, while to the Romans, a grant of *libertas* implied that the beneficiary would owe the same moral and legal obligations that a client would owe to his patron.[15] Largely because of this misunderstanding of principles, relations between the League and Rome steadily deteriorated over the next half century. In 147 B.C., the final crisis occurred when a Roman embassy met an assembly of the League at Corinth to arbitrate its conflicts with Sparta. The Romans threatened to detach the cities of Argos, Sparta, Oetean Heraclea, Arcadian Orchomenus, and even Corinth itself from the League, thus effectively destroying its power. The assembled Achaeans, enraged at the Roman threat, dismissed the ambassador with insults and abuse, and had all Spartans and suspected Spartans in the city arrested.

After a second embassy proved ineffective, the Romans were told to return the following year for another meeting with the League at Corinth.

In the spring of 146, the Roman governor of Macedonia, Q. Caecilius Metellus, sent two envoys to this assembly, which was thronged by a large and unruly crowd of manual laborers. The envoys were not even allowed to speak, but were shouted down and expelled. It had been Rome's policy in Greece and elsewhere to accomplish its political objectives through reliance on local aristocracies, often at the expense of the poorer classes.[16] This policy provoked the hostility of the Achaean League with its relatively democratic institutions and values, and the hostility was compounded by strong nationalist sentiment against the Romans.[17]

At this meeting, the assembled Achaeans declared war on Sparta, Rome's ally, and began to mobilize. The Romans quickly countered by sending the consul, L. Mummius by sea and Metellus by land to subdue the refractory Achaeans. After defeating them in three battles in central Greece and killing the League's general, Critolaus, a Roman army of 23,000 infantry and 3,500 cavalry moved towards the Isthmus, where the command was transferred to Mummius. Another Achaean army was raised under General Diaeus, who ordered 12,000 slaves to be freed from the League's cities and sent to Corinth armed for battle. With these reinforcements and requisitions of money levied from wealthy Achaeans, Diaeus was able to field a poorly trained and equipped, ramshackle army of some 14,000 infantry and 600 cavalry, for a last desperate defense of Greece. The two forces met at Leucopetra on the Isthmus where the Achaeans were annihilated. After the defeat, the city of Corinth was deserted by most of its inhabitants, but Mummius waited outside its massive fortifications for two days, probably thinking its deserted appearance was meant to lure his troops into a trap. When the army did enter the city, it was looted and burned; any men found within were killed, and women and children sold into slavery.[18] Thus ended the history of the great Greek city, renowned since the days of Homer:

> Corinth the Bright Star of Hellas.[19]
> Corinth, the Light of all Greece.[20]

Several contemporaries wrote epitaphs concerning the disaster that show the magnitude of the catastrophe for the Greek people:

> Lucius has smitten the great Achaean Acrocorinth, the Star of Hellas
> And the twin shores of the Isthmus.
> One heap of stones covers the bones of those felled by the spear;
> And the sons of Aeneas left unmourned by funeral rites the Achaeans who burnt the house of Priam.[21]

Another read:

> I, Rhodope, and my mother Boisca, neither died of sickness,
>    nor fell by the enemy's sword,
> But we ourselves, when fierce Ares burnt the city of Corinth,
>    our fatherland, chose a brave death.
> My mother slew me with the slaughtering knife,
> Nor did she, sorrowful woman, spare her own life,
> But tied the noose around her own neck, for to die in
>    freedom was better than slavery.[22]

Following the victory, Mummius called another assembly of the League and announced that all the Achaean cities were to be "free," with the exception of Corinth, whose inhabitants were to be sold, and walls and buildings demolished. The wealth from the looted Greek city, most of it used to adorn public buildings in Rome, became proverbial. Its land became *ager Romanus,* and was farmed for the Roman government by the Sikyonians, who also undertook the direction of the Isthmian Games.[23]

From 146–46 B.C., central and southern Greece were nominally free, but in fact under the close watch of the governor of Macedonia. Although the Romans had sacked the city, the destruction of its buildings was far from complete. While many had suffered from neglect, if not willful destruction, most still stood during this period. The city was largely deserted, although some descendants of the old Corinthians still lingered like ghosts among its ruins.[24]

Cicero visited the site of the city probably between 79 and 77 B.C.:

> I have seen too in the Peloponnese in my youthful days some natives of Corinth who were slaves. All of them could have made the same lament as that in the *Andromacha:* "All this did I see . . . ," but by the time I saw them they had ceased, it may be, to chant dirges. Their features, speech, their movements and postures would have led one to say they were freemen of Argos or Sikyon. The sudden sight of the ruins of Corinth had more effect on me than the actual inhabitants; for long contemplation had a hardening effect on their souls.[25]

## The Roman Colony

Shortly before his death in March of 44 B.C., Julius Caesar ordered the colonization of Corinth and of Carthage, which had also been destroyed by Roman forces in 146 B.C.[26] Both cities were destined to flourish once again as commercial centers, as they had in the past. Caesar probably had many reasons to refound Corinth. Most of Corinth's colonists were from Rome's freedman class, urban plebs, and Caesar's veterans. By removing part of these politically disaffected and volatile groups from Rome, he probably earned the gratitude of many in the capital. Since the land was not taken from Italian landowners, no doubt they were also appeased as well. In choosing a site where they would have an excellent chance to prosper, he would increase the loyalty and devotion of these groups, and especially his veterans, to himself.

Caesar probably recognized that the new foundation would soon become a major commercial center, as it had been throughout its history, and so would help revive the economy of Greece, exhausted by wars and extortion by Roman governors. Thus, he would earn the support of the entire province.

Finally, its geographic position and its excellent harbors would make it a vital strategic center and communications link for his projected campaigns into Dacia and Parthia. Caesar also planned a canal through the Isthmus which would not only facilitate trade but also expedite the movement of warships, supplies, and communications to the Black Sea. The new colony was named Colonia Laus Julia Corinthiensis in honor of its founder.

No "constitution" or civic charter exists for the colony of Corinth, but we are able to form a good idea of its political institutions from numerous inscriptions, coins, and from comparisons with civic charters that have survived for other colonies. The populus of Corinth was comprised of its citizens (*cives*)—the colonists themselves and their descendants—and resident aliens (*incolae*). Citizens and perhaps some resident aliens had the right to vote, but as a rule the latter were not allowed to hold office. For voting purposes, the populus (citizens and resident aliens) was divided into a number of tribes that voted in the *comitia tributa* (Gk. *ekklesia*). So far, the names of twelve tribes are attested in the city.[27] Full citizenship in the community could be acquired through birth, adoption, or manumission by a Corinthian citizen, or through a gift of the Emperor or the local senate (*decurio*, Gk. *boule*).[28]

By the time Corinth was founded, the *comitia* no longer had legislative functions, although it retained the important right to elect the magistrates of the city at least until the early third century A.D. Thereafter, officials were elected by the *decurio*. Individual tribes could also bestow honors on deserving individuals.[29]

In Roman colonies, the local senate had wide-ranging powers. Among other things they authorized the building of new aqueducts, chose new festival days, audited municipal accounts, authorized the sending of embassies, passed legislation regarding public expenditures, public buildings and roads, granted citizens the right to use waste water from reservoirs, and called out the militia in times of emergency.[30] The prerequisites for membership in the *decurio,* which probably had one hundred members, were a substantial property qualification, or election to the aedileship or duovirate. Members were chosen by the *duoviri quinquennales* from among these ex-magistrates and if there were not enough to make one hundred members, they would select other distinguished individuals. Those members of the *decurio* who had not previously been elected magistrates had to have been thirty years old; those who were magistrates had to have been twenty-five or perhaps twenty-two.[31] Membership was highly prized, at least until the end of the second century A.D. In the third and fourth centuries however, when cities lost much of their independence and autonomy, membership in the *decurio* became hereditary and compulsory. During this era, the local senates became little more than agents for the imperial government insuring the collection of taxes from their communities.[32]

The chief magistrates of the colony were the two *duoviri iure dicundo,* elected annually by the *comitia tributa*. They presided over meetings of the *comitia* and *decurio,* and carried out the measures passed by the latter body. Every fifth year (when they became *duoviri quinquennales*) they took the census of the colony and named new members to the *decurio*. They were also the chief justices for civil cases in the city, but gradually this power was removed from them by the imperial governors, who always had jurisdiction in criminal cases.[33] Their names appeared on the city's bronze coinage, which was minted when need arose, and forty-seven duovirs are known from this source alone.[34]

Initially, Caesar allowed freedmen to be duovirs of the colonies he founded, however this privilege was revoked by Augustus and henceforth all were free born.[35] To hold office, they needed the same property qualification as a decurion, they must never have been convicted of a crime, nor have followed an ignoble trade. Another qualification may have been their previous election to the aedileship, although occasionally the emperor or some other distinguished non-Corinthian may have held the office.[36]

Two aediles were also elected annually, and were the city's business managers. They were in charge of maintaining public buildings and streets, supervising the marketplace, and were responsible for the public revenues derived from these sources. They also served as judges for commercial litigation.[37] In Corinth, the aediles were also probably responsible for supervising the local games in the city's theater and amphitheater. In other colonies they often funded these events from their own personal resources and perhaps this was the case in Corinth as well.[38]

The international Isthmian Games, Caesarean Games, and the Imperial Contests were under the supervision of an *agonothetes* who was assisted by a board of ten *hellanodikai*. The office of agonothete was considered to be the highest attainable by a Corinthian citizen. They were elected biennially, and were expected to contribute personally to the game's expenses; hence they must have been among Corinth's wealthiest citizens.[39]

The political institutions of Corinth, like those of other classical cities, conferred significant benefits on its citizens. Even as late as the third century A.D., the Corinthian populus, rich and poor alike, still elected their magistrates. Although they could not formulate the law for their city, they retained the right to elect the officials who would administer and interpret the law among them. The magistrates were accountable to the people as a whole, and they often had to make extravagant promises (kept at considerable personal expense) to win election. This right to elect the highest magistrates checked the abuse of political and economic power by the Roman elite that became characteristic of the late Empire. Once it was lost, the powerful in each city began to oppress their poor neighbors with impunity. This decline of classical political values contributed to the end of the classical city and its replacement by the despotic type of the late Empire.

Before the formation of the province of Achaea in 27 B.C. by Augustus, affairs of Greece fell under the purview of the governor of Macedonia. In 42 B.C. Marc Antony was given general authority of the eastern provinces, and he fully appreciated Corinth's strategic position in his operations against Octavian.[40]

By September of 32, Antony and Cleopatra's huge force of 500 warships with crews totaling some 150,000 men, approximately 75,000 infantry, and 12,000 cavalry, had occupied a line from Corcyra to Methone in Messenia to defend Greece from the impending attack of Octavian. The provisioning of this vast force relied on grain transports from Egypt. During the winter months of 32/31, ships sailing from Egypt to the western Peloponnese would encounter dangerous winds (see table 6), and thus most, if not all the supplies were probably shipped through the Aegean, where the winds were calmer, and over the Isthmus to Antony's forces in western Greece. Hence, Corinth was a vital strategic point, and Antony confided it to one of his most trusted lieutenants, Theophilus. The capture of Corinth and other Peloponnesian cities by Agrippa early in 31 was a severe setback for Antony, whose huge force, now blockaded in the Gulf of Ambracia, was slowly being starved.

Because of its dependence on trade, Corinth probably never had a chance to thrive during the civil wars that followed Caesar's assassination. But the victors of Actium treated the city well, and it experienced a veritable refoundation under Augustus. Many of Corinth's public buildings were constructed or restored during his reign, the Isthmian Games were returned to Corinthian control in 6 or 2 B.C., and the city probably became the capital of the new province of Achaea.[41]

During the early empire, the provincial status of Achaea changed several times. In 27 B.C. Achaea became a new senatorial province, but in 15 A.D., Tiberius, after hearing complaints about high taxation, converted Achaea and Macedonia into imperial provinces attached to Moesia. Both of the former provinces were returned to senatorial control by Claudius in A.D. 44.[42]

It was during the reign of Claudius that Paul's missions to the city were undertaken. Corinth was a logical place to establish a strong Christian church, for its numerous trade connections would assure the rapid propagation of the new religion, and quite soon it came to dominate the other churches of the province. Corinth also had an important Jewish community, and whenever Paul entered a new city, he would always begin preaching at the local synagogue. (Moreover, the Corinthian people were more receptive to the new message than the inhabitants of many other mainland Greek cities, as we shall see in chapter 5.)

Greece bestowed many honors on the emperor Nero during his visit to the country, and even awarded him victories in the competitions at Olympia and the Isthmia. In gratitude, Nero proclaimed freedom for the province of Achaea (A.D. 67) from the stadium at Isthmia—the identical location Flamininus had used to make the same declaration some 250 years earlier. The grant of freedom would give Achaean cities autonomy over their local affairs, and a tax exemption. Nero also sought to stimulate the economy of Greece by cutting a canal through the Isthmus, an attempt that might have succeeded had the emperor lived (see map 4). These favors were also a way to strengthen the imperial basis of support in Greece against old-line Republican aristocrats, and were no doubt responsible for Nero's popularity in Achaea and Asia even after his death, as the enthusiastic reception of the false-Neros indicates.[43]

Vespasian however, was not pleased by the Greeks' adulation of his predecessor, or with their quarreling, and withdrew the gift of freedom, saying that the Greeks had forgotten how to be free. Achaea was once again made a senatorial province. But Vespasian was not slow to demonstrate his clemency after the disastrous earthquake of 77, which leveled much of Corinth. In gratitude for his aid, the thankful citizens renamed their city Colonia Julia Flavia Augusta Corinthiensis. After the quake, the city was rebuilt anew, this time with marble instead of limestone, a testimony to Corinth's importance as a focus of imperial patronage and to its economic revival during the first century.[44]

On his way to the Jewish wars, Hadrian stopped in the city and presented it with a new bath and an aqueduct to supply the city's increased population with water. It was during the second century A.D., from all indications, that Corinth reached the apogee of its size and prosperity.[45]

Little evidence survives concerning the city during the third century. The Christian community founded by Saint Paul, had grown to be one of the most important in Christendom (see chapter 5). As elsewhere in the Roman Empire, the Third-Century crisis caused a reaction against the Christians for their apparent disloyalty, and church records reveal several martyrdoms.

Otherwise, Corinth escaped many of the ill effects of the military anarchy and barbarian attacks that devastated so many other cities. In 267/68, an invasion of Herulians sacked Byzantium, Chrysopolis, and Cyzicus, and destroyed the city of Athens, but they seem to have had little impact on the Peloponnese or Corinth; either the city was mercifully spared by the invaders or they mounted only a small raid against the city.[46]

Under Diocletian, Corinth remained the capital of Achaea, now part of the diocese of Moesia. Under Constantine, Achaea became part of the new diocese of Macedonia in the prefecture of Illyricum. After the establishment of Constantinople in 330, the administrative supervision of Achaea gradually moved from Rome to the new capital on the Bosphorus.[47] The authority of the city was enhanced during the mid-fourth century when the city-state of Argos was added to its territory. The Corinthians abused their power by levying unlawful taxes on the Argives, in part to fund wild beast hunts in their theaters—a situation that required the intervention of the Emperor Julian in 362.[48]

Corinth was also the seat of the metropolitan bishop of Achaea, and the letters written to Bishop Epictetus by Saint Athanasius and to Bishop Alexander by Saint John Chrysostum reveal the leading role of the Corinthian see in the Church as a whole. Saint John, writing shortly before the sack of the city by Alaric, described Corinth as the first city in Greece in population, wealth, and also in wisdom.[49]

In 365 and 375, the city was shattered by two severe earthquakes, and received its coup de grace from Alaric in 395 when, "burning Corinth . . . heated the waves of her two seas."[50] Table 11 can only suggest the massive destruction of the city's buildings that occurred in the late fourth century; the cost in human life was appalling, including the murder of Corinth's leading citizens.[51] The mass graves left from Alaric's destruction are the silent testimony of the end of classical Corinth.[52]

# 2
# Agriculture and Manufacturies

Not houses finely roofed, or stones of
walls well built, nor canals nor dock-
yards makes the city, but men able to
use their opportunity.

ALCAEUS, Frag. 28 Edmonds

By the first century A.D., Corinth had grown from a small colony of perhaps 3,000 colonists to the first city of Greece, "the common emporium of
Asia and Europe."[1] Contemporaries were impressed by the city's bustling
harbors, thronged with visitors to the "Propylaea of the Peloponnese," and
the "Promenade of Hellas."[2]

This chapter examines the contributions of agriculture and manufacturies to the economy of the Roman city, and attempts to answer the following questions: can a marketing system be observed for the Corinthia from
the types and locations of settlements in its hinterland? To what extent was
Corinth dependent on the agricultural rents of its countryside for its existence? What was the role of manufacturies the city provided to the residents
of its local hinterland, merchants, and travelers?

## Human Geography

An analysis of the settlement patterns of the Corinthia may help to
understand the region's agricultural economy during the Roman era. Plato
and Aristotle were among the first to recognize that people choose their
settlements with care regarding strategic requirements, easy access to natural resources and productive agricultural land, requirements of public
health, communication with the sea, and other economic factors.[3] Aristotle
observed that a city ought to be well situated with regard to sea and land
transport, so that crops, timber, and other products could be easily brought
in. It should also be convenient for the defense of the region. He further
noted that a town must have sufficient arable land in the vicinity to support
its population, and that communication with the sea is desirable to provide
the town with necessities that could not be produced by its own territory. It
should have a pure and abundant supply of water for the health of its citizens, and should be located in a healthy region (e.g. remote from swamps
and other poorly drained areas).

Since the time of Aristotle, there has been a vast body of research on
economic geography undertaken in all areas of the globe from the earliest

eras of prehistory to the present day.[4] The consequence of these studies has been to demonstrate that the sites of human settlements are not random dots on a map, but represent the conscious decisions by members of a society to fulfill basic needs.

Since earliest times, settlements have fulfilled military or strategic functions. These functions include the commanding of a strategic pass or river crossing, or the occupation of a precipitous acropolis used as a place of refuge during an attack. If the country is endangered by sea-borne raids, there may be a tendency for settlements to move away from the sea. As Thucydides noted;

> The cities which were founded in more recent times, when navigation had at length become safer, and were consequently beginning to have surplus resources, were built right on the sea shore, and the isthmuses were occupied and walled off with a view to commerce and the protection of the several peoples against their neighbors. But the older cities, both on the islands and on the mainland, were built more at a distance from the sea because of the piracy that long prevailed, for the pirates used to plunder each other and any others dwelling near the coast who were not sea farers, and up to the present they still dwell inland.[5]

A desire for easy access to fishing resources may also be reflected in patterns of coastal settlement. In table 2 we find that the percentage of sites recorded to have occupied coastal locations in the Roman era was somewhat smaller than in the preceding classical era, although larger than in the Geometric-Archaic era, when piracy may have been more of a problem.[6] The percentage of sites with easily defended, strategic locations was also relatively low in the Roman era and the classical period compared to earlier times, reflecting an era of relative peace.

An analysis of the continuities and discontinuities in settlement patterns from one era to the next may illuminate changes occurring in the agricultural system.[7] This can be examined in three different ways: as a percentage of sites occupied in one period that were occupied in the next, a percentage of new sites occupied in a given era, and a ratio between a random pattern of continuity (where every site occupied in a given period has an equal chance of being occupied or unoccupied in the next, and every unoccupied site has an equal chance of being occupied or unoccupied in the next) and the actual continuity.[8] For our purposes, the ratio between random and observed continuity yields the most significant information. Table 4 indicates a comparatively high rate of settlement continuity from the Classical and Hellenistic to the Roman eras, and this may indicate that the Roman colonists made few changes in the pattern of exploitation.[9]

The high degree of settlement continuity receives further confirmation from an analysis of the microenvironments of ancient Corinthian settlements. For over a hundred and fifty years it has been recognized that farmers will intensively exploit land only within a limited radius of their settlement.[10] This is because, by the law of diminishing returns, at a greater distance more and more time, labor, and transport outlays become necessary for the production of a given crop, until the return from that crop is no longer an adequate compensation for the outlays necessary to produce it. It has often been demonstrated that the most intensive cultivation of a surrounding territory occurs within a radius of four kilometers from a settlement under many different conditions of technology and geography.[11] Therefore, by examining the microenvironment within a four-kilometer radius of a settlement, one may determine the types of soil and other natural resources preferentially exploited by its inhabitants. Moreover, an analysis of the microenvironments of all the sites of a region through time may yield important information on the region's changing agricultural economy.[12] Table 5 shows that a comparatively high proportion of sites in the Classical, Hellenistic, and Roman eras exploited similar territories, and this once again indicates that the Roman colonists made few changes in the subsistence system.[13] As in other regions of Greece, Corinthian settlements throughout antiquity show an overwhelming preference for neogenic soils.[14] This reflects not only the dominance of this soil type in the central Corinthia (where most settlements have been located throughout history) but also its suitability for the ancient farmer and his agricultural practices. Outlines of centuriation (the division of land into square fields) have not been observed for Corinthian fields as in other Roman colonies, and this may mean that the freedmen-colonists may have left the cultivation of the land to their Sikyonian tenants.[15]

Like other large cities in the classical world, such as Athens, Rome, Jerusalem, and Carthage, the city of Corinth was immediately surrounded by a zone of villas, gardens, and prosperous farmsteads.[16] To date, six villas have been located within a mile radius of the city limits.[17] Further out from this zone, we find towns, villages, and the occasional isolated farmhouse.[18]

The open pattern of settlement (where farmers live in individual farmsteads) near the city of Corinth and the more nucleated pattern (where farmers live in villages) commonly seen throughout the rest of the countryside seem to reflect the impact of the city's large market for agricultural products. It will be argued below that, in general, the peasants and farmers of classical city-states produced for the markets of their cities, not merely for their own subsistence, and they had a substantial surplus remaining for themselves with which to purchase urban goods and services. This was true for both the farmers living on prosperous villas near the cities and for peasants living in towns and villages further away (see appendix 1).

No town or village of the Corinthia was more than a day's journey from the city (most settlements were within a one-day's round trip journey), so their farmers would not be priced out of the market through high transport costs. Since the distances were short and high speeds unnecessary, heavy transport, such as ox carts could be used. Corinth provided a huge market for agricultural surplus whose size had far outstripped the ability of its hinterland (*territorium*) to supply. This assured that local farmers would always have a market for their surplus, probably at a good price. Furthermore, the ubiquitous presence of small harbors all along the Corinthian coasts meant that even in remote regions, farmers would be able to transport their goods to the market by sea, thus lowering transport cost still further.[19]

Hence, the different settlement patterns—an open pattern near the city and a nucleated pattern further away—does not mean that the nearer farms were producing cash crops for the urban market, while the villages further out produced for their own subsistence, although this may have been partially true. Rather, the differences seem to reflect a higher demand and a higher price for agricultural land near the city. The price of agricultural land increases significantly near large cities both today, and from all available evidence, also in antiquity.[20]

In a market economy, the price or rents of agricultural land are largely determined in the following manner.[21] Take some farmers grouped around a hypothetical market where they sell many of their products. If one product is wheat, and the produce of one acre sells for 100 sesterces (HS) at the market, while the costs of production are 50 HS per acre, a farmer growing wheat for the market will make a profit of 50 HS per acre. But, if it costs him 5 HS per mile (in time, labor, and transport outlays) to ship an acre's produce, he would operate at a loss at a distance greater than 10 miles.

Now, take a second farmer growing flowers. Since this product is perishable, and harder to produce and transport, he can get 150 HS per acre's produce at the market, but the costs of production are 75 HS, and the transport costs per mile are 10 HS. This means that at a distance greater than 7.5 miles from the market, the flower grower will not realize a profit.

These relationships are graphed in figure 1 below. It will be seen from the graph that flower growers can bid higher prices, or rents, in the range of 0–5 miles from the market; further out, wheat farmers will bid higher. Segments *MT* of the rent-bid curve for flower farming and *TS* for wheat farming will be the effective rents, while segments *RT* and *TN* represent unsuccessful bids. The process continues indefinitely for other crops until the rent-bid lines resemble a curve.

A market economy, therefore, influences to a large extent the price of land, the types of crops produced, and the type of settlement pattern near a city. This may explain why Roman agricultural writers recommended growing garden products, and other perishables that fetch a high price at the market, but cost a great deal to produce, near the city.[22] Indeed, the

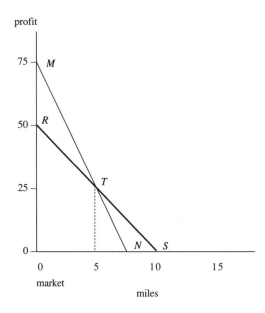

Figure 1.

price of agricultural land near the city of Rome was roughly ten times more than the price of ordinary agricultural land in Italy.[23] If the price of agricultural land rose near the city, one would expect an open settlement of prosperous villas and farmsteads nearby. When the farmer lives on the land he cultivates, the time and transport costs necessary to produce the crops are reduced and this enables the land to be exploited more intensively. In a nucleated settlement, such as a town or village, the farmer must often travel considerable distances to his fields, making their intensive cultivation more difficult.[24]

This view of a rural market economy organized on a rational (if not capitalistic) basis, is in conflict with the current primitivist notion that Greco-Roman agriculture was pre- or nonrational, and uninterested in profit. It is often maintained that, since a system of double-entry bookkeeping, (with separate accounts kept of profits and expenditures for different parcels of land) was not applied to agricultural production until A.D. 1770, when Arthur Young published his book, *A Course of Experimental Agriculture* (although this view may be challenged), no system of rational exploitation was possible before that date, because profits and losses could not be calculated.[25] Nevertheless, the empirical rules long in existence before 1770 assured many farmers a profit. Several good rules were recommended by Roman agricultural writers: grow labor intensive crops near the city and less intensive crops further out, analyze which crops are grown successfully and unsuccessfully on neighboring farms, economize on labor and materials where practicable, and above all understand the demands of the urban market.

The work of G. Mickwitz on rationalism in Greco-Roman agriculture is often cited by the primitivist school in favor of their arguments. But even he concluded that, "under this empirical system of farm management, it was . . . possible for the Romans to get a general idea of the average profits to be gained from farming."[26]

A rational system of agricultural markets is reflected in the advice of Roman agronomists concerning the different types of crops that are most suitable at various distances from the city. It is also reflected in the settlement patterns observed near ancient cities such as Corinth, and in the marketing networks that joined the cities to the towns of the region discussed in appendix 1.

## Agriculture

To assess the contribution of the city's agricultural *territorium* to Corinth's economy, the relationship between the maximum agricultural production of the territorium and Corinth's total population must be examined. The *territorium* of the city state of Corinth was about 825 square kilometers (318 square miles), and the area seems to have been the same in both the Greek and Roman eras.[27] Of this land, only about 207 square kilometers (80 square miles) is capable of supporting any kind of agriculture, and is therefore a *maximum* figure.[28] Modern climatological and geological research has confirmed that the climate, pedology, and forestation of modern Greece is similar to that of the Greco-Roman era.[29]

Even with high yields of 16 hectoliters per hectare (18 bushels per acre) of barley, 207 square kilometers (80 square miles) of cultivable land would scarcely support 17,600 people, giving each one a mere 1.2 kilogram (2.65 pounds) of grain per day, or about 2,600 calories.[30] This allowance gives each individual the production of just 1.17 hectares (2.9 acres) for support, and includes grain that was wasted, spoiled, that went for animal feed, and any surplus needed to pay for shelter, equipment, clothing, entertainment, taxes, and rents. In a two-field system, only half the 1.17 hectare would be under cultivation at any given time. Even individuals growing cash crops such as vine products, fruit, vegetables, and flowers may not have been able to support themselves with such a holding, since 1.17 hectares is probably a considerable underestimate for the average needs of each individual: it only allows for a minimal diet, ignores all other needs, and assumes maximum yields for a region with marginal rainfall. Hence, the figure of 17,600 individuals that could have supported themselves through agricultural production in the ancient Corinthia is an absolute maximum.[31] When surplus grain needed to provide maintenance is included, the actual number of individuals supported by agriculture would have been considerably less—perhaps 8,000. However, it will be argued in chapter 4 that the total population of the city and its territory approached 100,000 by the second century, approximately the size of the old Greek polis.[32] This implies that a maximum of 17 percent of Corinth's population could have earned a subsistence living through agricultural production directly, or indirectly through rents.

Furthermore, the maximum numbers of individuals living in the city of Corinth who were directly supported by agricultural production probably never exceeded 10,000, and the actual numbers supported were probably considerably less. This is because 10,000 individuals will need the yield of a minimum of 117 square kilometers (45 square miles) of cultivable land to support themselves.[33] The radius of a circle with an area of 117 square kilometers is 6.1 kilometers (3.8 miles) and hence, a farmer living in the city and cultivating land on the periphery of the 117 square kilometer circle would have to walk a total of about 12.2 kilometers (7.6 miles) round-trip to his fields and back.

For Corinth, however, a circle with a radius of 6.1 kilometers with the city at its center would include vast stretches of the Corinthian Gulf, much land not suitable for cultivation, and the urban area of Corinth itself, which was not under cultivation, except perhaps for garden plots. In fact, a circle with a radius of 6.1 kilometers contains about 25 square kilometers of the Corinthian Gulf, 10.4 square kilometers occupied by the city of Corinth and Lechaion, and about 34 square kilometers of uncultivable wasteland— land whose slope is too steep, and soil too thin to allow cultivation at present and presumably also in the past.[34] Because of these factors, one needs a circle with an area of about 285 square kilometers (110 square miles) and a radius of almost 10 kilometers (6 miles) to contain 117 square kilometers of cultivable land. This would require a journey of over 19 kilometers (12 miles) round trip for an urban farmer with fields near the periphery of the 10-kilometer radius.

Distance is only part of the problem the urban farmer would encounter in cultivating fields in the countryside; another is time. While it is easy to walk to fields along the flat coastal plain at a pace of five to six kilometers per hour (three to four miles per hour), it is much more difficult to attain that speed to reach fields south of Corinth, where one must contend with the steep slopes of Acrocorinth and Pentaskouphi. A journey from the forum area of Corinth to the saddle between these two heights takes about an hour, and a detour around them to the south takes even longer.[35] Thus, a farmer living in the ancient city would add two or more hours to the round-trip journey to fields south of Corinth.

A third factor that would limit the distance the ancient farmer could walk to his fields was the probable fragmentation of his holdings. The partible system of inheritance used by the Greeks and Romans would promote the divisions of land owned by a family when the land was bequeathed to more than one individual.[36] The existence of dowries would further tend to fragment a family's holdings by adding parcels of land held by other families whose holdings were not necessarily contiguous to those of the husband's family.[37] Certainly the fragmentation of land holdings is a reality in much of Greece and Italy today, and it has important consequences for agricultural production.[38]

It was also important for the ancient farmer to live as close as possible to his fields because the labor of women and children as well as men was needed in farming, and the processes of production often required the close integration of farmstead and fields for manuring and other activities. The farmer had to transport his tools, draft animals, seed, and the produce itself at harvest, as well as protect his land from predators, especially when cash crops easy to steal and transport were grown. Modern agricultural economists analyzing distances farmers walk to their fields have shown that the extreme distances are only about 6 kilometers (3.73 miles) and the average distances only about 1 kilometer (.6 mile). When farmlands are heavily fragmented, as in modern Greece and Italy, the average distances from house to fields is only .3 kilometer (.18 mile) to 1.8 kilometers (1.12 miles) at the extreme, and these farmers often use modern means of transportation (small tractors or other mechanized vehicles) that were unavailable to the ancient farmer.[39] Clearly, it is not reasonable to assume that ancient farmers would travel greater distances to their fields than their modern, mechanized counterparts in a variety of differing cultural, economic, and geographical circumstances.

For these reasons, Davis concludes that no more than 3,000 to 5,000 in any given community could have been supported by farming during pre-industrial eras.[40] It is highly improbable that this figure was exceeded in Roman Corinth or any other Greek or Roman city. Certainly, a figure of 10,000 would be an absolute maximum for the city of Corinth, given the geographical realities of the site and the fact that the grain allowance for the diet and maintenance of the 10,000 individuals was calculated as a bare minimum. The human response to these problems has been the widespread distribution of agricultural villages that minimize the farmer's journey to his fields. There were great numbers of these villages in the ancient Corinthia and throughout the ancient world. Thus, Corinth could not have been an agro-town.

Of course, one need not have been directly engaged in agricultural production to have been supported by that occupation. Landlords retained a portion of their tenants' surplus in the form of rents, and many may have resided in the city of Corinth, or in their villas in the surrounding countryside. If we want to know how many Corinthians living in the city supported themselves through agriculture, we will have to include them too. But, the total numbers of landlords living from the rents of tenants in the Corinthia probably were not large. This is because rents in the Greco-Roman world seem to have seldom exceeded 10 percent of the tenant's produce and many peasants in the classical era were peasant proprietors who paid no rent.[41]

It is possible to calculate approximately the maximum number of landlords the *territorium* of Corinth could support for different ratios of landownership between landlords employing tenants or slaves and free peasants. For the sake of argument, let us assume that 90 percent of the land of the Corinthia was owned by landlords and 10 percent of the land by free peasants.[42] If more than 90 percent of the Corinthia was owned by landlords employing tenants or slaves, slightly more landlords could subsist on their labor; if landlords owned less than 90 percent, their numbers would be fewer. The reader is free to employ whatever proportion he chooses.

Some landlords used slaves as well as or instead of tenants, but this difference in the mode of production does not significantly alter the analysis, since slaves are like tenants in that they surrender a portion of their production to someone else. They differ in that the tenant was responsible for his own maintenance while slaves received their maintenance from their owners. Nor were slaves necessarily more efficient workers than tenants; they may not have produced more net surplus to their owners (their net production minus their maintenance) than tenants produced in rents for their landlords. If slaves were more efficient, we would expect Roman agriculture during the Imperial era to have been dominated by slave labor, but this was not the case.[43] In fact, under many circumstances, tenants were thought to be more efficient than slaves. Therefore, it is unlikely that the net surplus slaves provided their owners far exceeded the rents provided by tenants to their landlords.

If 90 percent of Corinth's cultivable land was owned by landlords, this would amount to 18,616 hectares (46,080 acres). If 20,685 hectares (the total cultivable land area of the Corinthia) supported a maximum of 17,600, then 18,616 hectares would support a maximum of 15,840 individuals, giving each one about 1.17 hectares (2.9 acres) to supply the minimum nutritional requirement necessary for survival.[44] In a two-field system, only half of the 1.17 hectares would be under cultivation at any given time. It should be stressed that the 1.17-hectare figure is a gross underestimate, since it excludes any surplus needed for *anything* besides food. Even those growing cash crops (such as vine products, fruit, vegetables, flowers) would probably need a larger holding, while those cultivating land in barren, rocky regions would need far more.

To estimate the maximum number of landlords for this proportion of landownership, we shall only allot to each one the net production of 1.17

hectares. Thus, a landlord by this definition will be someone who ekes out a bare subsistence from rents. In reality of course, many landlords received considerably more than a minimum subsistence from their rents, so their actual numbers were probably far lower than their maximum number. One can make any number of assumptions concerning the ratio of the numbers of landlords to the numbers of slaves and tenants for the 15,840 souls who were supported from the 18,616 hectares. But, different assumptions will have an effect on the rents (or the surplus produced by slaves), which seem to have averaged about 10 percent of the gross production. In fact, the tenants' rents can be estimated for different ratios of landlords and tenants, when the total cultivable land area of a given region is known, and each landlord receives a given portion of a tenant's production. In this case, the landlord will receive the bare minimum of production necessary to sustain life: the net yield of 1.17 hectares. Again, this will give us the *maximum* numbers of landlords supported entirely by agriculture.

To estimate the rent, let us make an assumption about the ratio between landlords and tenants. We may make any assumption we wish, but first let us assume that there were 14,000 tenants and slaves and 1,840 landlords earning a living from our 18,616 hectares. First, we divide the total land area owned by landlords (18,616 hectares) by the number of tenants. This gives us 1.33 hectares (3.3 acres), as the actual amount of land each tenant will be farming. Next, we subtract the amount of land needed for the tenant's own minimum maintenance (1.17 hectares) from the amount of land he is farming (1.33 hectares) leaving .16 hectare, the produce of which is the tenant's rent. Expressed as a percent of the tenant's holding, we divide .16 by the size of the tenant's holding (1.33) and derive a rent of 12 percent. If we assume there were 13,000 tenants and 2,840 landlords, we would divide 18,616 by 13,000 (= 1.43), then subtract 1.17 (= .26), and divide .26 by 1.43 to obtain a rent of 18 percent, and so on.

These relationships can be expressed by the following formula:

$$R = \frac{\dfrac{L}{T} - A}{\dfrac{L}{T}}$$

where $R$ = the rent, $L$ = the total land area involved, $T$ = the total numbers of tenants and/or slaves, and $A$ = the minimum allotment of land needed to sustain a human life (it may be adjusted if the reader chooses).

Furthermore:

$$T = \frac{L - PA}{A},$$

where $P$ = the number of landlords, and

$$P = \frac{L - TA}{A}.$$

Finally,

$$R = \frac{PA}{L}.$$

In other words, for a given region supporting a given number of landlords and tenants, the rent rate expressed as a percentage of gross production will also give the percentage of landlords in the population, when the assumption is made that each individual receives a bare minimum subsistence. Therefore, it is unlikely that the maximum numbers of landlords deriving their maintenance from lands in the Corinthia ever exceeded 1,400, with an agricultural rent of about 12 percent; their actual numbers would have been considerably less. Doubtless, some landlords living in the city of Corinth probably owned land outside the Corinthia. But, at the same time, Herodes Atticus, living in Athens, owned considerable properties in the Corinthia, and the rents from these would have been removed from Corinth's economy (some portion to be sure, returned to Corinth in the form of the benefactions he made to the city.)[45] Thus, Corinth could not have been a consumer city either.

Little is known about animal husbandry in Roman Corinth. The Corinthia had always been a breeder of horses and the majority of the known victors in the hippic contests at the Isthmian Games in Roman times were Corinthians.[46] This indicates the prosperity of Corinth's elite, who were wealthy enough to raise, train, and equip winning teams of horses. Remains of pigs and cattle were found in excavations in the Roman city and Saint Paul and his companions Priscilla and Aquilla were employed in the city making tents, awnings, and perhaps sails, of goat hair.[47] Doubtless there were also sheep, donkeys, and bees. For comparison, in 1961 some 54.31 square kilometers (21 square miles) of the region occupied by the ancient city-state was devoted to pasturage supporting 5,132 mules, horses, and donkeys; 394 cattle; 34,238 sheep and goats; 360 pigs; and 2,787 bee hives.[48] There are also large fish runs of tuna, sardines, and mackerel in the Saronic Gulf during the spring and fall that attract fishermen today from all over the Aegean basin.[49] Doubtless, many Corinthians earned a seasonal livelihood from this source, and access to fishing areas may help explain the occupation of otherwise desolate and remote harbors on the Saronic Gulf in the Roman era.

In conclusion, it seems highly improbable that more than 10,000 individuals living in the city of Corinth could have been supported by agricultural production. Nor was it possible for more than about 3,000 more individuals residing in the city (or elsewhere) to have earned even a minimum living from the rents of tenants. However, the population of the urban areas of Corinth and Lechaion seems to have been about 80,000. Twenty thousand more may have lived in rural settlements in the countryside (see chapter 4), and hence, only about one-eighth of the population at most could have maintained themselves directly or indirectly through agriculture.[50]

Here, it must be stressed that (whatever M. I. Finley may have said) a town whose economy is based on urban farmers commuting to their fields and back, and those who produce goods and services for these farmers is an *agro-town*. A town whose economy is based on a *rentier* class and those producing goods and services for that class is a *consumer city*. It is important to keep these two types separate. Corinth was not an agro-town and could never have been a consumer city, whether its population was eighty thousand, forty thousand, or even ten thousand.

There were scores of populous city-states with geographical locations along the sea, similar to Corinth, and with similar-sized *territoria*;[51] probably none were consumer cities, and few if any would have been agrotowns. It would not be difficult to apply the same analysis to most other ancient cities and reach the same conclusion. This seems to require that almost all classical cities be removed from Weber's category of "consumer city." How, then, did the vast majority of Corinthians earn their living?

## Manufacturies

Many Corinthians probably worked in the city's manufacturies. Although the record for most of them has perished, some evidence survives for lamp and pottery manufacture, work in bronze, and marble sculpture—only a small fraction of the vast variety of goods that would have been manufactured in a large city such as Corinth. As a major trading center, and a convenient destination for many merchant voyages, Corinth was ideally located for manufacturies requiring the reprocessing or combination of goods, since materials from different regions could be easily collected in the city. Bronze manufacture (requiring the mixture of tin and copper) and perfume making (mixing scents and oils from different regions) are two recorded examples; there were doubtless many others.

### Lamps and Pottery Manufacture

The manufacture of terracotta lamps is the best documented of Corinth's industries.[52] In many ways, lamp-making may serve as a paradigm for Corinth's other manufacturies whose record is lost, and help illustrate principles of economic growth in ancient cities.

During the first decades of the colony, Corinth's tiny lamp industry struggled to meet the demand for cheap, coarse products for the local market. Fine, mold-made lamps are found in greater numbers in Corinth than in any other city on the Greek mainland in the late first century B.C. But most of the fine lamps used in Corinth during the first decades of its existence were imported from Asia Minor, and are often called "Ephesian lamps," because their place of manufacture seems to be in that city, or perhaps elsewhere in Ionia.

Corinth's own industries produced cheap, wheel-made products of poor quality, purchased by those who did not wish to buy the more expensive imports from Asia. In the last years of the first century B.C., the Ephesian imports began to decline at Corinth, and their place was taken largely by imports from Attica (Type 20 lamps). A little later, more artistic, mold-made, lamps went into production in Italy, and quickly drove both the Ephesian and Attic lamps from the export market at Corinth. These large, elegant, Italian lamps, often with two or more spouts, were modeled after expensive metal prototypes, and their delicately molded relief designs have made them minor works of art. Italian lamps dominated the market for imported lamps at Corinth during the first three-quarters of the first century A.D. Notably, Corinth's own production of cheap, wheel-made lamps increased during this period, at least partially because the Italian imports were somewhat expensive. There were even a few Corinthian lamps exported. Close commercial connections with Italy are indicated by the great numbers of cheap Italian "factory lamps" imported into Corinth, and seldom found in the rest of Greece. The large imports of Italian lamps provide a glimpse of what must have been a significant trade with the new colony, whose colonists were of Italian origin, and who would naturally maintain contacts with their homeland.

During the reign of Domitian (81–96), Corinthian lamp-makers began manufacturing imitations of the expensive, glazed, Italian imports. However, the inability of glaze to adhere to Corinthian clay made the lamp-makers change to unglazed products that were specially treated to render them impervious to oil. Corinth, now with its own fine lamps, abruptly ceases importing expensive Italian lamps, and its own lamps now begin to be exported throughout the Eastern Mediterranean.[53] The exquisitely molded scenes on the discus of the lamps include representations of famous works of art (some located in Corinth), gladiatorial combats, exotic animals, erotic scenes, and religious subjects. Although local imitations of Corinthian lamps were made elsewhere (chiefly at Sparta and Athens), no other lamps were imported into Corinth through the early third century A.D. and Corinthian lamps formed a significant portion of exported lamps in many Eastern Mediterranean markets during this era.

The makers' names stamped on Corinthian lamps are significant in several respects. The majority are Italian names transcribed into the Greek alphabet, which indicates that not only was the city's elite of Italian (or at least Italianized Greek) origin, which we learn from inscriptions, but also these working-class entrepreneurs. It also indicates that much of the market for the lamps, whether at home or abroad, was Greek-speaking, and is evidence for Greeks in Roman Corinth, who were probably becoming a majority of the population. Moreover, nine names on Corinthian lamps are identical to those of Italian manufacturers.[54] Most of the names appear on the Italian factory lamps being produced concurrently with the Corinthian Type 27 lamps which bear the same names. This may be coincidence (the names are common), but it is possible that some Italian manufacturers established branches in Corinth or vice versa.

Early in the third century, Corinthian manufacturers began establishing branches in Athens to produce glazed imitations of Corinthian lamps. These branches stirred the local Athenian lamp-makers to greater efforts, and by the mid-third century, these imitation Corinthian lamps began to appear in Corinth itself. By the mid-fifth century, some 75 percent of Corinth's lamps were imported from Attica.[55]

A similar pattern of production can be detected in the manufacture of pottery at Corinth.[56] Most of the expensive terra sigillata wares found at Corinth from the earliest dated pottery deposits (A.D. 25–50) contain a predominance of Italian Arretine ware, and two forms manufactured in the East (Eastern Sigillata A from northern Palestine and Eastern Sigillata B), as well as some locally produced imitations. It is significant that during this period greater proportions of Italian Arretine ware were found in the pottery deposits at Corinth than at Athens or even Cenchreae or Isthmia.[57] In the next period (A.D. 50–150), we find many Eastern imports as well as Western imports from sigillata manufactures in southern Gaul and North Africa. In this era, the stamps on locally made Corinthian imitations changed from Latin names in the Latin alphabet to Greek names in the Greek alphabet, indicating a change in the makers and market that will be discussed in chapter 4. Also during this period, the decorative forms of Corinth's sigillata pottery changes from Western to Eastern types. Later in the second century and early third centuries A.D., local imitations of terra sigillata produced at Corinth predominate, and imports from the East and West virtually disappear.

In addition to terra sigillata, Corinth produced quantities of bowls with glazed relief, based on metal prototypes, which were exported throughout Greece from the mid-second to the end of the third century A.D., and the city always produced quantities of cheap cooking ware for every-day use in the local market.

During the rebuilding of the city, the demand for roof tiles was very great, and their manufacture at Corinth was a municipal monopoly. The early-type tiles bear the stamp COL(onia) L(aus) IVL(ia) COR(inthiensis), followed by the Latin initials of the manufacturer. From the second century onward, the tiles bear two separate stamps: KΛAI—an abbreviation for the name of the city—and a separate stamp with the name or abbreviation of the maker, also in the Greek alphabet.[58]

## Bronze manufacture

Corinth was a flourishing center of artistic production in the Roman period and, above all, its creations in the alloy called "Corinthian Bronze" were highly esteemed by Roman connoisseurs.[59] It will not be out of place to discuss the composition and production of this material, since it indicates the occasionally excessive entrepreneurial spirit of the Roman Corinthians.

One tradition stated that Corinthian Bronze was created from the accidental melting together of several statues of bronze, gold, and silver during Mummius' sack of the city in 146 B.C.[60] Whatever its origin, this so-called alloy of gold, silver, and bronze became popular in Italy after that date, and objects made from it fetched fabulous prices during the late Republic and early Empire.[61] There were three varieties of this alloy, a silver color where the proportion of silver predominated, a golden color where gold dominated, and an alloy of all three in equal proportion.[62] The distinction between bronzes of regular alloy and Corinthian Bronze was slight, and only experienced connoisseurs could distinguish the nuances of color (and even the odor) of the genuine alloy.[63] Pausanias adds that Corinthian Bronze was tempered by plunging the red-hot metal into the waters of the Fountain of Peirene.[64] Presumably the water was piped from the fountain to the industrial quarter, about one mile north of the fountain itself, where a bronze foundry has been located, since there was no foundry near Peirene in Pausanias' day.[65]

One problem for the study of Corinthian Bronze is that no example of this metal alloy has ever been found.[66] Moreover, it would have been impossible for the connoisseur to have distinguished the composition of a metal alloy by its variation in color or smell. Of course, the ancients were able to distinguish pure metals from alloys by using the principles of specific gravity (hence an element's atomic weight) developed by Archimedes, but it would not be possible for them to distinguish the properties or components of alloys.[67] This would require chemical, physical, or spectrographic analyses unknown to the ancient world. This leads one to suspect that if fraud could occur concerning the composition of Corinthian Bronze, it probably did occur.

Corinth did produce a high-tin bronze alloy (about 14 percent tin) in the classical Greek period, and again during the Roman Empire after the city was refounded.[68] This alloy is unique to Corinth; it is not even found at

Sikyon, a stone's throw away. I would like to suggest that the alloy called Corinthian Bronze was a forgery that may have begun in the following way. After the sack of the city in 146 B.C., numerous objects of Corinthian high-tin bronze were transported to Italy in Mummius' immense booty from the looted city. Some Corinthian bronze-workers, who knew the secret for the production of high-tin bronze, were sold as slaves in Italy along with other captives. When it was noted that the color of Corinthian Bronze was different from bronze of standard alloy, the story of the fortuitous mixture arose, probably promulgated by a bronze-worker. Roman connoisseurs accepted the story as the explanation for the lighter color of Corinthian Bronze, and since it was impossible for them to have known the true composition of the alloy, it became a point of honor and prestige among them to determine the genuine alloy by its color and smell. Corinthian high-tin bronze gave the hardness and lightness of color to the Corinthian Bronze noted by the experts.[69]

Pausanias' report about quenching the bronze in Peirene seems to reflect the process necessary to forge high-tin bronze by repeatedly heating it to 650° C, quenching it in water, and hammering. This process would render the alloy workable in a cold state into the decorative motifs for which Corinthian Bronze was famous, and is indicated by the microstructure of the preserved specimens of bronze found in Corinth.[70] However, in the process of producing high-tin bronze, the chemical composition and impurities of the water is of no importance (although the bronze-workers might have thought it was) and the report seems to reflect a common belief that the qualities of different metals could be attributed to the water in which they were quenched.[71] Hence, the Corinthian bronze-workers' report was an attempt to protect their local product from the competition of "Corinthian Bronze"–workers elsewhere by insisting that the genuine alloy could only be produced at Corinth, since Peirene's waters imparted a certain quality to the alloy.

Regardless of the metallurgical composition of Corinthian Bronze, Roman Corinth remained an important center for the manufacture of bronze of standard alloys, as it had been during the Greek era. Many of the numerous works of bronze sculpture in the city noted by Pausanias and represented in the city's municipal coinage were probably produced at Corinth.[72] Some bronzes were probably exported.[73] In fact, Corinth's school of bronze-workers was so influential, it seems to have affected the styles of the marble-sculptors in the city.

### Marble Sculpture

The work of at least three different Corinthian schools has been detected in the surviving fragments of marble sculpture found in the city. Above all, Corinth was an important center for the production of portrait sculpture for both official representations of emperors and their families and for private individuals. At first, the city imported its sculpture (and perhaps sculptors) from Athens, but by the first century A.D., a local workshop developed which followed Athenian models and techniques.[74] This school of portrait sculptors flourished until the fifth and sixth centuries A.D.

Of the imperial portraits probably produced by this school, those of Gaius and Lucius Caesar are among the finest that have survived, and both show the influences of bronze-working techniques.[75] Both stand with a chalmys draped over the right shoulder and forearm and hold a staff or spear in the right hand. The crumpled and wrinkled folds of the chalmys are characteristic of modeling style, a style derived from modeling in clay or wax for reproduction in bronze rather than carving in marble. The pose, the powerful, heavy torso, the massive, sloping shoulders, the thick roll of muscle above the groin line on the hip, all reflect the influence of the Polycleitian school of bronze athletic sculpture. Significantly, the hair with its stiff and accurate locks has an engraved quality similar to that of the Doryphoros of Polycleitus, originally a bronze statue. The eyes also, with their well-defined lids, have an inlaid appearance. Both seem to have been either modeled after bronze originals or under the strong influence of bronze-working techniques.

Influences of bronze production may also be detected in marble sculptors inspired by Aphrodesian or Pergamene models, such as the great altar of Zeus at Pergamon. Two torsos removed from the former church of St. John in the west side of the forum exhibit Pergamene influence in the extraordinary exaggeration of the musculature, especially the rib cage, which resembles "a sack of nuts or potatoes rather than a portion of the human body."[76] The two torsos show a remarkably high polish, not only on the nude surfaces but also on the drapery. The glassy polish given to marble surfaces by sculptors during the Roman era was intended to reproduce the metallic reflection and highlights of works of bronze.[77]

Another example of Pergamene influence has been recognized in a torso in vigorous action which resembles the figure of Apollo on the altar of Zeus at Pergamon.[78] A head of Zeus or Asklepios dating to the second century A.D., found near the Gymnasium, is a version of the Otricoli-type Zeus, and Pergamene inspiration is reflected in the rope-like locks of hair and the restless mass of the beard. The heavy brow ridges resemble those of several figures in the Pergamene altar, especially Klythios.[79] A gigantomachy frieze from the theater dating to the reign of Hadrian is also of Pergamene conception.[80]

A workshop of Neo-Attic style may have flourished in Corinth in the second half of the first century A.D.[81] A product of this school can be recognized in the winged Nike acroterion from the South Basilica. In particular, the modeling lines along the left leg, the illusory transparency of the drapery of the right leg, and the catenary lines of the drapery on the bust, are all typical devices for the representation of drapery in the best Attic work of the fifth and fourth centuries B.C. Neo-Attic work is also represented in the east pedimental sculpture of Temple E, which seems to imitate deliberately the Parthenon pediments, changed only to meet the requirements of a smaller-scale building. All the traditions of fifth century drapery style—motion lines, modeling lines, catenary and transparency lines—are represented in the figures from the pediment.

In the development of Corinth's manufacturies, we see the process of import replacement, occurring when a city replaces its imported goods with those manufactured locally. Undoubtedly, this process occurred for many other Corinthian goods and services whose record has been lost. The process has two important consequences for Corinth's early economic growth.[82] First, it creates new jobs that were not present in the city earlier (i.e. lamp, pottery, and sculpture production), and, second, it adds more money to the local economy, since money previously used to pay for the imports now remains in the city. In turn, the growing local economy creates a demand for more local goods and services.[83] This process also changed the nature of Corinth's imports from finished products (lamps, pottery, bronze, and marble statues) to raw materials (copper, tin, marble blocks, and grain to feed its growing population). The higher demand for agricultural products in the growing city probably caused an increased efficiency of agricultural production in the countryside, reflected in the open system of settlements within a short radius of the Roman city.[84]

It has recently been argued that the importance of manufacturies, especially metal and cloth production, has been underestimated for the Greek and Roman economy.[85] Few of the urban or rural poor could afford the equipment necessary for cleaning, combing, spinning, weaving, and dyeing, which turned raw wool into cloth. In Pompeii, a town of 10,000, there were some forty large-scale cloth-producing establishments, and in Egypt professional guilds of weavers produced for the local and export market.[86] This implies that many households had to purchase manufactured cloth on the market. The high labor inputs required for mining, smelting, forging, casting, and transport of metals probably had significant consequences for the extent of ancient manufacturies and trade.

## Rents and Taxes

The consequences of the relatively low rent and tax rates for the Greco-Roman world before the fourth century A.D. have also not been considered, and this has caused the manufacturing and service sectors of the ancient economy to be underestimated. The current view is that tenants and peasants of the early Roman Empire produced very little surplus, perhaps only 2 percent over and above what they needed for their own maintenance,

seed, taxes, and rents.[87] This view is based largely on comparisons of the
surplus available in other pre- and nonindustrial societies. However, there
is some reason to question this comparison. Available evidence shows that
agricultural rents, exclusive of taxes, average between 20 percent and 40
percent of gross agricultural production in most subsistence agricultural
societies, with a few higher or lower exceptions.[88] Although the evidence
for rents is limited for the Greek and Roman world, rates of 10 percent of
gross production are indicated.[89] Land taxes for the late Roman Republic
and early Empire also averaged about 10 percent of production. The rate of
the land tax seems to have doubled between about A.D. 324 and 364, and
tripled the rate of the late Republic and early Empire by Justinian's day.
Furthermore, rents seem to have increased in the same proportion, so that
the tenant of the late Roman Empire was paying some 60 percent of his
produce to his landlord and to the state.

This tripling of taxes and rents has important consequences for the analysis of rents, taxes, and surpluses in earlier eras. If the tax and rent rate
tripled to around 60 percent, yet the tenant still managed to survive, still
managed to provide his maintenance, seed, taxes, and rent, what does this
reveal about the surpluses available to the tenant and peasant before the
rates increased? Does it not indicate that, before around A.D. 300, the peasant and tenant had about three times the surplus available to him beyond
what he needed for maintenance, seed, rents, and taxes than he had in
Justinian's day? If the peasant of the early Empire had a surplus of only 2
percent of his gross production at a tax rate of 10 percent, no peasant could
have been able to maintain himself when the rate increased to 30 percent.
Yet, although some peasants were driven to desperate flight in the late Empire, many managed to survive.

Another overlooked factor in the calculation of peasant-farmer productivity is the clear statement in Aristotle's *Politics* (1267a-1268b). Aristotle
is describing Hippodamus' ideal state where there are three equal classes:
the farmers, the workers, and the warriors. The farmers farm for themselves, the workers work, and the warriors fight. Aristotle criticizes the
scheme, and notes that farmers who produce only enough for themselves
(i.e., at a subsistence level) are useless to the state; they should reasonably
be expected to produce enough both for themselves and for the warriors:

> Furthermore, what use are the farmers to the state? There must be
> artisans, for every state requires them, and they can make a living
> as in the other states from the practice of their craft; but as for the
> farmers, although it would have been reasonable for them to be a
> portion of the state if they provided the class possessing the arms
> with its food, as it is they have private land of their own and farm
> it for themselves. . . . But, if one is to make those who cultivate
> the private and the common land the same people, the amount of

the produce from the farms which each man will cultivate will be scanty for two households. Moreover, why are not they [the farmers] both to take food for themselves and to supply it to the soldiers direct from the land and from the same allotments?[90]

In other words, the farmer ought to be able to provide for two households, provided that this does not involve the farming of public lands, which Aristotle thinks is unproductive.[91] Therefore, the classical peasant and tenant had between 30 percent and 50 percent of his surplus left over, and not 2 percent, and since these groups made up the majority of the population,[92] this had an important impact on the Roman economy. The overlooking of these important facts has given us an erroneous view of the productivity of Greco-Roman agriculture.

Both Aristotle and the tax increases of the late Empire tell the same story. The peasant had 50 percent of his gross surplus left over after he took care of the needs of his household. In classical Greece and Rome, most of this surplus was saved, invested, or spent on goods and services the peasant wanted. In the late Empire, the 50 percent was confiscated by the state and landlord. This enriched the state and landlord at the peasant's expense. In the classical era, the peasant was not a subsistence farmer. In the late Empire, because of brutal rents and taxes (and now even labor rents of two to three days per *week*), he became a subsistence farmer, with almost nothing left over for himself after he provided for his household's maintenance, rents, and taxes.

### Agricultural Surplus and Living Standards

A further reason why manufactures and services may have been underestimated is the simplistic comparison of Greek and Roman societies with those of the nonindustrial, non-Western world. This practice may promote fundamental distortions in our understanding of the amount of surplus available to the Greek and Roman peasant and their per-capita minimum daily caloric consumption. Figures for the classical world are sometimes derived from comparisons with modern societies where starvation, deprivation, and death are rampant.

One overlooked factor that may have contributed to larger surpluses among Greek and Roman peasants was a relationship between population and resources common to European societies. Historical demographers have noted that Western European populations from at least the late Medieval era onward limited their numbers well below their potential maxima in relation to the resources available to support them.[93] In non-European societies however (those with which the Greeks and Romans are frequently compared) population levels are much closer to the limits of the available resources. In other words, for any given level of resources, a West European population would have been much lower than a non-European one, giving the European population a higher per-capita living standard. This relationship does not seem to have been based on differences in political or economic systems, but to differences in the expectation of living standards. These expectations were in turn reflected in marriage patterns, fertility, and family structure. If this "European pattern" existed in the classical world (and the evidence suggests that it did), it would help explain the magnitude of the peasant's surplus, upon which the classical city was based to a large extent. It also serves as a warning not to compare Greeks and Romans with other pre- and nonindustrial societies in an uninformed way, and to be aware of significant differences that may exist.[94]

Nevertheless, although the peasantry's aggregate demand was probably substantial and their demand for goods and services has probably been underestimated previously, Corinth's rural population was limited in numbers, and could not have provided a market for large amounts of urban manufacturies. Therefore, as important as manufacturies may have been for other cities and the early growth of Corinth, they probably did not play the dominant role in its economy, nor were they responsible for most of Corinth's population engaged in nonagricultural occupations. There was a limit to which Corinth's local market could absorb manufacturies, and the sale of goods and services to Corinth's urban market would merely redistribute them and the money used to purchase them within the city. This would not earn the city income.[95]

Furthermore, there would only be a limited market for Corinthian exports of fine manufactured goods. This is because the goods manufactured at Corinth were also produced in most other large cities in the Roman world as well.[96] Even Corinthian claims about its bronze did not prevent "Corinthian Bronze" from being manufactured abroad.[97] Why purchase a lamp or bronze vessel from Corinth when one could purchase much the same thing made in one's own city, less the transport costs? For these reasons, ancient "factories" remained small, and the numbers of individuals employed in them few.[98] There seem to have been only about 30 manufacturers of fine lamps at Corinth during the first and second centuries A.D.[99] In an era of slow technological innovation, most manufacturing processes remained widely dispersed in towns and cities throughout the Empire.

It was the provision of services, both to the inhabitants of its local marketing region in the northeastern Peloponnese, and more importantly, to merchants engaged in long-distance trade, travelers, and tourists, that seems to have been the basis for Corinth's economy throughout its history.

The Corinth Canal. Originally begun by Emperor Nero, it was finished by a French company in 1893. The cut is made through a vast deposit of marl that underlies much of the
Corinthia.

The Coastal Plain looking Northwest from Acrocorinth. The fabulous productivity of the plain in antiquity owed more to the intensive agriculture practiced by Corinthian farmers than to its natural fertility.

Marl deposit with cap of Corinthian sandstone (poros). These deposits were essential for Corinth's tile, terracotta, and pottery manufactures. The strong, lightweight sandstone was a valuable building material. Rain water trapped by the impermeable layer of marl flowed north through cracks and fissures, and burst out in numerous springs in and near the city.

Vines growing in southern Corinthia. Corinth has always been a major producer of wine and grapes. The word "currant" is a corruption of "Corinthe" through French.

The Xerias River Valley and the Plain of Tenea. The landscape of the Corinthia was sacred to the Greeks. Visitors felt themselves in the presence of the gods and heroes who made the Corinthia their home, especially Poseidon, Aphrodite, Helios, Palaimon, and Bellerophon.

The Village of Archaia Korinthos from Acrocorinth. The ancient city lies below the modern village and its surrounding fields. The Archaic Temple is visible to the left.

The Fortification Walls of Acrocorinth with the Coastal Plain in the Distance. Corinth was a strategic center throughout its history, as these walls indicate. It not only controlled traffic through the Isthmus, but its acropolis was never taken by assault. The walls shown here are mainly Venetian and Turkish.

The Classical Tower on Acrocorinth. The bastion to the right of the gate retains masonry from the fourth century B.C. fortifications.

Statue, possibly of Lucius Caesar, produced in Corinth early in the first century A.D.

Mosaic from a Roman Villa depicting Dionysos. This splendid mosaic is an indication of the skill of Corinthian artists and the wealth of their patrons.

Restoration of the Corinthian Forum as it Appeared in the Second Century A.D. This north view shows the Archaic Temple overlooking the Northwest shops. The Captives Facade and the Propylaea are to the right. Surmounting the Propylaea are bronze statues of Helios and Phaëthon being drawn in chariots, one facing north, the other, south. The mountains of Helicon and Parnassus are in the distance. Courtesy, Charles K. Williams, II

The Lechaion Road with Acrocorinth in the Distance. Paved streets and covered drains not only added to the aesthetic appearance of the city, but were fundamental components of public health policy.

The Fountain of Peirene.

Corinthian Municipal Coin depicting a lighthouse, probably at Lechaion. Lighthouses, harbors, canals, roads, and commercial facilities all indicate that trade was important for the Greeks and Romans. Reprinted from Price and Trell (1977) by permission of the Wayne State University Press.

Coin Showing the Temple of Aphrodite on Acrocorinth. This temple was a major tourist attraction in the Roman era, although the sacred prostitutes of the Greek period no longer existed. Reprinted from Price and Trell (1977) by permission of the Wayne State University Press.

Coin Depicting Pegasus and the nymph Peirene. The myth of Pegasus and Bellerophon was localized at Corinth. The site associated with them on Acrocorinth was a center for pilgrimages and played a similar role to the shrines of saints in the Christian tradition. Reprinted from Price and Trell (1977) by permission of the Wayne State University Press.

The Temple of *Gens Julia*. This municipal coin depicts a Doric, hexastyle temple that may be the Archaic Temple, the largest temple known to have been standing in Roman Corinth. Reprinted from Price and Trell (1977) by permission of the Wayne State University Press.

The Archaic Temple of Apollo. Built in the mid-sixth century B.C., it may have been rededicated to *Gens Julia,* the family of the founder of the Roman city.

The Governor's Tribunal, or *Bema*, in the Forum. As Corinth was the capital of the province of Achaea, the governor and his staff were often present in the city on legal business. St. Paul was brought before Cornelius Gallio at this site in 51 A.D. by the Jewish community of Corinth.

# 3
# The Service Economy

> For the cocks began to crow and the
> country people that used to bring things
> to the market place would be coming up
> to town.
>
> Plutarch, *Life of Aratus* 8. 3

The service sector of ancient urban economies has been generally under-
rated by historians who have instead concentrated on agriculture and manufactures. However, both of these components are insufficient foundations
for Corinth's economy, and they are probably inadequate for other large
Roman cities as well. There seem to be two reasons why the role of services has been neglected in the study of ancient urban economies. First is
the frequent failure to separate the ancient polis into its urban and rural
components. While rural and urban regions of the polis were combined
politically, administratively, and judicially, the rural countryside and the
urban capital performed quite different economic functions. These different
functions are not always seen when the two regions are considered together. The second reason is the underestimate of the economic surpluses
kept by peasants and tenant farmers discussed previously. Service facilities, however, have left an impressive archaeological record, and their existence can be logically deduced from other evidence.

The city of Corinth provided many services which were unavailable in
the towns, villas, and villages of the countryside. These services may be
divided into two types, primary, or attractive services, and secondary services. Primary services would include religious, educational, cultural, and
judicial activities that brought rural residents into the city. While in the city,
these individuals would need secondary services such as food, temporary
lodging, or the use of a public bath or latrine. Secondary services would
not attract the rural resident to the city (few presumably would travel to the
city to use a latrine), but would fulfill his needs during his stay. Of course,
services offered by the city were also used by city residents, but this activity would only serve to redistribute funds in the city and not earn the city
new wealth. It is the services offered to non-residents which earned the city
income. What services did Corinth provide to its rural and urban citizens?

First, the city provided a large number of religious services for native
Greek cults, Roman cults, and cults of Oriental divinities.[1] Pausanias lists
more different religious cults practiced in Corinth than in any other city in

43

the Peloponnese.[2] As the largest city in Roman Greece, Corinth's population practiced a great number of different religions reflecting the diverse ethnic and national backgrounds, and social and economic statuses of its people.

Attendance at a religious shrine was often necessary for the proper worship of a divinity. This was especially true for cults that required initiation rites, such as Demeter and Kore, whose agricultural significance probably attracted great numbers of rural residents, and Isis and Serapis. The cult of Asklepios also required his worshipers to be present at his shrine while the rites were performed. Many worshipers at the city's shrines bought dedications of edible goods, or of terracotta, gold, and silver made by the city's craftsmen.

Connected with the religious cults of the city were the joyous and colorful festivals and processions, such as the one Apuleius describes for the cult of Isis and Serapis at Corinth.[3] The processions attracted large crowds, and they used many items that could only have been produced in the city or imported from abroad: flowers from local gardens, perfumes, scented oils, and religious utensils of gold and silver. All these activities would enhance the city's economy.[4] The development of pagan and Christian religions in the city of Corinth played a significant role in the city's life, and chapter 5 will be devoted entirely to them.

As the capital city of an important province, Corinth provided many administrative services not only to local residents but also to the whole province. Many provincials traveled to Corinth to attend the governor's law court when it met in the city or petitioned the governor and his staff concerning taxes or other administrative matters. The importance of Corinth's administrative functions are reflected in its buildings: not only was virtually the entire first floor of the 162-meter-long South Stoa converted to administrative functions by the Roman colonists, but the city possessed at least three large basilicas.[5] These structures were used for judicial and administrative purposes, and the fact that Corinth seems to have had more of them than any other city in Greece (at least in the excavated, central areas; Athens has one), testifies to the importance of administrative functions performed by Corinth as compared to other Greek cities in the Roman era, and is further evidence that it was indeed the capital of Achaea (see Plan 2).

Corinth was also the center for tax collection of the entire province. However it is unlikely that Corinth itself was able to benefit much from provincial taxes. The imperial staff at Corinth was small, consisting of the governor, quaestor, and their assistants, and they were frequently absent from the city on their circuit (*conventus*) or engaged elsewhere in the province on official business—especially the quaestor (or procurator when Achaea was an imperial province), who collected the taxes. Not much revenue from the province was spent in Corinth itself, and most probably went north and west to support the armies on the frontiers.[6] Any money that was peculated from the provincials by the governors and their staffs probably found its way back to Italy and Rome where most of them returned after their term of office was over. During the late Empire however, when cities became more parasitical, taxation and the abuse of taxation became an important source of income for Corinth and other cities.

The changing political-administrative status of Corinth during the first century A.D. probably had an impact on its economic history, although, direct evidence for the impact of these administrative changes on Corinth's economy is difficult to find. More coins from municipal mints during Nero's reign than from Claudius' or Vespasian's may indicate the growth of local commerce and exchange when work was begun on the Isthmian canal and the burden of imperial taxes was temporarily lifted (A.D. 67–69). Fewer municipal coins found at Corinth dating to the reigns of Tiberius and Claudius may dimly reflect a reduced amount of local travel to Corinth when it ceased to be the administrative center of Greece. The loss of status as a provincial capital had no observable impact on the city's building program however. Perhaps the sources of wealth that financed the construction of Corinth's buildings were not dependent on local commerce and exchange.

The educational services Corinth offered probably also attracted many inhabitants of the surrounding villas and towns into the city. Philosophers and rhetoricians were active in the Roman city: some, such as the Cynic Demetrius of Corinth (*fl.* late first century A.D.) were permanent residents, while others were temporary residents or visitors. Among the latter were Aelius Aristeides, whose Isthmian oration, *For Poseidon,* gives such a vivid picture of Corinthian life, Apollonius of Tyana, Dio Chrysostum, and the great writer and teacher Plutarch.[7] The Corinthians erected a bronze statue to the orator Favorinus in front of their library, "to stimulate the youth."[8] The library itself may be identified with the Southeast Building in the Forum (see plan 2), erected shortly after the refoundation of the city, and rebuilt in the mid-first century A.D.[9] The size and prominence of this structure in the civic center of the city reflects the importance of the services it fulfilled. A flourishing book trade was also present in the city.[10] As a large city, Corinth possessed primary schools, grammar schools, and schools of rhetoric that would attract many children of wealthy townsmen residing in the countryside.[11]

Fortunately, a few precious scraps survive from Plutarch, providing us with a rare glimpse of the rich social and intellectual life of Roman Corinth during the early Second Century A.D. Plutarch was a frequent visitor to the city, and described scenes from two dinner parties he attended in conjunction with the Isthmian Games, which attracted vast numbers of visitors to the city:

The pine, and why it was used for the crown at the Isthmian Games, was the subject of a discussion at a dinner given us in Corinth itself during the games by Lucanius, the chief priest. Praxiteles, the official guide, appealed to mythology, citing the legend that the body of Melicertes was found cast up by the sea at the foot of a pine. . . . On hearing these remarks, a professor of rhetoric, who was reputed to have a wider acquaintance with polite literature than anyone else, said, "In heaven's name! Wasn't it only yesterday or the day before that the pine became the garland of victory at the Isthmia? Formerly it was celery. This is evident from the comedy where a miser says: 'I'd gladly sell the entire Isthmian show for the price at which the celery crown will go' " . . . It seems to me that I have also read a passage on the Isthmia by Procles, in which the author records that the first contest was held for a crown of pine, but that later, when the contest was made sacred, they adopted the celery crown from the Nemean games.[12]

The second description occurs in the home of M. Antonius Sopsis, who was agonothete of the Isthmian Games twice during the reign of Hadrian:

During the Isthmian Games, the second time Sopsis was president, I avoided the other banquets, at which he entertained a great many foreign visitors at once, and several times entertained all the citizens. Once however, when he entertained in his home his closest friends, all men of learning, I too was present. At the clearing away at the first course, someone came in to present Herodes the professor of rhetoric, as a special honor, with a palm frond and a plaited wreath sent by a pupil who had won a contest with an encomastic oration. After accepting them, he sent them back again, remarking that he did not understand why, of the various games, each one has as a prize a different kind of wreath, but all use a palm frond. . . . Caphisias replied, "If you impose weight on a piece of palm wood, it does not bend down and give way, but curves up in the opposite direction, as though resisting him who would force it. This is the way with athletic contests too. Those who cannot stand the strain because of weakness and softness are pressed down and forced to bend, but those who stoutly bear up under training are raised up and exalted, not in body only but in mind as well."[13]

Corinth also supplied many health and recreational services not available in some of the towns and villages in the countryside. The city was adorned with at least five large and splendid bathing facilities, a testimony both to the city's plentiful water supply and its large population of Romanized immigrants who were accustomed to such amenities in Italy. One of the bath buildings, built on the Lechaion Road north of the forum in the second half of the second century A.D., may have been the largest bath in Greece.[14]

The temple of the Greek healing gods, Asklepios and Hygeia, was located on the northernmost ledge of the city. Bathing and exercise were often prescribed for worshipers at the shrine, which contained its own bathing complex. Both the Fountain of Lerna (Fountain of the Lamps), with its small baths and vast swimming pool, and the Gymnasium, which offered a place to exercise, were located conveniently near the temple (see plans 1 and 2).[15]

Many physicians practiced in the city, and provided services probably not generally available in the towns and villages of the countryside, with their smaller and poorer populations. One physician, Gaius Vibius Euelpistos (fl.ca. A.D. 175–230) was also a priest of Asklepios, and the city honored him for his services.[16] The *venatores* (hunters) who fought in the Corinthian amphitheater had their own doctors, and in honor of one of them, named Trophinus, they erected a bronze statue in the amphitheater by the gate from which the animals were let into the arena.[17] The great physician Galen also stayed some time in the city.[18]

Corinth was a major center of entertainment. One of the first building projects undertaken by the Roman settlers was the restoration of the old Greek theater to its former magnificence.[19] The structure, which held 15,000 spectators, was not only used for theatrical performances, but also for spectacles of all kinds such as the one described by Apuleius for the judgement of Paris.[20] This performance began with a Pyrrhic dance done by choruses of young men and women. Next came an elaborate performance of the judgement itself, complete with an artificial wooden mountain turfed and planted with trees. An artificial stream tumbled down the side of the mountain, and goats grazed on the grass. There followed a graceful ballet, with musical accompaniment appropriate for the judgement itself. The characters of Paris, Mercury, and the goddesses Juno, Minerva, and Venus entered, each accompanied by her appropriate attendants: Juno with Ceres and Proserpina, Minerva with Fear and Terror, and Venus with a crowd of cupids, graces, and seasons. When the thinly clad Venus entered the stage, portrayed with heavenly and marine attributes of her character, she was greeted with a roar of approval by the audience—a fitting response in the City of Aphrodite where dependence on the sea was so important. After Venus' alluring victory dance with her attendants, a fountain of wine mixed with saffron burst from the top of the mountain, showering the goats with the golden color associated with the flocks of Mount Ida. Even if the account is not strictly accurate, it gives an impression of the types of entertainment one could see in the theater. The theater was modified, perhaps by the mid-second century A.D. to function as an arena for wild-beast fights and further modified in the late third century for aquatic performances.[21]

Towards the end of the first century A.D., an odeon seating some 3,000 was built immediately south of the theater.[22] Apparently, the theater was no longer able to fulfill all the entertainment needs of the city by that date. The odeon could serve as a small theater or music hall, but after a disastrous fire in about 225, the structure was rebuilt as a small arena for gladiatorial contests and wild-beast fights.

Although gladiatorial contests and wild-beast hunts were popular in some cities of Roman Greece, the Corinthian enthusiasm for these spectacles was considered excessive by many of their compatriots,[23] and may reflect the Italian cultural influences of Corinth's first settlers. Certainly, Corinth's obsession persisted through the fourth century. Julian wrote that bears and panthers were still hunted in the arena, and that the city appropriated tax money from Argos to pay for the hunts, even though Corinth was prosperous enough to support the expense itself.[24]

At first the games were held in a ravine outside the city, then in the converted theater and odeon; but their popularity required the construction in the late third century of a large amphitheater, one kilometer (.62 mile) northeast of the Archaic Temple. The eliptical arena measured 98 × 63 meters (321 × 207 feet)—larger than the Colosseum in Rome (80 × 50 meters or 262 × 164 feet)—and the structure was described in the mid-fourth century as one of the most significant buildings in the city.[25] In some ways, gladiatorial games were a form of public revenge. Murderers and other criminals condemned on capital charges would fight as gladiators in the presence of the community they had victimized.

Besides formal entertainments such as these, the city offered numerous other amusements. Doubtless, some visitors succumbed to the allurements of the city's numerous prostitutes; indeed, the association of some of these women with the early Christian church provided moral and ethical dilemmas for Paul.[26] Additionally, there must have been a whole host of other entertainments the city offered for which the record has perished—jugglers, story-tellers, and street musicians—that made life in the city a daily festival and celebration.[27]

In addition, the city provided many services of an economic nature to the Corinthia. Corinth provided a huge market for the sale of agricultural surpluses produced in the countryside. Since the city consumed far more than its *territorium* could possibly produce, it had to import most of its food from abroad. Except in the unlikely event of a glut on the market produced by excessive imports, the Corinthian farmer could always find a ready market for his surplus in the city.[28]

The city also provided a market for the purchase of goods not manufactured in local villages. As noted in chapter 2, if the peasant or tenant only had 2 percent of his gross production remaining after paying for seed, maintenance, rents, and taxes, as is commonly believed, then, their combined purchases would have been of negligible importance for the city. But if, as I believe, the peasant and tenant had at least 30 percent of his gross production remaining for purchases (at least through the third century), then the economic consequences for the city would have been considerable. Purchased items may have been produced in the city or imported from elsewhere and distributed by Corinthian middlemen. Such items would include fine pottery and lamps, cloth and clothing, metal products and utensils, and farm equipment. These goods could have been purchased by individuals going directly to Corinth; they could have been provided by itinerant peddlers going from village to village; or perhaps purchased at rotating-market fairs. Regardless of the method of distribution, however, Corinth was the origin (either through manufacturing or importing) of most of the high-order goods purchased by country dwellers.

Furthermore, although the per-capita demand of peasants and tenants was low, their aggregate demand was high. If each peasant needed only one new cloak per year produced in the city, this could have produced an aggregate demand of 20,000 cloaks. The same is true of their purchasing power for other goods and services produced in the city. The aggregate peasant exchange of agricultural surplus for goods and services provided by the city probably contributed more to the urban economy than the aggregate rents collected by landlords. If the peasant and tenant retained a surplus of at least 30 percent of their gross production, their combined purchasing power would be greater than that of the landlords, who only retained about 10 percent of their tenant's production. If the peasant and tenant retained only 2 percent of their gross production, and spent most of it to purchase goods and services in the city, then the surplus of 50 peasants would be needed to support approximately one townsman. But if the peasant and tenant retained at least 30 percent of their gross production, then the surplus of only 3 peasants could support one townsman; a highly significant difference.

Corinth also provided a market for the spending of agricultural rents by its landlords on goods and services provided by the city or imported from elsewhere. Since at least some landlords were wealthy, their demands might include the services of mosaicists, painters, sculptors, and the manufacturers of other luxury goods.

Finally, the city offered migrants from the countryside opportunities to improve their social and economic status through employment in the bustling service economy of the city. The city's relatively high death rates caused by the spread of infectious diseases, would always insure that positions would be available to newcomers, as long as the city's service-oriented economy remained strong. And, the slight population surpluses in the country districts would ensure that migrants were always available to occupy those positions.[29]

While in the city, rural visitors might require secondary services, such as food, lodging, or the use of a public latrine (for which a fee might be charged).[30] Although the secondary services the city offered to its rural citizens were far less important than primary services, they were of a much greater importance for Corinth's economy when provided to traders, travelers, and tourists, who stayed in the city for some time, as we shall see shortly.

The close interdependence of the city and its countryside is reflected in Corinth's position in the marketing network of the northeastern Peloponnese. Furthermore, the city's geographical location as a central place within this region was one of the factors that promoted its economic growth both in Greek and in Roman times. The application of central-place theory to the settlement pattern of the northeast Peloponnese helps demonstrate the validity of these propositions.[31]

### Services Provided to Merchants, Travelers, and Tourists

"Corinth is called wealthy," wrote Strabo, "because of its commerce, since it is located on the Isthmus and is master of two harbors, one which leads straight to Asia and the other to Italy". He continued:

> The exchange of merchandise from both distant countries is made easier by the city's location. And just as in early times, the seas around Sicily were not easy to navigate, nor the high seas, nor was the sea beyond Malea because of the contrary winds. . . . It was a welcome alternative for merchants both from Italy and Asia to avoid the voyage around Malea and land their cargoes here. And also, the duties on what was exported by land from the Peloponnese and what was imported into it fell to those that held the keys. And this has remained ever so in later times.[32]

The provision of services to these long-distance merchants, travelers, and tourists was probably the most important basis of Corinth's economy. These services can be grouped into two basic categories similar to those provided for rural residents: primary services that attracted merchants and travelers to Corinth, and secondary services which these individuals wanted and needed while in the city.

It is well known that the natural situation of Corinth astride the Isthmus facilitated trade between the Aegean and the Gulf of Corinth: the situation of the city itself provided an important service to merchants and travelers. The only land routes between the Peloponnese and Central Greece passed through the Corinthia. Many goods imported into the city were distributed overland to inland towns north and south of the city (see Map 3).[33]

Corinth played a critical role in the sea-borne commerce of the eastern Mediterranean. Many vessels sailing between Asia and Italy unloaded their cargoes at one end of the Isthmus, had the cargoes hauled across, and then reloaded at the opposite end.[34] This was done both to shorten the six-day voyage around the Peloponnese and avoid the treacherous winds and currents around Cape Malea, especially in winter. The ancient proverb, "Round Cape Malea and forget about home,"[35] expressed the foreboding mariners felt when crossing this dangerous stretch of water. Saint Paul, when nearing the Cape, was caught in a frightful storm that blew his vessel all the way to Malta, where it was wrecked.[36] The ancient fear of the Cape was not without justification as modern research indicates. Table 6 clearly shows the dangerous winds of Kythira near the Cape, especially during December and January when some 40 percent of the days experience winds that equal or exceed Beaufort force 6, which would place an ancient sailing vessel in jeopardy.[37] Even in the relatively calm months of summer, winds of that velocity prevail 25 to 30 percent of the time. In striking contrast, at Corinth, only .02 percent of the days in January and February have winds exceeding Beaufort 6 and only .01 percent of the days in December. In fact, on the whole, Corinth has the lowest wind velocities in the areas of Greece and the Aegean measured on the table: it becomes clear why the word halcyon comes from the Halcyonic Gulf north of the city. These geographical and meteorological realities had important consequences for the city.

All our ancient sources wrote of the immense numbers of traders and travelers in Corinth and its ports: "the common emporium of Europe and Asia," and, "the market, common meeting place and festival of the Greeks."[38] Many of the traders were engaged in the transit trade between the eastern and central Mediterranean and used the city as a stopover point while their merchandise was being transshipped across the Isthmus. Other merchants traded directly with the city, fulfilling its large requirements for raw materials such as marble, metals and, above all, food. Doubtless, many of these merchants were Corinthians (it would be astonishing if this were not the case), and their income probably made a substantial contribution to the city's economy.[39] Cicero wrote that, in the Greek era, so many Corinthians were engaged in trade that agriculture was neglected.[40]

Many travelers passed through Corinth on their way to Italy or the East. It seems that travelers compelled to journey in winter always stopped at Corinth on their way, probably for the calmer winds there at that time of year.[41] There are numerous references to travelers using the city as a stopover, from men of letters such as Ovid, Propertius, Apuleius, Apollonius of Tyana, and Plutarch, to administrators and emperors such as Agrippa, Avillius Flaccus, Augustus, Titus, Hadrian and Lucius Verus, to name only a few.[42]

The city of Corinth was a major tourist attraction in itself, and visitors regarded a stay there as a participation in a joyous, continual celebration.[43] The Isthmian Games, one of the three most important religious and athletic festivals in Greece, were celebrated at the Isthmia every two years under Corinthian supervision.[44] These games attracted contestants and spectators from all over the central and eastern Mediterranean, as inscriptions listing the victors in the contests show. The contests were divided into three groups. First came the musical and literary competitions where contestants performed on trumpets, flutes, and lyres. There were also competitions among poets, encomiographers, and bards who sang traditional works accompanied by the lyre. Next came the hippic contests which included the maneuvering of chariots, the *apobatikon,* where one rider rode several horses leaping from one to another, and the *epibaterion,* leaping on and off moving horses or chariots. Horse races were also held with single horses, and two- and four-horse chariots. Finally, there were the athletic contests themselves which included foot races of different lengths, the pentathlon, wrestling, boxing, the pancration, and racing in full armor. The contestants for these competitions were divided by age into boys, youths, and adult men, and competitions would occur within each age group. Only the race in full armor was restricted to adult men. By at least 2 B.C., women and girls also competed in their own contests, of which only chariot racing and foot racing are known. It is likely that their contests included other athletic, hippic, and music contests as well.

Besides the biennial Isthmian Games, there were also the quadrennial Caesarean Games and the Imperial Contests, the former begun in the reign of Tiberius to honor the imperial family. When the Isthmian Games were celebrated alone as in 28, 24, and 20 B.C., they are designated the Lesser Isthmia, and when they were celebrated concurrently with the Caesarean Games and Imperial Contests (30, 36, 22, and 18 B.C.) they are called the Greater Isthmia. The Caesarean and Imperial competitions included contests for the best encomia to reigning emperors and their families, poetry, and singing contests.

Of course, visitors who came to these summer festivals would also be attracted to the other types of entertainment the city offered. Indeed, so important were these attractions to the city that they were advertised on its coins, which may be regarded in part as promotional devices. For example, many Corinthian coin types depict Aphrodite and her famous temple on Acrocorinth, reminding the bearer of one kind of entertainment all too freely available in the "City of Aphrodite." Next in number to her coin types are those depicting Poseidon and his sanctuary at the Isthmia. Pegasus and Bellerophon, whose first encounter occurred at Corinth, were also depicted for those with antiquarian interests.[46]

## Coinage

An analysis of the mints, dates, and denominations of the coins found at Corinth dating to the Roman era can help us understand the international character of Corinth's trade and tourism. It will also help us see how Corinth was affected by various economic trends that occurred throughout the empire (see tables 7–10).[47]

In the municipal coins issued by city mints, we see the closest economic connections with Corinth's nearest neighbors in the Peloponnese. The coins of Argos are the most numerous (81) followed by coins from other nearby Peloponnesian communities (45), reflecting in part, Corinth's role as a regional market for goods and services. The numbers of coins from municipal mints found at Corinth also reflect to some extent the output of the mints. For example, Megara, with 6 coins, is poorly represented despite its proximity to Corinth. Nevertheless, the general pattern is clear. In addition, Corinth's transit trade is reflected in the numbers of coins from Patrae (33) at the western entrance of the Gulf of Corinth, and from Eastern mints in the Aegean, Asia Minor, and Syria (30). The relative numbers of coins indicate that north-south trade between Egypt, North Africa and northern Greece was less important to the city than east-west trade.

The variation in the numbers of municipal coins through time may also be of significance, although this evidence is more difficult to interpret. This is because the number of coins lost in the city may reflect a time of crisis, and not the economic growth or strength of the city's economy. Large numbers of coins may be lost during an earthquake when the occupants of buildings flee without a chance to collect their valuables. When the buildings collapse, quantities of coins may be buried and lost in the debris. Furthermore, during times of political or military crisis—the threat or occurrence of a sack of the city—many coins may be lost in the debris of destruction or by deliberate burial of coins in hoards. Nevertheless, during periods of peace and security devoid of earthquakes, invasions, and high rates of inflation, variations in the numbers of coins dating to different reigns may reflect variations in economic activity in a limited way (see table 7). For the municipal issues, there is an increase in coins during the reign of Domitian. This increase may reflect increased economic activity at Corinth associated with the rebuilding of the city after the disastrous earthquake of A.D. 77 destroyed many of its buildings. There is a similar increase in the numbers of coins during the reign of Domitian at Athens, perhaps caused by similar circumstances.[48]

Another increase in coins occurs during the reigns of Hadrian, Antoninus Pius, and their immediate successors.[49] This increase may reflect Hadrian's building activities all over Greece and their economic consequences, which earned him the title, Restitutor Achaeae. Corinth benefited directly through Hadrian's construction of a bath building and a magnificent aqueduct which brought fresh water into the city from Lake Stymphalos, some 35 kilometers distant, as the crow flies.[50] He also widened the road over the Skironian Cliffs between Corinth and Megara,[51] and, significantly, the first coins from Megara occur a few years later in the reign of Antoninus Pius.

After the reign of Caracalla, the numbers of autonomous issues declines at Corinth, since the municipalities' right to coin was curtailed.

The imperial issues found at Corinth may also be helpful in determining the commercial relations of the city (see tables 8–10). There are few imperial coins from the first century A.D. and virtually all of those whose mint is recorded are from Rome, the most prolific mint of the period. Undoubtedly, the substantial output of Corinth's own municipal mint was more than adequate to meet the city's demand. Once again, we note an increase of coins in the reign of Hadrian and his immediate successors, probably for the reasons noted above.

In the third century, the patterns of imperial coin distribution and their interpretations become far more complex. First, there is a gradual increase in the numbers of coins lost per year after the reign of Caracalla and Geta, when Corinth lost the right to mint, an increase that has often been attributed to an increase in Corinth's "prosperity" during that era. However, part of this increase can be attributed to the loss of Corinth's own mint, and a larger portion reflects the massive inflation the Empire experienced throughout the third and fourth centuries.[52] This increase in inflation and the debasement of imperial coinage can be seen in the changing denominations of the coins lost in Corinth throughout the era. Of the 166 coins of known denomination dating to the reigns of Augustus through Philip II, there are 24 asses, 8 dupondii, 5 quadrantes, 103 sesterces, and 26 denarii.[53] The proportions of sesterces gradually increased, until the reign of Nerva and Trajan, when the proportions remain roughly 5 sesterces for every 1 as and denarius found.[54] Then, from the reign of Decius to Numerian (249–84) virtually all the coins whose denominations are known are given as double denarii or antoniniani, a new coin first introduced in 212 by Caracalla. After the reign of Numerian, through the reign of Theodosius (284–395), virtually all the coins found are small bronze alloy folles and smaller fractional coins.

To explain the changing denominations found in Corinth through the fourth century, it is first necessary to review a few basic numismatic principles.[55] From the reign of Augustus to Tiberius, the silver denarius contained roughly 97 percent silver. Nero alloyed the denarius to 92 percent silver, and the purity gradually declined in successive reigns, reaching 85 percent under Vespasian, increasing to 91 percent under Domitian, and then declining steadily until it reached 47 percent in the latter part of Septimius Severus' reign. The weight of the denarius remained roughly the same throughout the period at about 3 grams. The ratio in value of silver and copper was roughly 1: 100 in the ancient world and hence, a Roman silver denarius weighing about 3 grams and containing roughly 75 percent silver (as it did from about 161–193) was the equivalent of 225 grams of copper. The bronze sestertius weighed 24 grams, and 4 of them made the denarius, which is equivalent to only 96 grams of bronze per denarius. The bronze as weighed 10 grams, 16 of which made one denarius, the equivalent of 160 grams of bronze per denarius. The fractional denominations of the dupondius (2 asses) and the quadrans (¼ as) do not occur frequently at Corinth. It will be seen at once that the sestertius had a nominal value (¼ denarius) far in excess of its intrinsic value (24 grams of bronze, worth only ⅒ denarius in terms of silver), whereas the nominal value of the as was much closer to its intrinsic value in terms of the silver denarius. Therefore, it was much more economical for the Roman mint to coin sesterces, and the more the denarius was debased, the more economical it became in relation to the as and other denominations. Furthermore, because of its high intrinsic value, the denarius would probably be lost less frequently than the other denominations; their owners would take greater care not to loose them, and to find them after they had been lost. These factors partially explain the proportions of denarii, asses, and sesterces found at Corinth.

Antoniniani do not appear at Corinth (among the coins whose denominations are given) until the reign of Philip II (243–249), even though they were first introduced by Caracalla in 212. Their minting declined under Heliogabalus (218–222), was discontinued by Severus Alexander and Maximinus (222–238), and reinstated by their successors. Nominally, the antoninianus was a two-denarius piece, but actually it weighed only 5 grams, and was half alloy, so its intrinsic worth was only slightly higher than a denarius, a fact which did not escape the notice of Caracalla's subjects.[56] The reasons antoniniani are not found from 212–243 are their infrequent and irregular minting, and their high intrinsic and nominal valuations. For similar reasons, no gold aurei are found in the Roman city. From 238, the antoninianus suffered massive debasement; by 270 it weighed 2.75 grams and contained 10 percent silver, and could no longer support its official equivalent in bronze. This is why sesterces and asses were driven out of circulation by the debased antoniniani: although the former coins were still minted in great numbers,[57] their intrinsic value became greater than nominal.

The effects of inflation can also be seen in the increasing quantities of coins found at Corinth dating to the third century. During the second half of the century, there were massive increases in the minting of debased antoniniani by regional imperial mints, which were largely responsible for the increases in prices observed in that era.[58] The average numbers of coins per year increased from about 218, when the city ceased to mint its own coins, to about 275, after which a drop occurred to 305. Finally, there is a colossal increase in coins beginning during the reign of Constantine and peaking during the reign of Constantius II. Usually, this increase is taken to indicate the prosperity of the city during this era,[59] but it is far more likely that it reflects the astonishing inflation of small copper and bronze folles the Empire experienced at the time.[60] During this period, the imperial government made compulsory purchases of gold and silver in exchange for its officially overvalued folles (so called from the sacks necessary to transport them). Part of this increase may also reflect the series of catastrophes that overtook the city when these coins were in circulation: the earthquakes of 365 and 375, and the sack of Alaric in 395. These catastrophes were highly destructive for the city (see table 11), and doubtless many coins were lost and buried in the debris of fallen buildings. The brief decline in coins from 361 to 364 may partially reflect a decline in the city's economic activity, or perhaps a diminished output from imperial mints during the ephemeral reigns of Julian and Jovian. The last increase during the reign of Theodosius probably reflects the final catastrophe of the classical city, the destructive sack and slaughter of Corinthians by Alaric in 395. Thereafter, the numbers of coins diminish and the city enters a new era.

The changing mints of imperial coins found at Corinth may reflect the city's changing position in the trade patterns of the third and fourth centuries. From about 253 to 285, most of Corinth's imperial coins come from Western mints. There is also a concurrent decline of imperial issues found in the city from 275 to 285 and seen throughout the eastern Mediterranean, despite raging inflation and the flood of debased antoniniani.[61]

From 285, the trend reverses, with most of Corinth's coins originating from eastern mints, a trend that can also be seen in Athens and Aphrodesias.[62] This changing pattern of mints may reflect a diminished output of Western mints and a concurrent increase from Eastern mints, although this seems improbable.[63] More likely, the change represents a genuine shift in trade patterns caused in part by the profound social, economic, political, and military dislocations occurring throughout the empire during the latter half of the third century. The cruel and destructive invasions of Goths, Herulians, and Alamani swept across Roman frontiers from Spain to Asia Minor. In the East, Shapur brutally sacked Apamea, Seleucia, and even occupied Antioch. In 267, the Herulians left a trail of slaughter and destruction throughout Greece and the Aegean until they finally stopped at Athens, which they viciously sacked and burned. These shattering attacks were compounded by nearly continual civil wars, as rival emperors attempted to defend the regions under their control from invasions and restore stability. It is little wonder that these events had a detrimental effect on commerce and manufacturing in the eastern Mediterranean, reflected in Corinth's coins.

When stability began to be restored under Diocletian and the numbers of coins began to increase again, most of the mints are from the Aegean Basin and its immediate hinterlands. This change must reflect a diminution in the transit trade through Corinth, caused by grave economic dislocations, reduced population, and the localization of production which characterized the later Roman Empire. This change in trade patterns had serious consequences for Corinth's economy and will be discussed in detail below.

## Secondary Services

Since the provision of secondary services to merchants, travelers, and tourists was one of the principal underpinnings of Corinth's economy, it is worth examining this aspect in some detail, as Corinth's economic dependence on the transit trade has not always been understood.[64]

Merchants traveling to Corinth would have required a number of services for themselves, their crews, and their vessels. During their stay at Corinth (be it only for a day), they would need lodging in rooms and dwellings rented to travelers, sailors, and merchants by local Corinthians. They would also require the services of food preparers. Some would use the services of fullers, prostitutes, entertainers, and tavern keepers. Others would want religious services, especially to marine deities such as Poseidon, Aphrodite Euploia, and Isis. Some would use the city's baths, use the services of a doctor, or a barber, and perhaps a guide to see the sights.[65] Stevedores would be required to off-load and re-load vessels, both those trading directly with corinth and those with cargoes in transit across the Isthmus. Warehousemen would be needed to stock and manage the warehouses that lined the quays of the city's ports. If the warehouses were privately and not municipally owned, their owners would reap a profit from their use. If goods and vessels were to be transported across the Isthmus, this would require a whole host of services, ox drivers to pull the wagons, animal pasturing and breeding, leatherworkers to make and repair leather harnesses, wagon manufacturing and repair, rope making and repair, manufacturing of leather containers, cloth sacks, or ceramic vessels, and often the financial services of banking and insurance.[66]

Corinth was in an excellent position for the reprocessing of goods brought from abroad, perfumes and scented oils produced from products imported into the city, bronze manufacture, and perhaps weaving and dyeing using imported materials.[67] Tolls and fees collected by the city for the provision of these services doubtless played an important role in the city's economy.[68] In addition to these services which are either known or can be inferred from the known economic functions of the city, there were probably vast numbers of others whose record has entirely perished. Corinth was a logical place to repair, refit, and perhaps even build ships, and doubtless, there were Corinthians who did.[69]

Travelers and tourists would also require many of these services. Since the traveler and tourist of ancient times must have had some wealth to undertake a journey, it is likely they demanded and received a great many services. They may have wanted the use of a slave or servant during their stay. Since many tourists came during the summer months to attend the Isthmian Games, and lived out of doors in tents, rope and tent manufacturers would have been important for them.[70] The numbers of individuals supplying travelers, traders, and the local urban population with food alone must have been quite large: merchants and sailors who imported the food, stevedores, warehousemen, container manufacturers (for clay amphoras, and leather and cloth sacks) mill equipment manufacturing and import, oven baking equipment, fishing gear manufacture, fishing boat repair and refitting, chandlers, donkey- and mule-breeding to power the mills, millers, bakers, and distributers. So critical was the need to import food, especially grain, the city had its own official, the *curator annonae,* who was in charge of the aquisition of adequate supplies.[71] While staying in the city, many travelers would use the same services provided for the locals, the theater, gymnasiums, libraries, and schools.

### Commercial Facilities

The importance of Corinth's commercial services is paralleled and reflected in the city's commercial facilities. The port of Lechaion, some 2.5 kilometers north of the city's forum, was one of the largest man-made harbors of the Roman world, both in the perimeter of its quays (5 kilometers) and in the area sheltered in its harbor (15 hectares); its great lighthouse must have served as a beacon throughout the Gulf of Corinth.[72] Corinth's other major harbor, Cenchreae, "a safe harbor always crowded with visitors," was important enough to have its own temple of Aphrodite, and sanctuaries of Asklepios and Isis, as well as its own Christian church seperate from Corinth's.[73] Its harbor had an area of about 8 hectares and had about 1 kilometer of quays. The facilities were maintained throughout the Imperial era. Both Lechaion and Cenchreae were regular ports of call for travelers and merchants during the Roman era.[74] In addition to these large facilities serving the city and Mediterranean commerce, Corinth possessed several smaller harbors for local traffic (see plans 3–4).[75]

Another important commercial facility was the *diolkos,* a roadway for transporting ships and their cargoes across the Isthmus.[76] Originally constructed during the tyranny of Periander (late seventh to early sixth centuries B.C.), the road continued in use throughout the Roman era, and saved the merchant a six-day trip around the Peloponnese and treacherous Cape Malea. The vessels were unloaded at the eastern or western terminus, transported across the *diolkos* on trollies (*plaustra*), and reloaded at the opposite end. Alternatively, the cargoes of the vessels could have been unloaded, carted across, and reloaded on other ships at the opposite end. The roadway was constructed of immense slabs of hard, flinty limestone, some

3.5 to 5 meters wide, with two parallel grooves cut into the blocks 1.5 meters apart for the trolley wheels. The grade was only about 70 meters in 3 kilometers or .023 percent.

The road expands in width at the two termini to 10 meters, where the vessels or their cargoes were hoisted out of the water on rollers and hauled onto the trollies by hauling mechanisms (*holkoi,* presumably incorporating blocks and tackles). Unfortunately, we have no information on the trollies themselves or their motive power. The heaviest weight capable of being transported in antiquity by teams of tandem-yoked oxen (the method used for transporting heavy objects) was about 10 tons.[77] This would exclude the hauling of most Roman merchant ships, which averaged about 50 tons unloaded in weight,[78] and presumably, the *diolkos* would be used primarily for small cargo vessels with expensive cargoes, and warships. Of course, there was no limit to the weight of ship's cargo which could be transported across the Isthmus in seperate trollies and reloaded at the opposite end.

Whether a merchant would use the *diolkos* or risk a voyage around Cape Malea, probably depended on the type of cargo, the time of year at which he was traveling, and the amount of risk he was willing to take. The fees and tolls for transporting vessels and their cargoes were likely to have been high because of the labor involved. But, would it be preferable to pay the costs rather than face the risks of the Cape, where the merchant would face a 40 percent chance of encountering dangerous winds in winter and a 25 to 30 percent chance in other months? There is no doubt that many chose to pay the costs rather than take the risks, since our ancient sources (who are usually silent about economic activity) mention the journey across the *diolkos* as a routine matter.[79] Nor would the aborted construction of Nero's canal, (which pierced the *diolkos* on its western end, have permanently ended its use. It is doubtful whether the Corinthians would have let such a valuable facility fall out of use, nor was the task of bridging the 120 meter long, 20 meter deep cut through the *diolkos'* path an surmountable obstacle for Roman engineering.[80] In any event, Pliny the Elder, writing in the reign of Vespasian, recorded its use in his day, and its last recorded use was by the Byzantine admiral Nicetas Oriphas in 883.[81]

Another reflection of the vital importance of the transit trade for the economy of Corinth and the Mediterranean in general, was the attempt made to cut a canal through the Isthmus to facilitate travel. Attempts were planned by Periander, Demetrius Poliorcetes, by the philhellene Roman rulers, Caesar, Caligula, and Nero, as well as by the Athenian millionaire Herodes Atticus.[82] The Romans seemed aware of the beneficial effects the canal would have for reviving the economy of Greece and the Aegean after the ruinous civil wars and fiscal plundering during the last century of the Republic. Of all the attempts, that of Nero was the most notable. After his visit to the Isthmus in 66, he decided to undertake the task himself. The emperor began the operation by singing hymns in honor of Amphitrite, Poseidon, Melikertes, and Leucothea, all local divinities of the Isthmus, and he dug the first shovelful of earth himself with a golden spade. Work continued on the project for 75 days, the labor force was augmented by 6,000 Jewish prisoners sent by Vespasian. Soldiers dug the alluvial deposits along the coasts, while the prisoners cut into the solid rock at the center. The channel was between 40 and 50 meters wide, enough for two of the largest merchant vessels to pass abreast. In all, three large channels were cut: the western, from the Gulf of Corinth 2,000 meters inland; the eastern, from the Saronic Gulf, 1,500 meters inland; and the central channel through the rock, 100 meters long and 30 meters deep. In addition to the channels, a series of deep shafts cut into the rock along the line of the canal were sunk, some to a depth of 40 meters. Although the channels were partially filled in by 1,800 years of erosion and deposition, when measurements of Nero's canal were taken in 1881, there still remained an excavation of 500,000 cubic meters. The work was terminated during the uprisings at the end of Nero's reign and the project was abandoned until modern times. It is a significant tribute to Roman engineering that the French, after carefully measuring and surveying the Isthmus, determined that Nero's route was the most feasible, and the modern canal was superimposed on his excavation. The undertaking of this project to help revive commerce in the eastern Mediterranean was no doubt partially responsible for Nero's considerable popularity in the Greek world, even after his death.[83] Such an enormous task would not have been undertaken unless the need for it was very great (see map 4).

Finally, the importance of services for Corinth's economy is mirrored in the vast spaces alloted to service facilities within the city's shops and stoas. Comparative evidence shows that the primary function of these facilities was to provide the consumer with a broad range of services, from schools, retail stores, taverns, hotel space, and even brothels.[84] In Corinth, some 23,220 square meters of building space were devoted to stoas and shop structures in the central, excavated area of the city.[85] This compares to some 21,250 square meters of building space devoted to shops and stoas at Athens in the excavated areas of the Agora, Roman market, and the Stoa of Eumenes on the south slope of the Acropolis.[86] The area devoted to services at Corinth was also far larger than the market areas of Argos and Sikyon, as far as these are known. Nor should the vast, 14,000-square-meter area of Corinth's forum be overlooked. Far from being an empty space, archaeologists have found numerous cuttings for tent and awning posts where a variety of activities took place. Doubtless, there are many more shop structures to be found in Athens, Argos, and Sikyon, as well as in Corinth, yet it is significant that in their central markets devoted to economic and administrative activities, Corinth has more space devoted to these functions than these other, nearby cities. This is an indication of the comparative importance of services for Corinth's economy and the large numbers of residents and visitors who used them.

M. I. Finley wrote:

> (I)t seems commonly overlooked that the excavators of Tarsus have found no Cloth Hall, that all ancient cities lacked the Guild-halls and Bourses which, next to the cathedrals, are to this day the architectural glories of the great medieval cities of Italy, France, Flanders, and the Hansa towns, or England. Contrast the Athenian Agora with the Grande Place in Brussels.[87]

But, the South Stoa of Corinth, certainly the largest structure ever built in the city, tells its own story about the importance of the economic services it provided. The plan of any ancient city will show that the stoas were the largest and most numerous public structures built. These buildings *were* the Cloth Halls of antiquity and, unlike their medieval counterparts, they were far larger in overall size than the religious structures, the temples. The failure even to see these buildings, and to recognize their importance for the classical city, only shows how myth can blind the strongest minds.

### General Economic Trends

The economic vicissitudes of the city are best reflected in its buildings (see table 11). Many of Corinth's public structures were built by wealthy Corinthians as a service to their community. Others were repaired by them, or given marble revetments. Some structures may have been paid for by public funds acquired by the collection of tolls, harbor duties, or legacies. Still others were built or repaired by emperors: Hadrian built the city a bath and aqueduct, and Valentinian II restored the West Shops after an earthquake.[88] The structures are a reflection of the economic health of the city's elite and the growth of the city's social, economic, and administrative needs.

Many Corinthians were employed in the construction of the city's buildings as architects, contractors, engineers, specialized workmen, and manual laborers. Plutarch's statement concerning Pericles' building program for Athens, also applies to other cities:

> And the arts or trades that wrought and fashioned them were smiths and carpenters, moulders, founders, and braziers, stonecutters, dyers, goldsmiths, ivory-workers, painters, embroiderers, turners; those again that conveyed them to the town for use, merchants and mariners, and shipmasters by sea, and by land,

cartwrights, cattle-breeders, waggoners, leather-dressers, road makers, flax workers, shoemakers, rope makers, and miners. And every trade in the same nature, as a captain in an army has his soldiers under him, and its own hired company of journeymen and laborers belonging to it banded together as in array, to be as it were, the instrument and body for the performance of the service. Thus, to say all in a word, the occasions and services of these public works distributed plenty through every age and condition.[89]

The first years of the colony witnessed frenetic building activity as temples, stoas, and other public and private buildings rose to meet the city's needs. Old buildings of the Greek city beyond repair were dismantled and their blocks reused in new structures, while those still serviceable were cleaned of debris, given new roofs and other necessary repairs. The city reflects the Italian origin of many of its citizens in its architecture, from the Roman podium-style temples on the West Terrace down to details of the mouldings of its column bases.[90] The large and splendid Temple E, with its high podium and its broad precinct enclosed by colonnades, is another example of this influence, as is the formal layout of the forum and its paving in marble. Corinth's three basilicas—structures seldom found in Greece but popular in the Roman West—and its amphitheater, the only one in mainland Greece, also reflect Italian culture. Levantine inspiration can also be seen in its colonnaded streets and the zoomorphic column capitals from the West Shops, similar to those from Magnesia on Maeander.[91] Native Greek influence can be seen in some of the city's temples, both those of the Greek era restored by the Romans (the temple of Apollo, the Asklepion, the sanctuary of Demeter and Kore), and also in the new Temple E, with its Greek Peristyle.

Many of the buildings constructed from the Augustan era to Nero's reign were of Corinthian sandstone, often called "poros", which was easily available from local quarries and the ruins of old Greek structures. The devastating earthquake of A.D. 77 destroyed or damaged many of the city's buildings, and these were rebuilt not in sandstone as before, but in marble. This is an indication of the city's prosperity at the time, for the cost of transporting the marble was often equal to the cost of construction itself.[92] Polychrome marble revetments imported from Asia Minor, Africa, and elsewhere in Greece (Corinth has no marble of its own) were used to face the walls of new and older buildings alike, and the city must have had a dazzling appearance when reconstruction was complete, for every conceivable combination of colored marbles was used. Aristeides writing in the second century probably paid the city its greatest complement: "If a beauty contest among cities were held, just as they say arose among the goddesses, (Corinth) would rank with Aphrodite."[93]

Although the city's buildings were kept in repair during the second century, the pace of new construction slowed. Clearly, fewer new structures were needed in the second century than in the first, an indication that Corinth's economy and population had reached a plateau. From the third century through most of the fourth, new construction virtually ceases, and there are fewer restorations and repairs undertaken on older buildings. In the late fourth century, a series of catastrophes destroyed most of the city's buildings: the earthquakes of 365 and 375 had a devastating impact, and the sack of Alaric in 395 ended the life of the classical city. One of the most moving sights in Corinth is the ruins of the late-fourth-century fortification wall still preserved in parts along the city's northern plateau. One sees that the Corinthians had dismantled their own buildings and incorporated the pieces into the wall in a vain effort to defend themselves against the onslaught of Alaric and the Goths. Mass burials and destroyed buildings tell what happened.[94] There was no rebuilding program then as in 77; Corinth had entered a different world.

The causes of the city's great prosperity, mirrored in the expansion in the numbers of its buildings, can be attributed to the services it provided to local residents, merchants, and travelers. An additional factor was the growth in Corinth's manufactures. What were the causes for the decline in the city's growth in the third and fourth centuries and its inability to recover its former glory after the catastrophes of the late fourth? Doubtless, the city participated in the general social, economic, and political decline of the later Roman Empire; but there were several factors which probably had an adverse impact on long-distance trade and, hence, were important causes for Corinth's stagnation and decline.

Excessive taxation on an agricultural base and a reduced population lowered the demand for goods and services throughout the empire.[95] During the early fourth century, the tax rate doubled. Now, much more of the peasant's surplus went for taxes, and he had a smaller amount left to spend on goods and services provided by his city. Also, much land only marginally productive before the tax increases was probably removed from cultivation afterwards: the return from the land was no longer sufficient to counterbalance the greater cost of keeping it in production. Throughout history, higher taxes on land have reduced productivity. One of the major consequences of lower productivity was a reduced peasant population.[96] Combined with high taxation, the Empire as a whole experienced a general decline in population caused by a combination of political and military instability, a declining economy, and the deaths caused by barbarian attacks.[97] This reduced population had a lower demand for both agricultural goods and goods and services provided by cities. The lower population meant that more agricultural demand could be met locally without the need for imports. One consequence of lower population was smaller cities, where most of the demand for agricultural imports would occur. All these factors lowered the demand for imported agricultural products and other goods, and caused trade to diminish.

Another factor which caused trade to diminish was the increasing localization of production of agricultural and manufactured goods.[98] This process is reflected in the coins found at Corinth: from the reign of Diocletian onwards, most of the imperial coins found at Corinth were minted in the Aegean basin and its immediate hinterland. Very few coins now appeared from Western mints, which indicates that the transit trade with the West had diminished.

Part of the reason for the increased localization of production was the population decline, increased taxation, and political and military instability of the late Empire; but ironically, much of the problem was the result of the import-replacement process that had been responsible for some of the initial economic growth for cities like Roman Corinth. From the early Empire, more and more regions began replacing their imports with locally made and locally grown products. One of the most famous examples of this process was the development of viticulture in southern Gaul during the late Republic and early Empire. Gallic wine production lowered the demand for imported Italian wines, which hurt Italian vinters (and the merchants who transported their product).[99] An example of the process occurring for manufactures can be seen in the localization of the production of terra sigillata ware during the first century B.C. to the second century A.D. This type of pottery, usually red in color, apparently originated in the early first century B.C. in northern Palestine (near Tell Anata), whence it was exported throughout the eastern Mediterranean and even to the west. Later in the first century B.C., many regions began producing their own local imitations (some of very high quality); the most famous coming from Arretium in central Italy. Corinth also began manufacturing its own terra sigillata soon after the city was refounded. By the first and second centuries A.D., the production of locally made terra sigillata spread further to Gaul, North Africa, and the Aegean basin, so that by A.D. 150, mainly locally produced wares are found in Corinthian deposits and almost none is imported.

This process continued across the whole spectrum of agricultural goods and manufactures throughout the Roman Empire and no doubt caused a reduction in trade. The same process continues today but does not necessarily lead to such a reduction, at least among nations whose values and economic systems promote creativity and innovation. In these advanced industrial societies, ongoing technological innovation produces vast quantities of new industrial goods and services which are continuously manufactured, traded, and replaced by new manufactures. However, the process of technological innovation occurred only intermittently in the ancient world, despite its relatively advanced economy, its high degree of urbanization, and its sophisticated scientific base. Few techniques used in the fourth century A.D. were unknown in the first century B.C. Hence, another important reason for the reduction in trade during the later Roman Empire was the technological stagnation brought about in part by deep-seated social values of the elite which were inimical to the creative use of capital.[100]

# 4
# Society

What is the city but the people?
SHAKESPEARE, *Coriolanus*

One difficulty encountered in the study of cities is that they have been excessively reified. Although it may be convenient to say that the city taxes, or exploits, or provides goods and services, of course it is not the city itself that does these things, but the people in it. The city is not a cause but a consequence; not an active entity but an entity that is acted upon by its people. It is a mirror in which their social, economic, and political institutions and values are reflected. The city has been called "a poem composed by its people." Here one can see the institutions and values, the triumphs and failures expressed in their clearest, most succinct forms. What indeed is the city but the people?

This reification has also been a major obstacle to the understanding of classical cities. In a previous chapter, we saw good reasons to believe that Corinth and other large cities similarly located could not have been consumer cities whose economies were based on the collection of rents and taxes from peasants living in their *territoria*. It will be further argued in the summary that virtually no classical cities were of the consumer type. One reason why an inadequate model has been accepted for classical cities is that the cities have not been studied in their cultural context. A major goal of the present chapter is to explain why classical cities were not consumer types, but service cities. The answer will be found in the civic values of classical civilization.

The rapid economic growth that Roman Corinth experienced during the first two centuries of its existence was largely the consequence of the talent and creativity of its people. In this chapter, the society and culture of Roman Corinth will be examined, and the following questions will be asked: What were the social classes of the city and the ethnic groups they comprised? How and why did the ethnic composition of the city change through the Roman era? Regarding the demography of the city, how did public health factors, the differential mortality and fertility among preindustrial urban and rural populations, and patterns of migration affect the city's people? Can the size of Roman Corinth's population be estimated? What was the impact of Corinth's social and economic structure on the urban geography of the city? Finally, what were the cultural values shared by Corinth's citizens, and how did they affect the city?

## The People

In 44 B.C., Corinth received its first colonists from Rome's freedman class, urban poor, and some veterans of Caesar's campaigns.[1] We do not know their numbers, but in all likelihood there were not many, perhaps only 3,000.[2] When the colony was founded, the *territorium* of Corinth would have ceased to be *ager publicus* belonging to Rome and would have been distributed among the colonists, perhaps 10 to 12 iugera (2.53–3.0 hectares; 6.25–7.5 acres) per colonist. This was the size of the allotments made to Roman colonists in the *ager campanus* and the *ager Stellas* by Caesar,[3] and the size of the Corinthians allotments may have been similar. At first, there would have been few opportunities aside from agriculture to support the immigrants. All the city's commercial facilities—its harbor works, warehouses, shop buildings—and its other public and private structures had lain derelict for over a century, and were in need of major repair. Nevertheless, it did not take long for the new colonists to exploit every natural advantage the new city offered and to initiate the process of economic growth analyzed in chapter 2. In turn, this economic growth permitted a vast increase in the city's population during the first two centuries A.D. As was noted earlier, outlines of centuriation have not been observed for Corinthian fields as in other Roman colonies.[4] This may mean that the freedmen colonists who dominated Italian manufacturing and commerce left the cultivation of the land to the Sikyonians, who had been farming the territory as *ager publicus* for the Romans since the destruction of the Greek city by Mummius in 146 B.C., and who may have become tenants of the new colonists.[5] In any event, the system of agricultural exploitation seems to have remained the same after 44 B.C. as before; the new colonists did not change the pattern of rural settlement that prevailed before they arrived.

The freedmen, many of whom became Corinth's new citizens, had distinguished themselves in Italian industry and commerce, and so the city was inherited by workers and producers rather than literati,[6] a fact that annoyed the literary elites of surrounding communities. It was the talent and ability of these new citizens that established the commercial and manufacturing basis of the city's economy. Julius Caesar granted freedmen the exceptional right to hold magistracies and become senators (*curiales* or *decuriones*) in the municipal curiae of the colonies he founded. This privilege was revoked by Augustus, and, hence, all Corinthian magistrates after his reign were full Roman citizens as was the case in other Roman colonies.[7] Nevertheless, although freedmen were excluded from office, a civic career would be open to their sons.[8]

Many full Roman citizens probably migrated to the city with the freedmen during the first years of the colony. Two early duovirs have full Latin names, L. Aeficius Certus (duovir in 43/42 B.C.) and M. Insteius G. f. Tectus (duovir between 43/42 and 37/36, and again in 34/33 B.C.). They do not have Greek cognomens characteristic of most freedmen, nor do their Latin cognomens indicate servile origin.[9] The filiation in Tectus' name (the son of Gaius) is an indication of free and not servile birth. Some early migrants may have been Greeks who were granted Roman citizenship by Roman magistrates, including Julius Caesar. Two names of the first duovirs of the colony are G. Julius (_____) (43/42 B.C.; his cognomen is unknown), and G. Julius Nicephorus (duovir between 43/42 and 37/36 B.C.. They may have been the same individual).[10]

These Roman citizens and their descendants dominated Corinthian society at least through the early third century A.D., when the epigraphical evidence diminishes. They controlled the city's political and religious institutions and were also the city's great benefactors: not only were municipal officials unsalaried, but they were required to pay the city a large sum of money upon election.[11] Often candidates for office promised to perform important benefactions for their fellow citizens upon election—such as fund public works, games, and banquets—and distribute money from their own resources. They also undertook the administration of the Isthmian and Caesarean Games, and constructed many of the city's public buildings at their own expense.[12] Their assistance to the city was gratefully received by the rest of Corinth's citizens, as the numerous public statues and other dedications set up in their honor indicates.

Two members of Corinth's aristocracy are particularly worthy of note. The first is Gn. (Gnaeus) Babbius Philinus, in all probability one of Corinth's original freedman colonists. Although libertine status is not noted directly in any of the inscriptions about him, his cognomen Philinus or "Darling," is a strong indication of servile origins. He became aedile sometime during the reign of Augustus, duovir sometime between 7/8 and 12/13 A.D., and also pontifex.

During the reign of Tiberius, he constructed the so-called Babbius Monument on the West Terrace of the Forum. This structure—an elegant round tempietto with eight Corinthian columns—may have been dedicated to Aphrodite, or perhaps was part of an enclosure sacred to All the Gods. He was also associated with the erection of the Southeast Building (a Library?) and a nearby portico, as was his son Italicus. One daughter in the family (unfortunately we cannot be more specific), Babbia, married M. Publicius Rusticus, one of the most prominent men of the city.

The career of Babbius, sketchy as it is, provides a glimpse of what must have been an important phenomenon in Roman Corinth. He was originally a slave, given a humiliating slave name, but rose to become the chief magistrate of one of the largest cities of the Roman world and an important benefactor to its citizens. The social mobility of Babbius was probably repeated many times in the new city, and provides a hint of the abundant economic opportunities that must have existed during its early history.[13]

Corinth's most prominent son was probably Gn. Cornelius Pulcher. A friend of Plutarch, Pulcher had a long, distinguished career of public service to Corinth, Greece, and also to the emperors Trajan and Hadrian. He was the son of a Tiberius Cornelius Pulcher, and perhaps originally came from Epidaurus, where he served as agonothete of the Asklepian Games. He also lived in Corinth where he held all the most important magistracies including *duovir quinquennalis,* and agonothete of the Isthmian Games and the Trajanea festival. In Greece he served as hellenodarch of the Achaean League, High Priest of Greece, priest of Hadrian Panhellenius, and Panhellenic archon. In imperial service he was first a military tribune of the Fourth Legion, a procurator of Epirus, and *juridicus* of Egypt and Alexandria. Through his influence with Hadrian, he was able to get Corinth declared immune from taxes.[14]

Although their social origins were very different, both Babbius and Pulcher migrated to the city, attracted by the different opportunities it offered to people of talent and ambition. Both provide excellent examples of the civic-minded values that characterized Greco-Roman elites of the classical era.

Corinth's status as a provincial capital probably also contributed to the strong Roman identity of its elite. The political and judicial power of the governor (usually an ex-consul or ex-praetor) and his staff would reinforce the elite's view that social advancement and prestige was identified with the Latin language and Roman culture.

The city's working-class citizens also included many Romans and Italians. They left their Latin names on the lamps and terra sigillata were produced in the city.[15] The early Ionic and Corinthian column bases and moldings carved by the city's stoneworkers reflect Italian architectural traditions and indicate that the workers were of Italian origin or at least responded to the Italian public taste of the citizens.[16] This Italian-style base was not produced in any other city in Roman Greece.

The Italians left an indelible stamp on the character of the city. The founders of the colony named it Colonia Laus Julia Corinthiensis, avoiding the more common *-ius* or *-us* ethnic, which implies that the Italian colonists wished to distinguish themselves from the original Greek inhabitants of the city.[17] Roman Corinth always retained an Italian love of gladiatorial contests and wild-beast hunts that Greeks considered excessive,[18] and Italian culture left its imprint on the city's religions as well. The city's elite, at least through the early third century, were anxious to retain their Roman identity, since their names gradually changed from Latin names with Greek cognomens to wholly Latin names throughout the era.

The non-Romans residing in Corinth were legally classified as *incolae*. They were not citizens of the colony, and they could not vote, hold magistracies, or be members of the curia unless they were given a special grant of citizenship. One notable family that received this honor was that of G. (Gaius) Julius Eurycles (d. ca. 2 B.C.), his son G. Julius Laco, and their descendants. Eurycles built a fine bath for the city, and at one time or another, he and his descendants held all the major magistracies during the first century of the city's existence.[19] Most non-Romans in the city were probably Greeks. It is often difficult to categorize a Greek given Roman citizenship as either Greek or Roman, since the distinction is more legal than social or cultural. Moreover, a Greek cognomen does not in itself prove that the person was Greek. Only in rare instances when supporting evidence exists (as for Eurycles) can we be certain about an individual's ethnic identity.

Some Greeks in the Roman city were probably descended from the inhabitants of the old Greek city destroyed by Mummius in 146 B.C. As noted in chapter 1, Mummius' destruction of the city was not complete: some Corinthians escaped enslavement by Roman forces and remained in the city during its eclipse from 146–44 B.C.[20] Furthermore, the town of Tenea, which had revolted from the Corinthians and joined the Roman side, was spared by the Romans, and continued to be occupied during Corinth's abandonment. An oracle was recorded concerning a man who wished to move to Corinth. The oracle responded, "Blest is Corinth, but it's Tenea for me!"[21]

Perhaps the clearest evidence for the descendants of Greek Corinthians living in the Roman city is seen in the manufacture of bronze. As was noted in chapter 2, this high-tin alloy bronze was unique to Corinth, both in the Greek and again in the Roman era. It was not even produced by its neighbor Sikyon. Clearly, there were Greeks who retained important elements of their Corinthian heritage residing in the Roman colony. Doubtless other Greeks migrated to the city in large numbers, attracted by the opportunities provided by its growing economy. Although ethnic Greeks were a substantial portion of Corinth's population (the large audience for Paul's letters and sermons were mainly poor Greeks) unless they were granted Roman citizenship, they were not members of the elite. No building is known to have been built, repaired, or restored by an individual with a Greek name, and since they were not citizens, they could not control the city's political institutions or officiate in the Isthmian and Caesarean Games.

There were also numerous Easterners in the city: Jews, Anatolians, and Phoenicians.[22] Like the Greeks, they were not members of the city's elite, and were excluded from the magistracies and the senate unless granted Roman citizenship. No individual with an Eastern name was recorded to have constructed or restored a building or have held any religious or civic position in the city. Except for the Jews, very little evidence concerning Easterners survives. Two Jews mentioned in the New Testament (Crispus, the *archisynagogos;* and Titus Justus, a worshiper of God), had Roman names, as Paul did, himself; another, Sosthenes, Crispus' successor, had a Greek name. Other Corinthian Christians mentioned in the New Testament (Priscilla, Aquilla, and Phoebe) may or may not have been Jews before their conversion.[23]

Of the other Near-Easterners at Corinth, most of them probably had Greek names and spoke Greek, hence their presence would not show up in inscriptions. Many priests of the city's Oriental religions were doubtless themselves Orientals, although unfortunately, their names do not survive in the epigraphical record.[24] The religions of Isis and Serapis, Cybele (Mother of the gods), and Judaism fulfilled their spiritual needs in the city.

### Evidence for a Change in Ethnic Identity

The ethnic composition (or at least the ethnic identity) of the city's people gradually changed during the Roman era from Latin to Greek. Favorinus, in the second century, wrote that Corinth, "though Roman, has become thoroughly Hellenized."[25] Let us first look at the evidence for this process and then discuss the reasons for the change.

The change in ethnic composition (or identity) is seen most clearly in the change from Latin to Greek in Corinth's dated inscriptions, indicating that the audience for the inscriptions, and perhaps the authors, changed from Latin speakers to Greek speakers (see table 12).[26] Of the 104 texts written prior to the reign of Hadrian, 101 are in Latin, and only 3 are in Greek. Fifteen Greek texts and 10 Latin texts survive from Hadrian's reign, and in subsequent reigns through Gallienus, 24 Greek and 7 Latin texts remain. The few Latin inscriptions of the third century contain many grammatical and spelling errors absent from Greek inscriptions, indicating that its use was virtually forgotten.

A similar change can be seen in the tombstones found in Corinth, although they are more difficult to date. Of the 40 tombstones found and published that seem to date from 44 B.C. to the late third century A.D., 26 are in Latin and 14 in Greek.[27] All legible names on the Latin tombstones are Latin or Latin with Greek cognomens. Of the 14 Greek inscriptions, only 8 have Greek names (Greek personal name plus patronymic) and the rest are Latin names or Latin names with Greek cognomens. There are a large number of early Christian tombstones (163) that date from the late fourth to the early seventh centuries A.D. Unfortunately, most of the stones were not found in situ and so it is impossible to date them with more accuracy from the contents of their related graves. Of the 98 different names, all or partially preserved on the stones, all are written in Greek, and there are only 5 Latin names (Julianos, Konstantinos, Maximos, Rouphinos, Romanos). The rest are Greek or Judeo-Christian (e.g., Anastasia, Anna, Eusebios, Ioannes, Paulos). Paulos is the most common name, occurring 5 times, and the Christian connotations of the name, rather than the Roman, were more likely to have been important for naming a child, because of Saint Paul's missionary work in the city.

The social origins of the individuals named on the tombstones cannot be determined with accuracy. Some poor families may have wished to erect an expensive memorial to a departed loved-one while some wealthy families may have wanted only an inexpensive commemoration. The Christian graves were all cut by amateurs, and feature irregular letters and errors in spelling and syntax that show the semiliterate nature of the makers and owners.[28] Nevertheless, the families were able to purchase marble blocks, which had to be imported into the city, and to pay to have them inscribed. The tombstones may reflect the names of lower-middle-class Corinthians during the early Christian era.[29]

Private tombstones are likely to give a better indication of changing population trends in the city than the dated inscriptions on official monuments, and while it is difficult to assign them more than an approximate date, the same trend is clear for both types of evidence. Each humble monument was the personal expression of a bereaved family; they were not concerned with an elite public audience as were the official, public inscriptions.

Further evidence for a change in ethnic composition comes from the names of the makers of Corinthian terra sigillata ware. From the founding of the city to the mid-first century A.D., the potters had Latin names written in the Latin alphabet; after that date, Greek names in the Greek alphabet are found, indicating a change in the makers and market. Since these locally produced imitations were not exported in quantity, the change in names indicates a change in the ethnic composition of Corinth. During the first century A.D., the column bases, moldings, and architectural ornaments of Corinth's buildings change from the Roman to the Greek tradition,[30] which indicates at least a change in the public taste, if not a change in the ethnic origin of the marble-workers themselves. Finally, the religious preferences among Corinth's population changed during the first three centuries A.D. In this era, the inscriptions reveal a decline in the importance of specifically Roman cults and an increase in native Greek religions.[31]

On the other hand, the elite of the city show a countertrend. Our evidence here is poor, however, and future discoveries may change the picture. Among those Corinthians recorded to have held high civic positions or to have made important benefactions to their city, the proportion with

Greek cognomens declined through the early third century A.D.[32] The reasons for this trend are difficult to understand; doubtless several factors were responsible. It indicates that, while the general population was becoming Hellenized, the elite wished to emphasize their Italian identities and their status as full Roman citizens by abandoning Greek cognomens. These cognomens were often a degrading sign of freedman status, and freedmen parents would frequently abandon them in naming their children.[33] For example, we recall that Gn. Babbius Philinus, the wealthy Corinthian of freedman status named his son Gn. Babbius Italicus, probably in part to remove the stigma of the family's servile origins.[34] The changing cognomens through the early first century A.D. could also reflect the fact that, after Augustus' reign, freemen were excluded from office in the colony, although positions would be open to their sons. Since freedmen were likely to give their sons Latin cognomens, this would increase the proportion of Latin names among Corinthian magistrates. It could also mean that fewer Greeks were given Roman citizenship in the late second and early third centuries, or, of those Greeks that were given citizenship, fewer held high office at Corinth. In any event, by using purely Italian names, the Corinthian aristocracy, like other colonial elites, attempted to preserve the heritage of its old homeland.[35]

What were the causes of the changing ethnic composition or at least ethnic identity of the city's people? Part of the cause was the assimilation of the Italian immigrants into the Greek cultural milieu.[36] It would be difficult indeed for any community in the center of Greece to isolate itself from its surrounding culture, and this was especially true for Corinth—a major center of tourism and trade in the Greek-speaking eastern Mediterranean. Although the process of assimilation offers a partial explanation for the change in language, it does not fully explain the evidence for the changing ethnic proportions of the population indicated by the changing names. It is doubtful whether an Italian family (of whatever class) with a more prestigious Latin name, would give their children less prestigious Greek names. Instead, the changes indicate an increasing proportion of Greeks in the population.

One reason for this changing proportion was probably the migration of Greeks into the city from surrounding regions. The original number of Italian colonists was probably small, since there would have been few opportunities at first aside from agriculture to support them; but once the city's economy began to grow, large numbers of workers would have been needed to provide goods and services. As Aristeides astutely observed, one of the best proofs for the large size of Corinth was the fact that the city received immigrants, not from one or two regions, but from all over the Mediterranean world.[37] There is little doubt that many of these migrants were Greeks, since most rural-urban and inter-urban migration in preindustrial populations occurred over short and not long distances.[38] Their numbers would soon swamp the original Italians. A final reason for the diminishing influence of Italian culture in Corinth was the high death rates experienced by all urban populations before the late-nineteenth century.

## Public Health and Demography

The consequences of preindustrial demographic conditions for classical cities have seldom been discussed.[39] This is a potentially fruitful area of inquiry, and it can help explain many social, cultural, religious, and linguistic changes occurring in classical cities over time. What is valid for preindustrial cities in general will also be valid for Corinth and other classical cities. Indeed, it is difficult to understand any city, ancient or modern, without a basic knowledge of demography.

As in all preindustrial cities, Corinth's demographic structure was largely determined by public health factors, the differential fertility and mortality among preindustrial rural and urban populations, and patterns of migration.

For all cities up to the 1870s for which evidence is available, the death rates of those born in the city exceeded their birth rates.[40] This is primarily because urban populations are more frequently exposed to virulent communicable diseases than the inhabitants of rural regions. Communicable diseases spread in four basic ways: airborne droplets, spread through coughs and sneezes, broadcast diseases like tuberculosis, measles, and whooping cough; water contaminated by sewage or microorganisms spreads diseases such as typhoid, cholera, dysentery, and intestinal parasites; vectors (animals and insects) may transmit diseases such as bubonic plague and malaria; and direct contact between human beings may cause venereal disease or other infections.[41]

Individuals living in large communities are more likely to come into frequent contact with infectious diseases carried by airborne droplets than those living in small communities. There will always be a greater probability of encountering infected individuals in large crowds than in small groups. The number of possibilities for direct contact also increases in large groups. The populations of some vectors, such as rats, often flourish in urban environments, although in this case, their numbers were checked by the cats the Greeks and Romans introduced into Europe.

Moreover, many acute community infections, such as rubella, cholera, smallpox, mumps, and measles, require a minimum population of potentially susceptible individuals for the disease to be maintained in a given population.[42] It has been demonstrated that in small, isolated populations below 30,000, these diseases cannot be maintained, but must depend on external contacts to initiate their spread. Hence, the minimum populations necessary to maintain acute community infections are more likely to be found in large cities than in rural towns.

Populations of port cities located on major trade routes are also more susceptible to the spread of infectious diseases than those living in inland cities and towns.[43] Many acute community infections need very large populations, sometimes over a million, to maintain themselves in a given region. Few if any individual cities in the ancient world ever achieved this size, but when several large cities of 100,000 or more were closely linked through commerce and other contacts, the exchange of infections would be permitted, frequently with devastating results.

What Thucydides wrote concerning the spread of the Athenian plague was also true for the spread of communicable diseases in general in the preindustrial world:

> Certainly the plague broke out directly after the Peloponnesian invasion, and never affected the Peloponnese at all, or not seriously: its full force was felt at Athens, and after Athens, in the most densely populated of the other towns.[44]

In other words, since political, diplomatic, and economic contacts were broken between Athens and the Peloponnese, the disease (and this statement indicates that it was an acute community infection) did not spread there, but to the largest towns in contact with Athens.

Periodic famines, such as the one that may have affected Corinth in A.D. 51, were also more devastating for large urban areas than for smaller towns in the preindustrial world. In rural areas, population levels were more in balance with food production than in urban regions.[45] Cities were always chronically short of food because their large populations usually outstripped the production of their local territories, and imports were almost always necessary. Because of the limited capabilities of land transport, it was impractical to import food more than sixty miles overland, and so, rural areas with surpluses frequently could not bring food to urban areas suffering famine, even though profits would be high.[46] During times of food shortages, rural residents would be better able to live from their own resources than the residents of cities, since they could often turn to other sources of food such as edible flora, the bran and husks from milling, and the slaughter of farm animals or herds—survival strategies unavailable to their urban counterparts. It may be that during a famine, urban mobs could take any rural food by force, and no doubt this occurred. Nevertheless, in many cases, the peasants would flee beforehand, taking whatever they could with them. In part, food shortages could be alleviated for cities through the importation of food by water, since all large cities were on major navigable rivers or sea ports; however, that was not always possible. Even in the city of Rome, where the emperor himself made every effort to secure adequate food supplies, shortages were common and famines not unknown.[47] Most deaths during times of scarcity were not caused by starvation but by disease, since malnutrition weakens the body's ability to resist infection.

These facts about the spread of disease had important consequences for ancient cities in general and Corinth in particular. Since cities before the 1870s were unable to maintain their own populations, they depended on migration from the countryside and smaller towns. In general, larger urban centers attracted more migrants from diverse regions than smaller ones.[48] The pattern of migration may have tended to depress birth rates in large cities, since many of the migrants may have been single males and not single females or families. This localized imbalance in sex ratios could have depressed the birth rates in urban areas, but not in the population on the whole.[49]

For Corinth, these patterns of mortality, fertility, and migration meant that urban-based families would gradually decline in numbers through time. There is little doubt that many of the first Italian immigrants lived in the city rather than the countryside. The Italian elite controlled the city's political, religious, and economic institutions, and they needed to spend much time in the city where these institutions were concentrated. Working-class Italians were engaged in manufacturing and services in the city. Their numbers would be gradually depleted by the periodic epidemics and famines which decimated all preindustrial cities. Their places were taken by immigrants from the Corinthian countryside and further afield.[50]

Like other Greco-Roman cities, Corinth had what must be called a public health policy that sought to reduce mortality in the city as much as possible. These policies are reflected in the attempts made by the Corinthians to obtain abundant supplies of pure water, the sanitary arrangements made for waste disposal, and the acquisition of adequate food supplies for the city as far as possible through the office of *curator annonae*.

## Corinth's Water Supply

Unlike most preindustrial cities, whose water supplies were often taken from wells infected with typhoid and cholera, or rivers polluted with sewage and other wastes, the Corinthians and their contemporaries in other Greek and Roman cities took theirs from natural springs. Care was taken to obtain the water at its source, or as close to the source as possible to avoid the possibility of contamination as the water flowed away. This often required that large aqueducts be constructed to bring the water from considerable distances to urban centers.[51] Aqueducts then, are symbols of public health policies and public control of the institutions that created them.

Abundant quantities of potable water flowed from Corinth's springs; the largest of them, Peirene, produced an average of 18 cubic meters per hour. Besides Peirene, there were some sixteen other water sources in the city, some quite copious.[52] In the second century A.D., the abundant water from the city's own springs was no longer adequate for its population, and a major aqueduct was constructed by Hadrian to bring fresh supplies from Lake Stymphalos, some 35 kilometers away. The water system of Roman Corinth was one of the most complex and sophisticated in the classical world, every effort was made to tap all the sources of water within the city and distribute it through a network of reservoirs, distribution basins, channels, and terracotta pipes.[53]

The principles of water distribution used by the Corinthians are significant. The first priority was given, not to animals, manufactures, or waste disposal, but to human consumption. There were many fountain houses within the city where aquiferous strata were tapped and the water distributed. The reservoirs and draw-basins of the fountains were constructed so that water would be constantly flowing through them, and not stagnate and attract water-borne parasites. The reservoirs, draw basins, and distribution channels were periodically cleaned, which prevented the growth of microorganisms. The runoff from the fountains would then be used to supply swimming pools, as in the Fountain of the Lamps (Lerna) and Peirene; some was undoubtedly used for the city's large baths and other bathing establishments. After the water satisfied these needs, it was then used to flush municipal latrines (two of which are known) or used for industries such as bronze manufacture. Finally, the water flow that remained was perhaps used to irrigate the fertile fields north of the city.[54] Such meticulous attention to the use of water probably had a significant impact in reducing mortality caused by water-borne microorganisms.

The severest penalties were levied against anyone polluting or contaminating public water supplies.[55] Efficient disposal of human wastes may have reduced the populations of some vectors such as rats and parasites. Water contaminated by wastes in the city was not used for human consumption, a principle either unknown or forgotten in many cities outside the Greco-Roman era. All these practices helped reduce mortality caused by water-borne parasites and some vectors, but unfortunately, had no impact on air-borne droplets or direct contact.

Famine was a frequent threat to all preindustrial cities. Corinth, as other classical cities, had an official—the *curator annonae*—who was responsible for procuring adequate supplies for the city at a reasonable price; which often meant that he had to make purchases himself from his own funds. This institution would reduce the occurrence of famine in the city and the illness and mortality associated with malnutrition. Despite its all too frequent occurrence, neither later European cities, or regional, or national governments developed institutions that would reduce the threat of famine until the modern era.

These policies and the principles of public health that created them were more advanced than in European cities until the nineteenth century A.D. and were virtually unique in the pre- and nonindustrial world.[56] Even the public health policies and facilities of late-nineteenth-century London compare poorly with those of many Greco-Roman cities. As the Registrar General of the city of London wrote in 1862:

> The supply of water in London is derived from shallow wells, from deep wells, from the New River, and from the River Thames, or its tributaries the Lea and the Ravensbourne. The well waters are foul, and nearly all of them have in solution organic matter derived from cesspools. The Thames has during this period been the great sewer of London, and in the years of the cholera epidemic was found charged with organic matter of unquestionable origin . . . in every 10,000 inhabitants living in the districts supplied with water taken from the Thames at Kew and Hammersmith, 15 died of cholera; 48 died of cholera in districts supplied with the waters of the Amwell, the Lea, and the Ravensbourne; and that 123 out of the same number died of cholera in the districts supplied with waters taken from the foul part of the Thames between Battersea and Waterloo Bridge. . . . A gallon of the Southwark [company's] water contained 3.5 grains . . . of organic matter. . . . In five weeks [in 1854] 2,284 persons died of cholera in 40,046 houses supplied with the Southwark water.[57]

This litany of horrors could be continued to include many other cities and regions. The fact that public health policies and facilities were more advanced in Greco-Roman cities than in many other cities until the late nineteenth century requires an explanation; it implies not only a greater understanding that contaminated water causes disease (an understanding forgotten by later ages) but a greater willingness and ability (despite the limited economic means of classical cities) to devise and construct public health facilities based on this understanding. The reasons for this willingness and ability must once again lie in the nature of the classical city. The public valued cities that were as safe and pleasant for human life as possible, and since their political institutions served public needs and not merely the needs of a small elite, these values and needs were translated into public health policies and facilities. These urban amenities both attracted visitors and immigrants and insured that they would not die from cholera, dysentery, or typhoid from drinking contaminated water in the city. They also fulfilled the political elite's desire for status through the performance of public benefactions.

## Population

It is impossible to estimate the population of Roman Corinth with any degree of certainty, since we lack a census giving the population of the city. Such censuses exist only for two classical cities, Apamea and Alexandria, but historians and archaeologists for generations have used indirect methods to estimate ancient urban populations.[58] These methods have enabled us to estimate, within limited parameters, the populations of such cities as Rome, Ostia, and Pompeii. What evidence exists for Corinth?

Aristeides speaks of Corinth as the largest city in Greece during his day, the mid-to-late second century A.D.:

> Everything travels here from every place by land and sea, and it is because of this that the ancient poets sang of this place as wealthy, and also because of the delights always present and the happiness that always resides in it. For it is like the marketplace, the common meeting place and festival of the Greeks, which they crowd into, not every two years, as for the present festival, but every year and every day. And if, just as among men, there was the institution of guest-friendship among cities, then this city [Corinth] would be honored everywhere, for it hospitably receives everyone and bids them farewell again. It is the common refuge of all, just as some passageway and crossroads of all mankind, the common city of the Greeks . . . their metropolis. . . . What better proof could one make for the magnitude [of the city] than that it has been apportioned into all seas and colonized and settled from them, not from one or another, but from all of them alike. And the city is well governed, an administrative center, and still arbitrates justice among the Greeks. Indeed, such an abundance of wealth and prosperity pours into the city from every land and every sea, that they dwell in the midst of plenty that washes around them, just as some merchant ship filled with valuable cargo. . . .
>
> Which Greek city is still commemorated as the most brilliant in peace and war, esteemed by land and sea? Which is the most conspicuous in deeds and accomplishments? But the present era is peaceful . . . and when the Greeks celebrate festivals, they live in harmony together in this most splendid and renowned celebration [the Isthmian Games].[59]

Corinth is the common city and metropolis of the Greeks, always crowded with visitors and celebrants; it is their capital city arbitrating justice among them. The size of the city can be gauged by the fact that its settlers come from all over the Mediterranean world, not from one or two locations. (As noted above, only large cities attract immigrants from many regions.) Although one must allow for some rhetorical exaggeration, clearly it was not Aristeides' intention to have his oration greeted with ridicule and contempt by his Panhellenic audience. If he spoke of the city as the largest and most important in Greece in his time, it must have been an acceptable notion to his listeners. No other city in Roman Greece is spoken of in this way, not even Athens. Clearly, Corinth was a large city: but how large?

The vast extent of Corinth's economic and commercial facilities reflects the large population that used them. We have already seen that the port of Lechaion was one of the largest man-made ports in the Mediterranean, and more space was devoted to the city's commercial and service activities in its stoas and shops than in any other city in Greece, so far as these are known. Another notion of the city's size may be derived from the area occupied by its residents. It has been demonstrated many times that as the size of a city's population increases, the area it occupies increases also.[60] What was the extent of the inhabited area of Roman Corinth?

To determine this extent, I conducted an informal survey by crisscrossing the area of the city for surface occupation debris (pot sherds, building block, marble, and roof tile fragments). Some pot sherds can be dated to within a few decades of their manufacture by their color, glaze, and surface decoration,[61] and hence, their distribution provides some notion of the area of the city occupied in a given era. As we saw in chapter 1, the soil occupying the area of the ancient city is neogenic, that is, derived from the decomposition and weathering of underlying sandstones, limestones, marl, and conglomerate. It is not composed of alluvium washed in from elsewhere. Except near the steep north slope of Acrocorinth, most of the area of the ancient city was level, and there would be little probability of debris washing downwards for long distances within the city. Indeed, debris was found far up the northern slope of Acrocorinth and along the city's eastern edge, which slopes gradually to the west. This fact indicates that even after thousands of years, considerable debris has not yet washed down even from steep slopes, and that the area occupied by ancient buildings as revealed by surface debris has not been significantly distorted through time.

Heaviest concentrations of debris were found in an area extending 950 meters east of the forum in the eastern part of the city; in the north, extending all along the northern scarp of the city (near the old northern city wall) and north along the modern road to Lechaion for some 3 kilometers. Heavy debris extended to Anaplogas in the west, and in the south, along the modern road to Argos and along the edge of the road to Acrocorinth to about 100 meters west south west of the sanctuary of Demeter and Kore. Lighter concentrations of debris were found to the line of the Greek city walls in the east, gradually thinning out beyond the line of the walls to the Xerias gorge east of the city. In the north, light debris was found from 3.2 kilometers north of the city all the way to Lechaion along the modern road, and in the west, west of Anaplogas gradually thinning out to the western line of the city walls. In the south, light concentrations were found south of the road to Acrocorinth, along the steep northern slope of the citadel itself (see plan 1). Perhaps some of the debris along the northern slope of Acrocorinth washed down from the citadel above. There is little doubt that most if not all of the area where occupation debris dating to the Roman era was found, was indeed occupied during that era.

The best evidence for the extent of the area occupied by the Roman city is the excavations conducted by the Greek archaeological service in Ancient Corinth. Many new houses are continually being built throughout the modern town of Archaia Corinthos. Before each new house is constructed, the site is excavated and the finds recorded: wherever a new house is built, a structure from the Roman city lies beneath. Indeed, Pausanias noted that houses (of undetermined age) were located outside the perimeter walls of the city.[62] I suspect that future investigation will confirm these views.

An enormous area was occupied by the ancient city as indicated by occupation debris: about 525 hectares for the city itself and about 200 hectares for Lechaion and the area between Lechaion and Corinth, or 725 hectares in all. Of course, the inhabited area of the city did not remain static, but undoubtedly grew during the first three centuries of the colony's existence. Hence, the survey probably indicates the maximum extent of the area inhabited during the Roman era, probably in the second century A.D.

What was the density of habitation in Corinth? This depends on the type of housing constructed in the city. Those few houses so far excavated show that they were one or two stories high, like the dwellings of Pompeii, and not the four-story *insulae* of Ostia and Rome.[63] The density of habitation was likely to have varied within the city as well; in Ostia, there were considerably higher densities near the center of the town than in the outskirts.[64] In sixteenth-century Venice, densities varied from 450 to 510 persons per hectare near the central squares of St. Mark and St. Paul, to 175 per hectare in outlying regions.[65] Similar differentials in density are indicated for Corinth, at least so far as they can be determined by the densities of occupation debris.

Nevertheless, there are some parameters for the overall densities of urban habitation. On the upper level are towns and cities with high densities, such as Rome and Ostia, where the dominant type of housing was tenements of about four stories. For Ostia, with a population of about 27,000 and an inhabited area of 69 hectares, the overall density was about 390 per hectare.[66] Alexandria, with an inhabited area of about 920 hectares; was said to have contained 300,000 free residents (*eleutheroi*) in the first century B.C.,[67] for a density of at least 326 per hectare. The number of slaves in Alexandria is of course unknown, and the density would increase when their numbers are added. A minimum urban density would perhaps be represented by Pompeii, with a population of about 10,500 in an area of 64 hectares, or a density of about 164 per hectare.[68]

Roger Mols, in his exhaustive study of European demography from the late Middle Ages through the eighteenth century, has shown that the maximum average densities for the largest cities was about 500 per hectare. This is a higher density than is indicated for the largest classical cities, and the difference may be caused by the greater areas devoted to public buildings, such as theaters, baths, stoas, law courts, senate houses, public fountains, gardens, squares, and other public monuments in classical cities than in their later European counterparts.[69] The lowest average densities for smaller towns was about 100 per hectare.

Hence, even with an average density of 100 per hectare, perhaps the lowest figure for an urban center, the city of Corinth would have included some 52,500 people, and 72,500 people if the area of Lechaion were added. If Corinth had a density of 160 per hectare—similar to that of Pompeii, and a figure that seems justified by the limited excavation of houses in the city—then Corinth would have had 87,000 people (116,000 if Lechaion were added). For comparison, modern Larissa has 150 per hectare and Patras, 180.[70]

Some Corinthians lived in the countryside in forty or so settlements dating to the Roman era, and ranging in size from farms and villas to large towns.[71] Of the forty settlements, five were large towns: Crommyon, Cenchreae, Tenea, Ayios Charalambos (Assae?), and Asprokambos.[72] Without thorough excavation, the precise areas occupied by these towns and other settlements in the countryside cannot be determined with certainty. Cenchreae seems to have occupied an area of forty hectares, Tenea at least sixty hectares, and Ayios Charalambos at least nine hectares; Crommyon and Asprokambos also occupied large areas.[73] If we assume that the density of these towns was similar to the density of many small modern Greek towns, 110 per hectare,[74] then the population of Cenchreae might have been 4,400; Tenea, 6,600; and Ayios Charalambos, 990; or a total of almost 12,000. Crommyon and Asprokambos may have approached the size of Cenchreae and so the population of all five towns may have neared 20,000. In addition, there were several large villas (or small towns), harbors, and the great sanctuary of Isthmia. It is impossible even to estimate the populations of these other rural sites, but they undoubtedly contained several thousand souls. A minimum figure for the population of Corinth's *territorium* would be about 20,000.

The population of Greek Corinth during the fifth and fourth centuries B.C. also suggests that the population of Roman Corinth was large. The numbers of people living in a city-state ultimately depended on the extent of its economic resources and opportunities. Most of Corinth's population was dependent for its livelihood on services and goods provided to traders, travelers, and tourists in both eras.[75] Since the volume of Mediterranean trade seems to have increased from the fifth and fourth centuries B.C. to the late Republic and early Empire,[76] it is likely that Corinth's population was at least as large if not larger in the Roman era than in the Greek era.

J. Salmon has provided the most accurate figures for the number of citizens of Greek Corinth during the fifth and fourth centuries. He has shown that there were at most 15,000 free adult males between ages twenty and forty-nine.[77] In a population with a life expectancy at birth of twenty-five (which seems to have characterized the Greco-Roman world)[78] males between the ages of twenty and forty-nine comprise some 43 percent of all males.[79] Hence, if 15,000 males comprised 43 percent of all males, a total population of 34,883 is indicated for males. If we assume that, as in all viable human populations, the male-female ratio was about 1 : 1, then a total population of 69,766 is indicated for the free population. Salmon also believes that there was approximately one slave per free household on average in Greek Corinth, which would give a total population of about 85,000.[80]

The demand for agricultural land seems to have been at least as great if not greater in Roman times than in the Greek era. Some forty-eight settlements varying from villas to large towns were occupied in the Corinthian countryside during both Greek and Roman times. Of these, thirty-nine were occupied in the Greek era (fifth through second centuries B.C.) and forty in the Roman era. This indicates that the density of the rural population and the demand for their products by the city was similar in both eras. In the Greco-Roman era, settlements were inhabited that were considered marginal or unproductive in postclassical times and abandoned, because the reduced demand from the city's market made the sites unprofitable to farm. In other words, it was about equally as profitable to farm Corinthian land in the Greek as in the Roman era, because the city's demand for agricultural products (and hence its size) was similar in both eras.

The magnitude of the city's water supply also indicates that Corinth's urban population was quite large. As discussed above, the Corinthians of the Greek and Roman city made extraordinary efforts to tap spring water from every available source. They distributed this water to the city's public fountains, private houses, baths, industries, and latrines by one of the most sophisticated systems of distribution basins, channels, pipes, and drains in the ancient world. Such an elaborate system would never have been constructed and maintained unless the demand for water was very great. However, during the reign of Hadrian (117–38), Corinth's abundant supplies of water were no longer adequate for the needs of its people and an extensive aqueduct was constructed by that emperor to bring water from Lake Stymphalus, some 35 kilometers away. This aqueduct was a major undertaking, constructed at considerable expense, requiring substantial revenues to maintain, and would not have been built unless Corinth's need for more water was genuine.[81]

Only the roughest approximation of Roman Corinth's population can be attempted because of a lack of census data. Nevertheless, Aristeides wrote of Corinth as the largest city in Roman Greece, and evidence from the city's inhabited area, water supply, and comparisons with the population of the old Greek city all suggest a substantial population in the Roman era. Few would argue that Roman Corinth was not a large city and an urban population of 80,000 and a rural population of 20,000 does not seem unreasonable.

Even if these population estimates for both the Greek and Roman cities are wildly inaccurate and the actual figure only half these estimates— 40,000, or even only 10,000—this would still not affect the economic analysis. As we have seen, advocates of the consumer city view visualize the economy of the classical city as consisting essentially of two components. The first is the agro-town, where urban residents commute back and forth to their fields. The second component is the consumer city itself, in which the rentier class lives on the rents and taxes it collects from the peasant farmers. Nevertheless, these two components are quite different; it is the latter that makes a city a consumer city and not an agro-town.

As we have already seen, given classical rent rates and land tenure systems, a *maximum* of 2,000 to 3,000 landlords could have been supported in the Corinthia. This is only a miniscule proportion of the entire Corinthian population, whether it was 100,000, 40,000, or even 10,000. Surely, if 3,000 maximum were rentiers, and 10,000 maximum were urban farmers in ancient Corinth, this would describe an agro-town and not a consumer city. Even with an urban population as low as 26,000, Corinth could not have been either a consumer city or an agro-town.

An application of this type of analysis to other ancient cities would probably show that virtually none were consumer cities.

## Social and Religious Values

Beliefs influence behavior.[82] The social and religious values of the Greeks and Romans are at the heart of classical cities and go far to explain their unique characteristics. Since the time of Homer, the Greeks have displayed several characteristic patterns of thought and behavior. Some of these characteristics were transmitted to the Romans, and a few Roman ones were transmitted to the Greeks.

Several of these beliefs were central to the classical city. First and foremost was the basic respect given to even the most humble citizen. Homer recognizes this attitude among his contemporaries (eighth century B.C.), although he deplores it. During a rout of Greek troops before Troy, Odysseus addresses one of the common soldiers:

> Excellency! Sit still and listen to what others tell you, to those who are better than you, you skulker and coward and thing of no account whatever in battle or council. Surely not all of us Achaians can be as kings here. Lordship for many is no good thing.[83]

Even the commoners thought they were kings: that they ought to make autonomous, independent decisions for themselves, unrestricted by their betters. This concept is given its classical expression in a story attributed to Protagoras by Plato. Protagoras also wrote that "Man is the measure of all things."[84] During a crisis in an early stage of human development, Zeus asked Hermes to distribute justice (*dike*) and self-respect (*aidos*) to humans. Hermes asked:

> "Shall I distribute them as the arts were distributed—on the principle that one man skilled in medicine suffices to treat many laymen, and so with the other craftsmen? Shall I distribute justice and respect to men this way, or to all alike?" "To all alike," said Zeus; "let them all have their share. There could never be cities if only a few had a share in these virtues, as they do in the other crafts."[85]

Therefore, a sense of good judgement and self-respect are given to everyone, not just a select few. To the Greeks, these virtues were given by Zeus himself, and thus the concept had the highest religious sanction. This is also what Aristotle concluded about the public as a judge of art:

> For it is possible that the many . . . may yet taken altogether be better than the few, not individually but collectively, in the same way that a feast to which all contribute is better than one given at one man's expense. For where there are many people, each has some share of goodness and intelligence, and when these are brought together, they become as it were one multiple man with . . . many minds. So to in regard to the character and powers of perception. That is why the general public is a better judge of works of music and poetry; some judge some parts, some others, but their joint pronouncement is a verdict upon the whole. . . . There is no reason why in a given case we should not accept and apply this theory of the collective wisdom of the multitude.[86]

Indeed, Greco-Roman art was in every sense public art. Not only were the works themselves displayed in public places, but they were also judged and voted upon by the cities' councils. The same was true for the cities' public and private buildings. All works of public art and public and private buildings had to have the approval of the council, or they would not be erected. This meant that in ancient Athens, the common citizens (who were elected to the Council of Five Hundred by lot) passed judgement upon the great monuments of art and architecture that are now universally admired. The commoners also voted upon their favorite plays and helped ensure the survival of the masterpieces of Aeschylus, Sophocles, and Euripides.

Aristotle also concluded that the rulers are not the best judges of political institutions, but the ruled:

> There are tasks of which the actual doer is not either the best or the only judge, cases in which even those who do not possess the operative skill pronounce an opinion on the finished product. An obvious example is house-building; the builder certainly can judge a house, but the user, owner, or tenant, will be a better judge. So to the user of a rudder, the helmsman, is a better judge of it than the carpenters who made it; and it is the diner not the cook that pronounces upon the merits of the dinner.[87]

Because God has distributed justice and respect evenly, it is a sacrilege to deny good treatment to even the most humble.

Another expression of this value is in the kindly treatment of strangers (*philoxenia, hospitalitas*) that has characterized Greco-Roman societies from the beginning and is still common in Greece and Italy today.[88] "All strangers and wanderers are sacred in the sight of Zeus," said the Greeks.[89] When Odysseus, disguised as a lowly outcast, returns home and is ill-treated by the suitors, this is yet another sign of their impending doom. Telemachos expresses anger at the shame he feels in not being able to protect the humble beggar who has sought the protection of his house.[90] In Greek, the word for stranger (*xenos*) is also that for friend. Good treatment of even the most humble and outlandish strangers not only separates civilization from barbarism and good from evil, but also the godly from the ungodly. The gods themselves were thought to travel in the guise of poor strangers, and the treatment they received was rewarded or punished accordingly.

The Greek people shared the concepts of individualism, freedom, equality, distrust of authority, and most important, competition for honor, especially among the elite. In the Greek system, honor was not obtained solely by birth or family connections. It had to be earned through service to the community. Indeed, many high-born individuals were devoid of honor, since they had not fulfilled their obligations to their community (Paris, in the *Iliad*, is a good example). Honor for the Greek aristocracy consisted not in building pyramids, or in constructing a higher tower on one's palace than one's neighbor's, but in public service.

Since Homeric times, the Greek aristocrat obtained his honor only after displaying his ability to lead his community in war and peace. Kings were selected by the community on the basis of several criteria: family connections, relation to the former king, but above all, political and military leadership gained in competition with other aristocrats. This competition for honor was later formalized by elections (still called contests and races) which institutionalized the informal selection practices found in Homer and extended the vote to humbler citizens.

Democratic governments were the logical outgrowth of these values, and Aristotle noted that they dominated the Greek world during the fourth century. This form of government also received divine sanction, even as far back as Homer. In the idealized community of the Phaiakians, king Alkinoös held power that was given to him by his people. It was this community, among all those visited by Odysseus, that the gods had favored most.[91]

The Romans shared some of these values with the Greeks; but they never accepted democracy, because they never accepted equality. Nevertheless, the Greek aristocratic competition for honor found its analogue in the Roman world in the patron-client system. This was a system of acknowledged inequality, but, nevertheless, the patron was obligated to fulfill his responsibilities to his clients and promote their well-being. In exchange, the client gave his patron his political support and any other help he might require. The most successful political leaders often had the most clients to lend them their political support. In turn, large numbers of clients usually meant that the patron had performed *beneficia* for numerous individuals. The Romans did not see themselves as independent individuals, as the Greeks did, but as part of a nexus of social relationships. Once again, a Roman's political power was often determined by the breadth of his patronage, his service to others. While the Romans were not democratic, even the lowliest citizen had the right to vote and could determine legislation. Successful Roman leaders throughout the Republic and early Empire never forgot this fact.

Both systems, although different in some respects, shared common characteristics. Honor and esteem among aristocrats was given to them by their communities as a reward for public service in war and peace. Every citizen had judicial rights and the right to vote. He would only give his vote to those who had served his interests by providing *beneficia*.

As we saw in the introduction, these political and social principles were given philosophical form in the tenets of stoicism. Stoicism also added the concepts of natural law that stressed rationalism, spiritual equality (not social or economic), and brotherhood (*homonoia*) among all people. It was the duty of good stoic aristocrats, both men and women, to deliver services, based on these concepts, to their communities, and the public expected no less from its political leaders. These obligations were sanctified by the religious beliefs that all shared.[92]

In fact, the classical city is incomprehensible without an understanding of classical religious values. Later Stoicism promised that the good aristocrat who had fulfilled his duty to his fellow citizens could look forward to a blessed immortality in the heavens with other political notables and heroes, such as Heracles. Indeed, the greatest spirits among them, such as Scipio Africanus, were actually thought to be preexistent beings who came to earth in the service of mankind, and who returned to their heavenly abode when their tasks were fulfilled.[93]

What were the consequences of these virtues for classical cities? The laws of God are the laws of nature, and are not to be trifled with, ignored, or evaded. Indeed, evasion is futile in any event; the laws will prevail whether man wills it or not, just as summer follows spring. The good stoic believed that he and his community could only lead a just and virtuous life by obeying these laws and living in harmony (*harmonia*) with them: since natural law shows that drinking polluted water causes disease, expend every effort to obtain clean water at its source and bring it to the city, even if this means the construction of expensive aqueducts. If a clean body is a healthy one, construct public baths to keep the citizen body clean. If exercise is beneficial to health, construct gymnasiums where people can train. If paved streets, covered drains, sewers, and waste disposal systems help prevent disease, construct them. Allow all to use these amenities, men and women, free and slave, citizen and stranger, rich and poor, urbanite and farmer.

Since natural law shows that rats and mice carry dangerous diseases, do not make pets of them and massacre the cats. Favor the cats and let them help keep the rodent population under control. Avoid the threat of famine and malnutrition among the poor by guaranteeing adequate supplies of grain at reasonable prices. Hire public physicians to treat the poor for free or at reduced rates. If God has given everyone reason and justice, let all citizens have some role in the government. If Zeus gave all justice and respect, do not opress the poor with high rents and taxes. Treat slaves fairly, allow them to save money to purchase their freedom. Give them the right to escape ill-treatment and to bring charges against brutal masters. If criminals break these laws, punish capital crimes severely, even cruelly, in public, to deter others.

If nature is beauty and perfection, try to make the city correspond through public art and architecture. Indeed, individual cities competed with each other concerning the beauty of their physical appearance and their quality of life.[94] The classical city of the Hellenistic era and early

Roman Empire is the physical and institutional embodiment of stoic principles.

The Corinthians shared these values with their contemporaries, and exhibited a few others of their own. For a city like Corinth whose economy depended to a large extent on its ability to attract merchants, travelers, and tourists to use its services, hospitality was an especially important virtue. Pagan and Christian writers alike extolled the pervasive hospitality and warmth displayed by Corinth's people.[95]

The physical attractiveness of the city and its magnificent public structures attracted people to come and visit, just as they still do today. Numerous forms of public entertainment were available in the city: music, theater, athletic competitions, and gladiatorial contests.

The value placed on hospitality throughout the classical world assured that cities were as clean, healthful, and beautiful as resources permitted, and that there were many opportunities for visitors and guests to spend money as they wished. Wherever the traveler or tourist went, he was treated with a degree of respect and dignity.

Corinth's elite men and women showed a paternalistic concern for the city and its people, as can be seen in the many benefactions they made, for which they received public recognition in the form of inscriptions or other public monuments voted upon by the decurions and the assembly. They funded the construction of many of the city's public buildings, insured adequate food supplies for the city at reasonable prices (which often required that they make purchases from their personal funds), undertook the production of the Isthmian Games at their own expense, provided public banquets, public distributions of money, and other public and private benefactions to the city's people.[96]

There are a few values that were specific to Corinth, noted by many contemporaries. Among these was an emphasis on sensual enjoyment. To the Greeks and Romans, sex was part of nature, not against nature, as the later Christians believed. Although the one thousand sacred prostitutes of Aphrodite in Greek Corinth were no longer present in the Roman colony, Corinth was still the city of Aphrodite. As Aristeides wrote:

> And furthermore, there is no place where one might stay and rest as in the Mother of Seas [Corinth], no place is sweeter or friendlier, or offers such repose, refuge, and a place of safety for all that come to her. But clearly, her beauties, her passions, and her erotic pleasures attract many, as all are bound by pleasure, and all alike are kindled by her to find love, passion, companionship, and allurements. She beguiles their spirit and the wits from them . . . with the enchantments of the goddess, for clearly this is Aphrodite's city.[97]

No discredit was attached to these values by the Greeks and Romans—one need only walk down the streets of another City of Venus, Pompeii, to confirm this view—not even by the elite, who scorned the servile origins and mercantile values of Roman Corinth's population.[98] However, pleasure-seeking was not highly esteemed by the sterner teachings of Judaism and Christianity, and this conflict of values can be clearly seen in Paul's agonized letters to Corinth's early Christian community.

Since most of Corinth's first colonists were freedmen who had been engaged in commerce and manufacturing in Italy, it is not surprising that mercantile values were common among them.[99] Indeed, Aristeides compares the city in the mid-second century to a large merchant ship full of valuable cargo. The colonists were not slow to realize the economic potential the city offered, and their talents and abilities were largely responsible for the city's rapid growth. Nevertheless, their values were held in contempt by some of the elites of surrounding communities, with stagnant economies. One wrote:

> What inhabitants have you received, O luckless city
> and in place of whom? Alas for the great calamity of Greece!
> Would Corinth, that you lay lower to the ground
> and more deserted than Libyan sand,
> rather than wholly given to such scoundrelly slaves
> who afflict the bones of the ancient Bacchiadae.[100]

Indeed, some Corinthians were not above robbing the graves of their Greek predecessors and selling the contents to wealthy Romans.[101]

Despite all their individual failures and shortcomings, the Greco-Roman aristocracy did, in general, live up to its ideals, and delivered on its promises. Instead of spending money solely on themselves, which has been characteristic of many elites throughout history, the Greco-Roman aristocrats delivered public services to an extent seldom equaled. The proof lies not only in the thousands of honorary inscriptions set up to them by their grateful public throughout the Hellenistic era and Roman Empire, but in the works themselves that have survived. While we can no longer witness the private and public distributions of food or money, and the productions of musical and theatrical spectacles, the buildings have remained: shops, stoas, paved and colonnaded streets, public fountains, theaters, odeons, aqueducts, baths, swimming pools, triumphal arches, and beautiful, public monuments and statuary.

The traditional social and religious virtues were strong enough to survive the disasters of the late Roman Republic, lasting all the way to the late second century, and even later in some instances. After that date, political institutions became more autocratic at all levels, and an inevitable decline began, caused to a large extent by the corruption and abuse of power.[102] Social and religious values also changed among pagans and Christians alike: there was less of a concern for the future of the human community and more for the afterlife and the end of the world. An end was indeed approaching for the Romans of the Latin-speaking West. Since the end was thought to be near, there was an increasing emphasis on immediate self-enrichment, before it was too late, even at the expense of poorer citizens. Since there was no future, it was not necessary to maintain public buildings, and certainly no reason to construct new ones. There was no concern about obtaining honor from fellow citizens and from a posterity that would never exist. Now indeed, the quest for honor was called "vainglory."

Worst of all however, was the rejection of reason and natural law. The Christian church's greatest opponents were not Mithraism or state persecution, but these two great principles that had formed the basis of stoicism and indeed, classical civilization as a whole. In the struggle for men's minds, the church of the Latin-speaking West, if not the Greek East, was defeated by them. The Western church then announced that the use of reason and natural law were heresies. After it obtained police power under Constantine, the "heretics" were severely punished, a grim legacy that can still be felt today. The doom of the classical city was sealed, and it is not surprising that built upon its ruins, archaeologists find a few palaces and numerous hovels.[103]

# 5
# Religion

I have many people in this city.

ACTS 18:10

Since the Enlightenment, the West, and especially the United States, has maintained a political and intellectual separation between the secular and religious spheres. While this separation has benefited both, the ancient world made no such separation, and religion was a powerful influence on social, economic, and political institutions and values. Religion was an integral part of Roman Corinth as of other cities. The temples and shrines in the city attracted visitors and worshipers from all over the eastern Mediterranean. Religion is as important for the study of Corinth as the political institutions discussed in chapter 1.

Furthermore, Roman Corinth was one of the most important centers of early Christianity. Its importance is magnified by the fact that it is the best-known community, thanks to Acts and the letters of Paul. The social origins of Christian converts at Corinth is of prominent concern not only for those interested in Roman Corinth, but for Christianity in general. Christianity would have had no influence if it had no converts, so a few words about them will not be out of place.

One of the most important human needs religion fulfilled during the era of independent city-states (sixth to fourth centuries B.C.) was the spiritual unification of the citizen body through the worship of the city's gods. The need for spiritual unity was another reflection of the civic values of public-spiritedness that characterized the classical city. In fact, the fulfillment of their citizens' spiritual needs was one of the most important services provided by classical cities throughout their histories, even after they were incorporated into larger empires.

By the Hellenistic era and early Roman Empire, religious needs began to change. Important aspects of people's lives were no longer decided by themselves through the political institutions of the cities but by imperial administrations in Pella, Antioch, Alexandria, or Rome. Whether the state went to war, the rate of taxation, and which social classes participated in political institutions, were no longer decided locally, but in imperial capitals often far removed from the city. The consequences of these changes for religion were twofold. The first was the increasing loyalty to the new imperial cults of, for example, the emperors and Roma. The religious unity of the independent city-state was no longer as important, now that it was only a small part of a vast empire.

The second consequence was to promote the growth of personal religions. Since many important aspects of the individual's life were no longer under his control, there was an increasing need for individual spiritual fulfillment. Nevertheless, the old patterns persisted; the temples and shrines of the new gods were located next to those of the old revered deities in the cities. The focus of all religious activity was still the city.

This chapter analyzes the religions and religious trends in Roman Corinth, seeking answers to the following questions: What was the nature of the religious continuity between the Greek city and the Roman colony? What were the most important cults of the city and why? Which social groups worshiped which gods? What were the religious trends that occurred during the Roman Empire and what where their causes? Corinth became a major center of early Christianity through the missionary activities of Saint Paul. How did the problems Paul confronted in Corinth reflect the socioeconomic and cultural backgrounds of his converts? Why did Paul devote so much of his time to the rambunctious Corinthian church rather than to that of Athens or other cities on the Greek mainland? What was Corinth's role in the spread of Christianity in Greece?

These questions are difficult to answer because, in general, our sources are so poor. Our knowledge of the religious beliefs and practices of the city is based on four primary sources: inscriptions concerning priests and votive or dedicatory offerings to divinities; legends and images of deities on the coinage of the city; the remains of temples; and descriptions of religious cults by visitors to the city, especially Pausanias, who visited Corinth about A.D. 165. The numbers of different coin types illustrating individual gods can be considered, among other things, an indication of the relative importance to the city of the represented god. For example, there are more coin types of Aphrodite and Poseidon than any other divinities, and we know from other sources that they received the most honor and devotion.[1] The last two sources are often interrelated, since the identification of a temple will often rest on the description of its location by Pausanias. In addition to these literary sources, the book of Acts, First and Second Corinthians, Romans, passages in the *Ecclesiastical History* of Eusebius, First and Second Clement, and early church traditions preserved in the *Acta Sanctorum* and other works, provide evidence for the important Christian community in Corinth during the first four centuries of its existence.[2]

## Religious Continuity with the Greek City

There is strong evidence for the religious continuity of the Greek and Roman cities. The major divinities of the old Greek city, Aphrodite and

Poseidon, were also the most important in the Roman colony. Furthermore, some temples of the Greek era were rededicated to the same divinities in the Roman period, and one uniquely Corinthian cult, Athena the Bridler, survived into Roman times.[3]

But what was the nature of the continuity of religious cults from the Greek to the Roman city? Religious continuity may be defined in four different ways. First, specifically Corinthian cults may have been worshiped uninterruptedly during the city's eclipse from 146–44 B.C. by Corinthians who survived Mummius' sack of the city.[4] Second, Corinthians sold abroad as slaves may have retained some religious traditions from the old Greek city. When the city was refounded, the descendants of these slaves may have resettled in Corinth, bringing their traditions back with them. The continuity may reflect an antiquarian revival by Roman colonists and Greek settlers to the colony. Strabo and Pausanias writing in the Roman era were acquainted with a vast literature on the cults and rituals of Greek Corinth, and presumably, this literature would have been known to the new colonists as well.[5] Finally, the revival of the old Greek gods in the Roman city may have reflected a need the new colonists felt to worship the gods who protected the Corinthia, especially Aphrodite and Poseidon. From time immemorial, these two divinities were thought to dwell in the Corinthia, as Athena dwelt in Athens.[6] It would be to the colonists' advantage to pay special reverence to the powerful spiritual forces that fostered the well-being of their city.

It is probably misleading to emphasize the idea that the religious continuity observed at Corinth represents uninterrupted worship at the site or the preservation of Corinthian religious traditions by Corinthian slaves whose descendants returned to the city in 44 B.C.[7] It is more likely that the continuity of religions at Corinth reflects an antiquarian revival by the new colonists or their need to propitiate the gods who controlled the city. Certainly, it is an oversimplification to conclude that interest in the cult of Zeus in both Greek and Roman times implies a continuity of worship in the city.[8] Like any large city in Greece, Corinth would have had cults devoted to all the most important Greek gods in both eras. This fact alone does not demonstrate that the cult of Zeus was continuously practiced from the Greek to the Roman city.

Nor does the rededication of a few temples provide conclusive evidence for direct continuity for religion as a whole. Three Greek temples are known to have been rededicated to the same divinities in the Roman period: Demeter and Kore, Asklepios and Hygeia, and Aphrodite on Acrocorinth. Yet there appears to be no sign of religious activity in these temples during the period of the city's abandonment, and, indeed, the temples of Demeter and Kore and Asklepios (there is virtually no surviving archaeological evidence for the temple of Aphrodite) suffered heavy damage from neglect

and the theft of building materials during the period of the city's eclipse.[9]
It is also apparent that these temples' unique configurations, based on the
ritual requirements of their cults, would make the identity of the deities to
whom they were dedicated somewhat obvious. Take the example of the
temple of Asklepios and Hygeia on the north edge of the city.[10] Although
there was damage to the roof and colonnades when the Roman colonists
reoccupied the city, the structures survived more or less intact. There was
a small temple in the center of a courtyard surrounded by an *abaton,* or
stoa, where the patient would spend the night. Connected to the sanctuary
were dining rooms and a large fountain house, both of which were necessary for the cult. Additionally, there is the strong possibility that there were
inexpensive dedications to Akelpios lying around the precinct when the
Romans began cleaning the site. A large cache of such dedications belonging to the Hellenistic era was deliberately buried near the precinct.

A similar situation exists for the shrine of Demeter and Kore.[11] The
buildings of the shrine suffered heavy damage during the period of the
city's abandonment when they were not in use. But enough of the compli-
cated structures survived in 44 B.C. for the colonists to be able to identify
the deities involved. Again, we must not ignore the possibility that diag-
nostic dedications were strewn around the abandoned shrine. Although the
cult of Demeter and Kore would be more familiar to Greeks than Romans,
there were probably large numbers of Greeks in the colony from its incep-
tion.[12] The temple of Aphrodite on Acrocorinth was probably the most famous temple in Greek Corinth and its history was well known to Strabo;
would it not have been known to the colonists as well?

## The Pagan Cults of Roman Corinth

There were three currents of religious belief among the Corinthians of
the Roman era. First were the hallowed and traditional divinities of the
Greek and Roman pantheon.[13] These gods cannot be separated into Greek
or Roman categories, since by the first century B.C., the identification of
Greek gods such as Poseidon, Zeus, and Aphrodite with Roman gods such
as Neptune, Jupiter, and Venus, was so complete that for all practical purposes they were identical. There were, in addition, specifically Roman
cults, including the imperial cult, and oriental religions, including Judaism
and Christianity.

It is difficult to determine which were the most important pagan cults of
Roman Corinth, and whether different social groups worshiped different
gods. The literary, epigraphic, numismatic, and archaeological evidence
often yields seemingly contradictory views concerning the importance of a
particular cult. For example, there are more coin types depicting Poseidon
and Aphrodite than any other divinities, and this is one indication of their

importance for the city. However, the epigraphical evidence presents an entirely different picture. References to Aphrodite and Poseidon (or Venus and Neptune) are rare; instead, the overwhelming majority of dedications to divinities and references to priesthoods are to gods of the Roman state or the imperial cult. Nevertheless, the contradictory perspectives from different types of sources can yield important information about the religious preferences of different social groups within the city, as we shall see presently.

### The Cult of Poseidon

Poseidon's most splendid and renowned sanctuary was at the Isthmia, and there is no doubt that his worship was of great importance to the city's people. During the era of the city's eclipse, the Romans placed the sanctuary and the biennial Isthmian Games under the supervision of the Sikyonians, but when Corinth was refounded, the games and sanctuary were returned to Corinthian control.[14] The sanctuary itself consisted of the large Doric temple of Poseidon, a theater, and a stadium where the literary and athletic contests were held. There were also numerous auxilliary buildings: a bath, stoas, smaller shrines, and a hotel for visiting athletes (see plan 5).[15]

The major focus of the sanctuary was the great temple of Poseidon, measuring some fifty-six by twenty-two meters. Originally built during the mid-fifth century B.C. (and similar in size and proportions to the contemporary temple of Zeus at Olympia), the temple was badly damaged by fire, and rebuilt in 390 B.C. It was of limestone covered with a fine white stucco of marble dust, and had a roof of white marble tiles. During the second century A.D., the earlier cult statues of Poseidon and Amphitrite were replaced with a chryselephantine group dedicated by Herodes Atticus. This group consisted of Poseidon and Amphitrite in a chariot drawn by four golden horses with ivory hooves, and flanked by two gold tritons and Palaimon on a dolphin. On the base, Thalassa (the Sea), attended by Nereids, held the child Aphrodite. The temple precinct was surrounded by a grove of sacred pines, and portrait statues of victorious athletes lined the shaded walks. The dazzling white temple, shaded by the pines, must have been a magnificent sight to the visitors who thronged the Isthmia for the biennial games.

More different coin types were minted with the image of Poseidon (29) and the other divinities associated with him at the Isthmia than for any other divinity, reflecting the important role of the Isthmus and the Isthmian Games for the life of the city. The games attracted spectators and participants from all over the Mediterranean world, and what better way to lure them than to promote the importance of Poseidon and the Isthmian Games on the city's municipal coinage, which circulated throughout the region. The highest local honor obtainable for a Corinthian citizen was not the office of *duovir quinquennalis,* as in other Roman colonies, but that of *agonothetes*—the official in charge of producing the games. The international character of the games meant that he would receive the honor and esteem of the entire Hellenic world.

Since time immemorial, the Isthmus had been Poseidon's special home. In a city where so many earned their livelihood from the sea, and whose territory was periodically devastated by severe earthquakes, he would be the natural object of particular reverence. It is not surprising that the Roman colonists continued this tradition of reverence for the same reasons. Besides his temple at Isthmia, he had another at the port of Cenchreae, a sanctuary at Lechaion, as well as numerous statues, altars, and a fountain dedicated to him in Corinth itself.

### *The City of Aphrodite*

Of equal importance to the city of Corinth was the goddess Aphrodite. In Greek times, Corinth was the "City of Aphrodite," and her traditional status was maintained by the Roman colonists. No divinity received more devotion in the city than she, and, after Poseidon, Aphrodite had more different coin types than any other divinity (17). She had at least three sanctuaries within the city, two more in Lechaion and Cenchreae and, according to myth, she had been given possession of Acrocorinth as a gift by Helios. Her most famous shrine was on the top peak of Acrocorinth, and contained the famous statue of Armed Aphrodite (Aphrodite holding a shield before herself as a mirror). This small temple (ca. 10 by 16 meters) was originally built in the fifth century B.C., and may still have been standing when parts of it were used to construct a nearby church in the fifth century of the Christian era.[16] Although many modern works on early Christianity state that the one thousand sacred prostitutes of Aphrodite were still present when Paul visited the city (thus adding more lurid propaganda to their picture of morally depraved Corinthians), this venerable Near Eastern institution did not survive into Roman times.[17]

Another temple of Aphrodite, Temple F on the West Terrace, may have contained a cult statue by Hermogenes of Cythera (another important center for her worship). This marble Ionic temple, richly adorned with exquisite moldings, was built shortly before the mid-first century A.D.[18] Her third temple in the city, that of Black Aphrodite, was located in the Kraneion district near a cypress grove, a cemetery, and a precinct of Bellerophon. The close proximity of her shrine to a cemetery and a grove of cypress—a tree associated with death—shows that her epithet, *melaina*, referred to her as a goddess of the dead who would be invoked to partake of the libations offered there, like the Venus Libitina of the Romans.[19]

Aphrodite's prostitutes, who practiced in the Greek city, gave rise to numerous anecdotes and stories. They were temple slaves, over a thousand in number, who had been dedicated to the service of the goddess by both men and women. It was even believed that the city owed much of its wealth in the Greek era to their success in attracting visitors—especially sailors. Indeed, Corinthian prostitutes were the most highly esteemed in the Greek world, and some of the best rose to high social prominence. The tomb of Lais, perhaps the most famous prostitute of all, was still an attraction in the Roman era. Many stories and poems were repeated about Lais throughout the Hellenistic and Roman eras. One epitaphic poem was written by Antipater of Sidon:

> I contain her who in Love's company luxuriated in gold and
>      purple,
> more delicate than tender Cypris,
> Lais, citizen of sea-girt Corinth,
> Brighter than the white waters of Peirene,
> that mortal Cytherea, who had more notable suitors
> than the daughter of Tyndareus,
> all plucking her mercenary favors.
> Her very tomb smells of sweet-scented saffron,
> her bones are still moist with fragrant ointment
> and her anointed locks still breathe a perfume as
> frankincense.
> For her, Aphrodite tore her lovely cheeks,
> and sobbing Love groaned and wailed.
> Had she not made her bed the slave of gain
> Greece would have fought for her as for Hellen.[20]

Some even believed that the prayers of these prostitutes helped to avert the Persians from invading Corinth in 480 B.C.[21]

The goddess retained her importance in the Roman city: the founder of Roman Corinth, Julius Caesar, claimed descent from Venus, and the cult of Venus Genetrix became important during his lifetime. She was also the goddess of the sea; the base of the cult statue of Poseidon and Amphitrite at the Isthmia depicted Thalassa holding up the infant Aphrodite who, according to myth, was born in sea foam. In the theatrical performance at Corinth described by Apuleius, Aphrodite is portrayed as having her home in the sea.[22] Aristeides, writing in the mid-second century A.D. virtually identified Corinth with the goddess.[23]

The importance of Aphrodite in Roman Corinth reflected the values and needs of its people. The city was a mercantile center where many depended on the sea for their livelihood; a center for entertainment, not only for its local population but for the whole Hellenic world: it is little wonder that Corinth and Aphrodite were identified so closely. She fulfilled a variety of spiritual needs, and was not only the goddess of erotic love. Her pervasive influence in the city was respected by both Greeks and Romans, and does not malign the character of the Corinthians as some modern interpretations have claimed.

## Local Deities

The spiritual needs of Corinth's large mercantile and manufacturing population are reflected in the cults of Athena, Tyche (or Fortuna), and Hermes (Mercury). After Poseidon and Aphrodite, the heroes Bellerophon, with his famous horse Pegasus, and Melicertes, with his dolphin, Athena and Tyche appear most often on Corinthian coins. Athena was connected with the city through the legends of Bellerophon and Pegasus, and she always appeared on the obverse of the coinage of the Greek city, with Pegasus usually on the reverse. The goddess had helped Bellerophon tame and bridle Pegasus, and she had a shrine by the theater in the Roman era where she was called Athena Chalinitis, or Athena the Bridler.[24] Athena was the goddess of craftsmen, whose work was more highly esteemed at Corinth than any other Greek city and doubtless, her worship fulfilled the needs of many craftsmen and traders in the Roman colony as well.[25] Fortuna would also be an important goddess in a mercantile city, since ancient commerce was always attended by high risk, and she may have occupied Temple D on the West Terrace overlooking the forum. Hermes, the god of merchants and travellers also had a temple overlooking the commercial area of the forum.[26]

The myth of Pegasus and Bellerophon was localized at Corinth, and the divine pair were objects of special reverence. Bellerophon was the son of Glaucus and grandson of Sisyphus, kings of Corinth, and had to leave the city after he killed Bellerus (whence his own name, Bellerophontes) and his own brother. After many adventures, he came to the court of the king of Lycia who requested that Bellerophon kill the Chimera. Bellerophon consulted a seer, who informed him that the task could only be accomplished if he could capture and tame the winged horse Pegasus, beloved of the muses. Bellerophon found the horse drinking from the spring of Peirene at Corinth, and with Athena's assistance threw a golden bridle over his head and rode off to accomplish his task.

Numerous statues of the pair appear throughout the city, and they also had a sacred precinct near the shrine of Aphrodite Melainis. They were portrayed (somewhat sarcastically) in the sacred procession of Isis seen by Apuleius,[27] and were often depicted on municipal coinage, the number of their types coming after Poseidon and before Melicertes riding a dolphin. Again, this must indicate the importance of coinage as a promotional device. It seems that many tourists were attracted to Corinth so that they could see the actual location of Bellerophon's exploits, and the actual spot where Melicertes reached the shore on his dolphin. The locations themselves possessed almost magical powers as the dwelling places of potent spiritual forces.

Especially interesting in this context was the unofficial cult associated with the spring of upper Peirene on Acrocorinth. According to myth, the spring of Peirene, located east of the forum on the Lechaion Road, was created when Pegasus struck his hoof on a rock. However, after the reoccupation of the city by the Romans some confusion existed as to the exact location of this fountain; some identified it with the fountain of Peirene east of the forum, while others thought it was the spring on Acrocorinth. Under the influence of the Latin poets, the spring on Acrocorinth became more famous than the one below, and the name Peirene became attached to it, as recorded by Strabo. In the time of Pausanias, Peirene was again the lower fountain, and is so depicted on municipal coinage. To resolve the apparent contradiction, it was said that the source for both the upper and lower springs was the same, hence their identical names. Visitors to the spring on Acrocorinth in Roman times scratched dedications on its walls, often vicariously on behalf of those not present (a typical one might read, "Remember Euporos my brother, with good intentions, Hermios."), and similar ones are found on shrines throughout the Greek world, notably on the statue of the Singing Memnon in Egypt. These inscriptions were an act of vicarious worship to the powerful spirit of the place on behalf of those whose names were remembered." [28]

Corinth had always been a famous breeder of horses, and it is only fitting that the myth of antiquity's most renowned horse should be localized here.

The healing gods Asklepios and Hygeia were worshiped together in their temple on the north edge of the city. The temple, built largely in the late fourth century B.C., survived more or less intact into Roman times, when it was repaired and rededicated to the original divinities.

In the rites of Asklepios, the patient entering the shrine would sacrifice and purify himself by bathing. He would then spend the night in the *abaton* in the precinct, where the god would appear in a dream and either cure him on the spot or prescribe medication. Often, bathing or exercise would be prescribed, and the temple's own fountains, with their many draw basins, and the Fountain of Lerna, with its large swimming pool, were conveniently close by, as was the old Greek gymnasium. Dining rooms connected with the sanctuary were available for those who were given special diets. Often, a stay of several months was required for the treatment to be effective, and since the facilities at Corinth were only suitable for a brief stay—unlike the elaborate complexes at Cos and Epidaurus—this indicates that the sanctuary was primarily for local use. Asklepieia also served as training schools for doctors who were provided with ample opportunity for observing the sick and disabled. The Corinthian doctor Gaius Vibius Euelpistus was also a priest of Asklepios, and the famous doctor Galen may have used the facility during his stay in the city.[29]

The shrine and the nearby Fountain of Lerna were destroyed sometime in the late fourth century, when the general area became a large Christian cemetery. The temple precinct itself may have been converted into a church in the fourth century, but its site was scrupulously avoided as a burial place. At Corinth, Asklepios' healing functions were taken over by Saint Quadratus who was martyred in the mid–third century, and to whom the Cemetery Basilica was dedicated.[30]

A complex sanctuary dedicated to Demeter and Kore described by Pausanias was located on the north slope of Acrocorinth. Although the Greek sanctuary was desolate after Mummius' sack of the city, it was restored and rededicated to the same divinities at the end of the first century B.C. The sanctuary was considerably remodeled in Roman times when a new stoa, terrace wall, and several other structures were built. The small shrine was especially popular among the poor, as is shown by the quantities of inexpensive votive offerings found in Roman deposits. The sanctuary continued in use until the late fourth century.[31]

In a real sense old Greece was the holy land for the entire Greco-Roman world. It was here that all the great feats and achievements of gods, giants, and heroes were performed. In many ways, Greece fulfilled the same role that Israel does today for devout Jews and Christians.

## Roman Cults

Significantly, our knowledge of specifically Roman cults comes almost exclusively from dedicatory or votive inscriptions and inscriptions mentioning priests, almost all of which are in Latin, the language of Corinth's elite.[32] Of the thirty-eight extant dedications to divinities in Roman Corinth, thirty-two are in Latin and most of the Greek dedications (which date mainly from the late second to early third centuries A.D.) are poorly executed. The Latin dedications are all of marble, an expensive material in Corinth since it had to be imported, and generally record the dedications of marble or bronze statues or temples themselves. Furthermore, of the thirty-two Latin inscriptions, twenty or 63 percent are to the imperial cult, for which only one temple, that of Gens Julia is known to exist.[33] Another four dedications are to abstractions that became increasingly popular during the Empire: Victoria (1), Concordia (1), and the Genius of the Colony and Colonists (2). The rest of the Latin dedications are to Isis and Serapis (1),

Jupiter Optimus Maximus (1), Neptune (3), Venus (1), and Apollo (1). Fully twenty-five of the Latin dedications are to uniquely Roman gods or abstractions. The six Greek dedications are to Apollo (1), Asklepios (2), Hygeia (1), Tyche (1), and the Gods of the Beehive (1).

An even more striking pattern emerges from references to priesthoods in Roman Corinth. Of the thirty-one extant references, twenty-eight are in Latin and of these twenty are to priests of imperial cults.[34] Five are to uniquely Roman gods: Jupiter Capitolinus (4), and Janus (1), and the remainder are to Victoria (1), Saturn (1), and the Genius of the colony (1). The three Greek references to priesthoods are to Asklepios, Demeter and Kore, and Cronos, and date to the late second or early third century.

These epigraphical sources show the Corinthian aristocracy's devotion to (or even obsession with) the imperial cult. Even the Isthmian Games were linked to the imperial cult through the Caesarean Games and Imperial Contests. Many of these inscriptions were set up by the colonists or the descendants of colonists who were sent by Julius Caesar in 44 B.C. to refound the city, and who thus owed their high social position to the imperial house. Moreover, many of the duovirs and other magistrates, or their families, owed their freedom or citizenship to the imperial house, as can be seen from their names.[35] As did many colonial elites, the Corinthian aristocracy wished to retain the heritage and religious traditions of their homeland and to distinguish themselves from the Greek majority by worshiping gods of the Roman state. In general, the Latin-speaking aristocracy seems to have paid particular devotion to the gods of Rome, and after them, to the traditional gods of the Greco-Roman pantheon; they seem to have paid little attention to the Oriental and mystery religions. Since Corinth was the capital of the province of Achaea, it is obvious that special attention would be paid to the imperial cult. It was a wider projection of the old civic religion that expressed loyalty to the city's gods and hence, would gain the city favor in their sight. Therefore, provincial capitals would want to be seen as especially zealous towards the emperor; it was through such capitals and their governors that the divine emperors came most closely in contact with the governed.

## Eastern Religons

As residents of a major international entrepôt, many Corinthians worshiped deities and followed religions from the Orient. Two cults are known: that of Isis and Serapis, and Mother of the Gods (Cybele), as well as the religions of Judaism, and Christianity.[36] Unfortunately, nothing is known about the cult of Cybele at Corinth aside from the mention of her temple on Acrocorinth by Pausanias.[37] Our knowledge of the Egyptian cults of Isis and Serapis comes almost solely through Lucius Apuleius whose vision of Isis, experienced while sleeping on a beach near Cenchreae, is an imperishable monument of religious faith. His detailed description of the religion of Isis and Serapis at Corinth is one of the fundamental sources of information about their worship.[38]

The cult of Isis and her attendant deities, Serapis and Anubis, were important at Corinth. She had one temple in Cenchreae and two in Corinth itself which were adjacent to two temples of Serapis. The dispersion of these cults throughout the Mediterranean was achieved largely in the fourth and third centuries B.C.; the cults at Corinth may originally have developed at this time and been restored with the resettlement of the city.[39] Isis and Serapis were always worshiped together and were regularly named together in inscriptions. They were healing gods, often identified with Asklepios and Hygeia by the Greeks, since the process by which the patient was cured—incubation with a divine revelation—was similar in the two cults. Apuleius received his divine revelation concerning his return to human form while sleeping on a beach sacred to Isis near Cenchreae.

Isis' two shrines at Corinth concerned two different aspects of the goddess. Marine Isis (Isis Euploia or Pelagia) was responsible for rendering the seas safe for navigation during the sailing season, an ancient attribute, while her Egyptian aspect included Isis' more traditional roles as healer and provider of crops and fertility.

The initiation rites of Isis were also described by Apuleius in as much detail as religious prohibitions allowed. The devotee first had to live a chaste life, abstaining from foods forbidden by the cult. At the proper time, the would-be initiate received a dream from Isis, herself, telling him the proper time, place, and funds to be spent on the initiation ceremony. When the necessary (often substantial) funds were spent, the initiate was ritually bathed, after which he fasted for ten days, avoiding meat and wine. Apuleius' initiation ceremony began at sunset. The high priests led him into the sanctuary where:

> I approached the confines of death. I trod the threshold of Proserpine; and borne through the elements I returned. At midnight I saw the Sun shining in all his glory. I approached the gods below and the gods above, and I stood beside them, and I worshiped them.[40]

Apuleius was initiated because Isis told him:

> Neither is it aught but just that you should devote your life to her who redeems you back into humanity. You shall live blessed. You shall live glorious under my guidance; and when you have travelled your full length of time and you go down to death, there also

(on that hidden side of earth) you shall dwell in the Elysian Fields
and frequently adore me for my favors. For you will see me shining on amid the darkness of Acheron and reigning in the Stygian
depths. More, if you are found to merit my love by your dedicated
obedience, religious devotion, and constant chastity, you will discover that it is within my power to prolong your life beyond the
limits set to it by Fate.

In other words, the initiate received benefits both in this world and in the
next. In this, a long and glorious life and in the next a new life in the
Elysian Fields, where:

It is not the gods' will that you shall die . . . but the immortals
will convoy you to the Elysian Field, and the limits of the earth,
where fair-haired Rhadamanthys is, and where there is made the
easiest life for mortals, for there is no snow, nor much winter
there, nor is there ever rain, but always the stream of the Ocean
sends up breezes of the West Wind blowing briskly for the refresh-
ment of mortals.[41]

Lucius Apuleius left a vivid description of Marine Isis' procession to
open the sailing season at Cenchreae on March 5th. The description is
worth repeating in some detail, since it gives us the most vivid picture of a
religious procession in Corinth and, indeed, in virtually the entire ancient
world.[42]

At the head of the crowded procession were people dressed for different
roles in life—people one could see on the streets of Corinth: a soldier, a
huntsman, a woman, a gladiator, magistrate, philosopher, a bird catcher,
and a fisherman. A she-bear followed, dressed as a woman and carried in
sedan chair; next, an ape in a straw hat and a saffron-colored Phrygian
cloak, with a gold cup in its paws (a parody of Ganymede). Last came a
figure familiar to all Corinthians: a donkey with wings glued to its shoulders, ambling after a doddering old man—a caricature of Pegasus and Bellerophon.

After this came the procession proper, led by women crowned with flowers and scattering petals along the road. They were followed by women in
shining white dresses, carrying mirrors and combs to use on the statue of
Isis, and accompanied by other women sprinkling the road with perfume
and balsam. A company of men and women with torches and candles, all
addressing Isis as Daughter of the Stars, and a chorus of young choir boys
singing sacred hymns, preceded the initiates themselves: men and women
of all ages and classes, in their shining white linen garments, carrying sis-
trums of bronze, silver, and gold.

The leading priests carried emblems of Isis and Serapis: the first priest
carried a large golden boat lamp with a tongue of flame flickering from the

center, the second carried a miniature altar, and the third, a miniature palm tree with gold leaves and the serpent wand of Anubis. The fourth held up an emblem of justice—a raised left hand with the fingers extended—the left better suited for justice than the right, so the Egyptians thought, because of its lack of cunning and craft. He also held a gold vessel in the shape of a woman's breast, from which a thin stream of milk flowed, while the fifth priest held up a gold winnowing fan, the *vannus mystica*. Next followed images of the gods, first Anubis, with his jackal face blackened on one side and gold on the other to symbolize his power in heaven and hell, holding a herald's wand. He was followed by a priest carrying a statue of a seated cow representing Isis herself.

The procession led to a beach near Cenchreae, where the divine ship was anchored, its hull covered with hieroglyphics, while from its fir mast was spread a white linen sail inscribed with a prayer to the goddess for the protection of shipping during the new sailing season. The prow of the ship was gold plated, and the keel of polished citron wood. The initiates, or *mysticai*, stowed winnowing fans heaped with aromatics and other votive offerings, and poured a libation of milk into the sea before launching the ship.

On the celebrants' return to the temple, the images were returned to their places, and a scribe read out prayers for the emperor, the senate, the knights, the Roman people, and all sailors and ships under Roman jurisdiction.

The essential veracity of this description is suggested by Apuleius' accuracy in depicting other aspects of the city.[43] This joyous and colorful procession gives us an indication of the wealth and popularity of the cult of Marine Isis for Corinth, where many depended on the sea for their livelihood. Well might a visitor watch the spectacle and believe he was in a veritable Egyptian colony.[44]

The temple of Isis at Cenchreae has been excavated, and was found to contain some magnificent *opus sectile* glass panels dating to the late fourth century, depicting many Egyptian and Nilotic motifs.[45] Also at Cenchreae were sanctuaries of Aphrodite, Asklepios, and Poseidon, deities often identified with the Two Egyptians, and it was here that Paul underwent complete tonsure in fulfillment of a vow—a practice often followed by devotees of Isis.[46]

Serapis had two shrines at Corinth, located next to those of Isis, one of which was Serapis "in Canopus." The Serapion in Canopus, Egypt was his most hallowed shrine, and served as a school for the training of magi, or miracle workers. Men of high social standing often spent the night there to partake its miraculous cures on behalf of themselves or others.[47] Often Serapia, like Asklepieia, served as training centers for doctors. Isis and Serapis offered tenacious resistance to Christianity. Their shrines were some-

times converted into churches, and some of the saints may even have been
one of the Two Egyptians in disguise.

Two religious trends can be discerned for the pagan cults in Corinth from
the inscriptions written during the first three centuries A.D. First, there is
an increase in the proportion of inscriptions concerning priests and dedications to gods written in Greek rather than in Latin, and second, a relative
decline in the importance of the imperial cult and specifically Roman
gods.[48] These trends probably reflect the changing religious needs of Corinth's people. After several generations in a Greek cultural milieu, the appeal of the gods of the Roman state may have waned for the descendants of
the original Italian colonists. A second reason is probably the changing
ethnic composition of the city's people examined in chapter 4. After several generations, the ranks of the old Italian families had probably grown
thin, and they were replaced by Greek immigrants who migrated to the city
in vast numbers. The diminishing importance of Roman cults is paralleled
by the diminishing influence of Roman culture seen in other spheres at
Corinth.

From an examination of the archaeological, epigraphic, numismatic,
and literary sources, the pattern of religious preferences of Corinth's
people emerges. All the sources are unanimous that Aphrodite and Poseidon were the most important divinities in the lives of most of Corinth's
people. The Latin-speaking elite (whose religious preferences we know
best) were particularly devoted to Roman gods and the imperial cult, and
to a lesser extent, the gods of the traditional Greco-Roman pantheon. The
religious preferences of the poor are much more difficult to discern, since
they seldom wrote inscriptions. Moreover, the purpose of Corinth's municipal coinage seems to have been to advertize the venerable and respectable
gods and goddesses of the Corinthia and the minor heroes associated with
Corinth through myth and legend such as Melikertes (or Palaimon) and the
dolphin, and Pegasus and Bellerophon. Although Bellerophon was only a
hero, he and Pegasus are represented on twenty-five different coin types,
more than any god except Poseidon himself. The cults of Demeter and
Kore, Isis and Serapis, and Cybele however, did not possess tradition or
reputation, and therefore were not considered worthy to adorn the city's
coinage. Nevertheless, the evidence suggests that the cults of Demeter and
Kore, and Isis and Serapis were especially popular among the poor. The
immense numbers of inexpensive votive figurines in the excavations of Demeter and Kore's sanctuary are an eloquent if silent testimony. The crowds
in Isis' procession described by Apuleius contained men and women from
every social status, many of whom were probably poor. The location of
these temples along the Acrocorinthian road, far from the forum, may also
indicate that the ruling aristocracy did not wish these cults to occupy a

position of prominence within the city.[49] The oriental and mystery religions of the city offered a fertile milieu for the development of Christianity, since beliefs in a dying and reviving savior, faith healing, and a blessed afterlife for the initiate were shared by them all.

## The Christian Church at Corinth

We are fortunate to have more information on the early Christian church at Corinth than for any other Christian community. The book of Acts and the letters of Paul contained in First and Second Corinthians reveal an early church at the first critical stage of its development, when Christianity was being transformed from a Jewish sect to an international religion. Furthermore, our new understanding of Corinth's economy, society, and its pagan cults will help clarify the development of the city's early Christian church.

Perhaps the most important question concerning Paul's missionary activity in the city is the amount of time and energy he expended there compared to Athens, Thessalonica, and Philippi. His preaching in Athens fell largely on deaf ears, while Corinth proved to be one of his strongest and most successful foundations. Another question is the nature of the Corinthian converts themselves. Paul experienced many difficulties with them he did not experience with converts in other cities. How did these difficulties reflect the society, social values, and economic structure of the city? In other words, how did Paul's successes and problems reflect the fact that Corinth was a different kind of city than the others in mainland Greece where he had also preached?

In the spring of A.D. 50, Paul left Athens and journeyed to Corinth, where he founded its Christian church.[50] It was a fruitful scion from the start; the city's position as a central market for mainland Greece made it a natural site to establish a strong church from which the new doctrine could be dispersed. The church grew in prestige and power throughout the Roman imperial era until it exerted a general hegemony over the other churches in the province of Achaea.

Paul first stayed in a private house (that of Priscilla and Aquila, who may already have been Christians), which became the first assemblyplace for the new church, a common practice in early Christian communities.[51] The couple were originally from Pontus, then went to Rome, whence they were expelled by Claudius' decree, removing the Jews from the city, "on account of Chrestus."[52] The couple were tentmakers by profession as was Paul, but undoubtedly they also made awnings and sails which would be in great demand in the city.[53]

Roman Corinth possessed a substantial Jewish community, and Paul began his mission in their synagogue, as was his practice in other cities.[54] Although he converted the *archisynagogos* Crispus, and Titus Justus, a worshiper of God who lived next door, the Jewish community as a whole was hostile to Paul and his message. Because of his ill-treatment by them, Paul turned to the gentiles of the city, beginning his mission to them with fear and trepidation, no doubt because of Corinth's reputation as a worldly, cosmopolitan center.[55] Paul first despaired of success, but saw a vision: "Do not be afraid but go on speaking and do not be silent; for I am with you, and no man shall attack you or harm you; for I have many people in this city."[56]

Paul was highly successful in making converts among the pagan, urban poor of the city. He later wrote that among his converts there were not many who were wise, or powerful, and certainly not many well-born.[57] This is not to say that all Paul's converts in the city were poor: Chloe, whose people visited Paul in Ephesus may have been well-to-do, as was Gaius, who placed the hospitality of his household at the service of the church, and Erastus the aedile, another convert, who paved the theater at his own expense during the reign of Nero.[58]

Paul stayed at Corinth for a year and a half, in which time "many of the Corinthians hearing Paul believed, and were baptized."[59] The apostle would not have stayed so long in Corinth if the work had not been worthwhile:

> The Gospel had even spread to other towns of the province (Rom. 16:1, II Cor. 1:2 "the whole of Achaea"). The words which he heard in a dream, that the lord "had many people in this city" (18:9), show that the narrator feels that this church is among the first in numbers and vigor. It actually stood in the center of Paul's missionary career; it was the church which gave him the most trouble in love and grief, in labor and thankfulness; three times he visited it, he wrote to it at least four letters, and in Corinth, he composed the first letter to the Thessalonians, the letter to the Romans, and perhaps one to the Galatians. The church seems to have been unusually full of life, for Paul praises their enrichment "in all knowledge and in every kind of gift" (I Cor. 1:5f.). That does not simply mean that there were many religious personalities stirred and excited by religious zeal, but that all moral and religious attitudes had here a peculiar vigor and outspoken determination.[60]

However, Paul's mission was opposed by the Jews more than ever; they thought that he was attempting to persuade them to worship God contrary to Jewish law.[61] The Jews were troubled because the emperor Claudius had secured religious liberty for them once more by his famous edict of toleration (A.D. 41–45). By the terms of this agreement, they could now live in accordance with their law, but no new or irregular religious customs were to be introduced under the protection of this freedom. For only on such a condition did it seem possible for the magistrates to identify Jews and protect them as such. It was therefore in the interest of the Jewish community to denounce renegade coreligionists to the Roman authorities, in order to avoid being compromised by them. For in that case they lost the protection which a *religio licita* entitled them, and made them liable for prosecution.[62]

For this reason, some Jews brought Paul before the tribunal of the governor of Achaea, Cornelius Gallio, the brother of Seneca, between July and October of 51. Gallio would not hear the case, and dismissed the Jews, saying "If it were a matter of wrongdoing or serious crime, I should have reason to bear with you, O Jews; but since it is a matter of questions about words and names and your own law; see to it yourselves; I refuse to be the judge of such things."[63]

After the Jews' charges were dismissed, the bystanders attacked Sosthenes, the new *archisynagogos,* and beat him. Although the identity of the people who attacked him is not given, it seems likely that the offenders were gentiles rather than Jews, since Gallio criticized what he considered to be the groundless charges of the Jews against Paul.[64] It is also unlikely that the Jews would beat their own synagogue leader, even if he failed to win his case before the governor. This Sosthenes may have been later converted to Christianity and, according to church tradition, he became the second bishop of Corinth.[65]

After this incident, Paul stayed in the city for some time before leaving for Ephesus with Priscilla and Aquila via Cenchreae, which had its own church under the deaconess Phoebe. At Ephesus, Paul met Apollos, a Christian and a learned Alexandrian. Apollos was anxious to visit Achaea, and journeyed to Corinth where "he greatly helped those who through grace had believed, for he powerfully confuted the Jews in public, showing by the scriptures that the Christ was Jesus."[66] According to tradition, he was the first bishop of Corinth.

However, all was not well with the Corinthian church while Paul was away. In early 54, when at Ephesus, he received a message from Chloe's people that the church had divided into factions and was beset by numerous problems. In response, Paul wrote First Corinthians, and visited Corinth again later that year. His letter and visit were not entirely successful; many Corinthians, at the urging of "false apostles" and other apostles from the church at Jerusalem, did not accept the authority of Paul. So, Paul wrote another letter, "out of much affliction and anguish of heart and with many tears, not to cause you pain but to let you know the abundant love that I have for you."[67] He sent this letter (which does not survive) to Corinth with Titus in midsummer of 54. Titus reported back to Paul that his mission had been successful, and that the "false apostles" had been removed from positions of authority. In response to this welcome news, Paul wrote 2 Corinthians 1–9 in a spirit of reconciliation. However, Paul later learned that the situation in Corinth was more serious than Titus had represented to him, and in response to this new crisis, he wrote another letter (2 Cor. 10–13), reasserting his authority over the church, which he visited for the third and last time, perhaps in mid 55.

## Factions in the Church

Paul's problems with the Corinthians are usually portrayed as a conflict of superior understanding and legitimate authority against ignorance and recalcitrance.[68] This is indeed the impression obtained from reading Paul's letters. However, the Corinthian perspective of Paul is fundamental for the understanding of these problems, and this perspective is not always given in discussions of Paul's mission to the city.

To a large extent, the problems Paul encountered at Corinth were a reflection of the nature of the city's people. The Corinthian church, perhaps to a greater extent than Paul's other foundations, was a gentile church, and its members retained their traditional values even after they were converted.[69] First of all, the Corinthians displayed an individualism and independence of thought that Paul found excessive. In early 54, Chloe's people had informed Paul that the church was divided into four factions: those of Paul, Apollos, Cephas (Saint Peter, who visited Corinth during this period [Eusebius 2.25]), and that of Christ. Apparently the Corinthians had heard different messages from several sources, and had made no attempt to establish an orthodox or authoritative view, each individual following the message he deemed most appropriate. Of the factions, "Paul's group" was not defended by Paul himself, perhaps because they had exaggerated or falsified his views. Apollos the Alexandrian was learned and eloquent, and he may have inadvertently aroused some contempt for Paul, who was despised by some as a speaker.[70] The Cephas group probably represented Jewish Christianity based in Jerusalem. They may have promoted the observance of dietary laws and other legalisms, while questioning Paul's status as an apostle. The Christ party may have been those who wished to avoid factionalism. In Second Corinthians, a conflict of authority again appears when Paul's authority is challenged by representatives of the Jerusalem church, and by those he calls "false apostles."

This conflict between authority and individualism is ultimately a reflection of the Corinthian people themselves. Paul's largely pagan converts retained many of their former religious notions and social values. In paganism, there was no orthodox or authoritative dogma for the worship of any god. The worship of Isis, Cybelle, or Jupiter varied considerably from community to community and indeed from individual to individual; the individualism of worship reflected individualistic values.[71] Since the time of Homer, individualism and an innate distrust of authority had been a characteristic of Greek society. From Paul's view, the Corinthians were stubborn; but Paul's attempt to establish a hierarchical authority among them was completely alien to their culture and values. What gave Paul the right to assert his importance over others? Why should Paul, who had never seen Christ, be accorded greater authority than Peter, who had? Why not accept the message of Apollos who was at least an eloquent and persuasive speaker?

As in other aspects of their lives, it was for each individual to establish for himself the message he would follow. The Corinthians therefore, could not regard themselves as only a part of some larger body, but as independent, self-reliant individuals.[72] Each one had to find his own personal message of edification in the new religion.[73] The greater conflict of authority Paul experienced in Corinth, compared to the other Christian communities to whom he wrote, shows the greater proportion of gentile converts in the Corinthian church.

Paul also experienced difficulties with independent women, who prayed and prophesied in church, sometimes even with their heads uncovered—a disturbing practice to someone with Paul's cultural background.[74] Once again, this is a conflict of values between Jewish and Greco-Roman culture. Women who enjoyed many of the same civil rights as men (the right to divorce, inherit, bequeath, own property, and make contracts), and who played prominent roles in pagan and mystery cults, were unlikely to be as humble as Paul would have wished.

The sexual laxity Paul perceived in the City of Aphrodite was also troubling to him. Some Corinthians visited prostitutes and the church even tolerated a man living with his stepmother, a practice that broke both Jewish and gentile laws.[75] Prostitution was common in the Greco-Roman world (witness the grafitti on the walls of Pompeii) and little or no stigma was attached to the practice. Some courtesans, like Lais and Neara (Corinthians of the Greek era), and Aspasia, were held in high esteem by society in general. Nevertheless, the church's countenancing the relationship between the man and his stepmother must imply sexual standards in Aphrodite's City that most pagans would view as lax. Other practices that Paul found offensive among the Corinthians—litigiousness, the eating of meat sacrificed to pagan gods, and reveling during the sacred meal—had been characteristic of Greco-Roman culture since time immemorial.

Some attempts have even been made by New Testament scholars to portray the city as basically evil, apparently to legitimize the spiritual absolutism of the Apostle. According to this view, since the Corinthians are evil and depraved, naturally, they cannot think correctly for themselves, but must follow Paul. It must be remembered, however, that the Corinthians, for their part, are arguing for greater religious pluralism within Christianity, more social and religious toleration, and greater intellectual freedom. It was precisely the lack of these values that would cause great harm in the future.[76]

Paul's conflict with the Corinthians must also be seen from the perspective of his own social and cultural background, and not only from the view of orthodox theology. The only way the Jewish faith survived in a sea of paganism was through strict adherence to correct religious observances and laws. Only in this way was Judaism able to retain its integrity and indeed to survive at all, not only in the pagan, but also in the Christian world. Paul, therefore, thought it essential that the Corinthians follow his teachings with strict obedience: otherwise, Christianity would become diluted, like a small drop in a pagan ocean.

With such difficulties, it seems surprising that Paul made the valiant effort he did to convert the gentiles at Corinth; it almost seems that his initial fear and trepidation were justified. Yet, they were not, and Corinth's proved to be one of the most important and influential churches of the early Christian world.[77] Why then, did Paul devote so much time to a city that seemed so unpromising?

Some reasons have long been known. As a major destination for traders, travelers, and tourists in the eastern Mediterranean, Corinth was an ideal location from which to spread word of a new religion. The Isthmian Games celebrated in the spring of 51 when Paul was in the city were doubtless another reason Paul was attracted to Corinth.[78] Paul would encounter spectators and participants who could take word of the new religion to many distant places. Indeed, the importance of the games is probably reflected in this passage from 1 Corinthians 9:24–7:

> Do you not know that in a race all the runners compete, but only one receives the prize? So run that you may obtain it. Every athlete exercises self-control in all things. They do it to receive a perishable wreath, but we an imperishable. Well, I do not run aimlessly, I do not box as one beating the air; but I pommel my body and subdue it, lest after preaching to others I myself should be disqualified.

The "perishable wreath" in the passage is probably a reference to the victor's crown at Isthmia made of withered wild celery.

The city also offered Paul an opportunity to practice his own trade as tentmaker, since there was probably a high demand for his products: tents for sheltering visitors to the spring games, awnings for the retailers in the forum, and perhaps sails for merchant ships. Paul was not driven out of Corinth by Jewish hostility as he was in other locations. He had come to stay and his economic independence did not make him a burden on his new converts in the city.[79]

As important as these factors may have been in influencing Paul to remain at Corinth, they were probably not the most important. Ultimately, the Corinthian church was composed of Corinthians, and not transient merchants, travelers, and tourists. Nor were the spectators and participants at the Isthmian Games likely to be the best candidates for religious conversion. Most of Paul's converts in the city were poor and powerless, while many of the spectators and especially the athletes were of a high social standing, and had often traveled long distances at considerable expense to reach the Isthmia. It was the Corinthians who found his message attractive, and *they* were his converts in the city. Ultimately, if they were not convinced, Paul's mission would have been a failure.

Why should the urban poor of Corinth have been attracted to Christianity? Why did the Christian God "have many people in this city" and not in Athens? The large population of Corinth would ensure more potential converts here than in other cities; yet, Corinth's attraction for Paul was probably more qualitative than quantitative. He found a different kind of people in Corinth than in other cities: people who were more receptive to his message. A comparison between Roman Corinth and Roman Athens may be informative.

During the Roman era, Athens' economy was stagnant. Most of the religious and public buildings constructed at this time were built from imperial handouts, or by the millionaire Herodes Atticus, who obtained funds from inherited wealth or from rents collected from his vast estates all over Greece. The new structures do not reflect a strong local economy that produced sufficient surplus to construct them. This stagnant city could not attract immigrants from abroad: quite the contrary, the population seems to have been in decline, and was probably smaller than Corinth's during this era.[80]

Furthermore, Athens' religious traditions had never been interrupted, and remained a powerful influence throughout the Roman era. This is in contrast to Corinth, a new city, whose religious customs (despite antiquarian revivals) would have to begin anew. The leaders of Athens' philosophical schools commanded broad popular support within the city, probably to an extent unmatched anywhere else. Many philosophers found the Christian message, with its stress on faith over reason, to be in conflict with the Greco-Roman view of God as reason itself.[81]

Corinth, in contrast, throughout the first century A.D. had a dynamic and growing culture and economy that attracted immigrants from all over the eastern Mediterranean to work in its flourishing manufacturing, marketing, and service sectors, either as slaves or free immigrants.[82] Whatever their geographical origin, the new migrants had broken many cultural ties with their homelands and were probably more susceptible to a new and, in some respects, unconventional religious message. Most were probably poor (at least initially) and migrated, as people have always done, to improve their social and economic position in life. In many ways, Corinth was similar to Ephesus, where Paul also spent a considerable time:[83] a large, prosperous port city which would have attracted immigrants from afar. In contrast, this type of immigrant was probably absent from Athens, Thessalonica, Phillipi, and many other Greek towns during the Roman era, whose economies could not attract migrants from beyond their own hinterlands.

### Christianity's Appeal to the Poor

Many of Corinth's urban poor and new migrants worshiped oriental and mystery religions such as Demeter and Kore, and Isis and Serapis, which have some similarities to Christianity. All promised a blessed afterlife to the initiate, and in Serapis the worshiper would find a god who had suffered, died, and was miraculously reborn. When Paul compared the resurrection to a kernel of wheat for his Corinthian converts:

> . . . What you sow does not come to life unless it dies. And what you sow is not the body which is to be, but a bare kernel, perhaps of wheat or some other grain. . . .
> So it is with the resurrection of the dead. What is sown is perishable, what is raised is imperishable . . . [84]

he was speaking in terms familiar to the initiates of the Eleusinian Mysteries of Demeter.[85] And when he said, "Lo! I tell you a mystery (*musterion*). We shall not all sleep but we shall all be changed, . . . For the trumpet will sound and the dead will be raised imperishable, and we shall be changed. For this perishable nature must put on the imperishable, and this mortal nature must put on immortality . . . ,[86] it was not a coincidence that the message was similar to those of Eleusis, Isis, and Cybele.

Paul described one of his religious experiences in almost the same terms that Apuleius used to speak of his initiation into a cult of Isis:

> I know a man in Christ who fourteen years ago was caught up to the third heaven—whether in the body or out of the body I do not know, God knows. And I know that this man was caught up into Paradise . . . and he heard things that cannot be told, which man may not utter.[87]

Furthermore, the humble social origins of Christ would have attracted many of the city's working poor. In Christ they would find someone as socially and economically powerless as themselves, and who underwent suffering and deprivation, often at the hands of his political and social superiors. Yet he triumphed over death, as they might do if they followed his example.[88] Many were awed by the miracles Paul performed in the city.[89] Both Christ and Paul were workingmen, a carpenter and a tentmaker, the kind of people numerous in the city.

In other words, Paul's success in Corinth was based on the nature of the Corinthian people, and especially the urban working class, many of whom were recent immigrants. They found his message attractive, not because it offered them something different, but because it was similar to their own religious beliefs; a complete break with their past religious views was not necessary. What the Corinthians could not accept at first, and only reluctantly accepted later after a long struggle, were the notions of religious dogma and orthodoxy combined with a rigid structure of religious authority. These aspects of Christianity were antithetical to classical notions of individualism and the view that authority could only be accepted if it came from the people concerned; it could not be imposed from above.

Ironically, it was just these notions of dogma, orthodoxy, and authority that were responsible for Christianity's final triumph. Such authoritarian values were quite acceptable to Constantine and his autocratic successors. They recognized that Christianity, with its hierarchical power structure, could be controlled from the top—unlike pagan religions with their rampant individualism. When Constantine converted, he became the patron, not only of the pope, but also of all Christians, and they became his clients. This gave a legitimacy to the emperor's power that the pagan tradition could never match. The chance to control the religious beliefs of all Christians through the exercise of imperial power on the Church's hierarchy and (after Christianity became the official state religion), the beliefs of all imperial subjects, was too tempting for Constantine and later autocrats to resist. Left on its own to compete for converts on an equal basis with pagan cults Christianity might claim the devotion of a tenth of the Empire's population. But the authoritarian structure of the Church—a structure not shared by individualistic pagan religions—made it attractive to the imperial government. Its considerable political, military, social, and economic power was used to promote Christian beliefs among the entire population and made this triumph of Christianity inevitable. It is a wonder that paganism survived so long after Constantine.

A final reason for Paul's interest in Corinth was its position as a central market for much of the province. This explains why the Corinthian church was instrumental in the conversion of "the whole of Achaea." As is noted in chapter 3 and appendix 1, marketing centers serve many roles apart from economic ones. The culture of the Greco-Roman world was centered in cities, and larger cities played a greater role in cultural diffusion than smaller ones. Peasants and townsmen from the surrounding communities served by Corinth's market would come to the city frequently to take advantage of its numerous cultural, educational, legal, and economic services. Unlike transient merchants, travelers, and tourists, the peasants and townsmen looked to the city as their cultural and spiritual focus.

Corinth was probably the largest central market in mainland Greece, so that its economic and cultural influence would be enormous. This influence is, of course, similar to the influence of large cities of the present era. London, Paris, Rome, and New York all have profound effects on their marketing regions far beyond their mere economic roles, and often set cultural trends followed by their entire countries. By establishing a strong Christian community at Corinth, Paul assured that his message would be dispersed throughout the whole province in a way that churches in other communities could not match. Old Greece (Achaea) was still the intellectual and cultural focus of the Greek-speaking eastern provinces of the Roman Empire.[90] Therefore, the conversion of Corinth, the most powerful and influential city of Achaea, would have a profound effect, ranging far beyond the boundaries of the province. In this respect, the cities of Antioch and Alexandria, although far larger than Corinth in population, could not match it in influence. For these reasons, Paul's church at Corinth proved to be one of the strongest and most influential in the early Christian world.

## The Church After Paul

When Clement, the bishop of Rome, wrote his epistle to the Corinthians about 96, he described it as venerable, widely renowned, having a universally and deservedly cherished name, and displaying magnificent hospitality. Already, Paul's most valued foundation exerted a dignity beyond that of other churches in Greece.

> At the very beginning of the epistle, . . . we are told of many foreign Christians who came to Corinth, for of course the great trading city was visited by many foreigners. In Corinth, Christians who arrived from foreign parts could learn of the glorious and steadfast faith of the church which existed there, could marvel at its thoughtful and gentle piety, could proclaim widely the magnificent style of its hospitality and call the mature and perfect Christian knowledge of the Corinthians blessed.[91]

Then, about 96, two factions arose when "one or two headstrong individuals" removed some church officials, with the support of the majority of the community, thus abrogating the principle of apostolic succession and undermining the authority of the Church's law. The Corinthians, still possessing a perverse spirit of democratic individualism, naively believed that their church leaders ought to be accountable to the community as a whole. They were soon to be disillusioned. The leaders of this popular opposition relied on their charismatic spiritual gifts as prophets, teachers, and ascetics against the Church's authority. In many ways, the antithesis between spirituality and authority at Corinth was typical of the Church as a whole during this era.[92]

On the other side were the officials of the church, who had only a few followers. Since the Corinthian church was great and distinguished, and since it was hospitable and people visited it frequently, the news of its schism spread widely. Not only did Christians speak of the occurrence, but even the gentiles in the city of Rome.[93] For this reason, the Roman church of considered it proper to help resolve the dispute.

The church at Rome resolutely opposed the majority, and argued forcefully for the restitution of the deposed officials. Clement wrote that the right of appointing officials does not belong to the people but comes down through apostolic authority, and admonished the Corinthians to heed Paul's first epistle to them warning the church to abandon factionalism. Clement claims that the division created a danger to the church, since even the gentiles were aware of it. About this time, the first Corinthian martyr, Timon of Beroea, perished by crucifixion at the hands of the Greeks and Jews in the city.[94]

First Clement is important in providing a glimpse of church organization at an early stage of its development. Significantly, the monarchical episcopate, familiar in the later Church and in the early churches in Jerusalem, Syria, and Asia, did not spread to Corinth or to the West until probably about A.D. 150. At the head of the Corinthian church were several officials designated as elders or presbyters. They were formally installed, had definite positions and responsibilities within the church, and were usually accorded respect and obedience by its members. It was believed that their authority ultimately derived from God through Christ and the apostles who appointed them as successors. They led the congregation in prayers and the Eucharist, granted benevolences, and controlled finances. They were appointed for life by "approved men (church leaders) with the consent of the church."[95] In fact, it appears that the "approved men" made the actual choice, while the church merely confirmed it. They could only be removed from office for gross misconduct, but the Corinthians removed their presbyters because they were not content with them.[96]

Clement urged the church to accept his decision to restore the deposed presbyters, and sent three legates to Corinth to act as arbitrators. This first known use of the primacy of the Bishop of Rome to settle a dispute in another church was successful at Corinth, and Clement's letter received regular public readings in the Corinthian church at least through the second century.[97] At last, the obstinate Corinthian Christians had learned to obey authority.

During the second century, the prestige of the Corinthian church increased, thanks to the efforts of four Corinthian bishops: Apollonius, Primus, his successor Dionysius, and Bacchyllus. All played important roles in the formation of early Christian theology and the spread of the new religion, but especially Dionysius.[98]

Apollonius wrote denouncing the heresy of Cerdo, a presbyter in Rome at the accession of Antoninus Pius (138), who believed that the God of the Old Testament was not the father of Christ. Primus is mentioned in a letter of Hegisippus quoted by Eusebius (4.22) who wrote that the Corinthian church adhered to orthodoxy during this time, and that he was "refreshed by the true word while spending a few days in the city."

Dionysius was the most famous bishop of Corinth, active when Soter was pope, around 166–75. He was held in high esteem by the Christian world; even distant churches wrote to him for judgement and advice concerning their local problems. In addition to writing a church history (Euseb. 3.4), he was a prolific letter writer (Euseb. 2.25, 4.23). He wrote to the Nicomedeans denouncing the heresy of Marcion of Pontus, who elaborated upon the thesis of Cerdo; to Gortyn and the other churches on Crete; and to Amastris in Pontus, the home of Marcion. He urged the church at Knossos not to burden its members with unnecessary chastity, and to consider the weakness of the majority: a true son of the City of Aphrodite! Dionysius wrote to Soter, the bishop of Rome, and noted that Clement's epistle to them was still read in church on Sundays.

In Dionysius' letters as described by Eusebius, we see not only his personal ability but the authority of the old church of Corinth as well. The letters he sent to the churches of Athens and Lacedaemon are especially important in showing its prestige and influence. Although the church of Athens also traced its foundation back to Paul, and named Dionysius the Aeropagite its first bishop, it was quite insignificant compared to Corinth. Dionysius not only gives the church advice on its internal affairs, but strongly rebukes it for falling away from orthodoxy. Similarly, his letter to Sparta indicates that he considered Corinth the leading episcopate of Achaea. Corinth probably occupied this position from the beginning, and by the fourth century it had officially become the metropolitan church of Achaea and its bishops the archbishops of the province. This is why Bacchyllus, in the reign of Commodus, was able to convene and preside over a local synod of bishops to settle a dispute concerning the date of Easter (Euseb. 5.23).

## The Third and Fourth Centuries

The third century was a critical period for the development of Christianity in Corinth and throughout the Empire. Unfortunately, little evidence concerning Christianity or pagan religions survives from the city during this era. Not even the names of any bishops have been preserved. Church traditions have recorded some martyrdoms during this time however, the two most important being Quadratus and Leonides.

Quadratus' mother was martyred when he was a child, and he himself with five others perished in the reign of Decius or Valerian under a procurator named Jason. His relics were held in great esteem by the Corinthians, who revered them as the outer defenses of the city, and the church that held his relics became a place of healing.[99] The remains of this church have been identified with the Cemetery Basilica, north of the city, built in the late fourth century. A lintel bearing the name (Saint) Kodratos was found in the excavation, and numerous graves within the church testify to the importance of the martyr to whom it was dedicated. Among the distinguished individuals buried there was a Bishop Eustathius and a presbyter, Valerianus.[100]

About 258, Leonides and several others were martyred under a governor named Venustus. Leonides himself was hung over a fire and thrown into the sea; those who mourned him were tied to rocks and also thrown into the sea.[101] The baptistry of the great Lechaion Basilica may have originally been the martyrion of Leonides. The octagonal baptistry surmounted by a dome, a typical configuration of martyria, was constructed in the early fourth century, and is very close to the beach of Lechaion. The basilica itself was built later, about 450–60, and was rebuilt in the sixth century; perhaps it was dedicated to Saint Leonides and the drowned martyrs. It is the largest basilica yet found in Greece, measuring some 224 meters in overall length, only slightly smaller than St. Peter's in Rome, and no expense was spared in its lavish decoration of polychrome marbles and mosaics.[102] The Lechaion basilica is another indication of the importance of the Christian community at Corinth, and there may have been as many as five other early Christian churches, most of substantial size.[103]

Paganism still survived in Corinth during the fourth century, as we learn from the adventures of Aristophanes of Corinth, related by Libanius in an oration addressed to the emperor Julian in 362.[104] In the oration, Libanius requests that Julian show favor to Aristophanes, who has suffered unjustly at the hands of the Emperor's predecessor, Constantius II, and his notorious henchman Paul ("the Chain"). Aristophanes' vicissitudes in the imperial administration are an important source for that subject, but our interest in the oration is what it reveals about Corinth in the fourth century.

Aristophanes' father, Menander, was one of the leaders of the curial class in Corinth, and a worshiper of Hecate at Aegina and Poseidon at the Isthmia. He was enrolled in the Senate at Rome (which would have exempted him from performing municipal munera at Corinth), but preferred to remain a member of the Corinthian council. Menander's wife (unnamed) was a sister of the philosophers Hierius and Diogenes, friends of Julian. Menander entrusted his son's education to them, and, as part of his training, he was actively engaged in the cults of Demeter and Kore, Serapis, Poseidon, and Iacchus of Lerna. Aristophanes became duovir (*strategos*) and, helped by his father, spared no expense in performing benefactions for his fellow citizens. However, after Menander's early death, Aristophanes was cheated out of some property (according to Libanius) by Eugenius the agent of Constans; and he exiled himself to Syria. Charged with fraud and conspiracy to consult a soothsayer with the prefect of Egypt in 358, Aristophanes was tortured by Paul and forced to undertake the obligation of duovir for his native city in absentia. This position was now compulsory and hereditary, and burdened the official with considerable expense. In Libanius' appeal to Julian, he notes that Julian's father sought refuge at Corinth for a time under Constantine (325–330) and requests that Aristophanes be granted immunity from municipal public services, and be given a salaried position in the imperial civil service. Nevertheless, the pagan revival under Julian was short-lived and could do little to stem the power of the Christian Church.

The influence of the Corinthian church shows once again the importance of Corinth as a center for cultural diffusion throughout the province of Achaea during the Roman era. Its market not only satisfied material needs, but spiritual ones as well. John Chrysostum, writing shortly before the sack of Alaric, described Corinth as the first city of Greece in population, wealth, and also in wisdom.[105] In great cities such as Corinth, these three characteristics have always been found together.

# Summary:
# The Service City

But if you will work, soon will the idle
man envy your wealth; on wealth at-
tends goodness and fame.[1]

HESIOD, *Works and Days* 312–13

The present chapter will analyze to what extent the economic model developed for Corinth is applicable to other classical cities. We will also analyze classical views about taxes and rents. It will be shown that Greeks and Romans thought that high taxes promoted poverty and not economic growth as is currently believed. Let us summarize the arguments against the consumer-city and in favor of the service-city model.

First, there are good reasons to reject the idea that any city over 20,000 in population was an agro-town. It is improbable that the maximum number of individuals living in a city who supported themselves by farming ever exceeded 10,000, and the actual numbers were probably more like 3,000. This is because 10,000 individuals will need the yield of a minimum of 117 square kilometers (45 square miles) of cultivable land to support themselves at the most meager, subsistence level. The radius of a circle with an area of 117 square kilometers is 6.1 kilometers (3.8 miles) and hence, a farmer living in the city and cultivating land on the periphery of the 117 square kilometer circle would have to walk a total of about 12.2 kilometers (7.6 miles) round trip to his fields and back.

For an actual city however, the area would need to have been far larger, when we take into account local topography, land not suitable for cultivation, and the fragmentation of holdings through inheritance and dowries. The human response to these problems has been the widespread distribution of agricultural villages that minimize the farmer's journey to his fields.

It is unreasonable to assume that the Greek or Roman peasant walked farther than anyone else to his fields, and so, it is unlikely that more than 10,000 could have been supported by farming in even the largest ancient city-states. This number includes both those directly engaged in farming and any townsmen who provided farmers with goods and services. For many city-states in the Greco-Roman world, an area of about 285 square kms. (110 square miles) would have been needed to support 10,000 individuals, given the geographical realities of the Mediterranean region.

Nor could most cities have been consumer cities, no matter what their size. Given rent rates in the classical era and the comparatively widespread ownership of land, a maximum of 10 to 20 percent of those supported by agriculture could have earned a living from rents, even if all the land was owned by landlords. This will have been a miniscule proportion of the total population of most ancient cities. The relatively small territories of most city-states would further limit the numbers of landlords residing in cities, and, some landlords probably preferred to live in the small towns in the countryside rather than the city.

In general, rent rates for the classical era seem to have been comparatively low. As M. I. Finley has observed:

> In a city-state, furthermore, the land was in principle free from regular taxation. A tithe or other form of direct tax on the land, said the Greeks, was a mark of tyranny, and so firmly rooted was this view that they never allowed an emergency war tax, such as the Athenian *eisphora,* to drift into permanence (nor did the Romans of the Republic), Unlike the pattern with which other societies have been very familiar.[2]

A society in which the peasants did not tolerate taxes to be levied on themselves would be unlikely to tolerate high rents either. Isocrates wrote that in democratic Athens, landowners kept rents low.[3] The reason for this was probably because the Athenian peasantry would resist high rent rates politically, and if necessary by the threat of force, just as they had done under Solon. It is also likely that rent rates in other Greek democracies were kept low for similar reasons and as Aristotle noted, democracies were the predominant form of political system in Greece during his day.[4]

In general, agricultural rents are determined to some extent by the productivity of the land, labor, and the availability of nonagricultural opportunities.[5] Where the productivity of land and labor is high, and there are few opportunities for nonagricultural work, rents are generally high. The converse also seems to be true. However, the evidence also shows that social values and political institutions also have a role in determining rents, taxes, and the surpluses kept by peasants and tenants.[6] It is not a coincidence that for similar farming conditions, the highest rents occur in societies with the most oppressive social and political institutions. When peasants and tenants have even rudimentary rights, as in Greco-Roman culture before A.D. 200, they can resist high land taxes and rents.[7] And when, as in the later Roman Empire, these rights (and the memories of the rights) disappeared, and the values that supported the rights were forgotten, taxes and rents might have been increased with impunity by the State and rapacious landlords to the margin of the peasant's existence.

Nevertheless, it is theoretically possible to have a consumer city that is not an imperial capital, by excluding farmers from living in the *asty*, which would be reserved mainly for landlords. However, it seems arbitrary to assume that the proportion of farmers to landlords living in the *asty* was much different from the population of the polis as a whole, whether the ratio was 10 to 1 or 5 to 1. This should be true whether the polis had 1,000 people or 100,000.

Another theoretical possibility would be to increase the numbers of landlords living in the *asty* to more than 10,000, but this city-state would be rare, indeed. As we have seen, the maximum numbers of farmers that can live in any community is about 10,000 (more than that and the distance to fields and back becomes too great). So, if we had 10,001 landlords living in a city with 10,000 farmers, this would qualify as a consumer city. If we had 9,999 landlords, it would still be an agro-town. In theory, the numbers of landlords could keep increasing beyond 10,000, but the numbers of farmers could not, and a consumer city would be the result.

But, in order for there to have been 10,000 landlords, given classical rent rates and land tenure, we would need a total population of 111,110 engaged in agriculture, assuming that rent rates were 10 percent and the landlords owned 90 percent of the land. We must also assume that *all* landlords lived in the *asty* and that none lived in towns in the *chora*. Moreover, the city would obtain almost no revenue from providing goods and services to peasants in the *chora*, travelers, traders, or tourists. This strange community—we may call it the "Agro-Supergiant"—would have one of the largest populations of any ancient city state engaged in agriculture (Athens only had about 50,000 maximum).[8] But where would it exist? certainly not in Greece, Italy, Asia Minor, or North Africa; in the wilds of Gaul perhaps, or Britain?[9]

The maximum number of landlords in a given city-state would vary with the size of the *territorium* and the rate of rents, but probably seldom exceeded 5,000 for all but imperial capitals. The numerous small city-states, like Pompeii, had far fewer. In fact, (although the point needs to be investigated) there seems to be a proportional relationship between the size of a city's population and the extent of its *territorium*. With a rent rate of 10 percent of gross production, therefore, the largest ancient cities would still have no more than 2,000 to 5,000 of their urban residents supported at a bare minimum subsistence level, directly or indirectly through rents. This number also includes any individuals earning a living by providing goods and services to landlords. Nor could a city with a population above 20,000 to 25,000 have been an agro-town.

Furthermore, the widespread ownership of land, especially in the Greek world, would tend to limit the numbers of landlords. It is easy to see that in agrarian societies where landownership is concentrated in a few hands, tenancy would be widespread. In agricultural societies where landownership is dispersed, the need for tenancy is more limited.[10]

How did the city earn enough income to support the remaining people? Where did the remaining surplus come from?

Most of the income that supported cities seems to have come from peasants and tenants who did not live in the city but who participated in its political institutions and religious and cultural affairs. The current view that tenants and peasants of the early Roman Empire produced very little surplus, perhaps only 2 percent over and above what they needed for their own maintenance, seed, taxes, and rents is probably incorrect. It ignores the implications of the tripling of the land tax during the late Empire and the statement of Aristotle that the ancient farmer could support two households. Nor is it probable that higher taxes encouraged the peasant to become more productive. This is the view advocated by Keith Hopkins.[11] However, there are several problems with this notion.

First of all, in many cases, when taxes increase, the peasant will cut back his production. A farmer with a fixed amount of land, labor, and capital would face decreasing returns because of a higher tax. Eventually he reaches a point where additional labor and capital outlays will cost more than the value of the increased production. The imposition of a percentage tax on crops increases the cost of production: not only must the farmer pay for labor and capital, but he must pay the tax as well. He will begin to incur losses at a lower level of production than before. Hopkins's generalization is only true when the peasant is producing at substantially less than the optimum point (where additional inputs will cost more than the value of the resulting increase in production). Imposition of a tax would result in an increase in production only if the tax reduced the farmer's net production below bare subsistence level, on the assumption that the land could support such an increase. More likely, the tax will cause the peasant to appropriate part of the existing surplus to pay for it. The conventional view, that Greek and Roman peasants chose to produce only at the level of subsistence seems to be quite incorrect. Furthermore, one man's subsistence might be another's abundance; it all depends on how subsistence is defined, and what living standards are expected to be maintained.

Certainly, the ancient view was that higher taxes cause poverty and distress. As Aristotle observed:

> And it is the device of tyranny to make the subjects poor so they cannot maintain a military force and so that the people, being busy with their daily affairs, may not have time to plot against their ruler. Examples of this are the pyramids in Egypt, the votive offerings of the Cypselids, the building of the temple of Olympian Zeus by the Peisistratids, and the public works of Polycrates. All

these undertakings produce the same effect, constant work and poverty among the subject peoples. The levying of taxes in Syracuse under Dionysius also produced the same effect, for in five years, everyone had contributed the whole value of their property.[12]

It is probably wrong to assume that we know more about the ancient economy than our sources, when they do speak of economic matters, especially a source such as Aristotle. When he says a farmer can support two households and that high taxes cause poverty and not prosperity, he speaks from knowledge not ignorance.[13]

It would appear the Roman tenants and peasants of the early Empire (and *a fortiori* in earlier eras) had considerably more surplus at their disposal than is currently believed and since these groups comprised the majority of the Roman population, this has important consequences for the Roman economy and the classical economy in general.[14]

If the tenant or peasant proprietor had only 2 percent of his gross production remaining after paying for seed, maintenance, rents, and taxes, then their combined purchases would have been of negligible importance for the city. But if the tenants and peasants had 50 percent of his gross production remaining to purchase goods and services, then the economic consequences for the city would have been considerable. Cities also provided an vast range of religious, educational, cultural, and judicial services that would bring rural residents into the city. While in the city, these individuals may have needed other services such as food or temporary lodging.[15]

This participation of rural peasants in urban markets is reflected in the marketing systems of the northeastern Peloponnese and Roman Britain as revealed by central place theory.[16] These networks developed to give the rural consumer the widest range of primary markets physically possible. Adam Smith's observations concerning rural-urban trade in the industrializing but still largely agrarian Europe of his day are probably appropriate for the classical world as well:

> The great commerce of every civilized society, is that carried on between the inhabitants of the town and those of the country. . . . The country supplies the town with the means of subsistence, and the materials of manufacture. The town repays this supply by sending back a part of the manufactured produce to the inhabitants of the country . . . We must not. . . . imagine that the gain of the town is the loss of the country. The gains of both are mutual and reciprocal, and the division of labor in this, as in all other cases, advantageous to all the different persons employed in the various occupations into which it is subdivided. . . . The town affords a market for the surplus produce of the country, or what is over and above the maintenance of the cultivators, and it is there that the

inhabitants of the country exchange it for something else which is in demand among them. The greater the number and revenue of the inhabitants of the town, the more extensive is the market which it affords to those of the country; and the more extensive that market, it is always the more advantageous to a great number.[17]

Commercial cities located on major trade routes would also derive much income providing goods and services to long-distance traders, travelers, and tourists. These functions enabled many cities providing these services to grow larger than cities providing services only to their local hinterlands. A higher estimate of the surpluses available to peasants and tenants has important consequences for manufacturies and trade, since it gives tens of millions of people a higher standard of living than is now thought. Since at least some of this surplus would be used to pay for more goods and services, there may have been a higher demand for imported goods as well as those manufactured locally. Since commerce and manufacturing are essentially urban based operations, a higher demand would have promoted the growth of urban areas. It is well known today that agricultural production increases when the farmer is allowed to keep more of his surplus for himself rather than pay taxes and rents,[18] and this seems to have been true in antiquity. This situation would have encouraged an increased efficiency of agricultural production in general, and especially near large urban areas where demand was high (these relationships are depicted in diagram 1).

It would appear that far from being the dominant type of city in the Greco-Roman world, the "consumer city" was virtually nonexistent. Only imperial capitals that collected taxes and rents from vast areas, such as Athens during much of the fifth century B.C., Alexandria, Antioch, and Rome could have been of this type.[19] However, most classical cities did not have the same status as Athens or Rome, and another model must be found to explain their economies. Apparently, the classical city differed in fundamental ways from cities in other pre- and nonindustrial societies (with which Greek and Roman cities are often compared), and these differences were responsible for the surprisingly high degree of urbanization in the classical world.[20] These cities may be called service cities, and not consumer cities.

The fundamental problem with the consumer city model is not that it conflicts with the physical realities of classical city-states, but that it is in conflict with the values and institutions of classical culture.

Greek and Roman political institutions, social values, and law prevented the peasant and tenant from being exploited by extortionate landlords or tax collectors. In some Greek cities, the peasants and tenants *were* the gov-

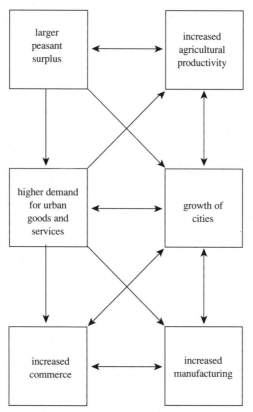

Diagram 1. Consequences of Larger Agricultural Surpluses for the Growth of Cities

ernment, and even where they were not (as in Republican Rome and in the cities of the early Roman Empire), the social values that affirmed their importance as human beings persisted until the late Empire. When these values and institutions disappeared to be replaced by others, the classical city disappeared with them. These institutions and laws, and the values that created them, assured that *in general* the peasant and tenant retained a substantial surplus as disposable income. Of course, this was not always the case, especially in the Empire: some tenants had cruel and oppressive landlords, some may have only had 2 percent of their gross income remaining after rents were paid, some even starved. Some peasants were exploited by the Roman imperial government through rapacious tax collectors and requisitions of draft animals and food.[21] Nevertheless, in general, they must have retained a substantial surplus for themselves, because it was through them that classical cities attained such large sizes and vast numbers.

The same institutions and values that prevented his exploitation also encouraged the peasant's participation in the life of his city, where he spent much, if not all of his surplus. This surplus was not confiscated from him by taxes and rents to be spent in the city by landlords and government officials, but was spent by himself to purchase the goods and services he wanted. The classical city was not parasitical, but was maintained to a large extent through the voluntary exchange of the peasant's agricultural surplus for urban goods and services. The peasant *was* the city and the city reflected his needs. The nature of city life attracted many peasants and tenant farmers, as well as travelers and tourists, to participate in its social, economic, and cultural affairs. The urban-based religions also encouraged participation in the joyous festivals, rituals, processions, and celebrations held in the city. Most city-states were small in size, to allow the peasants to visit the city frequently.

The social, economic, and political institutions and values of classical society were reflected in the physical patterns of the city's buildings and facilities. Law courts and assembly buildings mirrored political institutions, water supply systems reflected public health policies, and commercial facilities mirrored the urban economy. To some extent, the physical appearance of a city reflects a society's institutions and values as the biological structure of a living organism reflects its functions in the natural world. The ancient city may be compared to a fossil organism that perished long ago. Nevertheless, the fossil city once lived and its people's institutions and values shaped its physical form in the same way that modern institutions shape modern cities. We must try to reconstruct the urban systems and the values and institutions that created them from the archaeological remains (the fossil record as it were), just as the paleontologist attempts to reconstruct the biological systems of fossil organisms.[22]

Since the time of Homer, Greco-Roman aristocrats had competed with one another for the honor and esteem of their communities by performing services. Originally, these services were of a military nature, but by the Hellenistic and Roman imperial eras, this age-old tradition reexpressed itself in the provision of public services. In the early communities of Greece and Latium, the peasantry, led by their aristocratic neighbors, had played an important role in the cities' armies. This fact helps explain the importance of the peasantry in classical political and military institutions and the willingness of the aristocracy to serve their needs. Nevertheless, military necessities cannot explain the persistence of this relationship through the Hellenistic and Roman imperial eras. Therefore, we must look deeper for the explanation, and this is to be found in social and religious beliefs.

These values were deeply embedded in classical culture. They stressed the essential dignity of all men and women, and aristocratic service to the community. The principles received the highest religious sanction and were given philosophical form by stoicism. In serving his community, the good stoic was fulfilling the laws of nature and of God. From his community, he received honor (often expressed in election to office), the remembrance of posterity, and perhaps, personal immortality with the great spirits of the past.

The Greek and Roman aristocrat of the early Empire, strolling down the main street and market place of his community, would see hundreds of honorary inscriptions and statues dedicated to the public servants of the past, some perhaps, his own ancestors, extending back for centuries. This must have made an profound impression, and reinforced the spirit of civic virtue, and the expectations of the community.

The public-spiritedness of the Greco-Roman elite is not often found in the elites of other cities. The public controlled the classical city to a far greater extent than in many other cities; it even controlled the attitudes of the aristocrats, by rewarding their benefactions on behalf of the city with public honors and esteem. Large, impersonal economic institutions that dominate many modern cities were absent from the classical city, and since the cities were secular, they were not dominated by priests or temples or other religious institutions. Nor were classical cities characterized by the selfish individualism of their aristocracies.

There were many different types of cities in the classical world. Large commercial cities such as Corinth provided a vast array of goods and services to merchants and travelers. Smaller, more agricultural cities such as Mantinea or Plataea provided goods and services primarily to their local urban and rural populations, and contained a higher proportion of landlords and urban farmers. One aspect that most shared, however, was that the provision of services was the basis of their economies and not the collection of rents from an exploited peasantry.

To a large extent, the classical city was the product of a unique system of interdependent institutions and values. Values that stressed the importance of the peasant as a human being assured that he would have a substantial surplus at his disposal. Cities in turn were attractive places to spend the surplus: they were clean, healthy, physically attractive, and offered many goods and services wanted by the peasant and the rest of the community. The dominant attitude of *philoxenia,* literally "the love of strangers," ensured that a filthy, unhealthy, and ugly city would have been a collective insult and dishonor for the whole community. The fact is, whatever their origins, few aristocrats in other eras of history display such civic-minded values. Political institutions were also important in maintaining the cleanliness, health, and physical attractiveness of classical cities. It is not that the public in other cities did not value these amenities, but they lacked the institutions to translate them into reality. The classical city then, was also the consequence of democracy, or at least broadly based political institutions that served the needs of the public and not just a small elite. All these factors combined to promote the most extensive urbanization seen in the West until early modern times. The city then, was the creation of society; it was the servant of society and not its master.[23]

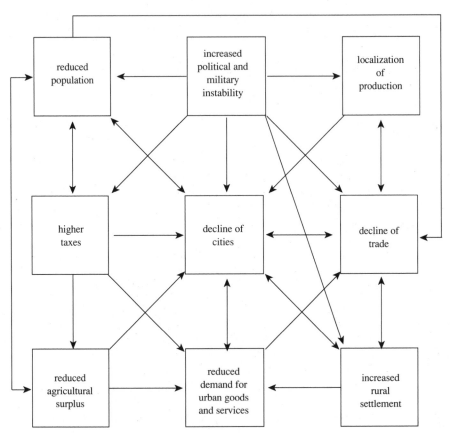

Diagram 2. Factors Leading to the Decline of the Classical City

# Conclusion:
# The Myth of the Consumer City

> The purpose of studying economics is
> not to acquire a set of readymade an-
> swers to economic questions, but to
> learn how to avoid being deceived by
> economists.
>
> JOAN ROBINSON[1]

One would expect that the consumer city theory, that makes such fundamental claims about the relationship between urban and rural regions and
that has won almost universal acceptance, would have the strongest analyt-
ical basis. One would expect to find rigorous examinations of the major
principles of the theory; relationships among tax rates, rent rates, the size
of city-state territories, and urban populations. Instead, we find that the
opposite is the case. The same facts are now marshaled in its defense that
were put forth forty and even fifty years ago. Many recent discussions of
the consumer city consist only of a sentence, a paragraph, or at most, perhaps half a page.[2]

In this chapter, we will analyze the evidence used to support the theory
and try to explain why it has been so widely accepted.

## Evidence for the Consumer City

In the Hellenistic East, Greek and Macedonian settlers often encountered systems of dependent labor and, hence, cities that were supported by
this type of agricultural system were more likely to have been of the consumer than the service type. In these cities, the Greco-Macedonian urban
aristocracies were more likely to have exploited the non-Greek tillers of the
soil through high rents and taxes. Nevertheless, I believe that, except for
Egypt (which was probably always dominated by consumer-type cities),
the cities of central Anatolia and Syria (if not Judaea) were also service
types. There are several reasons for maintaining this view.

First of all, the aristocracies of these Hellenistic (and later, Roman) cities
often included many Hellenized natives, especially after generations of immigrants had entered the cities and the original Greco-Macedonian urban
elites had died off. Furthermore, as cities in the Hellenistic East were
granted polis status, the dependent peasantry became free tenants or peasant proprietors. They could then form their own political organizations
(*politeuma*), and even become citizens of the polis through the successful

completion of a course of study in the gymnasium.[3] Finally, the peasants of both the Hellenistic East and the Latin West had to absorb the tripling of their taxes from the first century to the sixth century A.D. This must mean that they had a considerable surplus at their disposal, at least through the second or third centuries, and much of this surplus was spent in their cities, as we have seen.

Therefore, the cultural differences that can be discerned in the Hellenistic East between the Greco-Macedonian aristocrats of the cities and non-Greek peasants in the countryside were probably not as great as they may appear. Only in Judaea did the native peasantry offer fierce resistance to Hellenistic culture. Nor does the survival of native tongues (especially Aramaic) among village populations in the Hellenistic and Roman East constitute evidence that they did not share in the economic and cultural life of their cities.[4] I have heard modern Greek villagers in the area of ancient Corinth speaking Albanian, the language of migrants who settled that region some 160 years ago. This does not mean that they are "exploited," or that they do not share the culture of modern Greece. In fact, they are bilingual, speaking Albanian to each other in the village and Greek to others. Doubtless, many of the natives in the Hellenistic East were bilingual (as are some modern Greeks), using their native tongues in the village (as those speaking Aramaic still do), and Greek (perhaps only "pidgin" Greek) to communicate with the landlord and tax collector. Saint Paul was multilingual, speaking Hebrew, Greek, and probably Aramaic; there were doubtless many others.

Nor is the survival of native place names in the Hellenistic East of much use in determining cultural survivals or cultural antagonisms. I lived in Massachusetts, and many of the communities that surrounded me had Indian names (Natick, Cochituate, Quabin, etc.). This does not mean that the citizens of Massachusetts and the residents of these towns share Indian culture, or speak Indian dialects, or are hostile to American culture. Nor can we infer that in present-day Massachusetts, Indian culture dominates towns with Indian names, or that the citizens of Natick are exploited by the English-speaking citizens of the nearby cites of Worcester or Boston. Corinthos, the Greek name for Corinth, is a pre-Greek name; does this mean that the citizens of classical Corinth were "pre-Greeks" who were exploited by their Greek-speaking neighbors in Argos and Megara? The survivals of language and place names are poor indicators of cultural identification, let alone of the exploitation of one culture by another.

Evidence for the consumer city also comes from the projection of the late Roman political economy into the early Empire and, indeed, into the Greek and Hellenistic eras. However, the late Roman political economy was fundamentally different from those of earlier times. How valid is this anachronistic procedure?[5]

Famines and food shortages sometimes afflicted classical city-states. Occasionally, under severe stress, mobs from the city would roam the countryside and take food, sometimes from the peasantry. Is this really evidence for the consumer city? Furthermore, classical cities often took important measures to prevent famine and food shortages. How do these measures compare with those of later eras?[6]

It is often claimed that the Roman (and Greek) peasants were exploited by their landlords and their cities. If we really want to know if the classical peasant was exploited, we need to ask another question: exploited compared to whom? Was the Roman peasant who paid his 10 percent land tax, poll tax, and a 10 percent rent rate (assuming he was a tenant and not a proprietor) more or less exploited than the French peasant of the eighteenth century who had to pay up to 50 percent shares of his crop (as a *méteyer*), 10 percent to the church (the *dîme*), the *taille*, the *corvée*, plus innumerable feudal duties and royal taxes? Was he more or less exploited than the Egyptian peasant who was liable to be beaten and drowned, and his family enslaved, for failure to pay his 50 percent to the state, plus innumerable other duties? Until we are willing to ask these questions, we will not come to grips with the question of peasant exploitation in the Roman Empire.

It is often claimed that the classical economy was primitive, and that the peasants had little or no surplus left over to pay for urban goods and services. Therefore, cities must have been based on the collection of rents. We have already seen reasons to question the commonly held primitivist assumptions: massive commercial facilities, Aristotle's statement that the farmer should be able to support two households, and the peasant's absorption of the tripling of rents and taxes during the late Empire.

Marxist development theory will not help us to understand whether the ancient economy was primitive or advanced. If we want the answer, we must ask again: primitive compared to whom? Numerous comparative studies are needed on all aspects of classical society, economy, and political institutions. We must compare commercial facilities (roads, harbors), lighthouses, and commercial structures of antiquity to those of other eras. How do the commercial facilities of Pompeii compare with those of a similar-sized town of the Middle Ages or the Renaissance? How do the sizes of merchant ships, the complexity of commercial law, agricultural knowledge and practice, technology, and the size of manufactures compare? All this work must be done for us to answer this question. Only then can we say that the classical economy was more advanced than $x$ but more primitive than $y$. It is my view that the classical economy will compare favorably to that of fifteenth to sixteenth century Italy or mid-nineteenth century Japan.

Another important study would be to compare the economic ideas of classical literature to those of other eras. Since time immemorial, the literati have avoided any connection with the practical concerns of earning a livelihood. Classical literature, despite its brilliance and lasting impact, shares this same anti-economic bias. What needs to be done is to examine the economic ideas of the literature of other cultures whose economies are better known. Early modern China and Japan would make good comparative studies, as well as the literature of seventeenth-century England. If we only had the works of Shakespeare, Dunne, Milton, and Locke, what view of the English economy would we obtain? How would it compare to the real economy of seventeenth-century England, as seen in other sources: the types of sources that have not, with some important exceptions, survived for the classical world?[7]

None of this evidence—differences in language, anachronistic projections, famines, and ex silentio arguments from a literary tradition devoid of much interest in the economy—seems very convincing. The final question addressed in this work is to explain why the primitivist, consumer-city paradigm is so widely accepted, regardless of the rather limited evidence for it. The reasons seem to lie in the widespread preconceptions Western man has had concerning cities since the late Roman Empire and early Dark Ages (ca. A.D. 285–600). These preconceptions include a view that cities and city people are evil, and the country and country people are good. Another is the concept of primitivism—the belief in the superiority of non-industrial societies to those of more advanced cultures—which has contributed to the view that the classical world was innocent of the market forces that later characterized the West.

Since classical men and women did not regard their cities as the focus of evil, where did the notion come from?

## The Dark-Age View of the City

There have been some attempts to find generalized anti-urban values in the Old Testament, in the stories of Sodom and Gomorrah, and Babylon; but these have not been convincing.[8] In the West, the first genuine evidence for the view that cities were morally evil occurs in Christian authors of the fifth century. Indeed, by this time, the old values and institutions that made the classical city had been destroyed forever. The terrible failures and defeats of the late Roman Empire convinced many thoughtful pagans and Christians that judgement had been passed on a wicked and evil humanity. The devastation and destruction occurring daily before their eyes was ample proof of divine punishment. This is the view maintained by Saint Augustine (d. A.D. 430) in his *City of God*. Man is conceived in evil through original sin (he even calls infants "a mass of perdition") and cannot possibly be saved through good works, but must rely solely upon God's grace, given only to a predestined few. Since humanity was now evil, cities were regarded as the focus of evil in the world. Augustine believed that Cain built the first city, while his brother Abel was a herdsman and country-dweller.[9] Cain slew Abel in much the same way that urban-dwellers plunder and oppress the herdsman or farmer.

The view that cities were evil was also expressed by Saint Jerome (d. A.D. 420), Augustine's contemporary. Judaea was lost, Jerome believed, when rural tribesmen were forced by Chaldean attacks to enter the cities. An imaginary interlocutor in one of Jerome's letters asks: "What, shall all those perish who live in cities?" Jerome responds that, in order to escape temptation and defilement, one must flee to the country: "but to me a town is a prison, and the wilderness a paradise."[10]

By the fifth century, mankind was not only evil, but also ignorant. Man could not grasp the true nature of God, nature, or himself, and if he attempted to do so using principles of reason and natural law he became a heretic, often with unfortunate consequences.[11] Naturally, under these circumstances, Man was held incapable of self-government or making laws for himself. He had to be governed by his "betters": an emperor anointed by God as a Thirteenth Apostle, or a king who ruled through God's grace by divine right.[12] During this era, cities were no longer centers of self-government but had become centers of imperial administration, tax collection, conscription, and, in the end, economic oppression.

The Dark-Age view of humanity, nature, and civilization has had a powerful impact on later thought. Among the most important philosophers who secularized Jerome's view that "the town is a prison and the wilderness a paradise," was Jean Jacques Rousseau, prominent among the founders of the "Anti-Enlightenment."[13] According to Rousseau, man had been born good in a state of nature, but had been corrupted through the development of reason and civilization. The city is not therefore the highest creation of nature and reason, as Cicero thought, but is a product of the human corruption of nature. Reason ought to be subordinate, not to faith as in earlier eras, but to natural instincts. Nature itself is pure, sacred, and liberating. Human manipulation of nature to provide food, clothing, shelter, metals, and other natural products is a corruption of nature: the pinnacle of this corruption is the city.

Rousseau had a lasting impact on later thought concerning the conflict of nature and reason as can be seen in both Nietzsche and Max Weber. The modern view of the consumer city was developed by Weber, in part from his study of the towns and cities of East Elbian Germany in the 1880s and 1890s, and in part from his own philosophy of history. In the late nineteenth century, East Elbian agriculture had been the subject of intensive research and debate by Weber, Werner Sombart, and others.[14] In this region, landed aristocrats, called Junkers, operated vast, semifeudal estates worked by serfs. The Junkers lived in the towns and competed with the urban elite for social status. Weber also saw the conflict between the authoritarian Junkers and the more liberal political movements of his own era as a paradigm for the whole of history. He regarded history as a progressive ascent from absolutist social, economic, and political systems, represented by the Junkers, to more progressive systems advocated by Weber and many of his contemporaries. Hence, Weber may have seen the ancient city as resembling an East German town dominated by landowners who were maintained by income from their serfs.

The consumer-city view was heartily approved by Karl Marx and also by those employing Marxist interpretations of history. Notions of class struggle represented by urban-rural conflicts were too enticing to be ignored (regardless of the fact that no such conflicts are mentioned in *ancient* sources). Similar views of the classical city were held by A. H. M. Jones in several works and by Rostovtzeff concerning cities of the late Roman Empire.[15]

The recent revival of the consumer-city model owes most to M. I. Finley,[16] who suggested it as a possible model for the ancient economy in various works written during the 1970s. Because of his dominant position in the field of ancient economic history, Finley deserves the credit for making the concept attractive to Marxist and non-Marxist historians alike.[17]

But it was the influence of Marxist development theory and anticolonial sentiments that were particularly strong during the 1930s, that were the most important factors contributing to the modern idea that classical cities were consumer cities. Coupled with these trends was a growing appreciation and respect for primitive, precolonial, non-market economic systems. These trends in turn, exercised a powerful influence on the field of anthropology, especially economic anthropology. Karl Polanyi, one of the leading exponents of these new ideas, had a profound influence on the thought of M. I. Finley, and through him, on that of many of his followers.[18]

Inasmuch as Marxist development theories have played an important role in forming modern ideas about classical cities, we need to understand their origins, development, and consequences for developing countries, economic anthropology, and the study of economic history in our own field.

## Marxism and Anticolonialism

During the 1920s and 1930s, anticolonial movements grew stronger in many Asian and African colonies. They received support from Marxist theories concerning colonialism, imperialism, and underdevelopment, based on the thought of Lenin and ultimately Marx himself. These theories in turn influenced the ideas of anthropologists working in those areas.

Marxist development economics and anthropology mutually supported one another, from the twenties and thirties until the present day, but the main thrust came from development theory. There were many strands of thought that characterized this complex movement; only a few of the most important will be considered here.

The first was an understandable hostility towards and rejection of the West, especially its capitalist, market-oriented economic system. According to Marxist views, capitalism was not only to blame for imperialism and colonialism, but also for underdevelopment and class exploitation in the colonies themselves.[19] Associated with this notion was a desire to rediscover authentic precolonial, native economic traditions. This search was aided by the anthropologists. It was claimed that Asian and African societies had once enjoyed a pristine era of harmony, prosperity, and economic cooperation until they were rudely disrupted by Western economic imperialism.[20]

A closely associated idea was the rejection of modernism or modernization theory. According to this theory (which was initially accepted by almost all segments of the native, educated elite), the past was to be rejected as primitive and backwards. The only hope for development lay in the use of new technologies in trade, agriculture, and industry. The ignorant, backward peasants needed to be instructed in the new technologies by the Western-educated elites. Folk traditions and folk wisdom concerning agriculture and crafts were rejected. It is easy to see why this elitist, patronizing view was rejected by many in the emerging world during the 1960s and 1970s.

The last important factor was a deep-seated hostility towards cities and urban development. Cities were often seen as alien importations and centers of economic exploitation, both by imperialists and a "new" class of luxury-loving, rapacious landlords, usurers, and profiteers.[21] The fact is however, that many cities in the colonial, and, indeed, precolonial eras of the developing world, *were* parasitical, and frequently in a state of undeclared war against the countryside.[22]

Many of the same cities remain parasitical in the postcolonial era. This is because the urban ruling classes of many of these nations steal up to 80 percent of the foreign aid that is sent to their nations, hence, these classes are frequently called "kleptocracies."[23] Moreover, the aid that is sent in the form of loans is repaid, not by the military-bureaucratic urban elite, but by the poor rural farmers. The urban elite often live quite handsomely from the theft of the loans, some individual political leaders have stolen more than one billion dollars.[24] Their poor, rural compatriots often do not fare as well, since they are the ones who must repay the loans. Foreign aid in the form of food is also consumed by the urban elite, or sold by them on the black market for considerable profit, leaving the starving peasantry with nothing.[25] Sometimes, food aid is distributed free-of-charge to the urban residents, so when the rural farmer comes to the market to sell his produce, he finds no demand for it. "Land reform," often involving compulsory re-settlement of the peasantry in collective farms provides little incentive for the peasants to be productive and care properly for their land. This pro-vides further disincentives for agricultural production.

Anthropology helped to buttress Marxist development theory. Beginning in the 1920s and 1930s, the anthropological literature was replete with studies "proving" that primitive peoples lived in harmony with nature and with each other with no envy, jealousy, class oppression, or destructive wars.[26] These delusions about the developing world were understandable (if not acceptable as scholarship) in the context of World War I, the Great Depression, and above all, the enormous cultural, economic, and religious dislocations caused by Western Expansion into developing regions. The tragic consequences of these delusions would not be fully realized until the 1960s and 1970s.

Indeed, primitive and non-market economies were a popular subject of analysis up until the 1970s and early 1980s. Such systems were thought to impart moral superiority to their societies and to provide excellent models, not only for developing, but even developed nations. They "lived accord-ing to nature" and did not consume valuable resources. Unfortunately, those countries that attempted to become primitive were the greatest fail-ures.[27]

Many members of the colonial native elite were educated in Western universities, especially in France, England, and the United States. There they learned the principles of Marxist development economics and the as-sociated anthropological theories. As the emerging nations of Asia and Af-rica gained their independence during the 1960s and 1970s, it was only natural that some of these educated elites should attempt to put into prac-tice the theories they had learned. Unfortunately, these theories concerning the causes of underdevelopment, class formation, the market system, the processes of economic development, and even their own precolonial past were all based on simplistic, fatally flawed assumptions. Indeed, it has been the perpetuation of these myths that has been the greatest cause of suffering, death, and deprivation in the developing world during the last twenty years. The great tragedy is that this has been discovered by emerg-ing nations only recently.[28]

Two nations in particular are instructive in this regard, since they fol-lowed the precepts of development theory and economic anthropology to their logical conclusion: Democratic Kampuchea (Cambodia) and Tan-zania.

The leadership of Democratic Kampuchea (which ruled from 1975 to 1978), Pol Pot (Saloth Sar), Khieu Samphan, and Nuon Chen all received their educations in Paris during the 1950s, where they absorbed Marxist development theory and radical anticolonialism. The most important of the group was Khieu Samphan whose dissertation, "Cambodia's Economy and Industrial Development" earned him the *licencié* from the University of Paris in 1959.[29] This document provided the Khmer Rouge with the theoretical basis and blueprint for political and economic action, it is therefore, the bible of Cambodian genocide.[30]

According to Samphan and his colleagues, Hon Yuon, Nuon Chen, and Pol Pot, the Khmer people once lived in rural purity in a state of primitive communism. There were no cities in this era to corrupt the people. This system was gradually replaced by feudalism which introduced serfdom and the growth of cities. The feudal system grew stronger under colonialism and the introduction of the Western market system. However, under colonialism, cities became even greater centers of parasitical, luxury-loving profiteers, who lived by plundering the peasantry.[31]

Since these were the problems, the solutions were terribly simple. Since cities were centers of oppression and nonproductive parasitism, simply remove the urban dwellers to the countryside and make them perform useful work. In the countryside, recreate the pristine, prefeudal, and precolonial stage of the authentic Khmer past. From the solid base of "genuine" Khmer agricultural institutions, untainted by any foreign influence, the country would grow and prosper in its own unique way and could hope one day to become a world leader in agriculture. The experiment cost between two and three million lives.[32]

A similar sequence can be seen in Tanzania under its leader Julius Nyerere. As in the case of Pol Pot and Khieu Samphan, it was not Nyerere's intention to cause harm to his own people, he simply implemented standard development theories taught in institutions of higher learning throughout the West.[33]

Nyerere received his Western education at Edinburgh from 1949 to 1952, where he learned the latest trends in development theory (much had changed from the days of Adam Smith, we may be sure). Nyerere was originally a "modernist" in his approach to development, but soon succumbed to the spell of primitivist myths. In 1967 he implemented his famous Ujamaa Experiment, the compulsory villagization of the Tanzanian population, to return it to its authentic precolonial, non-urban past. The consequences were much the same in Tanzania as in Cambodia, although on a much more modest scale: starvation, high death rates, and deprivation.

There were many other countries that took the ideas of development theory and economic anthropology seriously, but these are only among the most extreme cases. All the experiments shared the same conceptual bases: a hatred of cities, delusional glorification of the primitive past, rejection of market forces and of modernism, and a belief that one could only develop by becoming primitive. They replaced a condescending, educated elite that imposed modernism on the peasantry (as in Stalinist Russia, and Maoist China in the 1950s) with a condescending, educated elite that imposed primitivism.

Karl Polanyi was instrumental in transferring Marxist development theory and economic anthropology to the ancient world and is therefore the éminence grise behind our current primitivist and anti-urban notions. The debate as to whether the classical economy was advanced or primitive extends back to the mid–nineteenth century, and has yet to be resolved. The primitivist view has received strong support from the theories of economic anthropology as applied by Polanyi, Finley, and others.[34] According to this view, cities were ultimately based on a subsistence agricultural economy. Cities cannot have been supported through commerce, manufacture, or the provision of services to the rural population because of primitive technology, general poverty and corresponding lack of purchasing power, and lack of markets.

According to H. W. Pearson,

[Polanyi] passionately opposed an economic sociology that would attempt to foist upon primitive and archaic economies the concepts of an economic theory valid inside a market system and nowhere else. To do so, he held, amounted to hampering the autochthonous development of the world's non-market societies, thereby being instrumental to neocolonialism and acting in its interests.[35]

Furthermore, Polanyi thought,

Whether we look to the evidence from anthropology or history, it is clear that the competitive market-money-price complex, operating in its legal context of primitive property and free contract and its "economizing" cultural context, has either been absent or has played a subordinate role through most of man's history.[36]

As we have seen this view also contains contradictions and shortcomings. In general, if agricultural productivity was low and market opportunities were few, how did ancient cities grow so large and attain such vast numbers? And why did the Greeks and romans continually employ terms such as *emporion, forum,* and *nundinae,* "markets" and "market days," for hundreds of years if markets were unimportant or nonexistent? Finally, why did classical cities construct immense commercial structures (stoas), often far larger than other public or religious buildings in their cities? Why did they devote vast spaces to commercial markets? Why did they construct impressive harbor complexes (Caesarea, Carthage, Corinth) if trade was not important?

Supporters of the primitivist school often accuse supporters of the modernist school of having a hidden agenda, the promotion of capitalism,[37] and this may be true. But, what kinds of political economies have been supported by the ideas of economic anthropology and its alliance with development economics?[38]

It is frequently overlooked that Polanyi himself, in his later years, saw the origin of the market system in sixth-century Greece, although the administered market, especially for grain, also existed. He even considered the classical economy to be an early type of capitalist system:

> The outstanding facts are . . . that trade and money, mainly through the use of small coin, were linked with market elements in the Athenian agora. . . . The significance of this development, important in itself, is greatly enhanced by its formative influence on Rome, and, eventually, on the whole of Europe and North America. . . . The conclusion can hardly be resisted that the Greeks of antiquity, whose genius was already credited with giving birth to our politics, philosophy, science, and art, were also the initiators of all advanced human economy.[39]

Therefore, we conclude that the consumer city model and the primitivist view of the ancient economy are themselves modernizing assumptions, largely based on the current theories of economic anthropology, and on the need of Western man since the Dark Ages to see cities as a focus of evil. Economic anthropology combined Marxist development theory, an understandable anticolonialism, Western guilt, and Third World resentment. It placed an important emphasis on the rediscovery of what were believed to be "genuine" native, precolonial cultural systems.

Through Karl Polanyi, both development economics and economic anthropology have influenced the field of ancient history. This can clearly be seen in the anti-urban, primitivist, and non-market concepts that now inform the field. Above all, it is reflected in the intense desire to return the classical world to its pristine, pre-market status. Just as Asia and Africa were colonized by the West with its markets and capitalist economic system, so the classical world was "colonized" by the modernists who wished, once again, to impose capitalism where it did not belong. Just as leaders of emerging nations attempted to de-colonialize and de-Westernize their economies, so Polanyi and the rest wished to de-colonialize and de-Westernize the ancient world.

So, by a curious sequence of intellectual trends, anticolonial Marxist thought has become dominant in the now de-colonialized world of classical antiquity. A few questions arise however. Is it possible to de-Westernize the classical world, whence come Western, freemarket institutions? In de-colonializing the classical world, has it not been primitivized to excess in some recent interpretations? Finally, what has Athens to do with Phnom Penh? While Ancient historians have avoided the egregious and even humorous excesses of development economists, we would do well to re-examine these assumptions.

*Leges sine moribus vanae* wrote the Romans, *laws without values are worthless.* The classical city was firmly based on the classical ideal of man: that he was capable, reasonable, and had an innate sense of justice. All that was needed was a system of education that would bring out these characteristics in everyone. These values—not the concept of original sin—are the foundation of self-government. If we are innately stupid and depraved, we cannot possibly govern ourselves, but must rely upon our "betters." [39] If people are essentially reasonable and just, they can manage their economy by themselves without "help" from "experts."

When the classical conception of humanity disappeared during the traumas of the third and fourth centuries A.D., the classical city disappeared with it. People now thought they were stupid and evil, and hence, incapable of either self-government or economic self-management. Their "betters" now ran things for them, for a service charge of 60 to 70 percent of the product of their labor, forcing them to the margin of human existence.

# Maps, Plans, and Tables

145

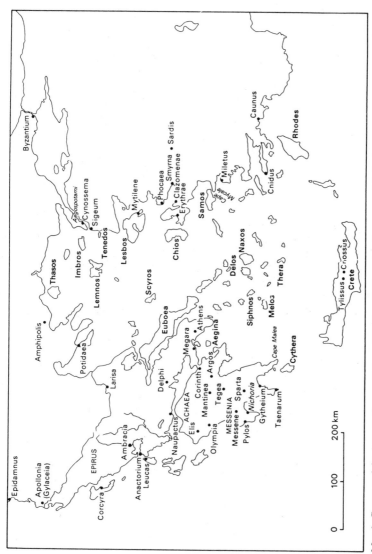

Map 1. Greece and the Aegean. *Source:* Salmon (1984), p. 2. Reproduced courtesy of Oxford University Press

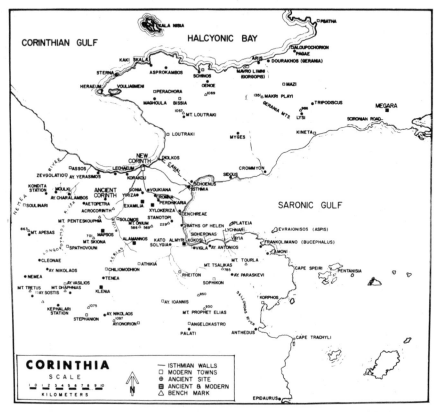

Map 2. The Corinthia. *Source:* Wiseman, *LAC*, p. 44. Reproduced courtesy of Professor Wiseman.

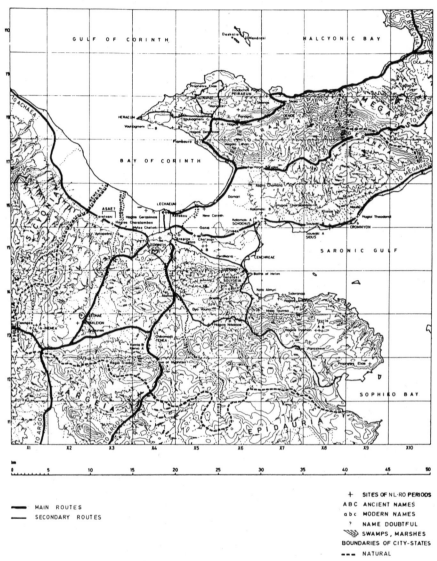

Map 3. The Corinthia, Natural Routes. *Source:* Sakellariou and Farklas (1971), fig. 9. Reproduced by permission of Athens Center of Ekistics, Athens.

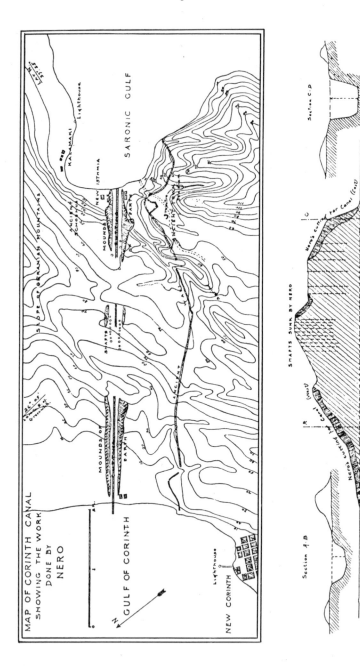

Map 4. Nero's Canal. *Source:* Fowler and Stillwell, *Corinth* 1.1.

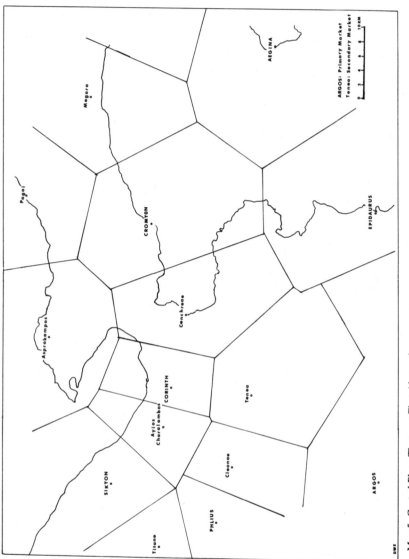

Map 5. Central Place Theory—First Abstraction

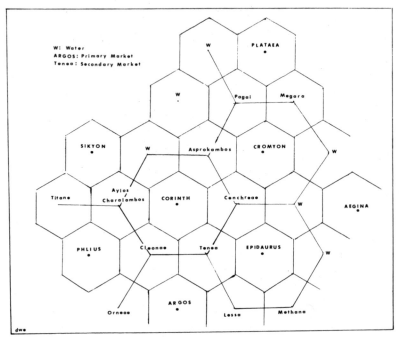

Map 6. Central Place Theory—Second Abstraction

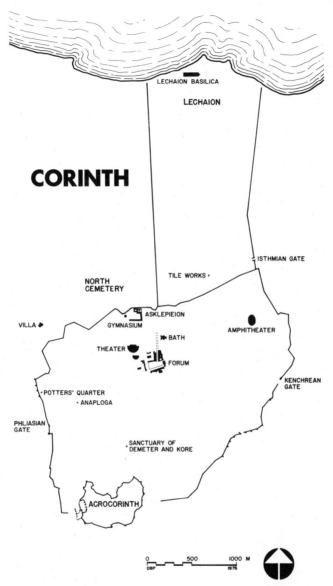

Plan 1. City Area. *Source:* Bookidis and Stroud (1987). Courtesy of the American School of Classical Studies at Athens.

A. Fountain of Poseidon or Neptune
B. Dionysion
C. Temple C
D. Temple D, Tyche or Fortuna
E. Temple E
F. Temple F, Aphrodite or Venus
G. Temple G, Clarian Apollo
H. Babbius Monument
I. Archaic Temple (Apollo in Greek era? Gens Julia in Roman?)
J. Theater
K. Temple K
L. Odeon
M. Roman House
N. Fountain of Glauke
O. West Shops
P. North Market
Q. Northwest Stoa
R. Northwest Shops
S. Basilica
T. Market
U. Public Latrines
V. Peribolos of Apollo
W. Fountain of Peirene
X. Lechaion Road
Y. Triumphal Arch, Propylaea
Z. Julian Basilica
1. Shop
2. Southeast Building (Library?)
3. Central Shops
4. Governor's Tribunal or Bema
5. Shop
6. South Stoa
7. Shop
8. South Basilica
9. Senate House or Bouleuterion
10. Temple of Hermes or

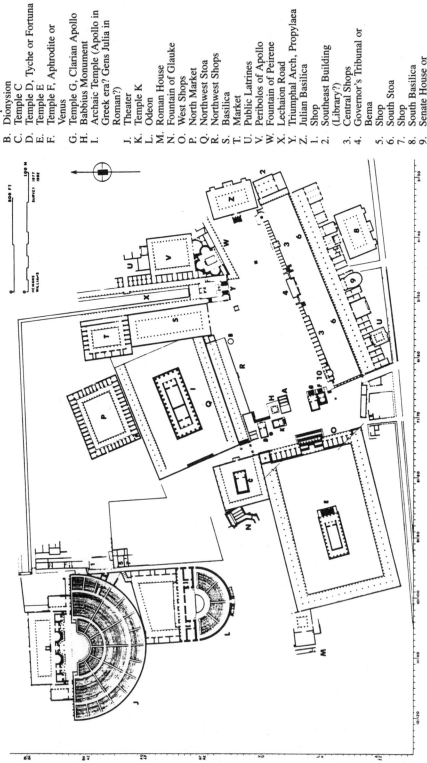

Plan 2. Forum Area. *Source:* Williams and Zervos (1989). Courtesy of the American School of Classical Studies at Athens.

Plan 3. Lechaion. *Source:* Paris (1915).

Key

| | |
|---|---|
| AA′ | Protected basin of outer port |
| MM′ | Remains of break-waters |
| JJ′ | Outer jetties |
| PP′ | Access passages to inner port |
| EE′ | Turning areas for ships in inner basins |
| N | Passage between basins E and E′ |
| D₁–D₃ | Inner basins |
| Π | Islet |
| Φ,Σ,T,Y | Remains of quays |

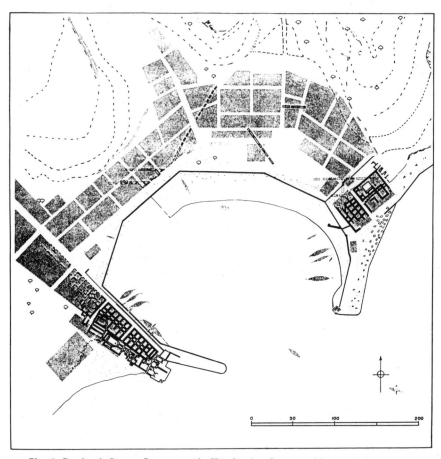

Plan 4. Cenchreai. *Source:* Scranton et al., Kenchreai 1. Courtesy of E. J. Brill, Leiden.

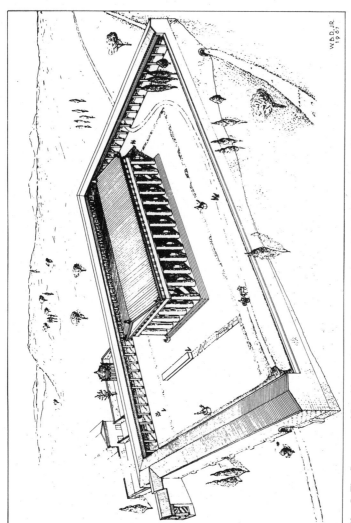

Plan 5. The Sanctuary of Poseidon at Isthmia. *Source:* Bronner, *Isthmia* 2. Courtesy of the American School of Classical Studies at Athens.

Table 1. Percentage of Sites Occupying Strategic Locations

| | | |
|---|---|---|
| Early Helladic | 58.3 | (N = 24) |
| Middle Helladic | 60.0 | (N = 15) |
| Late Helladic | 45.5 | (N = 22) |
| Geometric-Archaic | 28.6 | (N = 14) |
| Classical-Hellenistic | 22.2 | (N = 45) |
| Roman | 22.7 | (N = 44) |

Table 2. Percentage of Sites Within One Kilometer of the Coast

| | |
|---|---|
| Early Helladic | 50.0 |
| Middle Helladic | 53.3 |
| Late Helladic | 54.5 |
| Geometric-Archaic | 35.7 |
| Classical-Hellenistic | 48.9 |
| Roman | 46.5 |

Table 3. Percentage of Sites Occupied in One Era that were Occupied in the Next

| | |
|---|---|
| Early Helladic—Middle Helladic | 50.0 |
| Middle Helladic—Late Helladic | 73.3 |
| Late Helladic—Geometric-Archaic | 27.3 |
| Geometric-Archaic—Classical-Hellenistic | 92.8 |
| Classical-Hellenistic—Roman | 80.0 |

Table 4. Ratio of Random and Observed Patterns of Continuity

| Eras | Random | Observed | Ratio |
|------|--------|----------|-------|
| Early Helladic—Middle Helladic | 4.62 | 12 | 2.6 |
| Middle Helladic—Late Helladic | 4.46 | 11 | 2.47 |
| Late Helladic—Geometric-Archaic | 4.28 | 6 | 1.40 |
| Geometric-Archaic—Classical-Hellenistic | 5.34 | 13 | 2.43 |
| Classical-Hellenistic—Roman | 11.12 | 36 | 3.24 |

Table 5. Percentage of Sites with the Following Soil Types Within a 4-Kilometer Radius (2 kms. for lithosoils in mountainous regions)

| Era | Neogen soils derived from limestone, sandstone, and marl (rendzina) | Neogen soils derived from conglomerate | Alluvium | Lithosoils derived from limestone |
|-----|-----|-----|-----|-----|
| Early Helladic | 79 | 33 | 67 | 54 |
| Middle Helladic | 87 | 20 | 80 | 47 |
| Late Helladic | 77 | 27 | 77 | 45 |
| Geometric-Archaic | 71 | 21 | 57 | 57 |
| Classical-Hellenistic | 69 | 18 | 67 | 53 |
| Roman | 64 | 14 | 61 | 57 |

Table 6. Mean number of days with wind forces at least Beaufort 6 (22–27 knots)

| | Jan | Feb | Mar | Apr | May | Jun | Jul | Aug | Sep | Oct | Nov | Dec |
|---|---|---|---|---|---|---|---|---|---|---|---|---|
| Corfu | 2.2 | 2.2 | 1.1 | 0.6 | 0.2 | 0.4 | 0.3 | 0.3 | 0.3 | 1.1 | 1.6 | 3.4 |
| Zakynthos | 5.4 | 4.8 | 4.8 | 2.9 | 2.9 | 1.1 | 1.2 | 0.9 | 2.0 | 4.6 | 3.2 | 7.4 |
| Sitia (Crete) | 1.7 | 2.0 | 2.5 | 1.9 | 1.9 | 1.8 | 3.0 | 2.2 | 0.9 | 0.4 | 1.1 | 2.4 |
| Kythira | 12.2 | 9.4 | 11.0 | 9.9 | 8.3 | 8.4 | 7.5 | 8.4 | 9.3 | 11.6 | 6.3 | 12.3 |
| Rhodes (Maritsa) | 4.7 | 4.9 | 7.4 | 5.3 | 2.3 | 3.4 | 5.7 | 4.0 | 2.5 | 0.8 | 1.6 | 5.8 |
| Naxos | 12.1 | 10.9 | 10.6 | 7.8 | 4.3 | 3.7 | 7.0 | 9.4 | 9.2 | 10.5 | 5.4 | 11.8 |
| Athens (Hellenikon) | 2.4 | 1.7 | 1.7 | 1.3 | 0.8 | 0.5 | 2.0 | 1.5 | 1.0 | 1.0 | 1.3 | 2.3 |
| Corinth | 0.8 | 0.8 | 0.5 | 0 | 0 | 0 | 0.2 | 0.2 | 0 | 0.7 | 0.2 | 0.3 |
| Skopelos | 6.1 | 4.3 | 2.5 | 1.4 | 0.6 | 0.8 | 1.7 | 1.7 | 2.2 | 3.3 | 2.7 | 4.8 |
| Limnos | 12.5 | 10.4 | 8.4 | 6.0 | 3.3 | 2.5 | 5.7 | 6.5 | 6.3 | 8.8 | 7.1 | 11.9 |

*Source*: Air Force Command, Hellenic National Meterological Service

*Note*: Data are derived from observations made at 0800, 1400 and 2000 hrs., over the period 1961–70. For present purposes, Beaufort 6 ( = Strong Winds) is held to be an uncertain and risky sailing condition for ancient vessels. Modern small craft, with sophisticated sails, rigging and steering mechanisms, are capable of sailing under Beaufort 7 (28–33 knots) conditions, but this is considered marginal. Beaufort 8 ( = Fresh Gale) is clearly unpleasant and often dangerous for small vessels.

Table 7. Municipal Coins Found at Corinth

| Emperor | Mint | | | | | | | | | | | | | | |
| --- | --- | --- | --- | --- | --- | --- | --- | --- | --- | --- | --- | --- | --- | --- | --- |
| | Athens | Megara | Argos | Sparta | Patrae | Other Peloponnese | Cent. Greece | N.W. Greece | Thessaly | Macedonia | Thrace | Aegean, Asia Minor, Syria | Alexandria | Mint not given or other | Total |
| Caesar, Augustus 44 B.C.–A.D. 14 | | | | 2 | 2 | 2 | 3 | 2 | 3 | 3 | | 7 | 2 | 1 | 27 |
| Caligula 37–41 | | | | | | | | | | | | | 1 | | 1 |
| Claudius 41–54 | | | | | 1 | | | | | | | 1 | | | 2 |
| Nero 54–68 | | | | | | 1 | 3 | | | | | 1 | | | 5 |
| Vespasian 69–79 | | | | | | | | | | | | 1 | | | 1 |
| Domitian 81–96 | | | | | 3 | | 19 | | | 1 | | | | 2 | 25 |
| Trajan 98–117 | | | | | | | | | | | | 1 | 1 | 1 | 3 |

| | | | | | | | | | | | | | | | Total |
|---|---|---|---|---|---|---|---|---|---|---|---|---|---|---|---|
| Hadrian 117–138 | | | 4 | 5 | 5 | 2 | 2 | | | | | 2 | 2 | 3 | 5 | 28 |
| Antoninus Pius 138–161 | | 2 | 28 | 1 | 2 | 1 | | | | | | | | | 1 | 36 |
| Marcus Aurelius 161–180 | | | 13 | 2 | 5 | 2 | | | | | | 3 | | | 1 | 26 |
| Commodus 180–192 | | | 3 | 3 | 7 | 2 | | | | | | | 1 | | | 16 |
| Septimius Severus 193–211 | 1 | 2 | 24 | 1 | 3 | 22 | 2 | 1 | | 1 | | 2 | | 2 | 61 |
| Caracalla, Geta 198–217 | | 1 | 5 | 1 | 5 | 11 | 1 | 1 | | | | 3 | | 1 | 29 |
| Heliogabalus 218–222 | | | | | | | | | 2 | | | | | | 2 |
| Gordion III 238–244 | | | | | | | 2 | 2 | 2 | 2 | | 2 | 1 | | 7 |
| Gallienus 253–268 | | | | | | | | | | | 1 | 1 | 1 | | 3 |
| Others or unknown | 25 | 1 | 4 | | 2 | 2 | | | | 2 | 2 | 6 | 1 | 6 | 48 |
| Total | 26 | 6 | 81 | 16 | 33 | 45 | 30 | 6 | 4 | 9 | 4 | 30 | 9 | 21 | 320 |

Table 8. Imperial Coins Found at Corinth

| Emperor | Mint | | | | | | | | | | | | | | | | | | | Unknown or unrecorded | Total |
| | Rome | Milan | Aquileia | Ticinum | Carthage | Trier | Lugdunum | Arelate | Siscia | Sirmium | Serdica | Thessalonica | Asia | Constantinople | Heraclea | Nicomedia | Cyzicus | Antioch | Alexandria | | |
|---|---|---|---|---|---|---|---|---|---|---|---|---|---|---|---|---|---|---|---|---|---|
| Augustus 27 B.C.–A.D. 14 | 3As 2Q | | | | | | 1D | | | | | | 1D | | | | | | | 13 | 20 |
| Tiberius 14–37 | 2Dp | | | | | | | | | | | | | | | | | | | 2 | 4 |
| Caligula 37–41 | 1Q 2As | | | | | | | | | | | | | | | | | | | 1 | 4 |
| Claudius 41–54 | 2S 2Q 1As | | | | | | | | | | | | | | | | | | | 8 | 13 |
| Nero 54–68 | 1As 1D | | | | | | | | | | | | | | | | | | | 3 | 5 |
| Vespasian and Titus, Galba 69–81 | 1D | | | | | | | | | | | | | | | | | | | 1D 5 | 7 |
| Domitian 81–96 | 2D 1S | | | | | | | | | | | | | | | | | | | 6 | 9 |
| Nerva and Trajan 96–117 | 3S 1D 1Dp | | | | | | | | | | | | | | | | | | | 8 | 13 |

162

| Emperor | | | | |
|---|---|---|---|---|
| Hadrian 117–138 | 9S 1D | | 16 | 26 |
| Antoninus Pius 138–161 | 3D 13S 1As 2Dp 3 | | 19 | 41 |
| Marcus Aurelius 161–180 Lucius Verus | 1D 24S 4As 1Dp 1 | | 21 | 52 |
| Commodus 180–192 | 1D 9S 3As 1 | | 15 | 29 |
| Septimius Severus 193–211 | 4D 1As | | 10 1D | 16 |
| Caracalla, Geta 198–217 | 2D 4S 2As | | 6 | 14 |
| Heliogabalus 218–222 | 1 | | 2S 2 | 5 |
| Severus Alexander, Maximinus 222–238 | 5S | 3D 20S 3As | 1S 1Dp 19 | 52 |

Table 8. Imperial Coins Found at Corinth (continued)

| Emperor | Mint — Rome | Milan | Aquileia | Ticinum | Carthage | Trier | Lugdunum | Arelate | Siscia | Sirmium | Serdica | Thessalonica | Asia | Constantinople | Heraclea | Nicomedia | Cyzicus | Antioch | Alexandria | Unknown or unrecorded | Total |
|---|---|---|---|---|---|---|---|---|---|---|---|---|---|---|---|---|---|---|---|---|---|
| Pupienus, Gordion III 238–244 | 3D 8S 1Dp 2As 1 | | | | | | | | | | | | | | | | | | | 14 | 29 |
| Philip I and II 243–249 | 2A 5S 1Dp 1As | | | | | | | | | | | | | | | | | | | 10 | 19 |
| Decius 249–251 | 6 | | | | | | | | | | | | | | | | | | | 4 | 10 |
| Trebonius Gallus, Volusian 251–253 | 5 | | | | | | | | | | | | | | | | | | | 4 | 9 |
| Valerian, Gallienus 253–268 | 21 | 7 | | | | | | | 5 | | | 1 | 11 | | | | | 3 | | 97 | 145 |

| | | | | | | | | | | | | | | | |
|---|---|---|---|---|---|---|---|---|---|---|---|---|---|---|---|
| Claudius II 268–270 | 4 | 4 | | | | 2 | | 2 | | | | | | 16 | 26 |
| Aurelian 270–275 | 7 | 3 | 1 | 1 | 12 | 4 | | | | | | | | 66 | 94 |
| Tacitus, Florus, Probus 275–282 | 11 | 6 | 1 | 11 | 1 | 6 | | | | | | | | 38 | 73 |
| Carus, Carinus, Numerian 282–284 | 8 | 1 | 1 | 1 | | | | | | | | | | 9 | 19 |
| Diocletian, Maximian 284–305 | 1 | 3 | 1 | 1 | 33 | 32 | 3 | | | | | | | 87 | 161 |
| Constantius Chlorus 305–306 | 1 | 2 | 1 | 6 | | | | | | | | | | 7 | 17 |
| Galerius, Maximian II 305–313 | 1 | 1 | 2 | 2 | 7 | 3 | 15 | 2 | | | | | | 27 | 60 |
| Licinius, Maxentius 307–323 | 4 | 1 | 7 | 4 | 5 | 5 | 2 | 2 | | | | | | 20 | 50 |
| Constantine and Family 307–337 | 16 | 2 | 5 | 2 | 4 | 34 | 18 | 2 | 45 | 23 | 63 | 36 | 18 | 5 | 527 | 805 |

Table 8. Imperial Coins Found at Corinth (*continued*)

| Emperor | Mint | | | | | | | | | | | | | | | | | | | | Unknown or unrecorded | Total |
|---|---|---|---|---|---|---|---|---|---|---|---|---|---|---|---|---|---|---|---|---|---|---|
| | Rome | Milan | Aquileia | Ticinum | Carthage | Trier | Lugdunum | Arelate | Siscia | Sirmium | Serdica | Thessalonica | Asia | Constantinople | Heraclea | Nicomedia | Cyzicus | Antioch | Alexandria | | | |
| Constantius II and Family 337–361 | 17 | | 8 | | | | 3 | 4 | 13 | 5 | | 61 | | 96 | 35 | 107 | 111 | 33 | 6 | | 2021 | 2520 |
| Julian, Jovian 361–364 | 2 | | 2 | | | | 1 | 1 | 1 | 2 | | 8 | | | 9 | 3 | 2 | 3 | | | 141 | 174 |
| Valentinian I, Valens, Procopius, Gratian 364–383 | 24 | | 1 | | | 4 | | | 19 | | | 78 | | 32 | 2 | 22 | 11 | 8 | 7 | | 702 | 912 |
| Valentian II 375–392 | 10 | | 2 | | | | | | 2 | | | 70 | | 18 | 1 | 6 | 11 | 8 | 1 | | 400 | 529 |
| Theodosius 379–395 | 12 | | 3 | | | 1 | | | 2 | | | 111 | | 50 | 9 | 19 | 84 | 9 | 3 | | 872 | 1175 |

*Note:* Denominations are given where recorded through Philip II. As = as; Q = quadrans; Dp = Dupondius; D = Denarius; S = sestertius; A = Antoninianus.

Table 9. Number of Coins per Year of Reign

| Emperor | Reign | Municipal | Imperial |
|---|---|---|---|
| Augustus | 27 B.C.–A.D. 14 | .66 | .49 |
| Tiberius | 14–37 | 0 | .17 |
| Caligula | 37–41 | .25 | 1.0 |
| Claudius | 41–54 | .15 | 1.0 |
| Nero | 54–68 | .36 | .36 |
| Vespasian and Titus | 69–81 | .083 | .58 |
| Domitian | 81–96 | 1.67 | .60 |
| Nerva and Trajan | 96–117 | .14 | .62 |
| Hadrian | 117–138 | 1.33 | 1.24 |
| Antoninus Pius | 138–161 | 1.56 | 1.78 |
| Marcus Aurelius | 161–180 | 1.37 | 2.68 |
| Commodus | 180–192 | 1.33 | 2.42 |
| Septimius Severus, Caracalla, and Geta | 193–217 | 3.75 | 1.25 |
| Heliogabalus | 218–222 | .50 | 1.25 |
| Severus Alexander and Maximinus Thrax | 222–238 | 0 | 3.25 |
| Pupienus and Gordion III | 238–244 | 1.167 | 4.83 |
| Philip I and II | 243–249 | 0 | 3.167 |
| Decius | 249–251 | 0 | 5.0 |
| Trebonius Gallus and Volusian | 251–253 | 0 | 4.5 |
| Valerian and Gallienus | 253–268 | .20 | 9.67 |
| Claudius II | 268–270 | 0 | 13.0 |
| Aurelian | 270–275 | 0 | 18.80 |
| Tacitus, Florus, and Probus | 275–282 | 0 | 10.43 |
| Carus, Carinus, and Numerian | 282–284 | 0 | 9.5 |
| Diocletian and Maximian | 284–305 | 0 | 7.67 |
| Constantius Chlorus, Galerius, Maximian II, Licinius, Constantine, and Family of Constantine | 305–337 | 0 | 29.13 |
| Constantius II and Family | 337–361 | 0 | 105.0 |
| Julian and Jovian | 361–364 | 0 | 58.0 |
| Valentinian I, Valens, Procopius, Gratian, Valentinian II, and Theodosius | 364–395 | 0 | 84.39 |

Note: Numbers are averages of the actual number of coins found divided by the number of years of reign.

Table 10. Eastern and Western Mints of Coins Found at Corinth
Valerian to Theodosius

| Emperor | Eastern | Western |
|---|---|---|
| Valarian and Gallienus 253–268 | 15 | 33 |
| Claudius II 268–270 | 0 | 10 |
| Aurelian 270–275 | 5 | 23 |
| Tacitus, Florus, and Probus 275–282 | 7 | 28 |
| Carus, Carinus, Numerian 282–284 | 0 | 10 |
| Diocletian, Maximian 284–305 | 69 | 5 |
| Constantius Chlorus 305–306 | 6 | 4 |
| Maximian II, Galerius 305–313 | 29 | 4 |
| Licinius 307–323 | 21 | 9 |
| Constantine and Family 307–337 | 226 | 52 |
| Constantius II and Family 337–361 | 454 | 45 |
| Julian, Jovian 361–364 | 27 | 6 |
| Valentinian I through Theodosius 364–395 | 552 | 82 |

Table 11. Building Activity at Corinth (B = Built; R = Rebuilt, Repaired, Remodeled; D = Destroyed, Abandoned, Heavily Damaged)

| Building | 44 B.C. | A.D. 1 | 50 | 100 | 150 | 200 | 250 | 300 | 350 | 400 |
|---|---|---|---|---|---|---|---|---|---|---|
| Asklepieion | —R— | | | | | | | | | D |
| Odeon | | | —B— | | | D,R | | | —D,R— | D |
| Upper Priene | | —R— | | | —R— | | | | | D |
| Temple of Aphrodite | | —R— | | | | | | | | D |
| Theater | | —R— | R | —R— | | —R— | —R— | | | D |
| South East Building | | —B— | | —R— | | | | | | D |
| Julian Basilica | | —B— | | | —R— | | | | | D |
| South Basilica | | —B— | | D,R | | | | | | D |
| Mosaic House | | | | | B | | | | | D |
| South Stoa | —R— | | | | | | D,R | | | D |
| Temple G | —B— R | | | | | | | | | |
| Temple D | | —B— | R | | | | | | | |
| Babbius Monument | | B | | | | | | | | |
| Temple F | | B | | | | | | | | |
| Fountain of Poseidon | | B | | —B— | D | | | | | |
| Temple K | | | | —B— | | | | | | |
| Temple H | | | | | | B | | | | |
| Temple J | | | | | | B | | | | |
| Central Shops | | —B— | | | | | | | | —D— |
| Bema | | —B— | | | | | | | | —D— |
| Propylaea | | —B— | —R— | | R | | | | | D? |

Table 11. Building Activity at Corinth (B = Built; R = Rebuilt, Repaired, Remodeled; D = Destroyed, Abandoned, Heavily Damaged) (continued)

| Building | 44 B.C. | A.D. 1 | 50 | 100 | 150 | 200 | 250 | 300 | 350 | 400 |
|---|---|---|---|---|---|---|---|---|---|---|
| Captives Facade | | | | | | | | | | D,R |
| Northwest Shops | | | | —B— | | | | | | |
| Stoa South of Peirene | | | | | —B— | | | | | |
| Roman Market (North Market) | | —B— | | | | | | | | D,R |
| Glauke | —R— | | | | | | | | | |
| Peirene | | | —R—— | | —R— | | | —R— | | |
| Roman Bath near Lechaion Road N. of Forum | | | | | | —B—— | | | | |
| Semi-Circular Building | | —B— | | | | | | | | —D— |
| W. Colonnade Lechaion Road | | —B— | | | | | | | | |
| West Shops Lechaion Road | | —B— | | —R— | | | | | | |
| Peribolos of Apollo | | —B— | | | | | | | | —R— |

| Building | | | | |
|---|---|---|---|---|
| Lechaion Road Basilica | B | —R— | | D? |
| Gymnasium | —R— | —B— | | D |
| Fountain of the Lamps (Lerna) | —R— | —R— | —R— | D |
| Demeter and Kore Sanctuary, Building T | -R- | —R— | | -D- |
| Demeter and Kore Sanctuary, Theater | | —B— | | -D- |
| Demeter and Kore Sanctuary, Building G-1, 2 | | —B— | | -D- |
| Cellar Building | D,R | B | | -R- |
| West Shops | —R— | B | | D,R |
| Roman House, S.W. area of Forum | —R— | -R- | | D,R |
| Long Rectangular Building | | —B— | | D |
| Ampitheater | | —B— | | |

Table 12. Greek and Latin Inscriptions

| Emperor | Greek | | | Latin | | |
|---|---|---|---|---|---|---|
| | Date Certain | Date All But Certain | Total | Date Certain | Date All But Certain | Total |
| Augustus | 1 | 0 | 1 | 7 | 7 | 14 |
| Tiberius | 0 | 1 | 1 | 8 | 11 | 21 |
| Caligula-Claudius | 0 | 0 | 0 | 19 | 8 | 27 |
| Nero | 0 | 1 | 1 | 9 | 2 | 11 |
| Vespasian | 0 | 0 | 0 | 3 | 2 | 5 |
| Titus-Domitian | 0 | 0 | 0 | 1 | 7 | 8 |
| Nerva-Trajan | 1 | 0 | 1 | 9 | 6 | 15 |
| Hadrian | 12 | 3 | 15 | 6 | 4 | 10 |
| Antoninus Pius | 4 | 3 | 7 | 3 | 0 | 3 |
| Marcus Aurelius | 2 | 4 | 6 | 0 | 1 | 1 |
| Commodus-Gordian | 2 | 1 | 3 | 2 | 0 | 2 |
| Philip-Gallienus | 2 | 2 | 4 | 1 | 0 | 1 |

*Source:* John Harvey Kent, *Corinth*, Vol. 8, pt. 3.

# Appendix 1
# Central Place Theory and the Marketing Network of the Northeastern Peloponnese

Since this is the first attempt to apply central place theory to a region in mainland Greece, a word on methodology may be appropriate.[1] Applying this theory to the Corinthia may demonstrate, first, whether a regional marketing network existed for the area. In the absence of such a network, the larger and smaller sites would be distributed throughout the countryside without any pattern or order. Such a finding would not be without significance in attempting to understand the nature of Corinth's economy. If a network did exist, the application of the theory may reveal the principles of its organization. Second, central place theory may help explain why some Corinthian settlements grew large while others remained small. Not every site enjoying one or more natural advantages, such as a fine natural harbor, abundant supplies of water, or proximity to a large, fertile plain, achieved size or importance. Other sites, with fewer natural advantages, may have prospered. One of the reasons for this divergent pattern of development may have been the location of the sites within a stable regional marketing network; those with an advantageous commercial position grew, while those without did not (see maps 5, 6).

This theory, which has been empirically tested in over a thousand case studies, is based on a few general principles. First, if a consumer of goods and services is to calculate the real cost of an article or service in time, money, or opportunity costs, he must add to its price the cost of his visit to the market and his return home. By the law of diminishing returns, the cost will increase the further he must travel, until at a certain distance, the cost of a particular article or service will be so high that the demand for it will drop to zero. This distance is called the article's maximum range.

The range of some goods and services differs substantially from the range of others. For example, a Corinthian household in the classical era might require various agricultural products, such as olives, wine, or cheese, quite often and yet be unwilling to travel very far to get them, since their availability is ubiquitous. The suppliers of these items may be satisfied with the demands of a relatively few consumers because, in the course of a year, each household will buy a great deal of his produce, even though the individual transactions may be small. These articles are called "low-order" goods and services.

"High-order" goods and services are those which have a wider range. Examples would include the purchase of furnishings or articles of fine clothing, or attendance at a religious festival, theatrical performance, or judicial hearing. Because the value of these goods and services is high, the proportional cost of travel is smaller than for low-order goods. Hence, the consumer would be willing (or compelled) to travel greater distances for them. There are fewer marketing centers that produce high-order goods and services, since they are used infrequently and their cost may be high. They require a large population from a wide area to maintain their producers (the product's minimum range).

A regional marketing network arises in response to the supply and demand of high- and low-order products in a given area. Low-order goods will always be provided in the same markets as high-order goods; but since the maximum range of low-order goods is shorter than the maximum range of high-order goods, more centers for low-order goods will develop, until no demand will remain unfulfilled in the region.

Market centers providing high-order goods will be located approximately in the center of the regional market it serves. In this way, the consumer's traveling distance is minimized, since a central location is most easily accessible from all parts of the surrounding region, and the providers of goods and services can be assured of the maximum possible trade. Concentration of goods and services in a central location will aid the trader in attracting potential customers to his own service, and also the consumer by assuring that all the goods and services he needs are located in one place. The pattern of distribution of the smaller marketing centers, providing low-order goods, will vary from region to region depending on topography, transport facilities, and the nature of the social, economic, and political interrelationships between the large cities and the nearby smaller towns.

## Application of the Theory to Corinth

The first task in the application of this method is to distinguish the high-order and low-order market centers in the region. There is no doubt that Corinth itself was the major high-order market in the Corinthia; to say more would be to belabor the obvious. For the second-order centers, I have chosen the chief towns in the Corinthia next in size to Corinth itself, but larger than the numerous village, villa, and fortress sites in the region. Settlements that provided essentially religious services, such as Isthmia, Nemea, and Heraeum, were omitted from the analysis, and they also seemed smaller in size compared to the large towns.[2] Those sites selected as second-order markets are Crommyon, Cenchreae, Tenea, Cleonae, Ayios

Charalambos (Assae?), and Asprokambos. These are the largest town sites known to exist in the Corinthia from the surveys of the region.[3] It is also possible to include village sites of still lower order into the analysis and have third- and even fourth-level market centers. However, there are almost one hundred smaller sites in the Corinthia alone, and without thorough excavation of each one, at an immense cost, it is often impossible to tell whether a given site is a villa, a village, a farmstead, or a small fort. Because of the uncertainty in ranking these smaller sites, they are not included in this analysis, but they may well be included in a future analysis, when the evidence concerning them becomes better. Here, only one settlement hierarchy is examined—that between the largest cities and the largest towns of the region—although the analysis could extend downwards or upwards almost indefinitely.

The next problem is to determine whether the first- and second-order settlements form a pattern, or whether they are randomly distributed throughout the countryside. There are three possible ways of determining their distribution: using quadrant counts, nearest neighbor analysis, or Thiessen polygon techniques. Some combination of these techniques could also be used. For the present analysis, only the polygon technique has been employed for the following reasons. (1) Quadrant count analysis requires that a regular lattice of squares by superimposed on a map of the region and a count made of the number of sites within each square. The counts are then checked with a mathematical formula (The Poisson probability function) to determine whether the point counts are random or nonrandom. However, this method of analysis may not be applicable to a region where the topography is broken up by large mountains, inlets, and bays. Any pattern of settlement distribution may not be seen for these reasons when using this method, although it may be applicable to other ancient regions with more regular terrain. (2) Nearest neighbor techniques suffer from similar problems when applied to a region such as the Corinthia. This method analyzes the distances between nearest settlements for regularities or randomness and has been used successfully by Hassall and Hodder for Roman Britain. However, the method is probably of limited use for regions with varied terrain, where water transport was frequently used. For example, Cenchreae may have been much closer to Tenea than Aegina but travel to Aegina was probably immeasurably easier because of the facility of water transport compared to land transport. Hence, distance between towns varied from place to place not because of their position within a market network but because of the available means of transport, and locations physically more distant may be in closer social, economic, and political contact than those closer together.[4]

Thiessen polygons have the merit of demonstrating whether a pattern of distribution between high- and low-order markets exists, and also of showing visually how the pattern appears.[5] The polygons are constructed by drawing two arcs of a circle from two adjacent sites. A line is then drawn between the two points where the arcs intersect. This line will be the perpendicular bisector of a line drawn between the two sites. The process is repeated for all adjacent sites of the region. The polygons which result correspond roughly to the marketing regions of each of the sites for low-order goods: each location within the polygon will be closer to its central market than to any other (see map 5).

Next, the Thiessen polygons are fitted into a lattice of hexagons, so the relationships inherent in the region's settlements can be seen more clearly. Problems arise when the region subject to analysis contains large bodies of water or mountain ranges, where one might theoretically expect a market to exist, but geography makes it impossible.[6] For the Corinthia, where the adjacent polygons of Asprokambos, Sikyon, and Ayios Charalambos meet entirely over water, a hexagon of water was placed between them; similarly for Aegina. Skinner had followed a similar procedure for rural Szechwan Province, in China, where an intervening mountain range separated two adjacent marketing areas. The market regions of Cleonae, Tenea, and Ayios Charalambos have been placed adjacent to that of Corinth in the hexagon lattice, although only the latter two are adjacent to Corinth in the polygon abstraction. It will be noted, however, that the region of Cleonae is separated from that of Corinth by only 600 meters. The market polygon for Corinth was drawn from the center of the city, and if it were drawn from 600 meters south of the center, still well within the boundary of Corinth's urban area, then the two regions would adjoin. Similarly, the boundary between the market area of Corinth and Asprokambos are not shown over water in the hexagons as they are in the polygons. Once again, if the center of Corinth's market were shifted twelve hundred meters to the northeast (well within the city's limits), then the two regions would meet over land.

The boundaries of the polygons are not immutable, but only rough approximations of reality, especially when a market center itself has as large an area as Corinth has. The general relationship between the sites is clear and corresponds to a $K = 3$, or marketing pattern in which each low-order market is adjacent to three high-order markets, where geography allows.

In map 6, a few suggested sites were added to the hexagonal regions. Lessa was mentioned by Pausanias as a town (*kome*) lying between Argos and Epidauros, and perhaps it served as a small regional market.[7] Methana was described by Pausanias as a small city (*polisma*) and it probably served also as a small regional market.[8] In the classical era, Orneai was a large, walled town between Argos and Phlious, destroyed by Argos in 416 B.C. and later in 352 B.C.[9]

The application of this method raises some interesting questions. On the whole, the theory predicts rather well where large and small market centers are located within the regional marketing network: the high-order markets correspond to city-state capitals, and the smaller centers to either large towns or small capitals (usually absorbed by one or more of their larger neighbors during some period of their history, e.g. Cleonae). But it is also clear that other economic and political factors played a role in the growth of towns in the region. For example, Orneai twice lost its status as a large town through its destruction by Argos. The theory predicts that Crommyon should have a status of a high-order market, but perhaps it was prevented from attaining that status by the political and economic power of its greater neighbor, Corinth. Megara too has a higher status than predicted, and this fact may reveal imperfections in the theory—especially when applied to coastal regions—but it may also indicate that the talents and abilities of the Megarans raised the status of their community through their own efforts. In the time of Pausanias, at any rate, Megara had declined in importance.[10]

Perhaps this theory may be of some value in explaining the development of boundaries of the classical city states. Perhaps the boundaries were determined in part by the extent of the capital cities' regional markets, the areas of the surrounding territory that looked to the asty for high-order goods and services. Perhaps the marketing pattern of this region was to some extent responsible for its political instability in the Archaic and Classical eras (also characteristic of the rest of Greece). Each secondary market such as Cleonae, Orneai, and Tenea looked not to one, but to three city-state capitals for high-order goods and services. This might have reinforced the centrifugal nature of Greek regional conflicts, with border towns like Cleonae allied now with Corinth, now with Argos, to defend itself from incorporation into its larger neighbors. The theory may also help explain the process of cultural transmission in a given region. The fact that Cleonae's alphabet incorporated letters from both the Corinthian and Argive alphabets may be a reflection of its position in the marketing network which looked to both larger cities for goods and services.[11] Ultimately however, the people made the marketing system, not vice versa.

It is also significant that the settlements in the northeastern Peloponnese seem to reflect a marketing pattern ($K = 3$). This pattern is most effective in fulfilling the needs of rural consumers, since the ratio of high-order markets to low-order ones is at a maximum. Each low-order market was approximately equidistant to three higher-order markets depending on terrain.

Hence, the site of Corinth was conveniently located in relation to the other city states of the region to become a large and prosperous center for the distribution of high-order goods and services. It also confirms the central importance of the city for the transmission of culture to the countryside. The ancient city was above all, a center for communication between god and worshiper, shipowner and sailor, magistrate and citizen, and teacher and pupil. Almost all communication in antiquity was face to face, and these personal contacts occurred in the city. To the Greek or Roman, participation in the affairs of his city—its political institutions, festivals, religious, and cultural events—affirmed his importance as an individual, whether he lived in the city or in a remote village. The importance of this participation is reflected in the pattern of settlements in the Corinthia.

# Appendix 2
# Corinth's Population and Water Supply

The purpose of this appendix is to explore the possibility of using Corinth's water supply to estimate its population. When other sources of evidence are lacking, such as census lists and surveys of the area an ancient city occupied, this method may be of some use. Previous attempts have used estimates of water brought to the city by aqueducts, and this may be a valid method under certain conditions.[1] For Corinth, the flow rates of its springs will be used.

The flow rates from Corinth's springs were considerable. Today, the Fountain of Peirene has a rate of flow varying between 7 to 12 cubic meters per hour to a maximum hourly rate of 20 cubic meters. Since the modern fountains of Deke (Tekke) and Mourat Aga tap the same sources as ancient Peirene, the total flow in antiquity was probably equal to the combined rates of flow of all three fountains, or an average of 18 cubic meters per hour. Besides Peirene, there are some sixteen other water sources in the city, some of them quite copious, such as Hadji Mustafa and Kokkinovrisi, as well as the ancient fountains of Glauke, the Asklepieion, and the Fountain of the Lamps (Lerna).[2] Unfortunately, the flow rates of these other sources have not been measured, but they were probably quite large.[3] It is likely that a relationship existed between the sizes of the reservoirs and the flow rates of Corinth's major fountains, Peirene, Glauke, and the Asklepieion. Fountains with large rates of flow would need large reservoirs to hold and distribute the water, and fountains with lower rates of flow probably needed smaller reservoirs. For Peirene, reservoirs with a total capacity of 456 cubic meters were needed to hold and distribute an average flow rate of 18 cubic meters per hour. If a similar ratio existed between the capacity and flow rates for Corinth's other fountains then perhaps their approximate flow rates can be estimated. Glauke's reservoirs had a capacity of 527 cubic meters and if the ratio between capacity and the rate of flow was similar to Peirene, then an average flow of 20.8 cubic meters per hour is suggested. The Asklepieion's reservoirs had a capacity of 341 cubic meters and a similar ratio yields a flow rate of 13.4 cubic meters per hour.[4] In any event, it will be a considerable underestimate to assume that the rate of flow for all

Corinth's springs was only twice that of Peirene, or an average of about 36 cubic meters per hour.

How many people could have been supported by this amount of water? This depends on the proportion of the water used for nondomestic purposes and the average per-capita consumption of Corinth's population. In the city of Rome during the reign of Nerva (96–98), some 20 percent of the city's water supply went to public buildings and ornamental fountains, and not for direct consumption.[5] Since Rome apparently lavished some 1,135 liters per day (300 gallons) on each inhabitant (more than any other city in the world before the late twentieth century), it is likely that the percentage of water going to nonessential purposes in Corinth was lower than at Rome. Hence, a figure of 20 percent would probably be a maximum figure for water devoted to nondomestic purposes in Corinth.

The water-consumption rate of Corinthians in ancient times is of course unknown, but, as for urban densities, there are parameters to suggest minimum and maximum per-capita rates. In arid regions, where water supply and consumption are minimal, it has been estimated that minimum per-capita needs are 1.5 cubic meters per person annually, or about 4.1 liters per person per day.[6] This is a very low rate of consumption, and probably represents a minimum rate for any settled population. A maximum rate may be found by comparing urban water consumption in London and Paris from about 1790 to 1820. During that era, modern household plumbing devices, such as showers, flush toilets, and running water were first introduced, extravagances generally absent in the classical world. Furthermore, steam-driven pumps and extensive water-supply systems were constructed during this era which partially promoted and partially met an increasing per-capita demand.[7] Hence, the per-capita water consumption of cities using these devices was probably higher than in most classical cities. In London and Paris, per-capita water consumption increased from about 5 liters per day during the mid–eighteenth century to 12 to 14 liters a day between 1792 and 1823.[8] If the Corinthians used a low per-capita rate of water consumption, 1.5 cubic meters a year, then a population of 168,192 could have been supported by Corinth's springs—a maximum estimate of their population. If they used a high consumption rate of 4.5 cubic meters a year (12.3 liters a day), then 56,064 people could have been supported— a minimum figure.[9]

Water from any rain-water cisterns or wells that may have been used by the Corinthians has been omitted from the calculation; this will keep the population estimate at a minimum. Nor was much water wasted at Corinth; runoff from the fountains went to the city's baths and swimming pools, runoff from them was probably used for industrial purposes or to flush latrines, and any remaining water was then probably used for irrigation.

Of course, because the water supply was sufficient for a population of

56,000 people at a high rate of consumption, this does not exclude the possibility that there could have been considerably fewer people in the city. Hadrian's aqueduct however, implies that the city's own supply was no longer adequate for its needs and it would not have been built unless the need for more water was great. Unless the climate of Greece was drier in Hadrian's reign, and the flow from Corinth's springs lower—for which there is no evidence[10]—the conclusion that Corinth's population increased beyond at least 56,000 during his reign seems a probable one.

# Appendix 3
## Urban Geography

One of the promising new methodologies historians and archaeologists are now applying to ancient cities is urban geography.[1] In general, the social, economic, and political institutions and values of an urban society are reflected in the physical patterns of the city's buildings and facilities as well as in its overall pattern of spatial organization.

The pattern of urban residences and commercial facilities reveal social stratification, urban transport and communications systems, urban rent structure, and accessibility to the city's services. Obviously, the more that is known about a city's urban layout, the more meaningful the interpretation of that layout will be. Pompeii, Rome, and Ostia offer the most fruitful fields for the application of these principles.[3]

Unfortunately, little is known about the residential patterns of Roman Corinth; nevertheless, it seems worthwhile to say a few words about the evidence we have. As was noted in chapter 2, the city was ringed by villas in the zone of intensive agriculture immediately surrounding the city.[4] Within the city proper our evidence is poor: only four probable houses dating to the Roman era have been excavated and published, the Mosaic House near the South Basilica; the large Roman House on the northwest corner of the precinct of Temple E; the Roman house with glass panels east of the theater; and the Cellar Building, near the south end of the West Shops.[5] At least three of the four houses were elite dwellings. The splendid mosaics in the Mosaic House date to about A.D. 200 (the house may have been built earlier); the large Roman House had an atrium paved with marble; and the house east of the theater had magnificent glass panels (perhaps for a door) and frescoed walls. The Cellar Building may have been an elite dwelling as well, although its fragmentary remains are difficult to interpret. The two-story structure had pithoi sunk in the basement floor for storage—a common feature of many Greek and Roman houses—and the cooking and baking wares found in the remains also suggest that it was a house. Fragments of plaster reveal that the walls were painted in fresco secco technique, indicating a house of some pretensions.

Greek archaeologists excavating the sites of new houses before the foundations are laid continue to find portions of what appear to be houses of the

Roman era in diverse parts of the city.[6] As in other large Greco-Roman cities, Corinth's commercial, religious, civic, and administrative structures were concentrated in the forum, near the geographical center of the inhabited area of the city.

What are the explanations for the residential pattern, and the patterns of civic and commercial structures seen in Roman Corinth? Since only four probable houses have been excavated and recorded for the Roman city so far, any reconstruction of the city's residential pattern is tentative. Yet, these houses were elite dwellings located near the city's Forum. In Rome and Athens, elite dwellings are also found clustered around their civic and commercial centers: on and near the Palatine Hill in Rome and south of the Agora in Athens.[7] In many other preindustrial cities, the residences of the elite cluster around the town centers, and it may well be that future excavations will confirm a similar pattern for Corinth. The location of the residences of Corinth's poor is unknown. As in many other preindustrial cities, they may have lived in an area between the central zone of elite residences and the zone of agricultural villas ringing the city.[8]

One cause of the residential pattern may have been the limitations of ancient urban transportation and communication. Travel in ancient urban areas was hazardous, as the evidence for Rome indicates.[9] Unpaved streets turned into rivers of mud after a heavy rain, and the pedestrian had to compete with large crowds, pickpockets, troops of soldiers, wagons carrying heavy construction materials, and (by night) gangs of thieves and muggers. Methods of transport were limited to foot or at best a litter or horse. Street conditions could be unsanitary: Roman law codes indicate that the contents of chamber pots were sometimes emptied into the street and sometimes on the hapless pedestrian. Only the wealthy, who could afford a troop of slaves carrying torches, ventured out at night without risk. Although the distances were not great, and Corinth's main arteries were constructed in a radial pattern which facilitates travel to and from the central area, it would still take considerable time and inconvenience to go from the edge of the city to the central region where the civic, commercial and religious activities were located.

The urban aristocracy controlled the city's religious and political institutions which were clustered in the forum area. A residence easily accessible to them would be desirable and convenient, since it would reduce the need for long walks through unsafe streets. A centrally located residence would also be convenient to the city's retail facilities which were also located in the forum. For example, the lack of effective means of preserving foot meant an almost daily trip to purchase some food items.

The need for frequent, personal communication among the Roman urban elite would also encourage the clustering of their residences in one location. The daily visit to one's friends was not only an amenity for the Roman aristocrat and his family, but frequently a social and political necessity.[10] A major occupation of rising politicians was the daily morning call at the homes of their patrons, and all houses of rich and important members of Roman society were always open to the visits of their friends and clients. Since this form of communication was necessarily limited to face-to-face contact, the desirability for the clustering of elite residences around a central core is clear.[11]

There were also a variety of reasons for the commercial and civic land-use patterns observed for Corinth and other classical cities. A central location for a commercial facility is more accessible to consumers in all regions of a city than any other point. The radial street pattern observed for the city's main thoroughfares, with the Forum at their hub, would increase its accessibility to other regions. The limitations of ancient transport and communications would also promote the concentration of commercial activities in a central region. In this pattern, producers, middlemen, and consumers can most readily interact. "How much business could a seller of hides transact in a day if his perspective customers, the leather workers had their shops helter-skelter about the city?"[12] An agglomeration of civic and commercial facilities is not only convenient for producers but also for middlemen and retailers. The social, religious, and political activities of the forum area would attract large numbers of potential customers to the nearby shops, as the close proximity of other retailers would attract customers to one's own establishment. With a lack of modern methods of communication, only close proximity to civic, religious, and other commercial functions could attract large numbers of potential customers to the retailer. If he were to locate in a region not frequented by traffic and potential customers, he would have little possibility of attracting them by advertizing. As in Rome, speciality shops (such as jewelers, gold- and silversmiths) were doubtless concentrated in the most frequented region of the Forum, since, more than other retailers, they needed large numbers of potential customers to sell goods that were of little interest to most of the people.[13] Other retail activities, such as itinerant food vending, that had a high consumer demand in all regions of the city and did not require high transport outlays, could probably be found in many or all neighborhoods.[14]

Consumers would also benefit from the agglomeration of commercial functions in one area. It was both convenient to the city's other services and it would save the consumer many laborious side trips through crowded streets. In this way, only one journey would have to be made for a whole range of goods and services.

Most of the city's civic and religious services were clustered in the forum area for similar reasons. Such a location would encourage worship at temples and attendance at the theater and odeon, as well as the use of other nearby facilities. Since the purpose of the classical city was to serve the public that created it, measures were taken to ensure that their facilities had the maximum accessibility. The only major exception to this principle for Corinth is the location of the amphitheater, about one kilometer east of the Forum. In the city of Rome, the Colosseum was centrally located, although in Pompeii, it was constructed on the eastern end of town. Perhaps the Corinthians felt that such a structure, devoted solely to wild beast hunts and gladiatorial contests, was not a suitable neighbor for the city's temples and law courts. Or, perhaps the structure was located in a poor neighborhood so they would be the ones to bear the noxious odors and noise of the arena.

Some temples were located far from the civic center as well. The temple of Asklepios and Hygeia on the northernmost scarp of the city was probably located there to use the abundant water supply of the area's springs, since bathing was an important ritual of the cult. Other temples, such as Demeter and Kore's sanctuary on the north slope of Acrocorinth, may have been located on ancient cult sites, distant from the city's center, and were perhaps built before Corinth itself.[15]

# Appendix 4
# The Use of Archaeological Surveys

The use of archaeological surveys for the Corinthia makes only a modest contribution to the present work. In general, the use of such surveys has proven much more valuable for the prehistoric era, where other forms of evidence is poor, than for the classical period. Nor are the surveys essential for the application of central place theory, since the sites used here are all well-known primary and secondary market centers. Nevertheless, the surveys for the Corinthia seem to indicate that intensive agriculture was practiced near the city, as one would expect in a market system, and this is important. In chapter 2 we saw other literary and archaeological evidence that indicate a similar pattern near other ancient cities. Perhaps surveys could prove to be of some value for other regions of classical Greece, as they have been for many areas of the Greco-Roman world, for clarifying the agricultural economy, and cultural and economic continuity.

The purpose of this appendix is to survey the conceptual development of economic geography and some more recent applications that may be of value to our discipline. Finally, I want to discuss the limitations of such applications. For a full analysis of the methodologies used by this field, the reader is urged to consult the works discussed herein, especially Renfrew (1972).

As we saw in chapter 2, the conceptual origins of human geography can be found in the works of Thucydides, Plato, Aristotle, and the Hippocratic corpus. The next advances were not made until 1826, with the publication of von Thünen's *Der Isolierte Staat in Beziehung auf Landwirtschaft und Nationalökonomie*. From von Thünen's experience in operating his estate, Gut Tellow, he was able to show that the patterns of different crops grown on the estate changed as the distance from it increased. Crops requiring large amounts of time, labor, and transport outlays were grown close to the farm while those requiring less were grown further away. By the law of diminishing returns, the profitability of growing a given crop will decline as the distance from the farmer's residence increases, since more time, labor, and transport outlays are necessary for its production. Therefore, at increasing distances, crops requiring less time and labor outlays will be grown. Von Thünen applied his discoveries to a hypothetical isolated town, and was able to demonstrate the causes for the differing prices of land (called rent structure by economists) in differing locations, the patterns of agricultural land use surrounding a settlement, and the geographical reasons for locating settlements in given areas.

All subsequent research on economic geography is based on von Thünen's seminal work, and has taken three general directions. The first is central place theory, which received its first systematic explication by Christaller in 1933 (see Christaller 1966), and was further developed by Lösch (1954), Isard (1956), and others (see appendix 1). A second line of development has sought to apply von Thünen's theories to urban rent structure and land use patterns. These relationships were first explored systematically by the great Chicago School of urban economists, represented by the publications of Park and Burgess (1925), Burgess (1929), and Hoyt (1939) (see appendix 3). Even today, the discipline of urban economics retains a strong geographical basis, its legacy from von Thünen.

The third division of economic geography, the one that is of most concern to ancient historians, has continued and refined the ideas of von Thünen in agricultural economics. Despite the huge bibliography on the economic geography of human settlements since von Thünen's day, this method of analysis has only recently been applied to ancient settlements. Anthropologists have been the first to understand the implications of these methodologies for ancient societies, perhaps because of their traditional use of interdisciplinary approaches. Two works in particular, one by a geographer and the other by an economist have had a major influence on this recent intellectual trend: P. Haggett, et al., *Locational Analysis in Human Geography* (London, 1965, new ed. New York, 1977) and M. Chisholm's *Rural Settlement and Land Use: An Essay in Location* (London, 1962; new ed. 1968). It was C. Vita-Finzi (1969), in his now classic article, "Early Man and the Environment," who first demonstrated that an analysis of the local environment surrounding ancient settlements could help to understand the subsistence economies of their people. He was followed shortly thereafter by Lee (1969), Vita-Finzi and Higgs (1970), Renfrew (1972), and more recently by Davis and Cherry (1981), Renfrew (1984), and many others.

As historians, we are often confronted with the fact that our evidence is not perfect, and this is no less true for site surveys than for our literary, epigraphical, and archeological evidence. Yet, as we are not deterred from the judicious use other evidence, so, the careful use of site surveys should not be an insurmountable obstacle.

There are several limitations in interpreting data derived from site surveys. When certain types of easily discoverable sites, such as hills or prominent ridges, were occupied preferentially in certain periods, a site survey will be more inclusive for these periods than for other eras. Some burial practices in certain eras, such as the use of tholos or chamber tombs, will enable the burials to be found more easily than will cremation and pithos burials. All sites may not have been occupied simultaneously throughout the length of a specific period, and hence studies on density and continuity will yield maximum figures. Absence of finds from a site will not demonstrate abandonment, since this can only be determined through excavation. Surveys can only indicate the presence of occupation during certain periods and not the absence. The picture during eras for which few sites are found is more likely to change with the accumulation of new evidence.

Nevertheless, for some types of analysis, it is not necessary for every site occupied in a given era to have been recorded, for a site survey to yield understanding about the settlement history of a region. Analyses of strategic requirements in certain eras, or access to the sea, certain types of cultivable land, or other natural resources, require only a representative sample of sites.

The more exhaustive the survey, the more useful the evidence will be. In the case of the Corinthia, the region has been under intense study for a century. The two surveys we possess at present, Sakellariou and Faraklas (1971) and Wiseman, *LAC* represent the culmination of generations of research in the region, as well as the authors' own thorough investigations, in which I was partially involved. The conclusions drawn from these surveys are probably valid ones.

Recent advances in methodology will also be of help to us. In the United States, infrared aerial photography is proving of great value in the discovery of ancient sites. Because of their higher levels of organic residue, the sites of human settlements tend to absorb moisture to a slightly greater extent than their surroundings. This will slightly lower the temperature of the inhabited area—a differential that can be detected in the infrared wavelengths. This procedure may one day be perfected for the climatic conditions of Greece, where it would be of great help in locating ancient sites.

# Appendix 5
# Rents and Taxes

Since rents are supposed to be the economic basis of the polis, one would expect to find a massive quantity of research devoted to the subject, especially for rent rates. Instead, we find very little.[1] This is not as surprising as it seems, since the known rent rates show that most cities could not have been supported by rents in the classical era. Furthermore, the economic implications of the tax increases, especially of the *tributum soli* of the late Empire, and the high tax rate levied on Judaean peasants, have not been considered. The present appendix will address these issues.

There is abundant evidence concerning leases in classical and hellenistic Greece, especially for Delos and Attica,[2] but very little for rent rates. Our best indication for rent rates is for the *hectemoroi* in early-sixth-century Attica.[3] Although the term *hectemoros* could mean that he paid five-sixths and kept one-sixth for himself, this is unlikely, and it is more probable that he kept the five-sixths. A rent rate of five-sixths, or 83 percent, would be the most horrific known to man.[4] It seems unreasonable to assume that Athenian peasants would have paid much more in rent than their counterparts living in lush, fertile lands under oppressive autocracies. Even the Egyptian peasant, who was liable to be beaten, tied up, and thrown into a canal (not a happy prognosis) and his family enslaved for underpayment, only paid 50 percent in rent and taxes.[5] Indeed, the Egyptian peasant had less food remaining to feed himself after his payment than Cato's chained slaves.[6] It is probable that even the Egyptian peasant, who barely survived a 50 percent rent rate in his agricultural El Dorado, would have succumbed to an 83 percent rate.

After Solon's reforms, the *hectemoroi* became free peasant proprietors, owning their own lands.[7] Land rents doubtless declined after the reforms, because when landownership is widespread, there is less need for leasing.[8] We remember that Isocrates said that Athenian landlords kept rents low,[9] the Athenian peasant would resist high rents, by force if necessary. A. Jardé has suggested that the average land rent during the fourth century was 8 percent of gross produce.[10] Although this is only a suggestion, Jardé has certainly earned the right to make it.

It is significant that for Athens, the leasing of land to landless tenants is

not mentioned in our largest body of evidence, the leases of land from
public organizations.[11] Instead, the leases are often to members of the organization that owned the land (the deme, phratry, or local priesthood), and
therefore, lessor and lessee often came from the same rural district.[12] Frequently, the lessee had to provide a guarantor, who would be liable for rent
payment if he defaulted. In many instances, the guarantor was close kin to
the lessee, or expected to receive some form of payment from the lessee.[13]
On other occasions, the lessors themselves guaranteed to make payments
to their fellow demesmen if the lessee defaulted.[14] The leases fulfilled the
functions of a mutual (collective) aid society within the organization. Lessees were often honored by their fellow demesmen, since they assured de-
pendable incomes for the performance of cult and the entertainment of the
organization's members. The amount of public land available to lease was
also limited, amounting to some 10 percent of the arable total.[15] The situation revealed by the leases hardly fits the picture of evil urban landlords
exploiting an oppressed rural peasantry.

We are on somewhat firmer grounds for the Roman era. Appian wrote
that the rent charged to individuals farming the *ager publicus* was 10 percent of the cereal crops and 20 percent of the fruit crops.[16] It is unlikely
that the Romans of the Republic (seldom noted for their humanitarian excesses) would have charged substantially less than the market would bear.
The land belonging to the *ager publicus* was extensive in Italy and the
provinces, and included the *territorium* of Corinth before its refoundation
in 44 B.C.

There is also the famous emphyteutic lease from imperial estates in
North Africa dating to the reign of Trajan.[17] Since the *coloni* of the estates
paid both their taxes and rents to the imperial treasury, the payments recorded probably included both.[18] The payments are one-third of the wheat
and barley, one-fourth of the beans, and one-third of vine and oil crops. We
know from Hyginus (205L) that Africa paid eighths as taxes to the treasury.
That would leave rental payments of 20 percent of the grains, vine, fruit,
and oil crops and 12.5 percent of the beans.

The emphyteutic lease gave many benefits to the lessee not available
from other leases, if he improved the land. First of all, the *coloni* received
remissions from rent for the first five harvests for orchard crops and ten
harvests for olives. The demand for this type of lease was high, since usually (as in this instance), the leases were perpetual instead of short term (as
for Delos and Attica)—they could even be bequeathed—hence, lessees
would be willing to pay higher rents for them.[19] Given all the benefits, the
rents seem low.

Finally, some church lands in Ravenna during the reign of Justinian
(527–65) made a combined rent and tax payment that has survived on papyrus.[20] The taxes paid were 57 percent of the total sum. If taxes were 33
percent of the gross produce in Justinian's time, then the rent rate would be

about 25 percent. Furthermore, the *coloni* on the estates now had to pay a rent in their labor of two to three days per *week*. The *coloni* on the North African imperial estates had to make a labor payment of six days per *year*. The landlord and the state now take most of the peasants surplus from him; much has changed from the classical era.

The low rates of return on capital invested in Italian farm land also suggest that rents were usually low.[21] In general, it seems that a 6 percent per annum return was considered normal, but that investment in vineyards might yield 7 to 10 percent. Although some of the returns on capital recorded by our sources included lands cultivated by slaves rather than tenants, the return on capital invested in land cultivated by slaves is similar to the return on land cultivated by tenants. This is because both are the incomes accruing to the landowner after the maintenance of the producers, their buildings, seed, and equipment are deducted. Also, the tenant paid for the amortization of his buildings and equipment from his surplus, just as the slave did, since he was expected to maintain them in the same condition in which he received them.[22]

From all available evidence, rents from the classical era averaged 10 to 20 percent of gross production. They were probably higher in the late Empire, as the evidence for Justinian's reign indicates. The low rates of return on investments in agricultural land show that rents were low too. In fact, they are basically rents when the lands are cultivated by tenants. Although our evidence is limited, it comes from reliable sources and indicates that the burden of proof lies with those who would argue for higher rates between 500 B.C. and A.D. 200.

Taxes are much better known than rents. Because of the extensive research on the topic, there is no need for a full discussion here.[23] Our concern is to document the tax increases that occurred throughout the Empire from the reign of Vespasian through that of Justinian. We also want to look at the high rates paid by Judaean peasants during the Hellenistic era. Both aspects have been overlooked in assessing the surplus available to the peasant in ancient times.

The Romans inherited many diverse systems of taxation that were used in the lands they conquered, especially in the East. In the Seleucid Empire and the kingdom of Pergamon, tenths of gross produce were common, although eighths were also levied.[24] In Sicily, tenths were common, and even high-rent, high-tax Ptolemaic Egypt only levied a tenth on landowners.[25] The Romans generally kept the same systems intact when they took over, although they made modifications. Caesar lowered the taxes for Judaea, and Pompey levied a 1 percent annual tax on property for Syria.[26] A. H. M. Jones is probably correct that the Syrian tax is the equivalent to a 10 percent tax on produce.[27]

Under Vespasian, the *tributum* was raised and in some instances doubled.[28] Dio Chrysostom (d. ca. A.D. 117) wrote that Bithynia still paid tenths during his time,[29] and Hyginus (205) noted that under Trajan (98–117) some provinces paid fifths, some sevenths, and Africa eighths.

There is abundant evidence that tax rates increased during the late Empire. Lactantius, Aurelius Victor, Themistius, Emperor Valentinian III, and Procopius all wrote that taxes increased, and had a detrimental effect, especially for agricultural productivity.[30] In addition to these authors, there are numerous complaints from nameless peasants and landowners.[31] Although our sources speak of increases, Themistius quantifies the rate: taxes doubled between 324 and 364. In Egypt during the reign of Justinian, the landowner paid 33 percent of his produce in taxes.[32] In Ptolemaic times, we remember, he had paid only 10 percent. Jones suggested that the church lands in Ravenna also paid 33 percent in Justinian's time.[33] The numerous complaints about high taxation are in striking contrast to the situation during the early Empire. Then, even Vespasian's doubling of some taxes scarcely provoked complaint. The tax increases of the late Empire must have been real and punishing.

Finally, it has often been overlooked that the Judaean peasant paid one-third of sown crops and one-half of fruit crops as tax during the Seleucid era.[34] This very high rate of taxation may have been a legacy of Ptolemaic rule over the country, since it approximates the high rents and taxes paid by Egyptian peasants. In any event, the high tax rates were inherited by the Romans when they conquered the country under Pompey, but were reduced to one-fourth of the sown crops, with complete exemption every seventh year (the Sabbatical Year) in 47 B.C. by Caesar.[35] Here, one confronts the same problem posed in chapter 2. If the average Greek and Roman peasant of the early Empire had only 2 percent of his surplus left over at a tax rate of 10 percent, how did the Judaean peasant survive a tax rate of 33 percent?

The evidence from rents and taxes is consistent with Aristotle's statement that the peasant farm had half of its gross surplus remaining, after it met its own needs. In the classical era, this surplus was spent, saved, or invested by the household. By the late Empire it was confiscated by the state and landlord.

# Abbreviations

Titles listed below are abbreviated throughout the notes. For ancient sources, the initial reference in each chapter is spelled out; thereafter it is abbreviated. Abbreviations follow H. G. Liddell and C. Scott, *Greek-English Lexicon*, for Greek works, and C. T. Lewis and C. Short, *A Latin Dictionary*, for Latin works.

| | |
|---|---|
| ANRW | *Aufstieg und Niedergang der römischen Welt* |
| Ath. Mitt. | *Mitteilungen des deutschen archäologischen Instituts, Athenische Abteilung*, 1876-. |
| BCH | *Bulletin de Correspondance Hellénique* |
| CIG | *Corpus Inscriptionum Graecarum* |
| CIL | *Corpus Inscriptionum Latinarum* (1863–). |
| Corinth | *Corinth, Results of Excavations Conducted by the American School of Classical Studies at Athens.* Numbers refer to volume and part. |
| 1.1 | H. N. Fowler and R. Stillwell, *Introduction, Topography, Architecture* (Cambridge, Mass., 1932). |
| 1.2 | R. Stillwell, et al., *Architecture* (Cambridge, Mass., 1941). |
| 1.3 | R. L. Scranton, *Monuments in the Lower Agora and North of the Archaic Temple* (Princeton, 1951). |
| 1.4 | O. Broneer, *The South Stoa and its Roman Successors* (Princeton, 1954). |
| 1.5 | S. S. Weinberg, *The Southeast Building, The Twin Basilicas, The Mosaic House* (Princeton, 1960). |
| 1.6 | B. H. Hill, *The Springs: Peirene, Sacred Spring, Glauke* (Princeton, 1965). |
| 2 | R. Stillwell, *The Theater* (Princeton, 1965). |
| 3.1 | C. W. Blegen, et al., *Acrocorinth: Excavations in 1926* (Cambridge, Mass., 1930). |
| 3.2 | R. Carpenter and A. Bon, *The Defenses of Acrocorinth and the Lower Town* (Cambridge, Mass., 1936). |
| 4.2 | O. Broneer, *Terracotta Lamps* (Cambridge, Mass., 1930). |
| 6 | K. M. Edwards, *Coins: 1896–1929* (Cambridge, Mass., 1933). |
| 8.1 | B. D. Merritt, *Greek Inscriptions, 1896–1927* (Cambridge, Mass., 1931). |
| 8.2 | A. B. West, *Latin Inscriptions, 1896–1927* (Cambridge, Mass., 1931). |

| | |
|---|---|
| 8.3 | J. H. Kent, *The Inscriptions, 1926–1950* (Princeton, 1966). |
| 9 | F. P. Johnson, *Sculpture 1896–1923* (Cambridge, Mass., 1931). |
| 9.2 | M. Sturgeon, *Sculpture: The Reliefs from the Theater* (Princeton, 1977). |
| 10 | O. Broneer, *The Odeum* (Cambridge, Mass., 1932). |
| 12 | G. R. Davidson, *The Minor Objects* (Princeton, 1952). |
| 14 | C. Roebuck, *The Asklepieion and Lerna* (Princeton, 1951). |
| 16 | R. L. Scranton, *Medieval Architecture in the Central Area of Corinth* (Princeton, 1957). |
| 17 | J. C. Biers, *The Great Bath on the Lechaion Road* (Princeton, 1985). |
| Dar.-Sag. | Ch. Daremberg and E. Saglio, *Dictonnaire des antiquités grecques et romaines d'après les textes et les monuments* (1877–1919). |
| Finley, *AC* | M. I. Finley, "The Ancient City: From Fustel de Coulanges to Max Weber and Beyond." *Comparative Studies in Society and History* 19 (1977): 305–27. |
| Finley, *AE* | M. I. Finley, *The Ancient Economy* (Berkeley, 1973). |
| *IG* | *Inscriptiones Graecae* |
| *ILS* | *Inscriptiones Latinae Selectae* |
| *Isthmia 1* | O. Broneer, *Isthmia I: The Temple of Poseidon* (Princeton, 1971). |
| *Isthmia 2* | O. Broneer, *Isthmia II: Topography and Architecture* (Princeton, 1973). |
| *Kenchreai 1* | R. Scranton, et al., *Kenchreai, Eastern Port of Corinth, I: Topography and Architecture* (Leiden, 1978). |
| *Kenchreae 2* | L. Ibrahim, et al., *Kenchreai, Eastern Port of Corinth, II: The Panels of Opus Sectile in Glass* (Leiden, 1976). |
| *Kenchreai 3* | R. L. Hohlfelder, *Kenchreai, Eastern Port of Corinth, III: The Coins* (Leiden, 1978). |
| *MEFR* | *Mélanges d'Archéologie et d'Histoire d'Ecole Française de Rome* |
| *OGIS* | *Orientis Graeci Inscriptiones Selectae* |
| *RE* | Pauly-Wissowa, *Real-Encyclopädie der classischen Altertumswissenschaft.* |
| *SHA* | *Scriptores Historiae Augustae.* |
| Wiseman, *CR* | J. Wiseman, "Corinth and Rome, I: 228 B.C. to A.D. 267." *ANRW* II, 7.1 (1979): 438–548. |
| Wiseman, *LAC* | J. Wiseman, *The Land of the Ancient Corinthians* (Goteborg, 1978). |

# Notes

### Introduction

1. In a future work, I hope to differentiate more clearly between the different types of service cities: commercial cities, agricultural cities, and other types. I also want to examine the regional variations and temporal limits of the service city. But this is a major undertaking, and requires its own separate study.

2. Finley, *AC,* 325.

3. Finley, *AC,* 310. Cf. the cogent arguments of S. Dyson, "New Methods and Models in the Study of Roman Town-Country Systems," *The Ancient World* 2 (1982): 91–95.

4. Finley, *AC,* 309.

5. Ibid., 324–25.

6. The history of the concept will be discussed in the conclusion.

7. Of course, the record is not blank as the seminal work by Chester Starr, Michael Jameson, Keith Hopkins, Philippe Leveau, Thomas Figueira, and others shows. But, compared to other eras, our thinking has been limited.

8. *More Letters of Charles Darwin,* ed. F. Darwin and A. C. Steward (London, 1903), 1:195.

9. Philip Morrison, "The Ring of Truth," Public Broadcasting System television program, 24 November 1987; J. Hogan, "Cosmic Complex," *Scientific American* 259 (January 1988): 20–21.

10. For a recent restatement of this view see P. Garnsey and R. Saller, *The Roman Empire, Economy, Society, and Culture* (Berkeley, 1987), 48–49; and J. Stambaugh, *The Ancient Roman City* (Baltimore, 1988), 143.

11. It is significant that class antagonisms appear frequently in the political works of Plato and Aristotle, but they are never expressed in terms of rural-urban conflict. Even the conflict between Eupatrids and Hectemoroi in Solon's poems is not expressed in this way. For the religious unity of Athens and Attica, see A. Henrichs, "Between Country and City: Cultic Dimensions of Dionysos in Athens and Attica," *American Philological Association Abstracts,* 1987 annual meeting.

12. 1 Corinthians 3:16.

13. Cicero, *De Legibus* 1.7.22–1.8.24. Reprinted from Cicero, *De Republica, De Legibus,* trans. C. W. Keyes (New York, 1928).

14. Ibid., 1.14.40.

15. Ibid., 1.15.42–45. Cf. *De Re Publica* 1.25–26. (Fortunately, Cicero did not live to see the criminal justice system of the modern era.) To Cicero, who no doubt

reflected widespread cultural attitudes toward cities, man joined associations to form cities, not from fear of his fellow man or nature, or from compulsion, but because of man's nature as a social being.

## Chapter One

1. The geological works consulted in the research for this section are B. von Freyberg, *Geologie des Isthmus von Korinth*, Erlanger Geologische Abhandlungen 95 (1973); A. Philippson, *Griechische Landschaften*, Bd.3, t. 1 (Berlin, 1959), 71–91; A. Philippson, *Der Peloponnes* (Berlin, 1892). See also J. B. Salmon, *Wealthy Corinth: A History of the City to 338* B.C., 1–37.

Some useful maps are: B. von Freyberg, "Geologische Karte des Isthmus von Korinth, 1:20,000," 2 sheets (Erlanger, 1973); A. Philippson, "Geologische Karte des Peloponnes, 1:300,000," (Berlin, 1892); Geographischer Dienst der Armee (German), "Truppenkarte, Griechenland, 1:100,000," Blatt 8-J and 8-H (1941); National Statistical Organization of Greece, "Nomos Corinthias, 1:200,000" (1962).

2. For the best account of routes and settlement locations in the Corinthia, see Wiseman, *LAC*.

3. Von Freyberg, *Geologie*, 25–56.

4. Ibid., 101–24. Geologically, this is a sandstone (Korinthischer bausand-stein), but is often referred to in the literature as a limestone, or "poros."

5. A. Burford, *The Greek Temple Builders at Epidauros* (Toronto, 1969), 16, 57, 61; Wiseman, *LAC*, 66–68.

6. Wiseman, *LAC*, 66–68.

7. For a detailed geophysical and geochemical analysis of soils from different areas of the central Corinthia, see K. Brunnacker, "Zur Bodengeschichte im Quartar Bei Korinth/Griechenland," in von Freiberg, *Geologie*, 161–67. This type of soil was well-suited for ancient agriculture: J. Bintliff, *Natural Environment and Human Settlement in Prehistoric Greece*, British Archaeological Reports, Supp. ser. 28, vol. 1 (Oxford, 1977), 99–104.

8. As all the geological maps of the region show.

9. Macedonius, *Anthologia Palatina* 6.40; Cicero, *De Lege Agraria* 1.2.5.

10. Athenaeus, *Deipnosophistae* 5.219a.

11. Wine press and oil settling tank: C. Williams, "Excavations at Corinth," *Archaiologikon Deltion* 18 (1963): 79. There are classical references to apples from Sidous: Athenaeus, *Deipno*, 3.82a–b; Corinthian radishes: Athenaeus, *Deipno*, 2.56f; wine (said to be harsh): Athenaeus, *Deipno*. 1.30f; and Corinthian violets used as medicine: Galen, *De Compositione Medicamentorum per Genera* 13.829. It is worth noting that the ship of Isis described by Apuleius near Cenchreae and perhaps built locally, was of citron wood: Apuleius, *Metamorphoses* 11.16.

12. Wiseman, *LAC*, 9–10.

13. Aristeides, *For Poseidon* 24.

14. Cicero, *De Republica* 2.3.

15. For the history of the Achaean League in the Hellenistic era and its relations with Rome, see J. A. O. Larsen, *Greek Federal States, Their Institutions and His-*

*tory* (Oxford, 1968), esp. 215–40, 303–498; F. W. Walbank, *A Historical Commentary on Polybius,* vol. 1 (Oxford, 1957); Wiseman, *CR,* 450–62; and E. Gruen, *The Hellenistic World and the Coming of Rome* (Berkeley, 1984), 2:448–528. For the economic consequences of Rome's intervention in Greece, see J. A. O. Larsen, "Greece," pp. 261–435 in T. Frank, *An Economic Survey of Ancient Rome,* vol. 4 (Baltimore, 1938). For the Second Macedonian War (200–196 B.C.), and Flamininus' declaration, see in addition to the works above, F. W. Walbank, *Philip V of Macedon* (Cambridge, 1940), 138–85; E. Badian, *Foreign Clientelae* (Oxford, 1958), 84–115; and N. G. L. Hammond and F. Walbank, *A History of Macedonia,* vol. 3 (Oxford, 1988), 411–557. Since these important events have been retold many times and since the focus of this work is on the Roman city, they are only outlined here.

For the earlier history of the city, see C. Roebuck, "Some Aspects of Urbanization in Corinth," *Hesperia* 41 (1972): 96–127; E. Will, *Korinthiaka: Recherches sur l'histoire et la civilization de Corinthe des origines aux guerres médiques* (Paris, 1955); J. G. O'Neill, *Ancient Corinth, with a Topological Sketch of the Corinthia* (Baltimore, 1930); J. B. Salmon, *Wealthy Corinth.*

16. For a recent discussion of this policy, see G. E. M. de Ste. Croix, *The Class Struggle in the Ancient Greek World* (Ithaca, N.Y., 1981), 523–29.

17. A Fuks, "The Bellum Achaicum and its Social Aspect," *Journal of Hellenistic Studies* 90 (1970), 78–89; cf. two works by E. Gruen, "The Origins of the Achaean War," *Journal of Hellenic Studies* 96 (1976), 46–69; and *The Hellenistic World and the Coming of Rome,* vol. 2, 520–28. Gruen attributes the cause to mutual miscalculation.

18. For these events, see Polybius, 38.9.1–18.12, 39.2.6; Diodorus Siculus 32.26.1–5; Pausanias, 7.14.1–7.16.10; Livy, *Perioche* 52; Zonaras, 9.31; Justin, 34.2.1–6; Florus, 1.32.4–7; Strabo, 8.6.23; Orosius, 5.3, in addition to the works cited above.

19. Diodorus Siculus 32.27.1.

20. Cicero, *Pro Lege Manilia* 5.

21. Polystratus, *Anthologia Graeca* 7.297, trans. W. R. Paton (New York, 1919).

22. Antipater of Thessalonica, *Anthologia Graeca* 7.493, trans. W. R. Paton (New York, 1919).

23. Cicero, *De Lege Agraria* 1.2.5, 2.51; Pausanias 2.2.2.

24. For the city during this era, see Wiseman, *CR,* 491–96. For the status of Greece between 146 B.C. and 27 B.C., see Larsen, *Greek Federal States,* 498–504; and Gruen, *The Hellenistic World,* 2:523–28.

25. Cicero, *Tusculanae Disputationes* 3.53. Reprinted from Cicero, *Tusculan Disputations,* trans. J. E. King (New York, 1927).

26. Appian, *Punica,* 136; Strabo, 8.6.23; Plutarch, *Caesar* 57.5; Cassius Dio 43.50.3–5; Pausanias 2.1.2. For a full discussion of the city's foundation, see chap. 4 below.

27. Resident aliens had the vote in some Roman colonies and municipia (see F. F. Abbott and A. C. Johnson, *Municipal Administration in the Roman Empire* [Princeton, 1926], 58; and G. H. Stevenson, *Roman Provincial Administration*

[Oxford, 1939], 171). At least in the municipium of Malaca, resident aliens who had either Roman or Latin citizenship were enrolled in the tribes for voting purposes (*Lex Malacitana,* cap. 53). Some *incolae* even entered municipal senates (Dessau, *ILS* 6916, 6992; cf. Pliny, *Epistulae* 10.114). The tribes are Agrippa, Atia, Aurelia, Calpurnia, Hostilia, Maneia, Vinicia, Domitia, Livia, Vatinia, Claudia; Sae- or Ae(lia). Some tribal names were associated with Julius Caesar (Aurelia, his mother; Calpurnia, his wife; and Vatinia, perhaps identified with his friend P. Vatinius) and the rest with Augustus (Atia for his mother, Livia for his wife, Agrippa for M. Agrippa, Domitia for Gn. Domitius Ahenobarbus, or his son Lucius, Vinicia for M. Vinicius, and Sae[nia]? for L. Saenius Babbius), or a later emperor (Claudia for Tiberius or Claudius and perhaps Ae[lia]? For Hadrian). See Wiseman, *CR,* 498, n. 221; Kent, *Corinth* 8.3, 23.

28. *Digesta* 50.1.1; *Codex Justinianus,* 10.40.7; *CIL,* 2, nos. 4277, 4249; F. F. Abbot and A. C. Johnson, *Municipal Administration,* 58.

29. Kent, *Corinth* 8.3, 23.

30. Abbot and Johnson, *Municipal Administration,* 67–68. From the surviving inscriptions at Corinth, only two (Kent, *Corinth* 8.3, no. 306; West, *Corinth* 8.2, no. 125) mention the council's supervision of city buildings. The other inscriptions concerning the council are usually devoted to the granting of public honors. However, there is no reason to suppose that the functions of Corinth's council differed markedly from those of other colonies and municipia.

31. For the property qualifications of decurions, see Abbot and Johnson, *Municipal Administration,* 66; H. Stevenson, *Roman Provincial Administration,* 173. At Comum, a decurion had to possess 100,000 sesterces (Pliny, *Ep.* 1.19.2; cf. Petronius 44). They also had to pay entrance fees and contribute to public entertainments (*Lex Colonia Genetiva Julia,* cap. 70; Apuleius, *Met.* 10.18; Pliny, *Ep.* 10.112–3). It is not known for certain at Corinth whether the duovirate or aedileship was the prerequisite for membership in the *decurio.* In the first years of the colony, of course, there would be insufficient ex-decurions and aediles to make up the necessary 100 members. Hence for these years especially, the quinquennales had to have selected nonmagistrates for the council.

32. A. H. M. Jones, *The Later Roman Empire* (Oxford, 1964), 2:739–57.

33. Abbot and Johnson, *Municipal Administration,* 60–61; W. Liebenam, *RE* s.v. Duoviri, 1798–1842.

34. K. M. Edwards, *Corinth* 6, 6–7; Wiseman, *CR,* 498.

35. S. Treggiari, *Roman Freedmen during the Late Republic* (Oxford, 1969), 106–10.

36. *Tabula Heracleensis,* 8–126; Abbot and Johnson, *Municipal Administration,* 59; Kent, *Corinth* 8.3, 23–24; Wiseman, *CR,* 498–99.

37. Kent, *Corinth* 8.3, 27–28; W. Kubitschek, *RE* s.v. Aedilis, 448–464.

38. I see no reason to suppose that the agonothete, who was in charge of the international Isthmian and Caesarean games, would also concern himself with the purely municipal games and festivals held in the city's theater and amphitheater. This is surely a great deal to ask of a single magistrate, and in other Roman colonies and municipia the decurions and aediles were required to perform these functions (*Lex, Col. Genet. Jul.,* cap. 70; Kubitschek, *RE* s.v. Aedilis, 462–63). Indeed, in

Apuleius *Met.* 10.18, a Corinthian *duovir quinquennalis* collects animals in Thrace for a spectacle. Even if the individual per se is fictional, the story indicates what Apuleius' readers expected a Corinthian magistrate to do. Cf. D. J. Geagan, "Notes on the Agonistic Institutions of Roman Corinth," *Greek, Roman and Byzantine Studies* 9 (1968), 69: "One would expect that the system prevalent in other Roman colonies was in use also at Corinth, and this fact may well explain the paucity of information about the civic agonistic institutions and the absence of *agonothetai* for games other than the Isthmia."

39. Kent, *Corinth* 8.3, 28–30.

40. See Plutarch, *Antonius* 67.7; Wiseman, *CR,* 502–3; W. W. Tarn, "The War Against the West," *Cambridge Ancient History,* vol. 10, 66–111.

41. Kent, *Corinth* 8.3, no. 153. There seems to be little doubt that Corinth did indeed serve as the capital of the province of Achaea. In addition to the literary sources of Acts 18:12–17 (where Paul is brought before Governor Gallio at Corinth), Apuleius, *Metamorphoses* 10.18 (where Corinth is described as the capital city or chief city of the province of Achaea: *caput est totius Achaiae provinciae*), and Malalas, *Chronikon* 10, 261 (where Corinth is described as the metropolis of Greece under Vespasian), there is the clear statement in Aelius Aristeides, *For Poseidon* 27: "and the city was a starting point for good order and still administers justice for the Greeks" (*kai men eunomias ge hormeterion he polis eti kai nun brabeuei ta dikaia tois Hellesi*). There are also a considerable number of inscriptions relating to provincial administration found in the city: see B. D. Meritt, *Corinth* 8.1, nos. 75, 76, 80–83; A. B. West, *Corinth* 8.2, nos. 53–75; J. H. Kent, *Corinth* 8.3, nos. 119–148. Cf. J. Wiseman, *CR,* 501–2.

42. Tacitus, *Annales* 1.76.4; 1.80.1; Suetonius, *Divus Claudius* 25.3.

43. For a good account of Nero's activities in Greece, see E. Cizek, *L'Epoque de Néron et ses controverses idéologiques* (Leiden, 1972), 213–24. For the false Neros, see Tacitus, *Historiae* 2.8.9.

44. See Wiseman, *CR,* 506–7; Kent, *Corinth* 8.3, no. 82; Edwards, *Corinth* 6, nos. 91–93, 96–106, 109. Unfortunately, we are unable to tell from the surviving evidence to what extent Corinth's rebuilding was the result of imperial patronage or the local economy. Doubtless, both contributed.

45. See the discussion in chap. 4, 79–84.

46. The ancient evidence for the Herulian invasion of Greece is, Zonaras, 12.26; *SHA, Vita Gallienus* 13.6–9; Syncellus, p. 717, Bonn ed.; Orosius 7.22.7; Eutropius 9.8.2; Aurelius Victor, *De Caesaribus* 33.3; Jerome, *Chronikon,* Olympiad 260; Jordanes, *Getica* 20.108.7; and Zosimos, 1.39.1. Of all these sources, only Syncellus wrote that Corinth, Argos, Sparta, and the rest of the Peloponnese were invaded. However, there seems to be little or no archaeological evidence for a destructive raid by Herulians in the Peloponnese (see table 11 for the destruction dates of Corinth's buildings). This is in striking contrast to the massive destruction at Athens caused by Herulians. Damage caused to several buildings during the mid-third century A.D. is attributed to an earthquake by the excavators.

47. Jones, *The Later Roman Empire,* 1:101–2, 2:1451–61. Anatolius, the praetorian prefect of Illyricum from 357 to 360, had general supervision over the province and the city (Libanius, *Orationes* 14.15).

48. Julian, *Ep.* 28 (198).

49. Saint John Chrysostum, *Homily on the First Epistle to the Corinthians,* Argument 1–2. See also chap. 5 below.

50. Claudian 5.190. For the destruction of Corinth's buildings in this era, see table 11. See also R. L. Scranton, *Corinth* 16, 4–5.

51. Eunapius' friend, the philosopher and artist Hilarius, was decapitated by the Goths while trying to escape (Eunapius, *Vitae Sophistarum* 8.2.2).

52. T. L. Shear, "The Excavation of Roman Chamber Tombs at Corinth in 1931," *American Journal of Archaeology* 35 (1931): 434–35.

## Chapter Two

1. Aristeides, *For Poseidon* 22–25; Strabo 8.6.20; Dio Chrysostum (Favorinus), 37.7, 37.36; cf. Dio Chrysostum 8.5.

2. Alciphron, 3.24.3; Apuleius, *Metamorphoses* 10.35; cf. Pindar, *Olympian Odes* 13.5; Scholia in Pindar *Olympian Odes* 13.4; Xenophon, *Hellenica* 7.2.17; Thucydides, 1.13.1–6.

3. Aristotle, *Politics* 7.5.1–7 (1327a–b); Plato, *Laws* 4.704–7; cf. Hippocrates, *Airs, Waters, and Places.*

4. See appendix 4 for a discussion of the problems of sampling and interpretation inherent in settlement surveys.

5. Thucydides 1.7. Reprinted from Thucydides, *The Peloponnesian War,* trans. Rex Warner (Baltimore, 1974).

6. At least if Homer, who mentions piracy and raiding frequently, may indeed partially reflect this era. A similar pattern emerges in Messenia as I hope to show in a future publication concerning the transition between the Bronze and Iron ages in the Peloponnese.

7. The first to recognize this was C. Renfrew, *The Emergence of Civilization: The Cyclades and the Aegean in the Third Millennium* B.C. (London, 1972), 245ff.

8. The random pattern of continuity from one era to another may be found by applying the formula developed by Renfrew:

$$\frac{Na \times Nb}{2(Na + Nb)}$$

where $Na$ = the number of sites occupied in the first era and $Nb$ = equals the number of sites occupied in the succeeding era (see Renfrew, *The Emergence of Civilization,* 244–48). In table 4, a ratio of 1 would indicate a random pattern of continuity; the higher the ratio, the higher the continuity.

9. The comparatively low settlement continuity between the Late Helladic and Geometric-Archaic eras may reflect fundamental changes in population and can also be observed in Messenia. The percentage of new sites occupied in a certain era is a figure that is difficult to interpret since it can have ambiguous implications. In a flourishing period with a high rate of population increase (whether from natural increase or immigration, many new sites may appear. However, during a military

catastrophe when the inhabitants flee their old homes and occupy new sites with strategic locations, many new sites may again appear. Also, if new immigrants almost entirely supplant an existing population, many new sites may again appear, since the new settlers may occupy completely different sites than their predecessors. An analysis of the percentage of sites occupied in one period that were occupied in the next may also yield ambiguous interpretations. If many sites were occupied in an era when a natural or man-made disaster struck, and far fewer sites were occupied in the following era, the percentage of reoccupied sites would be low; but this would mask the fact that most or all of the settlements of the second era were occupied from the preceeding era, and the level of continuity far higher than it seems.

10. See appendix 4.

11. M. Chisholm, *Rural Settlement and Land Use: An Essay in Location* (London, 1962; new ed. 1968), 43–66; J. Bintliff, *Natural Environment and Human Settlement in Prehistoric Greece,* British Archaeological Reports, Suppl. ser. 28, vol. 1 (Oxford, 1977), 112.

12. As is so well demonstrated by A. Ellison and J. Harriss, "Settlement and Land Use in the Prehistory and Early History of Southern England, A Study Based on Locational Models," pp. 911–62 in *Models in Archaeology,* ed. D. L. Clarke (London, 1972).

13. See chap. 4, p. 67.

14. Bintliff, *Natural Environment,* 104–33. The high proportion of sites with alluvium in their microenvironments (although present in only miniscule amounts) indicates a high percentage of coastal sites and also the settlements along major routes of communication which followed alluvial river valleys.

15. R. Chevallier, "Pour une interprétation archéologique de la couverture aérienne grecque: Note sur les centuriations romains de Grèce," *BCH* 82 (1958): 635–36.

16. Carthage: Diodorus Siculus, 20.8.3–4; Rome: Varro, *De Re Rustica* 1.16.3; Pliny, *Natural History* 18.29; Cato, *De Agricultura* 1.2.4–5; Jerusalem: Josephus, *Bellum Judaicum* 5.57, 107; Athens: A. French, *The Growth of the Athenian Economy,* (New York, 1964), 131–32, 193 n. 39. Cf. Plutarch, *Aratus* 7.2, 8.1 for Sikyon. See also M. H. Jameson, "Agriculture and Slavery in Classical Athens," *Classical Journal* 73 (1977–78): 126–30.

17. These are Kokkinovrisi (Wiseman, *LAC,* 84); Beyevi (*LAC,* 82); Pano Maghoula (*LAC,* 72–74); Spathovouni (*LAC,* 110); Southeast Suburb (*LAC,* 88); and Anaploga (*Hesperia* 41 [1972]: 332f). All these sites are partially or fully excavated and their functions known.

18. E.g., at Heraeum (*LAC,* 33), if indeed the structures represent a farmhouse and not buildings related to the sanctuary. For the size, function, and identity of the settlements in the outer zone, see Wiseman, *LAC,* and appendix 1 in this volume.

19. Even Hesiod (*Works and Days* 618f.) has advice for the peasant wishing to transport some of his goods to the market by ship.

20. In Rome, for example, the rent for a villa on the outskirts of the city was 11,500 sesterces (HS) per *iugerum,* or about 5 HS per square meter, over ten times the average rental price of land in Italy. See R. P. Duncan-Jones,"An Epigraphic

Survey of Costs in Roman Italy," *Papers of the British School at Rome* 33 (1965): 224–25; R. P. Duncan-Jones, *The Economy of the Roman Empire* (Cambridge, 1974), 345–46.

21. W. Alonso, "A Theory of the Urban Land Market," p. 155f. in *Internal Structure of the City*, ed. L. S. Bourne (New York, 1971).

22. Varro, *Rust.*, 1.16.3; Pliny, *NH*, 18.29; Cato, *Agri.*, 1.2.4–5; Finley, *AE*, 107.

23. See n. 20.

24. Chisholm, *Rural Settlement*, 43–66, 111–34.

25. Finley, *AE*, 107–10: "Lacking the techniques by which to calculate, and then to choose among, the various options, for example the relative economic merits of growing or buying the barley for slaves and the stakes for vines; lacking the techniques by which to calculate the relative profitability, under given conditions, of one crop or another, or of agriculture and pasturage . . . the landowners of antiquity operated by tradition, habit, and rule-of-thumb" (p. 110). This statement contradicts the Roman agrarian writers cited in n. 22, but also Finley's statement on p. 107 that farmers living close to urban markets produce specialty cash crops for the market. How would they know enough to grow specialty crops if they lacked any means of calculating profit? Why did ancient farmers behave as farmers in capitalist countries who grow for markets and not for subsistence? See also G. E. M. de Ste. Croix, "Greek and Roman accounting," p. 38 in *Studies in the History of Accounting*, ed. A. C. Littleton and B. S. Yamey (London, 1956). Of what value is it to learn that Greek and Roman agriculture was no more or less profitable than other agricultural systems before 1770? There are a considerable number of passages in Roman authors that show a knowledge of the need to balance revenues and expenditures: Suetonius, *Domitianus* 12.1; Tacitus, *Annales* 1.11, 78; 13.50; 15.18. One could add many other examples. At the risk of belaboring the obvious, how could Greek and Roman farmers remain in business for so many centuries if they had no knowledge of profit and loss?

26. G. Mickwitz, "Economic Rationalism in Graeco-Roman Agriculture," *English Historical Review* 52 (1937): 584, on the basis of Cato, *Agri.* 1.2.4, and Pliny, *NH* 18.29, and other passages. Mickwitz was writing in reaction to those who claimed that Roman agriculture was "capitalistic" or "scientific."

27. H. N. Fowler and R. Stillwell, *Corinth* 1.1, 23; F. Sage Darrow, "Corinth from Mummius to Herodes Atticus" (Ph.D. diss., Harvard University, 1906), 80, 131; Strabo, 8.6.22. Cleonae was not part of the Corinthia during the Roman era, (*RE*, s.v. Kleonai, 728). Where there is doubt about the precise boundary, I have chosen the line that gives the largest area. I measured the Corinthia by dividing it up into geometric shapes, usually triangles, calculated the areas, and added them up.

28. A. Philippson, *Griechische Landschaften*, Bd. 3, t. 1 (Berlin, 1959), 3:71–161, 1:948–64; J. Salmon, *Wealthy Corinth: A History of the City to 338* B.C. (Oxford, 1984), 23. This area is similar to the amount of land under cultivation in the towns and villages of the modern nome of the Corinthia that were also included in the area of the ancient city-state (the modern nome is considerably larger than the ancient city-state). See M. Sakellariou and N. Faraklas, *Corinthia-Cleonaea* (Athens, 1971), appendix 1, from the 1961 agricultural census of Greece.

29. Bintliff, *Natural Environment*, 1:51–74.

30. The yield rates are based on A. Jardé, *Les céréales dans l'antiquité, grecque* (Paris, 1925), 31–60; C. Starr, *The Economic and Social Growth of Early Greece* (Oxford, 1977), 153–55. Cf. Salmon, *Wealthy Corinth,* 130; Jameson, "Agriculture and Slavery," 130–31. The figure also assumes a ratio of 1: 3 for the return on seed or a net yield of 12 hectoliters per hectare (13.3 bushels per acre), a weight of 61.8 kilograms per hectoliter (45 pounds per bushel), and a two-field system where only half the acreage is under cultivation in a given year. Yield rates in Greece were lower than in other parts of the Empire (e.g., Italy), where climate and soil conditions were better. Barley is the crop most suitable for arid regions such as the Corinthia and Attica (Jameson, p. 130). One kilogram of whole, hulled barley contains 2,158 calories and approximately 2,600 calories per day are needed on average for an individual, amounting to 1.2 kilograms per day; 438 kilograms per year; or about 7 hectoliters (L. Foxhall and H. A. Forbes, "*Sitometreia,*" *Chiron* 12 [1982]: 41–90). One hectare will produce a *net* yield of 12 hectoliters of barley (741.6 kilograms) and in a two-field system (where one-half the hectare is out of production in any year) one hectare will produce 6 hectoliters per year, or 370.8 kilograms. Since each person needs 438 kilograms per year, then he will need the produce of about 1.17 hectares, or 2.9 acres of land planted in barley. If the Corinthia contains 20,700 cultivable hectares and each person needs 1.17 hectares of land, then 17,600 people can be supported. Wheat has a higher caloric value than barley, but since its gross yield is only about one half that of barley, far fewer people could be supported from a wheat crop than a barley crop. Salmon estimated (p. 130) that an average individual needed 3 hectoliters of barley per year, or 185.4 kilograms. However, this provides only 1,100 calories per individual per day, far below the starvation level. The 1.2 kilograms of grain used per individual per day (438 kilograms per year) includes grain that was used to feed farm animals, wasted, spoiled, or that went for other purposes. E. R. Wolf, in *Peasants* (Englewood Cliffs, N.J., 1966), 4–6, notes that many peasants in preindustrial societies regularly set aside about one quarter of their production for the feeding of farm animals. It has been estimated that another quarter of gross production is wasted in subsistence agriculture (A. Keys, "Minimum Subsistence," pp. 27–39 in *The Population Ahead,* ed. R. G. Francis [Minneapolis, 1958]). C. Clark and M. Haswell (*The Economics of Subsistence Agriculture* [London, 1970], 148) note that farm laborers living virtually on the margins of human of existence in Uganda spend only 55 percent of their income on food. No doubt someone will recall that old Cincinnatus the dictator supported himself and his family from a 4-*iugera* farm (2.5 acres or 1 hectare [Livy 3.26.8]), but I for one do not believe it. Also, some allotments given to Roman colonists were small, and in this respect they are like the ration figures given for ancient soldiers in some of our sources. Since the rations that were recorded were barely adequate to support a human life, the soldier was required to supplement them. Similarly, the colonist must have been expected to supplement his income through a trade or animal husbandry. The way I have derived the minimum allotment is to see how much food it takes to keep a human being alive and then calculate how much land it takes to grow this amount of food. Perhaps someone will show me a better way.

31. Some individuals may prefer a lower level of subsistence for the ancient

Greek and Roman farmer based on comparisons with Bangladesh or similar modern nations where starvation, malnutrition, deprivation, and high mortality rates are the norms. However, there may be some reason to question such comparisons.

32. See chap. 4 for the estimate of Corinth's population. Of the 100,000 or so individuals, some 80,000 seem to have lived in the city, and 20,000 in the country.

33. Using the yield rates and nutritional requirements already discussed. In a two-field system, 58 square kilometers (22 square miles) would be under cultivation in any given year at a net yield (gross yield minus seed) of 12 hectoliters per hectare. This would provide 69,600 hectoliters (78,300 bu.) per year × ca. 62 kg. per hectoliter (45 lbs. per bu) = 4,315,200 kg./yr. ÷ the 438 kg. (964 lbs.) consumption per person per year = 9,852 people.

34. These figures were obtained by measurement. The area of the Corinthian Gulf included in a circle with a radius of four miles with the center of Corinth as its center was obtained by drawing such a circle over a map and then measuring the area over water. The area of the city of Corinth enclosed by its walls was 840 hectares, or 3.24 square miles, most of which was probably occupied by buildings (see chap. 4). The area occupied by Lechaion and the built-up area between Lechaion and Corinth was about 2 square kilometers (.77 square miles). The area occupied by wasteland was determined by the use of a 30″ × 30″ Landsat satellite photograph of the eastern Peloponnese produced by the EROS Data Center of the U.S. Geological Survey, Sioux Falls, South Dakota, and by photographs taken by the author in the summer of 1979. The areas of the Corinthia under cultivation, or occupied by scrub vegetation or forests, are clearly defined in the satellite photograph. The areas of scrub and forest were checked against my photographs for accuracy and then measured as carefully as possible on a map of the region.

35. I have timed numerous walks to various destinations in the Corinthia from the approximate center of the ancient city to obtain these figures. A detour west around Pentaskouphi to the cultivated areas south of the city took about two hours (one way) and a detour around the eastern flank of Acrocorinth took about 1.5 hours. I walked the most direct routes I could find along modern roads and footpaths.

36. Finley, *AE,* 106; A. Burford Cooper, "The family Farm in Greece," *Classical Journal* 73 (1977–78): 164–68; J. Crook, *Law and Life of Rome* (Ithaca, N.Y., 1967), 118–32; A. R. W. Harrison, *The Law of Athens* (Oxford, 1968), 130–55.

37. Crook, *Law and Life,* 104; Harrison, *The Law of Athens,* 46.

38. Chisholm, *Rural Settlement,* 56–59, 113–15; K. Thompson, *Farm Fragmentation in Greece* (Athens, 1963); E. Friedl, *Vasilika: A Village in Modern Greece* (New York, 1963), 8, 48–68.

39. Chisholm, *Rural Settlement,* 43–66; J. M. Wagstaff, *Aspects of Land Use in Melos* (University of Southampton, 1976). Wagstaff has shown that the use of *spitaikia,* small dwellings located on the farthest parcels of the farmer's land and occupied only during seasons of maximum labor output, have extended the range of agricultural production for individual farmers on Melos. Nevertheless, even with the use of *spitaikia,* the mean distance between the farmer's home and his most distant field was found to be two hours, or about 10 kilometers. The national average distance is 2.5 kilometers, or a 30-minute journey (Wagstaff, 18). Moreover, as far as I can determine, there is no literary or archaeological evidence of the use of

these structures in antiquity (Laertes' estate in *Odyssey* 24 is obviously quite large). The use of these structures on Melos may have been determined by the relatively large distances between villages on that island. The question of how the use of *spitaikia* may have varied from village to village in Melos was not answered. Were they found in fields devoted to labor-intensive crops (as can be observed in the fruit- and vine-growing areas of the Corinthia), or did their use depend on distances to neighboring villages, or the local topography (hills, bays, etc.) which intervened between the farmer and his fields?

40. Kingsley Davis, ed., *Cities: Their Origin, Growth, and Human Impact* (San Francisco, 1973), 12. He considered only the time-distance problems involved.

41. As a community in a Roman province, Corinthians would ordinarily be responsible for the land tax of 10 percent of gross production, except during A.D. 67–69, when the province of Achaea was granted "freedom" by Nero, and when the community received special dispensations from the emperor. In general, see J. A. O. Larsen, "Roman Greece," pp. 440–41, 458–59 in vol. 4 of *An Economic Survey of Ancient Rome,* ed. T. Frank (Baltimore, 1938). See B. D. Merit, *Corinth* 8.1, no. 80, for a tax exemption granted to Corinth through the efforts of Gn. Cornelius Pulcher during the reign of Hadrian; and see appendix 5 for rents.

42. For the accumulation of large estates by a few wealthy individuals in the empire, see Finley, *AE,* 98–113; A. H. M. Jones, *The Roman Economy* (Oxford, 1974), 130; John Day, *An Economic History of Athens under Roman Domination* (New York, 1942), 322–37.

43. K. D. White. *Roman Farming* (Ithaca, N.Y., 1970), 404–5; cf. Finley, *AE,* 107. Interesting in this context is Aristotle's comment (*Pol.* 6.5.13, 1323A) that the poor, presumably including many farmers, do not own slaves. Pliny the Younger found it better to use tenants than chained slaves on his farms (*Ep.* 3.19).

44. See n. 30.

45. Paul Graindor, *Un Milliadaire antique, Hérode Atticus et sa famille* (Cairo, 1930), 52–54, 66, 88, 121, 131–32; B. D. Merit, *Corinth* 8.1, nos. 85, 86.

46. B. D. Merit, *Corinth* 8.1, no. 15. No doubt, some of the horses transported from overseas cities did not take the voyage well. Cf. Philostratus, *Vita Apollonii* 8.7.4; Lucian, *Adversus Indoctum* 5.

47. Paul, Acts 18:3; Edgar Goodspeed, *Paul* (New York, 1961), 18. On cattle, see James Wiseman, "The Gymnasium Area at Corinth, *Hesperia* 41 (1972): 19; on pigs, Ronald S. Stroud, "The Sanctuary of Demeter and Kore on Acrocorinth," *Hesperia* 37 (1968): 300; regarding goatherds, Kent, *Corinth* 8.3, nos. 556, 587.

48. Recorded in the 1961 agricultural census of Greece and found in Sakellariou and Faraklas, *Corinthia-Cleonaea* (Athens, 1971), appendix 1, pp. 4–18.

49. Bintliff, *Natural Environment,* 1:113–14. Fishhooks have been found in the city and piscinas have been found in Cenchreae: Davidson, *Corinth* 12, 190; R. Scranton, et al., *Kenchreai* 1 (Leiden, 1978), 1, 16, 25f.; cf. West, *Corinth* 8.2, no. 125.

50. Despite all the ancient evidence that Corinth's economy was based on trade (see chap. 3, nn. 32–34), Salmon, in his otherwise excellent book, improbably suggests it was based on agriculture (p. 153).

51. Argos, Thessalonica, Byzantium, Nicomedia, Heraclea, Sinope, Ephesus,

Miletus, Rhodes, Tarsus, Sidon, Tyre, Gaza, Cyrene, Carthage, Gades, Massilia, Ostia, Puteoli, Neapolis, Messana, Syracuse, Brundisium, Ravenna, Aquileia, and Dyrrachium come to mind. It will be argued in the conclusion that virtually all cities in the classical era should be removed from this category.

52. O. Broneer, *Corinth* 4.2; Judith Perlzweig, *The Athenian Agora,* vol. 7: *Lamps of the Roman Period* (Princeton, 1961); K. S. Garnett, "Late Roman Corinthian Lamps from the Fountain of the Lamps," *Hesperia* 44 (1975): 173–206; Philippe Bruneau, "Lampes corinthiennes," *BCH* 95 (1971): 437–501; P. Bruneau, "Lampes corinthiennes, II" *BCH* 101 (1977): 249–95. For lamp manufacturies in general, see W. V. Harris, "Roman Terracotta Lamps: The Organisation of an Industry," *Journal of Roman Studies* 70 (1980): 126–45.

53. Bruneau, "Lampes corinthiennes, II," 284–85; Broneer, *Corinth* 4.2, 88.

54. Broneer, *Corinth* 4.2, 88. The names are Karpos, Kreskens, Loukios, Markianos, Oktabios, Onesimos, Preimos, Sekoundos, and Zosimos.

55. Garnett, "Late Roman Corinthian Lamps," 186.

56. K. S. Wright, "Early Roman Terra Sigillata and Its Local Imitations from the Post-War Excavations at Corinth" (Ph.D. diss., Bryn Mawr College, 1977), esp. 453–73; D. C. Spitzer, "Roman Relief Bowls from Corinth," *Hesperia* 11 (1942): 162–69.

57. Wright, "Early Roman Terra Sigillata," 469.

58. O. Broneer, *Corinth* 10, 136.

59. Cicero, *In Verrem* 2.2.19; 2.4.23; 44, 59, 97–98; Cicero, *Tusculanae Disputationes* 2.14; Propertius 3.5.6; Petronius 50; Josephus, *Bel. Jud.* 5.201; Florus, 1.32; Plutarch, *De Pythiae oraculis,* p. 395C, D; Suetonius, *Divus Augustus* 70; Suetonius, *Tiberus* 34; Martial 9.59, 14.43; Pliny, *NH* 34.1–12, 34.48, 37.12; Pliny, *Ep.* 3.6.3; Athenaeus 4.128D, 5.199E; Orosius 5.3.

60. Pliny, *NH* 37.12; Florus, 1.32; Plutarch, *De Pyth, or.* 395C records two other stories in which the mixture "Corinthian Bronze" was discovered before the destruction of the city in 146 B.C.

61. Pliny, *NH* 37.12; Martial 14.43; Suetonius, *Aug.* 70; Josephus, *Bel. Jud.* 5.201; Propertius 3.5.6.

62. Pliny, *NH* 34.8.

63. Martial 9.59; Petronius 50; Pliny, *Ep.* 3.6.

64. Pausanias 2.3.3.

65. There was a bronze foundry near the Peribolos of Apollo in the first century B.C. (Stillwell, et al. *Corinth* 1.2, 273). See Wiseman, *CR,* 512; C. C. Mattusch, "Corinthian Metalworking, the Forum Area," *Hesperia* 46 (1977): 380–89, for other bronze-working operations in Corinth. For an attempt to identify objects of standard-alloy bronze manufactured in Corinth, see E. G. Pemberton, "The Attribution of Corinthian Bronze," *Hesperia* 50 (1981): 101–11. For bronze-working at the Isthmia (the objects contain 5 percent tin): W. Rostoker and E. R. Gebhard, "The Sanctuary of Poseidon at Isthmia: Techniques of Metal Manufacture," *Hesperia* 49 (1980): 347–63.

66. Walter Sullivan, "Testing of Relics Results in Surprises," *New York Times,* 24 May 1981 (Sunday), Science and Education section, p. 39, records a discovery by P. T. Craddock of a plaque consisting of an alloy of gold, silver, and copper, and purple in color. Craddock is recorded to have suggested that the plaque could be an

example of Corinthian Bronze. However, the deliberately produced dark purple color of the object is in striking contrast to the Corinthian Bronze described by our sources as having a color so similar to ordinary bronze that only connoisseurs could distinguish the difference through nuances of color and odor (above, n. 61). This find may be an example of Pliny's liver-colored bronze (*hepatizon*), dark red-brown in color, made from a mixture of secret ingredients (*NH* 34.8).

67. For Archimedes' discovery, see Vitruvius, *De Architectura* 9, intro., 9–12.

68. E. R. Caley, "The Corroded Bronze of Corinth," *Proceedings of the American Philosophical Society* 84 (1941): 689–761, esp. 709, 719, 759; T. L. Shear, "A Hoard of Coins Found in Corinth in 1930," *American Journal of Archaeology* 25 (1930): 139–151.

69. Cicero, *Verr.* 2.4.44; Caley, "The Corroded Bronze of Corinth," 709.

70. Caley, "The Corroded Bronze of Corinth," 709, 719, 757.

71. Ibid., 759; cf. Pliny, *NH* 34.144.

72. Pausanias 2.1.7–2.5.1. The famous statue of Armed Aphrodite seen by Pausanias in her temple on Acrocorinth was of bronze (O. Broneer, "Investigations at Corinth, 1946–1947," *Hesperia* 16 [1947]: 245). For the coins, see F. Imhoof-Blumer and P. Gardner, *Ancient Coins Illustrating Lost Masterpieces of Greek Art: A Numismatic Commentary on Pausanias* (Chicago, 1964), 10–27.

73. Petronius 50.

74. C. E. de Grazia, "Excavations of the American School of Classical Studies at Corinth: The Roman Portrait Sculpture" (Ph.D. diss., Columbia University, 1973), 15–37.

75. E. H. Swift, "A Group of Roman Imperial Portraits at Corinth," *American Journal of Archaeology* 25 (1921): 363; B. S. Ridgeway, "Sculpture from Corinth," *Hesperia* 50 (1981): 422–48.

76. E. Capps, Jr., "Pergamene Influence at Corinth," *Hersperia* 7 (1938): 552.

77. R. Carpenter, *Greek Sculpture* (Chicago, 1960), 248.

78. Capps, "Pergamene Influence at Corinth," 541.

79. Ibid., 544.

80. F. P. Johnson, *Corinth* 9, 2, 5; M. Sturgeon, *Corinth* 9.2.

81. S. S. Weinberg, *Corinth* 1.5, 74.

82. J. Jacobs, *The Economy of Cities* (New York, 1970), 160–69.

83. In modern cities, the proportion of jobs providing goods and services to the local economy, to jobs in production, importing, and exporting, varies from 21: 10 in New York City to 6: 10 in Oshkosh (Jacobs, *The Economy of Cities,* 162). Doubtless, there was much variation in antiquity.

84. See above, pp. 24f.; cf. A. French, *The Growth of the Athenian Economy* (New York, 1964), 131–32.

85. In the important article by K. Hopkins, *Economic Growth and Towns in Classical Antiquity," pp. 35–77 in Towns and Societies,* ed. P. Abrams and E. A. Wrigley (Cambridge, 1978).

86. Ibid., 52. In New England in the 1830s, before the widespread distribution of machine-manufactured cloth, only about half the households in rural areas had looms, according to an Old Sturbridge Village, Mass., spinning and weaving exhibit.

87. K. Hopkins, *Conquerors and Slaves* (Cambridge, 1978), 17. Hopkins de-

serves credit for quantifying these proportions which had never been explicitly examined before for the Greco-Roman world.

88. C. Clark and M. Haswell, *The Economics of Subsistence Agriculture* (London, 1970), 105–7.

89. For rents and taxes, see appendix 5.

90. Aristotle, *Politics* 1268a–b. Why has this passage been ignored for so long? Aristotle knew more about the ancient economy than we do. Why is he not read and cited more frequently?

91. Ibid., 1261b–1264a. How many millions of lives would have been saved if Aristotle's advice had been followed?

92. P. Garnsey and R. Saller, *The Roman Empire: Economy, Society, and Culture* (Berkeley, 1987), 111; R. Macmullen, "Peasants during the Principate," *ANRW* 2, no. 1 (1974): 253. Alternatively, rents could have been higher and the ancient city would have provided more goods and services to landlords than to tenants. In any event, there must have been a considerable agricultural surplus (at least through the third century A.D.) for tenants, peasants, and landlords to have absorbed the tripling of taxes, and for large cities such as Corinth (which ultimately depended on the agricultural surpluses produced by others) to have existed in antiquity.

93. E. A. Wrigley, *Population and History* (New York, 1976), 35, 52, 90–92, esp. 116–43.

94. Anecdotes and hasty generalizations are also imperfect sources from which to derive information concerning peasant surpluses. For example, J. K. Evans, "Wheat Production and its Social Consequences in the Roman World," *Classical Quarterly* 31 (1981): 428–42, tries to demonstrate that, in general, Roman agricultural surplus was limited. He asks (p. 435), "Do we possess, in the voluminous testimony to abortion, exposure, infanticide, and the sale of free-born children into slavery, evidence of one response to marginal food productivity among the Roman peasantry?" The answer is not necessarily. The fact that some families exposed their children and practiced contraception and abortion, does not mean that peasant surpluses were inadequate in general. Furthermore, because some children were enrolled in the *alimenta* program in Italy during the late first and early second centuries, this does not indicate that most families were poor. At best, all this type of data shows is that some people engaged in these practices and that some of them were poor; at worst, the same data can be used to demonstrate opposite conclusions. Welfare programs in modern, industrialized societies do not indicate comparative poverty, but rather a large economic surplus available in general in them. If a well-to-do peasant with ten children wants to limit the further growth of his family by the means available to him, this does not mean that the peasant is poor but that he wants to maintain his standard of living. Take the *alimenta* program at Velia, for example. Here, some 300 children were enrolled: 264 boys below the age of eighteen, and 36 girls below the age of fourteen—the average ages at marriage for boys and girls in the Roman population. Let us assume for the sake of argument that the population of Velia was 10,000, probably a considerable underestimate, since Velia was a substantial city (R. Stillwell, et al., eds., *The Princeton Encyclopaedia of Classical Sites* [Princeton, 1976], s.v. Elea [Roman Velia]; P. C. Siestieri, "Greek Elea-Roman Velia," *Archaeology* 10 [1957]: 2–10), and had a life expectancy at birth of twenty-five years, similar to the Roman population as a whole (M. K.

Hopkins, "On the Probable Age Structure of the Roman Population," *Population Studies* 19 [1966]: 245–64). In such a population, the proportion of boys under eighteen years would be approximately 42 percent of all males, and the proportion of girls under fourteen years would be about 31 percent. If we assume that, as in all other stable populations, the ratio of males to females was about 1: 1, then for a population of 10,000; boys under eighteen would number 2,100 and girls under fourteen, 1,565, or a total of 3,665 (A. J. Coale and P. Demeny, *Regional Model Life Tables and Stable Populations* [Princeton, 1966], 30, 126). Hence, only eight percent of the boys and girls in the population would have been enrolled, a lower proportion than are enrolled in welfare programs in the United States. Far from showing that most families were poor, it shows that most were probably not poor and did not need assistance.

95. Jacobs, *The Economy of Cities*, 126; Finley, *AE*, 125; Finley, *AC*, 326.

96. Finley, *AE*, 133–39; Hopkins, "Economic Growth," 47–48.

97. E. Pottier, Dar.-Sag. s.v. Corinthium Aes, 1507–1508, n. 19; Mau, *RE* s.v. Corinthium Aes, 1234.

98. Finley, *AE*, 74.

99. These are the names of the known manufacturers of Corinthian lamps collected by P. Bruneau ("Lampes corinthiennes, II," *BCH* 101 [1977]: 285).

## Chapter Three

1. For the city's religions, see chapter 5.

2. By my count, he has listed twenty-four shrines, sanctuaries, and temples for Corinth, twenty-two for Argos, fifteen for Sikyon, six for Phlious, and two for Titane. Although not an exact enumeration of all the cults, the numbers do indicate the importance of religious services provided at Corinth compared to its neighbors. Pausanias has probably noted the most important temples and sanctuaries in the towns and cities he visited. For a more or less complete list of Corinthian cults, see R. Lisle, "The Cults of Corinth" (Ph.D. diss., Johns Hopkins University, 1955).

3. *Met.* 11.8–13. Whatever the historicity of his allegorical tale, Apuleius seems to have been an acute observer of Corinth and the Corinthians. Whenever his comments on the city can be checked against other sources, they are always in agreement. He casually mentioned the correct distance between Corinth and Cenchreae as 6 miles, and noted the shrines of Isis and Serapis at Corinth and alluded to the one in Cenchreae. His description of the doddering old man seated on the rump of a donkey with wings glued to his shoulders in the procession of Isis would immediately be recognized by Corinthians as Bellerophon and Pegasus, whose myth was localized in the city, and the pair figure prominently on municipal coinage and in statues in the city. The performances in the theater (10.29–32) with the patron goddess of the city, Venus, entering the stage to cheers from the audience could have been the description of an actual eyewitness. The duovir going to Thessaly to procure gladiators and wild beasts to be hunted in the theater agrees with what is known of Corinthians' love of such contests. The duovir himself, Thiasos, may have been an actual person, his name (an uncommon one) is found in an inscription from Epidaurus (*IG* 4.1.688). His correct naming of the city as *colonia Corinthiensis* (10.35) is a further indication of his accuracy, until recently the name

was thought to be Corinthus (O. Broneer, "Colonia Laus Julia Corinthiensis," *Hesperia* 10 [1941]: 388–90). Apuleius differs from the findings of modern scholarship in only one detail: his account of the theater being used as an amphitheater in the mid-second century, while the excavator proposed a date for its conversion in the reign of Caracalla. However, the evidence is meager, and, once again, Apuleius may be correct.

4. Cf. Acts 19:23–41; Pliny, *Ep.* 10.97.

5. South Basilica and Julian Basilica: Weinberg, *Corinth* 1.5; Wiseman, *CR,* 515; Lechaion Road Basilica: *Corinth* 1, 193–211; Wiseman, *CR,* 517.

6. Hopkins, "Taxes and Trade," 101–10.

7. Demetrius of Corinth: Tacitus, *Historiae* 4.40; Lucian, *Adversus Indoctum* 10; Seneca, *Epistulae* 20, 62; *De Vita Beata* 18; *De Providentia* 3.3, 5.5; Philostratus, *VA* 4.25; *Ep.* 36, 37; Aristeides: *For Poseidon,* 23; Apollonius of Tyana: Philostratus, *VA.* 4.25, 7.10; Dio Chrysostum: *Orationes* 31.121; Plutarch: *Quaestiones convivales* 8.4; cf. 9.5

8. Dio Chrysostum (Favorinus), *Or.* 37.8.

9. Weinberg, *Corinth* 1.5, 10–13; Wiseman, *CR,* 514.

10. Aristeides, *For Poseidon* 24; cf. Lucian, *Ind.* 5, *Verae Historiae* 17, 29, *Herodotus* 1.

11. Aristeides, Lucian, ibid.; Dio Chrysostum (Favorinus), *Or.* 37.8; Plutarch, *Quaest. conv.* 8.4.1.

12. Plutarch, *Quaest. conv.* 5.3.1–3 (675d–677b). Reprinted from Plutarch, *Moralia,* vol. 8, trans. P. A. Clement and H. B. Hoffleit (Cambridge, Mass., 1969).

13. Plutarch, *Quaest. conv.* 8.4.1–5 (723a–724b). Trans. P. A. Clement and H. B. Hoffleit.

14. J. C. Biers, *Corinth* 17; Wiseman, *CR,* 527.

15. Roebuck, *Corinth* 14; Wiseman, *CR,* 510–11.

16. Kent, *Corinth* 8.3, no. 206.

17. *CIG* 1, no. 106.

18. Galen, *De Anat. Admin.* 1.1; Kent, *Corinth* 8.3, no. 300, for the doctor and poet Thrasippus.

19. Stillwell, *Corinth* 2, 135; Wiseman, *CR,* 521.

20. Apuleius, *Met.* 10.29–32.

21. Stillwell, *Corinth* 2, 135–37; Wiseman, *CR* 521.

22. Broneer, *Corinth* 10; Wiseman, *CR,* 527. The odeum was remodeled in the late second century and the expense was paid by Herodes Atticus (Philostratus, *Vitae Sophistarum* 2.551).

23. Dio Chrysostum, *Or.* 31.121.

24. Julian, *Epistulae* 28.

25. *Corinth* 1.1, 80–81, 89–90; Anon., *Expositio Totius Mundi et Gentium* 52, in K. Muller, *Geographi Graeci Minores* (Paris, 1882), 524.

26. 1 Corinthians 5–7.

27. Aristeides, *For Poseidon* 23. Cf., Dio Chrysostum 8.9, for the Isthmian Games during the Greek era.

28. Aerial surveys in Attica and Rhodes suggest that considerably more land in those areas was cultivated in antiquity than in 1956 (J. Bradford, "Fieldwork on

Aerial Discoveries in Attica and Rhodes," *Antiquaries Journal* 36 (1956): 57–69, 172–80. If the same were true for Corinth, it would be an indication of high ancient demand. I am grateful to an anonymous referee for pointing this out to me.

29. E. A. Wrigley, *Population and History* (New York, 1976), 61–106, and chap. 4 below. See also E. A. Wrigley, "Parasite or Stimulus: The Town in a Preindustrial Economy," pp. 295–309 in *Towns in Societies,* ed. P. Abrams and E. A. Wrigley (Cambridge, 1978).

30. If the Corinthians followed the admittedly unpopular policy of Vespasian, who charged the fullers a fee for using the contents of urinals for their work (Suetonius, *Vesp.* 23).

31. See appendix 1.

32. Strabo 8.6.20 (reprinted from *The Geography of Strabo,* trans. H. L. Jones [New York, 1932]); cf. Aristeides 27.7. Hopkins has shown that trade during the Roman era was more extensive than commonly believed, especially for metals, cloth, and luxury items ("Economic Growth," 39–59). Moreover, the average interannual variation in the size of wheat crops in the modern nations which are the successor states to the Roman Empire is 28 percent (p. 48). This implies a considerable trade from regions with a surplus to those with poor harvests in any given year. It is also true that there would be an immense trade between those regions which consistently produced surpluses for sale on the market, such as Egypt, Sicily, and southern Russia, and large cities such as Corinth where there would always be a chronic shortage of grain produced locally.

33. For the routes, see Wiseman, *LAC,* 17–37, 113–25.

34. Strabo 8.2.1, cf. 8.6.22; Pliny, *NH* 4.10; Dio Cassius 51.5; Meritt, *Corinth* 8.1, no. 1; cf. Thucydides 3.15.1, 8.7, 8.8.3; Polybius 5.101.4, 4.19.7; Mela 2.3.

35. Strabo 8.6.20.

36. Acts 27, on Paul's journey from western Crete to the Adriatic.

37. Table 6 taken from E. N. Borza, "Alexander's Communications," *Ancient Macedonia* 2 (1973): 295–303.

38. Aristeides, *For Poseidon* 23; Strabo 8.6.20; Dio Chrysostom (Favorinus), 37.8; Apuleius, *Met.* 10.35; and chap. 2, nn. 1 and 2.

39. The city was even called "a merchant ship," by Aristeides (*Poseidon*), and "the prow and stern of Greece," by Dio Chrysostom (Favorinus) 37.36. Favorinus also wrote, "For you have accorded me this honor, not as one of the many who each year put in at Cenchreae as traders, tourists, envoys or passing travelers, but as to a cherished friend" (37.8). See Lucian, *Dialogi Mortuorum* 21 (11), for a wealthy Corinthian of the Greek era who owns a fleet of merchant ships. There were doubtless many such individuals in the Greek and Roman city.

40. Cicero, *De Republica* 2.3. That this was a commonplace does not make it any less true.

41. F. S. Darrow, "The History of Corinth from Mummius to Herodes Atticus" (Ph.D. diss., Harvard University, 1906), 43, 86; cf., Dio Cassius 51.5.2; Strabo 8.6.20.

42. Ovid: *Tristia* 1.10.9; 1.11.5; Propertius: 3.21.19–22 (an imaginary voyage); Apuleius: *Met.* 10.18–11.25 and n. 103; Apollonius of Tyana: *Vita A.* 4.25, 7.10; Plutarch: *Quaest. conv.* 8.4, 5.3; Agrippa: Dio Cassius, 50.13.5; Avillius Flaccus: Philo, *In Flaccem* 154–5; Augustus: Dio Cassius, 51.5.2; Titus: Tacitus, *Hist.* 2.1;

Hadrian: Aurelius Victor, *De Caesaribus, Ep.* 14.2; Lucius Verus: *SHA Verus,* 6.9; cf. Pausanias 2.3.5; Wiseman, *CR,* 511.

43. Aristeides, *Poseidon,* 23.

44. For the Games, see Meritt, *Corinth* 8.1, nos. 14–17; Kent, *Corinth* 8.3, 28–30, nos. 152, 153, 272; W. R. Biers and D. J. Geagan, "A New List of Victors in the Caesarea at Isthmia," *Hesperia* 39 (1970): 79–93; and chapter 5 in this volume. Victors came from as far as Sardinia, Syracuse, Alexandria, Antinoöpolis in Egypt, Caesarea, Laodicea, Miletus, Ephesus, and many other locations in Greece and the eastern Mediterranean.

45. For the comparative numbers of Corinthian coin types depicting different divinities, see chapter 5, p. 96ff.

46. T. L. Donaldson, *Architectura Numismatica* (Chicago, 1965); M. J. Price and B. Trell, *Coins and Their Cities* (Detroit, 1977).

Corinth was not the only city to depict its attractions on coins. Ephesian coins dating to the Imperial era frequently portray the great temple of Artemis, and Alexandrian coins the Pharos Lighthouse, another of the Seven Wonders of antiquity. The temple of Hera at Samos, Astarte at Byblos, the Acropolis and the theater of Dionysus at Athens were also portrayed on municipal coins of the Roman era. The greatest attractions of various cities were portrayed on their coins, not abstract symbols or mottoes. They would remind the owner of the famous monuments to be seen; many of them still attract modern tourists in great numbers.

47. The quantities of coins given in tables 7–10 represent over 95 percent of all coins found and recorded in the city from the Roman era, and constitute a valid sample from which legitimate conclusions can be drawn. Very few of Corinth's coins were found in hoards dating from the Roman era, and the few hoards that were found seem to have been hastily assembled in a time of hurried flight—the threat of a sack or earthquake—during the late Empire. This means that Corinth's coins provide a good indication of the coins actually in circulation in the city, and not those saved in hoards because of their intrinsic value. The autonomous coins minted by municipal mints are called "Greek Imperials" in the numismtic literature, but this is a confusing term for the general reader, since one is not sure whether they are coins minted by the imperial government in Greek municipalities or Greek municipal coinage minted in the Imperial era. The coins in the table are from Edwards, *Corinth* 6; K. M. Edwards, "Report on the Coins Found in the Excavations at Corinth during the Years 1930–1935." *Hesperia* 6 (1937): 241–56; J. Harris, "Coins Found at Corinth," *Hesp.* 10 (1941): 143–62; C. K. Williams and J. E. Fisher "Corinth 1970: Forum Area," *Hesp.* 40 (1971): 45–46; C. K. Williams and J. E. Fisher, "Corinth, 1971: Forum Area," *Hesp.* 41 (1972): 143–84; C. K. Williams and J. E. Fisher, "Corinth, 1972: The Forum Area," *Hesp.* 42 (1973): 1–44; C. K. Williams, J. E. Fisher, and J. MacIntosh, "Excavations at Corinth, 1973," *Hesp.* 43 (1974), 1–76; C. K. Williams and J. E. Fisher, "Corinth, 1974: Forum Southwest," *Hesp.* 44 (1975): 1–50; J. E. Fisher, "Coins: Corinth Excavations, 1976, Forum Southwest," *Hesp.* 49 (1980): 1–29; A. E. Beaton and P. Clement, "The Date of the Destruction of the Sanctuary of Poseidon on the Isthmus of Corinth," *Hesp.* 45 (1976): 267–79; R. L. Hohlfelder, *Kenchreai* 3; J. Dengate, *Hesp.* 50 (1981): 147–88; C. K. Williams and O. H. Zervos, *Hesp.* 51 (1982): 115–63;

J. E. Fisher, *Hesp.* 53 (1984): 217–50; C. K. Williams and O. H. Zervos, *Hesp.* 54 (1985): 55–96; C. K. Williams and O. H. Zervos, *Hesp.* 55 (1986): 129–83; O. H. Zervos, *Hesp.* 55 (1986): 183–205.

48. M. Thompson, *The Athenian Agora 2, Coins from the Roman through the Venetian Period* (Princeton, 1954), 83.

49. Also seen at Athens (ibid., 83).

50. Pausanias 2.3.5; W. R. Biers, "Water from Stymphalos," *Hesperia* 47 (1978): 171–84.

51. Pausanias 1.44.10.

52. For inflation see Jones, *Roman Economy,* 187–227; Hopkins, "Economic Growth," 39–41; C. H. V. Sutherland, *Roman Coins* (New York, 1974), 215–54; R. Reece, "Roman Coinage in the Western Empire," *Britannia* 4 (1973): 227–51.

53. Only a small proportion of Corinth's coins have their denominations recorded. Nevertheless, since whether coin denominations were recorded or not in a given catalogue depends on the person making the catalogue, it does not seem that the recorded denominations show any systematic bias for or against any particular denomination, and hence, those recorded are probably a representative sample.

54. I. Hodder and R. Reeece, "A Model for the Distribution of Coins in the Western Roman Empire," *Journal of Archaeological Science* 4 (1977): 1–18, have noted a similar trend in the distribution of sesterces in the West.

55. L. C. West, *Gold and Silver Standards in the Roman Empire, Numismatic Notes* 94 (New York, 1941); G. C. Boon, "Counterfeiting in Roman Britain," *Scientific American* 246 (December 1974): 121–30.

56. Dio Cassius 78.14.3–4. The purity of the silver was simple to measure by the principle of specific gravity discovered by Archimedes.

57. Sutherland, *Roman Coins,* 225.

58. D. Sperber, "Costs of Living in Roman Palestine, IV" *Journal of the Economic and Social History of the Orient* 13 (1970): 1–15.

59. E.g., by J. Harris, "Coins Found at Corinth," *Hesperia* 10 (1941): 159; Edwards, *Corinth* 6, 10; Hohlfelder, *Kenchreai* 3.

60. The price of one pound of gold increased from 96 denarii in the early second century to 50,000 denarii in the fourth century (Jones, *Roman Economy,* 200–225). This is called inflation, not prosperity.

61. D. J. MacDonald, "Aphrodisias and Currency in the East, A.D. 259–305," *American Journal of Archaeology* 78 (1974): 279–80.

62. Ibid., 283–86; Thompson, *The Athenian Agora 2,* 10–59.

63. At least, there is no recorded evidence for such a change.

64. For example, if some interruption or interference of the transit trade between the Aegean and Sicily and Italy occurred, Corinth's entire economy would suffer. The decline would effect not only the poor who worked as stevedores, sailors, and ox drivers, but also the elite who owned or controlled the means of distributing goods and transport services. They owned the dwellings in which travelers, sailors, and tourists would rent rooms; teams of oxen and mules to transport goods and ships across the isthmus; warehouses; and the ships themselves. Such a small portion of Corinth's economy was dependent on agriculture in any era of classical history, its elite must have been engaged in commercial and manufacturing activi-

ties, if only through ownership of the means of production and distribution. Such interference seems to have been caused by Corcyra in the mid-fifth century B.C., if not earlier, and I hope to analyze this problem in detail in a future publication.

65. Rooms for rent: Dio Chrysostum 8.4 (Greek period); food preparers and sellers: Alciphron 3.24.1; pickled vegetable merchant: Kent, *Corinth* 8.3, no. 551; fish and lobster catcher: Kent, *Corinth* 8.3, no. 551; pickle maker: Kent, *Corinth* 8.3, no. 540; poultrymen: Kent, *Corinth* 8.3, no. 542; food salesman: Kent, *Corinth* 8.3, no. 559; pheasant breeder: Kent, *Corinth* 8.3, no. 561; meat markets: West, *Corinth* 8.2, nos. 124–25; Kent, *Corinth* 8.3, no. 321; fullers: Kent, *Corinth* 8.3, no. 522; prostitutes: 1 Corinthians 6:15; entertainers: Apuleius, *Met.* 10.29–32; cf. Dio Chrysostum 8.9; innkeeper: Kent, *Corinth* 8.3, no. 525; taverns (*tabernae*, also called shops): West, *Corinth* 8.2, nos. 120, 185; Kent, *Corinth* 8.3, no. 324; bath attendents: Kent, *Corinth* 8.3, nos. 534, 547; barber: Kent, *Corinth* 8.3, no. 722; guide: Plutarch, *Quaest. conv.* 5.3. 110–12. For religious services, see chapter 5; doctors: nn. 16–18.

66. Teamster: Kent, *Corinth* 8.3, no. 530 (animals, harnesses, wagons, ropes, and containers were all necessary to haul ships and cargoes across the Isthmus, and if they were not produced by Corinthians, they would have to be imported); banker: Kent, *Corinth* 8.3, no. 722 (bottomry loans may have been used as a form of insurance); Plutarch, *De Vitando Aere Alieno* 831a.

67. Bronze manufacture: chap. 2, nn. 59–74; perfumes: Pliny, *NH* 13.5; Dioscorides 1.67; weaving and dyeing: Athenaeus 12.525D, cf. 1.27D; Dioscorides, 5.103.

68. Strabo 8.6.20.

69. Shipbuilding seems to have been an activity at Corinth during the Hellenistic era (Wiseman, *LAC,* 74, n. 21), and it may have been during the Roman era as well.

70. Tent makers: Acts 18:3. Some notion of the vast numbers of services offered to spectators of the Isthmian Games is given by Dio Chrysostum, who describes the scene in the fourth century B.C. during the time of Diogenes the Cynic: "That was the time too, when one could hear crowds of wretched sophists around Poseidon's temple shouting and reviling one another, and their disciples, as they were called, fighting with one another, many writers reading aloud their stupid works, many poets reciting thier poems while others applauded them, many jugglers showing their tricks, many fortune tellers interpreting fortunes, lawyers innumerable perverting justice, and not a few peddlers peddling whatever they happened to have" (8.6.9).

71. Kent, *Corinth* 8.3, nos. 158–64, 170, 177, 188, 227, 234–36, 238.

72. J. Paris, "Contributions à l'étude des ports antiques du monde Grec I. Notes sur Léchaion," *BCH* 39 (1915): 5–16; Wiseman, *LAC,* 87–88; R. Scranton, et al., *Kenchreai,* vol. 1 (Leiden, 1978), 14. J. Shaw in Scranton, et al., and Paris both measure the inner harbor of Lechaion as 10 hectares, while Paris measures the shelter of the outer harbor as 5 hectares, and Shaw, 1 hectare. From the plan of the harbor given in p. 7 of Paris's article, his measurement seems more accurate. Lechaion has a larger man-made harbor than Carthage (14 hectares) and it seems that only the great ports of Ostia (32.2 hectares), and Caesarea were larger among the man-made ports. Such a large port would not have been built unless it was justified

by a very great need. For the lighthouse depicted on a municipal coin, see Price and Trell, *Coins and Their Cities,* 84–85.

73. Apuleius, *Met.* 10.35; Pausanius 2.2.3; Romans 16:1. L. Ibrahim, et al., *Kenchreai* 2 (Leiden, 1976), 96, notes that one of the glass panels found in a building at Cenchreae dating to the late fourth century A.D. (panel 18) resembles a coin of Corinth from the reign of Antonius Pius depicting the port of Cenchreae. It may also be noted that the panel resembles the port of Cenchreae as actually excavated. The panel depicts a harbor scene with two prostyle podium temples on the ends of the two harbor moles, another temple in the left background, a warehouse stretching around the harbor, and on the left mole, two apparently semicircular buildings. The Corinthian coin depicting Cenchreae shows the two prostyle temples at the ends of both moles as on the panel, and the warehouses facing the harbor have been uncovered in excavations. The two semicircular buildings on the left mole in the panel are in exactly the same positions and are the same relative sizes as the two excavated apsidal buildings in the south mole of the harbor, which would appear semicircular, with their apses facing the viewer, from the perspective of the panel. The panel depicts the apsidal buildings just as they would appear from a ship entering the harbor, no doubt a familiar sight to many who saw the panels. The left-hand semicircular building has a wall between the apse and the side of the building with a door and a window (or two windows). From the angle of the windows, we see that the artist wished to depict them (and hence, the wall they were in) perpendicularly from the viewers' line of sight at the entrance of the harbor. The plan of the excavations of the south mole shows that the left-hand (or southernmost) building does indeed possess a wall between the apse and the side wall of the building which would be seen perpendicularly from the entrance of the harbor. The right-hand apsidal building possesses no such walls, and none are depicted on the panel.

74. Apuleius, *Met.* 10.35; nn. 7–8, 32–42.

75. Wiseman, *LAC.* The small ports of Schinos, Kaki Skala, Sterna on the Gulf of Corinth and Crommyon, Sidous, Schoenus (the eastern terminal of the *diolkos*), Kato Almyri, and Anthedus on the Saronic Gulf, were all inhabited in the Roman era.

76. For the *diolkos,* see Wiseman, *LAC,* 45–46; N. M. Verdelis, "Der Diolkos am Isthmus von Korinth," *Ath. Mit.* 71 (1956): 51–59; R. M. Cook, "Archaic Greek Trade: Three Conjectures," *Journal of Hellenic Studies* 99 (1979): 152–55; Fowler and Stillwell, *Corinth* 1.1, 49–55. Such an immense task of construction would not have been undertaken by an archaic Greek State with limited resources unless the need was real. See also, B. R. MacDonald, "The Dilokos," *Journal of Hellenic Studies* 106 (1986): 191–95.

77. For the capabilities of ancient heavy transport, see A. Burford, "Heavy Transport in Classical Antiquity," *Economic History Review* 13 (1960): 1–18, esp. 14.

78. L. Casson, *The Ancient Mariners* (New York, 1961), 119.

79. As Thorstein Veblen notes in *The Theory of the Leisure Class* (New York, 1953), since time immemorial the leisure class has distinguished itself by its ignorance of earning a livelihood. Any such knowledge is considered déclassé. This has led to a pronounced anti-economic bias in our literary sources, a bias that can be corrected with the help of archaeology.

80. The canal cut the *diolkos* diagonally, which is why the cut is 120 meters instead of 40 to 50 meters—the width of the canal. The cut could have been bridged or, more simply, filled in with stones and earth.

81. Pliny, *NH* 4.1; Hesychius, s.v. *diolkos;* Verdelis, "Der Diolkos."

82. For the canal, see Wiseman, *LAC,* 48–50; B. Gerster, "L'Isthme de Corinthe: Tentatives de percenant dans l'antiquité," *BCH* 8 (1884): 224–32; Fowler and Stillwell, *Corinth* 1.1, 55–59. Nero's attempt may be attributed to megalomania (but why not build a pyramid?); this cannot be said about Periander, Demetrius, Caesar, or Herodes. The numerous canals built to facilitate trade in the Roman era show an understanding of the importance of trade.

83. Tacitus, *Hist.* 2.8.9. A pretender who claimed to be Nero received considerable support in Achaea and Asia Minor, at least among some elements of the population.

84. For the functions of these structures, see R. E. Wycherly, *Athenian Agora,* vol. 3 (Princeton, 1957), 20–47; H. A. Thompson and R. E. Wycherly, *Athenian Agora,* vol. 14 (Princeton, 1972), 82–110; and O. Broneer, *Corinth* 1.4, 157–59, for the functions of the South Stoa at Corinth.

85. I have obtained this figure by measuring the roofed areas of these buildings on a plan of the city. While the measurements may not be accurate to the nearest square millimeter, they provide a good approximation of their sizes: North Market, 3,700 m$^2$; stoa surrounding Temple C, 672 m$^2$; West Shops, 1,420 m$^2$; Northwest Shops, 1,584 m$^2$; Central Shops, 552 m$^2$; South Stoa, 8,100 m$^2$; stoa south of Peirene, 240 m$^2$; Semicircular Building, 1,140 m$^2$; shops east of the Lechaion Road, 522 m$^2$; stoa around Temple E, 3,410 m$^2$; stoa west of Southeast Building, 150 m$^2$; stoa north of the Odeon, 1,031 m$^2$; stoa in front of the Theater, 702 m$^2$. These vast spaces for both Corinth and Athens, show the importance of services, for the urban populations and visitors combined.

86. The approximate areas are: Stoa of Attalos, 4,032 m$^2$; Middle Stoa, 2,610 m$^2$; Southeast Stoa, 550 m$^2$; shops in front of Library, 642 m$^2$; Stoa of Zeus, 616 m$^2$; Civic Offices, 427 m$^2$; Metroön stoa, 304 m$^2$; Royal Stoa, 136 m$^2$; East Building, 456 m$^2$; stoa south of the Panathenaic Way, 1,200 m$^2$; Roman Agora, 4,846 m$^2$; Stoa of Eumenes, 5,440 m$^2$.

87. Finley, *AE,* 137.

88. Kent, *Corinth* 8.3, 21, no. 504; Pausanias 2.3.5. Many of the dates in table 11 are approximate and the data taken from the standard publications in the *Corinth* series and preliminary reports in *Hesperia* and *Archaiologikon Deletion.* Buildings constructed by Emperors are not themselves an indication of the prosperity of a community, as the case of Athens shows.

89. Plutarch, *Pericles* 12.6–7, trans. Bernadotte Perrin (New York, 1916). Whether this statement represents the period of Pericles or a later era, and whether it was his intention to establish a public works program for indigent Athenians is immaterial here.

90. The Roman-style column base moldings are only found at Corinth in Greece and the eastern half of the Empire in general, and indicate that the city's marble workers were of Italian origin, working in Italian architectural traditions (L. Shoe, "The Roman Ionic Base at Corinth," pp. 300–304 in *Essays in Honor of Karl Lehmann,* ed. L. Freeman Sandler (New York, 1964).

91. W. L. McDonald, *Architecture of the Roman Empire* (New Haven, 1965), 210.

92. For transport costs of building materials, see A. Burford, "Heavy Transport in Classical Antiquity," 14–17; A. Burford, *The Greek Temple Builders at Epidauros* (Toronto, 1969), 185–206.

93. Aristeides, *Poseidon* 24.

94. For a mass grave of Corinthians slaughtered by Alaric, see T. Leslie Shear, "The Excavation of Roman Chamber Tombs at Corinth in 1931," *American Journal of Archaeology* 35 (1931): 424–41, esp. 434–35. For the destruction of Corinth's buildings, see table 11. Cf. Claudian 5.190, "burning Corinth . . . heated the waves of her two seas."

95. For the consequences of high taxation during the later Roman Empire, see Jones, *Roman Economy*, 82–84.

96. Ibid.

97. A. E. R. Boak, *Manpower Shortage and the Fall of the Roman Empire in the West* (New York, 1955). Cf. G. E. M. de Ste. Croix, *The Class Struggle in the Ancient Greek World* (Ithaca, N.Y., 1982), 453–503.

98. M. Rostovtzeff, *Social and Economic History of the Roman Empire* (Oxford, 1957), 174–78; Jacobs, *The Economy of Cities,* 176–79.

99. Cicero, *Rep.* 3.16; cf. Suetonius, *Dom.* 7.2.

100. F. W. Walbank, *The Awful Revolution: The Decline of the Roman Empire in the West* (Toronto, 1969).

## Chapter Four

1. Appian, *Punica* 136; Plutarch, *Caesar* 57.5; Dio Cassius 43.50.3–5; Strabo 8.6.23.

2. F. F. Abbott and A. C. Johnson, *Municipal Administration in the Roman Empire* (Princeton, 1926), 5. Three thousand colonists were sent to Carthage, which was reestablished in the same year as Corinth (Appian, *Pun.* 136).

3. Cicero, *Epistulae ad Atticum* 2.16.1; Suetonius, *Caesar* 20.3.

4. R. Chevallier, "Pour une interprétation archéologique de la courverture aérienne grecque: Note sur les centuriations romaines de Grece," *BCH* 82 (1958): 635–36.

5. S. Treggiari, *Roman Freedmen during the Late Republic* (Oxford, 1969), 106–10. See also Cicero, *De Lege Agraria* 1.2.5; Pausanias 2.2.2.

6. Treggiari, *Roman Freedmen,* 91–106; A. M. Duff, *Freedmen in the Early Roman Empire* (Oxford, 1928), 107–17. For the reaction of some Greek aristocrats to their new neighbors, see Crinagoras, *Greek Anthology* 9.284; Alciphron 3.24.

7. Treggiari, *Roman Freedmen,* 63–64.

8. Since the sons would be full Roman citizens.

9. Roman names in the late Republic usually had three parts. In the name Gaius Julius Caesar, Gaius is the *praenomen,* Julius the *nomen,* or family name, and Caesar, the *cognomen.* Roman slaves usually had Greek names, occasionally Latin names, often with distinctive erotic connotations or with connotations concerning luck or fortune (e.g., Philetos, Eutyches, and Eudaimon, for Greek names, and Amatus, Fortunatus, and Felix, for Latin names). When a slave was granted free-

dom, he took the praenomen and nomen of his former master or patron and retained his slave name as a cognomen. So, if a slave named Philetos was freed by Gaius Julius Caesar, his name would become Gaius Julius Philetos. Occasionally, inscriptions will preserve filiation or libertine status, although this is rarely the case at Corinth. For example, "G. Julius G. f. Caesar" means "Gaius Julius Caesar, the son of Gaius," and "G. Julius G. l. Philetos" means "Gaius Julius Philetos, the former slave of Gaius." A Greek granted Roman citizenship will have a name similar in form to a freedman with a Greek slave name. When Nicephorus was given citizenship by Julius Caesar, his name became Gaius Julius Nicephorus. Hence, it is often difficult to tell freedmen with Greek slave names apart from Greeks granted Roman citizenship by Roman magistrates unless filiation or libertine status is preserved. Greek names usually had two parts, a personal name, e.g., Hipparchos, and a patronymic, e.g., son of Theophilos. For the names of freedmen and Roman names in general, see Duff, *Freedmen,* 52–58; Treggiari, *Roman Freedmen,* 250–51.

10. Unfortunately, Nicephorus' name does not reveal filiation or libertine status, so it is not possible to determine his status with certainty. Nicephorus was not a common servile name. For the most up-to-date list of Corinthian magistrates as of the present writing, see Kent, *Corinth* 8.3, 24–31.

11. Abbot and Johnson, *Municipal Administration,* 87.

12. Ibid.; Kent, *Corinth* 8.3, 21, 28–31; cf. Apuleius, *Metamorphoses* 10.18.

13. For Babbius' life and career, see West, *Corinth* 8.2, no. 132; Kent, *Corinth* 8.3, 25, 27, nos. 155, 176, 259, 323. For the identification of the Babbius monument, see Scranton *Corinth* 1.3, 21–22, 72; *Hesperia* 44 (1975): 27.

14. For Cornelius' life and career, see Meritt, *Corinth* 8.1, 60–62, nos. 80–83; West, *Corinth* 8.2, 55–57, nos. 71–72; Kent, *Corinth* 8.3, 26, 31, nos. 138–43, 173, 223; A. J. Spawforth and S. Walker, "The World of the Panhellenion I: Athens and Eleusis," *Journal of Roman Studies* 75 (1985): 78–104, esp. 86–89.

15. Lamps: Broneer, *Corinth* 4.2, 88; pottery: K. D. Wright, "Early Roman Terra Sigillata and its Local Imitations from the Post-War Excavations at Corinth" (Ph.D. diss., Bryn Mawr College, 1977), 459–60.

16. L. Shoe, "The Roman Ionic Base at Corinth," pp. 300–304 in *Essays in Honor of Karl Lehmann,* ed. L. F. Sandler (New York, 1964); W. W. Cummer, "A Roman Tomb at Corinthian Cenchreae," *Hesperia* 40 (1971): 205–32. Lucy Shoe Meritt told me in 1973 that the Roman Ionic bases were more likely to have been the consequence of Italian marble-workers than Italian public tastes.

17. O. Broneer, "Colonia Laus Iulia Corinthiensis," *Hersperia* 10 (1941), 388–90. Festus, s.v. Corinthienses, p. 53, wrote: "They began to be called *Corinthienses* from the time they were led as colonists to Corinth—previously they were called *Corinthii*—just as we are still accustomed to call traders transacting business in foreign cities *Romanenses, Hispanenses,* or *Sicilienses.*"

18. Dio Chrysostum, *Orationes* 31.121; Julian, *Epistulae* 28.

19. For Eurycles and his family, see West, *Corinth* 8.2, no. 68; Kent, *Corinth* 8.3, no. 314; G. Bowersock, "Eurycles of Sparta," *Journal of Roman Studies* 51 (1961): 112–18.

20. Wiseman, *CR,* 493–96.

21. Strabo 8.6.22.

22. Jews: Acts 18:1–5; Anatolians: Kent, *Corinth* 8.3, no. 522; Phoenicians: Philostratus, *Vita Apollonii* 4.25.

23. Acts 18:1–5; Romans 16:1–3.

24. The high priest of Isis at Corinth had the theophoric name Mithras, according to Apuleius (*Met.* 11.25), and if genuine he may have been of Eastern origin, since the cult of Mithra and theophoric names based on Mithra are uncommon in mainland Greece.

25. Dio Chrysostum (Favorinus), 37.26.

26. Table 12 is taken from Kent, *Corinth* 8.3, 19. Inscriptions found subsequent to the publication of this splendid volume in 1966 have not altered the general trend.

27. Evidence for the tombstones has been taken from Meritt, *Corinth* 8.1; West, *Corinth* 8.2; and Kent, *Corinth* 8.3. Since they are difficult to date, there is no overlap with the dated inscriptions in table 12.

28. Kent, *Corinth* 8.3, 163.

29. Ibid.; cf. K. Hopkins, "The Age of Roman Girls at Marriage," *Population Studies* 18 (1965): 319, 322.

30. See note 16.

31. See chapter 5.

32. Of those named in Kent, *Corinth* 8.3, who constructed, repaired, or restored a building; were elected duovir or received an honorary duovirship; those elected aedile or received an honorary aedileship; or who became *agonothetai,* or honorary agonothete, the proportion with Greek cognomens recorded between the years 44 B.C. and A.D. 14 was 44 percent ($N = 34$); between A.D. 14 and 68, 39 percent ($N = 47$); between 68 and 117, 53 percent ($N = 18$); between 117 and 161, 29 percent ($N = 17$); and between 161 and the early third century, 22 percent ($N = 9$).

33. Duff, *Freedmen,* 50–58; cf. Dio Chrysostum 37.25, "for while the best of the Greeks over there [in Rome] may be seen inclining toward Roman ways, he [Favorinus, the author] inclines toward the Greek and consequently is sacrificing both his property and his political standing, and absolutely everything, aiming to achieve one thing at the cost of all else, namely, not only to seem Greek, but to be Greek too."

34. See note 13.

35. R. Syme, *Colonial Elites: Rome, Spain and the Americas* (Oxford, 1958).

36. Dio Chrysostum 37.26.

37. Aristeides, *Poseidon* 24: "What better proof could one make for the magnitude of the city than that it has been apportioned into all seas [i.e., it has sent out many colonies] and colonized and settled from them, not from one or another, but from all of them alike" (my translation).

38. Weitz, *Urbanism,* 7; R. Mols, *Introduction à la démographie historique des villes d'Europe du XIV au XVIII siècle,* vol. 2 (Louvain, 1955), 374–75.

39. Among the few exceptions are C. B. Patterson, *Pericles' Citizenship Law* (Chicago, 1978); and P. Garnsey, *Famine and Food Supply in the Graeco-Roman World* (Cambridge, 1988).

40. T. McKeown and R. G. Record, "The Reasons for the Decline of Mortality in England and Wales during the Nineteenth Century," *Population Studies* 16 (1962): 94–122; B. Benjamin, "The Urban Background to Public Health Changes

in England and Wales, 1900–1950," *Population Studies* 17 (1964): 225–48; K. Davis, "The Migrations of Human Populations," *Scientific American* 246 (September 1974): 95; R. Weitz, *Urbanization in the Developing Countries* (New York, 1973), 6–8; E. A. Wrigley, *Population and History* (New York, 1976), 95–106; D. V. Glass, "Some Indicators of Differences between Urban and Rural Mortality in England and Wales and Scotland," *Population Studies* 17 (1964): 263–67.

41. R. Boyd, "Urbanism, Morbidity, and Mortality," pp. 345–52 in *Man, Settlement, and Urbanism*, ed. P. Ucko (London, 1972).

42. T. A. Cockburn, "Infectious Diseases in Ancient Populations," *Current Anthropology* 12 (1971): 50–51; D. Brothwell, "Community Health as a Factor in Urban Cultural Evolution," pp. 353–62 in *Man, Settlement, and Urbanism*, ed. P. Ucko (London, 1972).

43. Wrigley, *Population and History*, 95–99; Cockburn, "Infectious Diseases," 51.

44. 2.54.5. Reprinted from Thucydides, *The Peloponnesian War*, trans. Rex Warner (Baltimore, 1974).

45. Wrigley, *Population and History*, 64–68. A severe famine in A.D. 51 may have affected Corinth (Tacitus, *Annales* 12.43.1; Suetonius, *Divus Claudius* 18.2; Eusebius, *Chronikon* 2, p. 152); there were doubtless many others.

46. Finley, *AE*, 126–27.

47. The evidence for famines, food shortages, and epidemics for the city of Rome is collected in L. Friedländer, *Roman Life and Manners Under the Early Empire*, vol. 1, trans. L. A. Magnus (New York, 1968), 24–29.

48. See n. 38; cf. Aristeides, *For Poseidon* 24, cited in n. 37.

49. Davis, "Migrations," 103.

50. This may explain why many urban elites fled the cities during the summer months when epidemics would be most frequent. A similar differential in rural and urban mortality may help explain why the Roman republican aristocracy gradually died out.

51. Frontinus, *De Aquaeductibus Urbis Romae* 1.10, 13, 14; Pliny, *Epistulae* 10.37; A. Burns, "Ancient Greek Water Supply and City Planning," *Technology and Culture* 15 (1974): 389–412. Since the time of Hippocrates, the Greeks and Romans had understood that drinking contaminated water caused disease (an understanding forgotten in later times). See Hippocrates, *Airs, Waters, Places;* Aristotle, *Politics* 7.11.2–3 (1330B); Frontinus, *Aq.* 2.88–94.

52. Peirene: Hill, *Corinth* 1.6, 17, 29; other sources: H. S. Robinson, "Excavations at Corinth" *Hesperia* 31 (1962): 96.

53. Virtually every excavation in the city reveals the remains of this extensive network. Some of the more important publications that cover aspects of Corinthian water supply are Hill, *Corinth* 1.6, for the fountains of Peirene and Glauke; Roebuck, *Corinth* 14, for the Asklepieion source; J. Wiseman, "The Gymnasium Area at Corinth," *Hesperia* 41 (1972), 1–42, for the Fountain of the Lamps (Lerna); C. C. Mattusch, "Corinthian Metalworking in the Forum Area," *Hesperia* 46 (1977): 380–81; and Stillwell, *Corinth* 1.2, 273, for water for bronze foundries; Broneer, *Corinth* 1.4, 151–53, for the latrine in the South Stoa; H. S. Robinson, "Excavations at Corinth," *Hesperia* 31 (1962): 120–30, for the Baths of Helen.

54. Frontinus, *Aq.* 1.14–16, 2.88–97, notes that the first priority given to the purest water from Rome's aqueducts was for drinking. Runoff from these outlets or from less pure water sources was used for bathing, fulling, and finally for watering gardens. A similar priority of usage prevailed at Corinth, as is revealed in the publications in n. 53. Why were not these fundamental principles followed in other pre- or nonindustrial cities, or indeed in Western industrial cities before the late nineteenth century? When they began to be followed in late nineteen-century London, dramatic declines in deaths from cholera, typhoid, dysentery, and diarrhea occurred (McKeown and Record, "Reasons for the Decline of Mortality," 96; A. Daley and B. Benjamin, "London as a Case Study," *Population Studies* 17 [1964]: 249–62).

55. Frontinus, *Aq.* 2.97, records fines up to 10,000 HS. No laws concerning Corinthian water supplies are known, but presumably they would not spend immense labor and money to construct and maintain an elaborate water system only to have its effectiveness destroyed by negligence or carelessness. Cf. *OGIS*, no. 483; Hesiod, *Works and Days,* 737–59; F. Wurst, *Historia* 3 (1954–55): 142.

56. For modern Hyderabad, cf. C. Bell, *The People of Tibet* (Oxford, 1928), 256: "A high majority of the citizens commit nuisance promiscuously in open spaces. . . . Public latrines are few and far between . . . [and] are not kept clean by the scavengers, and it is an annoying sight to see many a scavenger emptying his bucket full at some street corner or under a culvert." For Morocco and Afghanistan, G. Sjoberg, *The Preindustrial City* (New York, 1965), 94–95: "Inhabitants of Rabat have used the water conduits for bathing, washing their clothes, and watering their herds. Andkhui, a small urban community in northern Afghanistan, has long depended, for both drinking and cleansing purposes, upon a large water tank teeming with finger-length worms and other wriggling creatures. Facilities in Indian cities are still notoriously inadequate by industrial standards, a protected water supply being unavailable to a large portion of the citizenry."

In the Middle Ages, public health, sanitation, and personal hygiene were all regarded with contempt—Saint Jerome taught that taking baths was unchristian (Letter 125). This led to increases in the rat and flea populations. When combined with the massacres of cats, these practices were largely responsible for the death of half of the European population during the Black Death. Nature will not be mocked.

57. Quoted in Daley and Benjamin, "London as a Case Study," 251.

58. For example, many historians have attempted to estimate the populations of Ostia, Pompeii, and Rome by examining the areas occupied by the city and estimating their population densities. See, for example, J. E. Packer, "Housing and Population in Imperial Ostia and Rome," *Journal of Roman Studies* 57 (1967): 80–95; R. Meiggs, *Roman Ostia* (Oxford, 1960), 532–54; J. P. Russell, "Late Ancient and Medieval Population," *Transactions of the American Philosophical Society* 48, no. 3 (1958): 64–65.

59. Aristeides, *For Poseidon* 23 (my translation). He lived from ca. 126–81. Cf. John Chrysostum, *Homily on the First Epistle of Paul to the Corinthians,* Arguments 1, 2.

60. R. M. Adams, *The Land Behind Baghdad* (Chicago, 1965), 39–62, tables

10–18; R. M. Adams, *The Heartland of Cities: Surveys of Ancient Settlement and Land Use on the Central Flood Plain of the Euphrates* (Chicago, 1981), 142, 178; J. Ringel, *Cesarée de Palestine* (Paris, 1975), 91; W. A. McDonald, ed., *The Minnesota Messenia Expedition* (Minneapolis, 1972), 254–56; C. D. DeRoche, "Population Estimates from Settlement Areas and Number of Residences," *Journal of Field Archaeology* 10 (1983): 187–92.

61. For pottery of the Roman era in Greece, see H. S. Robinson, *Agora*, 5 (Princeton, 1959). Early Roman red wares (such as Pegamene and Samian) and late Roman spirally grooved wares predominated in the Roman pottery I saw. A future survey conducted with more manpower may find similar patterns of distribution.

62. *Archaiologikon Deltion* 28 (1973): 82; *Arch. Delt.* 29 (1973–74): 212; *Arch. Delt.* 31 (1976): 64. Pausanias (2.5.4) noted houses outside the walls.

63. Roman Cellar Building (perhaps a house): *Hesperia* 46 (1977): 59; elite dwelling at Anaploga: *Hesperia* 41 (1972): 332; Mosaic House: Weinberg, *Corinth* 1.5, 111f.; elite dwelling in Southeast Suburb: *Archaiologikon Deltion* 29 (1973–74): 212; Large Roman House on the northwest corner of the precinct of Temple E: J. K. Anderson, *Hesperia* 36 (1967): 1–12; elite dwelling east of the Theater: C. K. Williams and O. H. Zervos, *Hesperia* 51 (1982): 133–35, and *Hesperia* 55 (1986): 29–182.

64. J. E. Packer, "Ostia and Rome," 86.

65. R. Mols, *Introduction*, vol. 2, 93.

66. J. E. Packer, "Ostia and Rome," 86.

67. Diodorus Siculus 17.52.6, for about 60 B.C.: "The number of its [Alexandria's] inhabitants surpasses that of those in other cities. At the time we were in Egypt, those who kept the census returns of the population said that its free residents (*eleutheroi*) were more than 300,000."

This quote is particularly important because it probably refers only to the population of the city itself and not its *chora*. Because of the city's position on a narrow and restricted cape, the *chora* of the city was located some distance away in the Mareotic nome. There was little or no habitation outside the walls of the city because of its constricted position; extensive necropolises were located on its eastern and western sides, while the sea blocked the north and south. Since Alexandria was regarded as an entity distinct from the rest of the country (referred to as Alexandria by Egypt), it seems likely that Diodorus' figure includes only those living in the city itself and did not include those who lived in its *chora*, or territory. Furthermore, the figure is likely to have included both free males and females, because if only males were included, the free population would have been about twice as great (600,000), and the density (652 per hectare) beyond that of any human settlement known. Modern Calcutta has a density of only about 450 per hectare.

68. The population of the town of Pompeii (excluding its *territorium*) is usually given as 20,000 (e.g., by M. Grant, *Cities of Vesuvius: Pompeii and Herculanium* [New York, 1971], 45). This figure seems to be based on the 20,000-seat capacity of the community's amphitheater. However, it is probably misleading to rely on this type of evidence for town populations. Pompeii's amphitheater was a regional attraction, not only for the city and its own *territorium*, but also for surrounding communities. This is shown by the brawl in the amphitheater between spectators from Pompeii and neighboring Nuceria, that caused Nero, in A.D. 59, to ban gladia-

torial shows for ten years (Tacitus, *Ann.* 14.17). If Pompeii had a population of 20,000 in its sixty-four hectares, then it would have had a density of 312 per hectare. In Ostia, where four-story apartment houses were the dominant type of habitation, the density was only 390 per hectare; and so the density for Pompeii, with its one- and two-story houses, should have been considerably lower. J. C. Russell ("Late Ancient and Medieval Population," 64) estimated that the town of Pompeii had a total population of 10,584, and a density of 160 per hectare, which is probably closer to the truth. Russell estimated the population by counting the numbers of bedrooms in the excavated houses. This may give a minimum density, since more than one person can sleep in a room, but his method seems to me to be the most accurate.

69. Mols, *Introduction*, vol. 2, 98–100. From the preserved plans and contemporary pictures of Medieval, Renaissance, and even early modern cities in L. Benevolo, *The History of the City* (Cambridge, 1980), it is clear that far less space was devoted to public use than in classical cities.

70. C. A. Doxiades, *Ekistics: An Introduction to the Science of Human Settlement* (New York, 1968), figs. 70, 72.

71. The sites are given in Wiseman, *LAC*, and Wiseman, *CR*, 536–38. Forts, toll stations, mountain sanctuaries, and cemeteries with no related towns are not included in this figure.

72. See appendix 1.

73. Cenchreae: R. Scranton, et al., *Kenchreai* 4; Tenea: Wiseman, *LAC*, 92: "Almost the entire distance between the southern edge of Chiliomodhion and Klenia (ca. 2 km.), spreading east and west of the road for several hundred meters, was once occupied by an ancient settlement." Ayios Charlambos: Wiseman, *LAC*, 100; Crommyon: Wiseman, *LAC*, 19; Asprokambos: Wiseman, *LAC*, 34–36.

74. Doxiades, *Ekistics*, fig. 68.

75. See chapter 2.

76. K. Hopkins, "Taxes and Trade in the Roman Empire (200 B.C.-A.D. 400)," *Journal of Roman Studies* 70 (1980): 101–25, esp. 105–12.

77. J. Salmon, *Wealthy Corinth: A History of the City to 338 B.C.* (Oxford, 1984), 165–69. Cf. Herodotus 9.23.3; Wiseman, *LAC*, 10–11.

78. K. Hopkins, "On the Probable Age Structure of the Roman Population," *Population Studies* 19 (1966): 245–64; M. Hombert and C. Préaux, "Recherches sur le recensement dans l'Egypte romaine," *Papyrologica Lugduno-Batava* 5 (1952): 40–41, 159; A. E. Samuel, et al., *Death and Taxes*, American Studies in Papyrology, vol. 10 (Toronto, 1971); C. G. Merino, *Poblacion y Poblamiento en Hispania romana, El Conventus Cluniensis* (Valladolid, 1975).

79. A. J. Coale and P. Demeny, *Regional Model Life Tables and Stable Populations* (Princeton, 1966), 126.

80. For comparison, J. Beloch estimates Corinth's Greek population as between 80,000 and 100,000 (*Die Bevölkerung der griechisch-römischen Welt* [Leipzig, 1886], 86, 119–23); and Sakellariou and Faraklas estimate the population at between 66,000 and 73,000 for the Greek city (*Corinthia-Cleonaea*, 83–86).

81. See appendix 2.

82. No need to cite Max Weber here, the Bible, Greek philosophy, and Shakespeare express the concept much better. See also, M. I. Finley, *The World of Odys-*

*seus* (New York, 1978); A. W. H. Adkins, *Merit and Responsibility* (Oxford, 1960); D. Earl, *The Moral and Political Tradition of Rome* (Ithaca, N.Y., 1976).

83. Homer, *Iliad,* bk. 2, lines 193–204. Reprinted from *The Iliad of Homer,* trans. R. Lattimore (Chicago, 1961).

84. Cited by Sextus Empiricus, *Adversus Mathematicos* 7.60.

85. Plato, *Protagoras* 322B.

86. Aristotle, *Pol.* 1281B. Reprinted from Aristotle, *The Politics,* trans. T. A. Sinclair (New York, 1979).

87. Ibid., 1282A.

88. E. Friedl, *Vasilika, A Village in Modern Greece* (New York, 1963), 87; L. J. Bolchazy, *Hospitality in Early Rome: Livy's Concept of Its Humanizing Force* (Chicago, 1977).

89. Homer, *Odyssey,* bk. 6, lines 207–8.

90. Homer, *Odyssey,* bk. 16, lines 68–89.

91. Homer, *Odyssey,* bk. 7, lines 199–206.

92. The fulfillment of these obligations is what made men and women human and would lead to a life of piety, happiness, and inner peace. As the emperor Marcus Aurelius asked (*Meditations* 9.42): "What more do you want when you have done a man a service? Are you not content that you have done something conformable to your nature, and do you seek to be paid for it, just as if the eye demanded a payment for seeing, or the feet for walking? For as these members are formed for a particular purpose, and by working according to their individual constitutions obtain what is their own; so a man is formed by nature to acts of benevolence. When he has done anything benevolent or in any way helpful to the common interest, he has acted conformably to his constitution, and gets what is his own."

93. Cicero, *De Re Publica* 6.13: "Yet, Africanus, that you may be more zealous in guarding your country, be assured of this: All men who have saved or benefited their native land, or have enhanced its power, are assigned an especial place in heaven where they may enjoy a life of eternal bliss. For the supreme God who rules the entire universe finds nothing more pleasing than the societies and groups of men, united by law and right, which are called states. The rulers and saviors of states set forth from that place and to that place return" (reprinted from Cicero, *On the Commonwealth,* trans. G. H. Sabine and S. B. Smith [Columbus, Ohio, 1929]). For the revival of classical civic virtues in the United States, see G. Wills, *Cincinnatus: George Washington and the Enlightenment* (Garden City, N.Y., 1984). For the philosophical influences upon religious beliefs during the Empire, especially through the use of oracles, see R. Lane Fox, *Pagans and Christians* (New York, 1987), 162–64.

94. N. Lewis and M. Reinhold, *Roman Civilization,* vol. 2 (New York, 1966), 340–58; S. Dill, *Roman Society from Nero to Marcus Aurelius* (New York, 1957), 194–250.

95. Aristeides, *Poseidon* 23; Romans 16:23; 1 Clement 1.2.

96. Buildings: Kent, *Corinth* 8.3, 21; *curator annonae:* Kent, *Corinth* 8.3, nos. 127, 158–64, 169, 170, 177, 188, 227, 234–36, 238; *agonothetai:* Kent, *Corinth* 8.3, 30–31; public banquets: Kent, *Corinth* 8.3, no. 135; public distributions of money: Kent, *Corinth* 8.3, no. 306; other benefactions: Kent, *Corinth* 8.3, nos. 239–77.

97. *Poseidon* 23 (my translation).

98. E.g., Crinagoras, *Anthologia Palatina* 9.284. Cf. Alciphron 3.24.

99. Strabo 8.6.20–23; Aristeides, *Poseidon* 24. Mercantile is used here as the adjective of merchant; it does not denote the later concept of mercantilism.

100. Crinagoras, *Anth. Pal.* 9.284.

101. Strabo 8.6.23. This practice continues today in all parts of the globe.

102. R. MacMullen, *Corruption and the Decline of Rome* (New Haven, 1988).

103. S. P. Ellis, "The End of the Roman House," *American Journal of Archaeology* 92 (1988): 565–76.

### Chapter Five

1. The coin types, individual dies depicting the divinities, were taken from K. M. Edwards, *Corinth* 6. Poseidon has twenty-nine different types and Melikertes (Palaimon) and his dolphin, the hero in whose honor the games were founded by Sisyphus (Pausanias 2.1.3), had twenty-three different types. Aphrodite had seventeen. Both gods were especially honored in the Corinthia (Aristeides, *For Poseidon* 22–25).

2. Another source is sculptural representations of divinities, yet firm identifications are often difficult to make in the absence of specific attributes associated with the statue (which is often the case at Corinth).

3. See Pausanias 2.4.5. It has been maintained by R. L. Scranton in *Corinth* 1.2, 131–65, that the cult of Hera Akraia was still practiced in the Roman era, and that her temple was Temple C, built in the late Augustan or Tiberian times. The literary basis for her cult's survival is an anecdote in Aelian (*Varia Historia* 5.21), who lived there from A.D. 170–235. However, Pausanias, who visited the city in about 165, is quite certain that the cult perished with the Greek city in 146 B.C. (Paus. 2.3.6). Nor does the archaeological evidence present an overwhelming case that Temple C was dedicated to Hera.

4. Wiseman, *CR*, 493–96.

5. Pausanias (2.1.1), for example, cites Eumelos' *Korinthiaka*, and Strabo (8.6.21) cites Hieronymos and Eudoxos: doubtless there were many others.

6. Pausanias 2.1.6; Aristeides, *Poseidon* 22; Aeschylus, *Theoroi* 27 (see *Nachtrag zum Supplementum Aeschyleum*, ed. H. J. Mette [Berlin, 1949], kleine texte 169a).

7. E.g., by R. Lisle, "The Cults of Corinth" (Ph.D. diss., Johns Hopkins University, 1955), esp. 168; C. K. Williams and J. E. Fisher, "Corinth, 1970: Forum Area," *Hesperia* 40 (1971): 1–51; Wiseman, *CR*, 495.

8. Lisle, "The Cults of Corinth," 168. Nor is it easy to accept the antiquity (let alone the continuity in place) of the wooden image of Dionysus seen in the market by Pausanias (2.2.6), and said to have been made from the tree that Pentheus climbed to spy on the Theban women.

9. For the Asklepieion: Roebuck, *Corinth* 14, 82–84; Demeter and Kore: R. S. Stroud, "The Sanctuary of Demeter and Kore on Acrocorinth, Preliminary Report II, 1964–65," *Hesperia* 37 (1968): 300–310; N. Bookidis and J. E. Fisher, "The Sanctuary of Demeter and Kore on Acrocorinth," *Hesperia* 41 (1972): 284.

10. Roebuck, *Corinth* 14.

11. Stroud, "The Sanctuary of Demeter and Kore," esp. 300; Bookidis and Fisher, "The Sanctuary of Demeter and Kore."

12. See chap. 4, p. 70.

13. For a complete list of Corinth's gods, see Lisle, "The Cults of Corinth."

14. Kent, *Corinth* 8.3, no. 153.

15. For the Isthmian sanctuary, see O. Broneer, *Isthmia* 1 and 2; Kent, *Corinth* 8.3, no. 306; Pausanias 2.1.1–2.2.2.

16. Blegen, et al., *Corinth* 3.1, 21. Some modern guidebooks absurdly state that the one thousand sacred prostitutes of Aphrodite practiced in this temple.

17. Strabo's statement (8.6.20) makes it clear that the cult of Aphrodite's sacred prostitutes belonged to the past and was not practiced in the Roman city. Yet, many works on early Christianity state or imply that the cult was still practiced in the Roman era and that this implies degraded moral standards among the Corinthians of Paul's era. A good example of this confusion is in H. C. Kee, et al., *Understanding the New Testament* (Englewood Cliffs, N.J., 1965), 181: "Located atop Acrocorinth was a small structure that dramatized in grosser fashion the cultural mingling at Corinth. It was a temple ostensibly in honor of Aphrodite, the Hellenic goddess of love and beauty, but actually a center for the worship of Astarte, the sensual Phoenician deity whose orgiastic cults had shocked the sensibilities of the ancient Israelites. . . . So low was the level of morality in Corinth that the very name of the city had become synonymous with profligacy and degradation. 'To corinthianize' meant 'to debase.'" Kee does not note that this cult did not survive into the Roman era, or that the verb *korinthiázomai,* meaning "to have sexual intercourse" comes from Aristophanes writing in the early fourth century b.c. No source from the Greek or Roman eras states that the city had "become synonymous with profligacy and degradation."

Such distortions hardly contribute to our understanding of the New Testament, but contribute mainly confusion. In contrast, C. K. Barrett (*A Commentary on the First Epistle to the Corinthians* [New York, 1968], 2–3), observes that the reputation of old Corinth "may not be simply carried across a century. . . . In Paul's day, Corinth was probably little better and little worse than any other great seaport and commercial centre of the age."

18. R. Scranton (*Corinth* 1.3, 57–69) identified the temple as Tyche's, but a reexamination of the evidence by C. K. Williams in *Hesperia* 44 (1975), 25–29, makes Aphrodite a more sensible choice.

19. E. Will *Korinthika* (Paris, 1955), 224.

20. Antipater of Sidon, *Anthologia Graeca* 7.218, trans. W. R. Paton (New York, 1919).

21. For Corinth's prostitutes in the Greek era, see Strabo 8.6.20; for Lais' tomb, Pausanius 2.2.4; for the prayers during the Persian War, Athenaeus, *Deipnosophistae* 13.573c–f; Scholia in Pindar, *Olympian Odes* 12.32; and Plutarch, *De Herodoti Malignitate* 871a–b.

22. Pausanias 2.1.7; Apuleius, *Metamorphoses* 10.31.

23. *For Poseidon* 23 (above, p. 89).

24. Pausanias 2.4.1, 2.4.5.

25. Herodotus 2.167.2.

26. Scranton (*Corinth* 1.3, 67–72) had identified Hermes' temple with Temple D, but more recently C. K. Williams (*Hesperia* 44 [1975]: 25–27) has identified Temple D with Tyche, and the temple of Hermes with the small, three-roomed shrine on the southwest end of the Central Shops.

27. Pegasus and Bellerophon have twenty-five different coin types. Shrine: Pausanias 2.2.4; procession: Apuleius, *Met.* 11.8.

28. For the spring of Upper Peirene and the unofficial cult of Pegasus and Bellerophon, see Broneer, *Corinth* 3.1, 52–59.

29. Kent, *Corinth* 8.3, no. 206.

30. For Asklepios' and Hygeia's temple, see Roebuck, *Corinth* 14; for Saint Quadratus and the Cemetery Basilica, see *Acta Sanctorum*, March, vol. 2, p. 4; Wiseman, *LAC*, 85–86.

31. Preliminary reports on the sanctuary of Demeter and Kore appear periodically in *Hesperia*. See especially R. S. Stroud in volume 37 (1968, p. 300) for the votive dedications.

32. Chapter 4, p. 69. The inscriptions are taken from Meritt, *Corinth* 8.1, West, *Corinth* 8.2, and Kent, *Corinth* 8.3; T. Martin, *Hesperia* 46 (1977): 178f.; K. Bookidis, *Hesperia* 43 (1974): 278f. (a priestess of Demeter and Kore); *L'Année Epigraphique* (1971), no. 442. Of course, these are not all the divinities mentioned in inscriptions. But, the mere name of a divinity, without any context, is of little meaning for the understanding of the worship of that divinity. It only shows that a knowledge of that divinity existed.

33. The Doric, hexastyle temple can be seen in F. Imhoof-Blumer and P. Gardner, *A Numismatic Commentary on Pausanias* (Chicago, 1964), 22; B. V. Head, *Catalogue of Greek Coins in the British Museum, Corinth, Colonies of Corinth, etc.* (Bologna, 1963), pl. 16, nos. 1–3; K. M. Edwards, *Corinth* 6, nos. 41–43. The temple looks suspiciously like the great Doric temple overlooking the Forum and commonly attributed to Apollo—to whom it may have been dedicated in the Greek era. Pausanias (2.3.1) described a large temple of Octavia overlooking the forum (*uper de ten agoran*), and it may have been the same temple. Only one Doric, hexastyle temple is known to exist in Roman Corinth: the temple of Apollo. Dedications to the imperial cult are, Livia, Julius Caesar, Tutela Augusta, Augustus, Diana Pacilucifera Augusta, Gens Augustae, Lares Augusti, Nemesis Augustae, Genius Augusti, Tiberius, Titus, and Nerva. Many have more than one dedication.

34. The priests of the imperial cult are Divus Julius, Mars Augustus, Apollo Augustus, Saturn Augustus, providentia Augusta et Salus Publicae, Domus Augustae, Divus Claudius, and Victoria Britannica. Some have more than one dedication. The sample of religious inscriptions we possess, although small, is probably representative. The city has been under excavation for about one hundred years now, and the forum area, where most of the temples, altars, and dedications were located, has been thoroughly investigated. There is no reason to expect any given type of cult to be either under- or overrepresented owing to the accidents of discovery. After almost a century of excavation, it is doubtful that new information will alter the picture substantially, and there is little doubt that the religious pattern derived from the inscriptions is generally accurate. It is also supported by the evidence for different social and ethnic groups in the city, discussed in chapter 3.

35. See chap. 4, 68ff.

36. As is the rule in mainland Greece, the worship of Mithra does not appear in Corinth from any source. It is possible that the Syrian goddess Atargatis (often identified with Aphrodite or Astarte) was worshiped at Corinth; she may be represented in a fragmentary statue (Lisle, "The Cults of Corinth," 123; F. P. Johnson,

*Corinth* 9, no. 229). Attis was the husband of Cybele, and frequently appears with her on Corinthian-made lamps (P. Bruneau, "Lampes corinthiennes," *BCH* 95 [1971]: 483–91).

37. Pausanias 2.4.7.

38. Apuleius, *Met.* 11.

39. A Hellenistic dedication to Isis and Serapis has been found some 400 meters below the shrine of Demeter and Kore on Acrocorinth, near the location of the Roman temples to these gods given by Pausanias (2.4.7): see L. Vidman, *Sylloge inscriptionum religionis Isiacae et Serapiacae* (Berlin, 1969), no. 34a.

40. These passages are from Apuleius, *Met.* 11.23, 11.6, reprinted from *Apuleius, The Golden Ass*, trans. J. Lindsay (Bloomington, Ind., 1971), 238–39, 249. Cf. the statement of Paul in 2 Corinthians 12:2–4: "I know a man in Christ who fourteen years ago was caught up to the third heaven—whether in the body or out of the body I do not know, God knows. And I know that this man was caught up into Paradise . . . and heard things that cannot be told, which man may not utter."

41. Homer, *Odyssey*, bk. 4, lines 561–69. Recent revisionist work in Greco-Roman religion has focused on the social aspects of the mystery religions, and has deemphasized the religions' promise of a blessed afterlife. R. MacMullen, in his splendid book, *Paganism in the Roman Empire* (New Haven, 1981, 53–54) believes that there was no promise of a blessed immortality for the initiate of Isis. Although he discusses this passage from Apuleius in great detail, and gives many quotes from it, he does not discuss the only phrase in this important passage that suggests that a blessed immortality was indeed promised to the initiate (11.6): *campos Elysios incolens ipse, tibi propitiam frequens adorabis* (you will adore me frequently for my favor to you in the Elysian Fields). Since the time of Homer, the Elysian Fields were known as a place where mortals went, who did not die, but lived at ease. Furthermore, there are immense numbers of references that show that a blessed afterlife was granted to the initiates of the Eleusinian Mysteries of Demeter; see W. K. C. Guthrie, *The Greeks and Their Gods* (Boston, 1955), 284–94. The evidence for the Eleusinian Mysteries is ignored by MacMullen, but the Greek sources are unambiguous (as far as religious prohibitions allowed) that initiation gave the hope of a blessed immortality: see esp. Isocrates, *Panegyricus* 28; Sophocles, fr. 753, ed. Nauk; and Aristophanes, *Frogs* 154–58. The Eleusinian Mysteries remained immensely popular in the Roman era (as even the evidence at Corinth attests) and few would argue that the beliefs of the cult had changed markedly from the Greek to the Roman eras.

42. *Met.* 11.8–17.

43. See chapter 3, n. 85. R. Scranton, et al. (*Kenchreai* 1, 72) believe that Apuleius' description of the Iseum at Cenchreae could refer to obvious features of the sanctuary as excavated.

44. F.-J. de Weale, *Corinthe et Saint Paul* (Paris, 1961), 86.

45. L. Ibrahim, et al., *Kenchreai* 2.

46. R. E. Witt, *Isis in the Graeco-Roman World* (Ithaca, N.Y., 1971), 191. It was also a Nazirite practice; see Numbers 6:1–21.

47. Witt, *Isis in the Graeco-Roman World,* 121.

48. Of those inscriptions concerning priests or dedications to divinities that can be dated, in the first century A.D. thirty-eight of forty-seven, or 81 percent, are to

the Imperial cult or to specifically Roman Gods; in the second century, three of eleven, or 27 percent; and in the third century, one of four, or 25 percent. Of these same inscriptions, none were written in Greek in the first century A.D.; four (44 percent) were in Greek in the second century; and three (75 percent) in the third century. The evidence for the second and third centuries is admittedly poor, and future discoveries may disprove this trend. Nevertheless, the trend is consistent with the ethnic and cultural changes discussed in chapter 4.

49. Cf. the Roman Senate's attempts to exclude altars and temples of Isis from the city of Rome (S. K. Heyob, *The Cult of Isis Among Women in the Graeco-Roman World* [Leiden, 1975], 18). In general, the cult of Isis was popular among the urban poor, slaves, and freedmen and women (MacMullen, *Paganism,* 114; Heyob, *The Cult of Isis,* 11–18).

50. The chronology of Paul's missionary activities in Corinth has been frequently discussed; see Wiseman, *CR,* 503, n. 255. The chronology of C. K. Barrett (*A Commentary on the First Epistle to the Corinthians* [New York, 1968], 4–16) is followed here. Although the exact dates may be off by as much as a year, Paul spent considerable time in the city—eighteen months on his first visit alone (Acts 18:11)—and when the duration of his other two visits to the city are reckoned (2 Cor. 13:1), he may have spent more time in Corinth than in any other city. This fact is more important than the exact dates of his visit. All New Testament references and translations are taken from the Revised Standard Version of the New Testament. It is not the purpose of this section to discuss Paul's theology; for this, the reader is referred to Barrett and the other works cited below.

51. Romans 16:3–5; cf. Acts 16:15, 17:5–9. Titus Justus' house was next to the synagogue, and may also have been used for preaching (a situation not without its own humor); see Acts 18:7.

52. Acts 18:1–2; Suetonius, *Divus Claudius* 25.4.

53. E. Goodspeed, *Paul* (New York, 1961), 18.

54. Acts 18:4. The Jewish community at Corinth is also mentioned by Philo (*ad Gaium* 281).

55. 1 Cor. 2:3.

56. Acts 18:9–10.

57. 1 Cor. 1:26, 12:1–3. For the humble social origins of many early Christian converts, see C. F. D. Moule, *The Birth of the New Testament* (New York, 1962), 156ff; R. Lane Fox, *Pagans and Christians* (New York, 1987), 293–301. For a different view of the social status of the early Christians in Corinth and elsewhere, see W. Meeks, *The First Urban Christians: The Social World of the Apostle Paul* (New Haven, 1983). Meeks believes that Paul's converts for whom we have explicit information, were from various social and occupational groups within the cities he visited: free artisans, small traders, freedmen and their descendents, wealthy independent women, and wealthy Jews. Most were characterized by high status inconsistency; their achieved status was often higher than their attributed status (p. 73). Nevertheless, it is probably an oversimplification to assume that the individuals specifically referred to by Paul were representative of the Church as a whole. The individuals mentioned may have had "high status inconsistency"; but what of the rest? Paul's statements in 1 Cor. 1:26 and 12:1–3 show that *in general,* his converts were powerless, low-born, and ill-educated. These passages, the only ones in

which Paul gives his own views on the social status of his converts, have not received the attention they deserve from Meeks. A deemphasis on the urban poor among Paul's converts also has implications for Meeks' views on the reasons for conversion to Christianity (pp. 173–74). He believes that the values and worldview of these status-inconsistent individuals may have facilitated their conversion (and perhaps it did); but what about the views of the majority of the Church who were poor? Why were they attracted to Paul's message?

Furthermore, Meeks discusses the relatively high social and economic status of Greco-Roman women (pp. 23–25), but later says that many Corinthian women converts "broke through the normal expectations of their female roles" (p. 71). Normal from whose perspective? not that of their society, but the perspective of Paul. Nevertheless, these are minor quibbles with an important, thought-provoking book. Perhaps recent migrants may also be categorized as status-inconsistent individuals.

58. Chloe: 1 Cor. 1:11; Gaius: Rom. 16:23; Erastus the aedile: Rom. 16:23, Kent, *Corinth* 8.3, no. 232. See also Meeks, *The First Urban Christians*, 51–72.

59. Acts 18:8.

60. J. Weiss, *Earliest Christianity*, vol. 1 (New York, 1959), 293.

61. Acts 18:12–13.

62. Weiss, *Earliest Christianity*, 304–5.

63. Acts 18:14–15. See J. Murphy-O'Connor, *Saint Paul's Corinth: Texts and Archaeology* (Wilmington, Del., 1983), 141–50.

64. Indeed, some of the manuscripts at Acts 18:17 read, "all the Greeks," instead of "all"; cf. Barrett, *Commentary*, 31.

65. Barrett, *Commentary*, 1 Cor. 1:1.

66. Acts 18:24–28.

67. 2 Cor. 2:4.

68. E.g., by H. C. Kee, et al., *Understanding the New Testament*, 182–90.

69. 1 Cor. 12:2; Acts 18:6.

70. 2 Cor. 10:10, 11:6; cf. Acts 18:24–28. Apollos is described as an *aner logios*. For an attempt to see gnostic influences in Paul's opponents at Corinth, see W. Schmithals, *Gnosticism in Corinth* (Nashville, 1970).

71. MacMullen, *Paganism*, 1–18.

72. 1 Cor. 12:13–30.

73. 1 Cor. 14:2–5.

74. 1 Cor. 11:5–7, 14:34–35. The latter passage may be a later interpolation; see Barrett, *Commentary*, 330.

75. 1 Cor. 5:1; cf. Lev. 18:7–8.

76. One of the more egregious attempts to portray the city as a den of iniquity is by H. J. Mason, "Lucius at Corinth," *Phoenix* 25 (1971): 160–65. The article is notable in projecting the practices of a few individuals onto the whole community; projecting the past onto the present (Aphrodite's sacred prostitutes again); its use of fiction (i.e., Apuleius) as absolute fact; and mistranslations (*toiouton se thomen politen Korinthion*, shall we make such a one as you a Corinthian citizen, for example, is translated as "a man with your perversions should be a Corinthian").

77. 1 Clem. 1–2.

78. Weiss, *Earliest Christianity*, vol. 2, 827–28; O. Broneer, "The Apostle Paul

and the Isthmian Games," *Biblical Archaeology* 25 (1962): 2–31. Cf. Dio Chrysostom (8.5–9, 9.1–2) on Diogenes the Cynic's reasons for attending the Isthmian Games in the Greek era: "For he observed that large numbers gathered at Corinth on account of the harbors and the hetaerae, and because the city was situated as it were at the cross roads of Greece. Accordingly, just as the good physician should go and offer his services where the sick are the most numerous, so, said he, the man of wisdom should take up his abode where fools are thickest in order to convict them of their folly and reprove them. So, when the time for the Isthmian Games arrived, and everybody was at the Isthmus, he went down also" (8.5).

79. Broneer, "The Apostle Paul and the Isthmian Games," 5; Acts 18:3; 1 Cor. 9:12–18.

80. The doleful picture of the economic decline of Athens in Roman times has been painted many times, most recently in the excellent article by D. J. Geagan, "Roman Athens: Some Aspects of its Life and Culture I: 86 B.C. to A.D. 267," *ANRW* 7, no. 1 (1979): 371–437, esp. 385–86. Cf. J. Day, *An Economic History of Athens under Roman Domination* (New York, 1942), 177–83. The third-class towns of Thessalonica and Philippi were probably not much different. For Philippi, see P. Collart, *Philippes, ville de Macedone* (Paris, 1937). Buildings in a city constructed by emperors tell us nothing about the strength of the local economy.

81. R. Wilken, *The Christians as the Romans Saw Them* (New Haven, 1984), 68–163.

82. Chap. 4, 73ff. Cf. N. Rich, *The Age of Nationalism and Reform: 1850–1890* (New York, 1977), 26: "A population concentrated in cities was more accessible to the influence of new ideological trends than a population scattered throughout the countryside. The man who had severed his traditional local ties to live in the impersonal and anonymous city searched for something he could identify with, for new loyalties and attachments." Among these new loyalties were new religious sects.

83. Acts 19:1–10.

84. 1 Cor. 15:36–42.

85. Guthrie, *The Greeks and Their Gods,* 284–94.

86. 1 Cor. 15:51–53.

87. 2 Cor. 12:2–4.

88. Meeks, *The First Urban Christians,* 51. From the beginning, many Romans thought Christianity was a lower-class conspiracy. In the Beatitudes, Christ taught that the poor are blessed.

89. 2 Cor. 12:12. The performance of miracles was an important factor in winning converts in antiquity for pagans and Christians alike. See MacMullen, *Paganism,* 96, 134.

90. The powerful cultural influence of mainland Greece on the Greek-speaking world, especially during the Second Sophistic, is well known and abundantly documented. See A. J. Spawforth and S. Walker, "The World of the Panhellenion I: Athens and Eleusis," *Journal of Roman Studies* 75 (1985): 78–104, and "The World of the Panhellenion II: Three Dorian Cities," *Journal of Roman Studies* 76 (1986): 88–105; G. W. Bowersock, *Greek Sophists in the Roman Empire* (Oxford, 1969). The closest modern parallel would be the role of Israel for the Jews.

91. Weiss, *Earliest Christianity,* vol. 2, 828.

92. Ibid., 831.

93. 1 Clem. 47:7.

94. *Acta Sanctorum,* April, vol. 2, p. 616.

95. 1 Clem. 44.3.

96. 1 Clem. 44.3–6, 3.3–4.

97. Eusebius, *Ecclesiastical History* 4.23.11.

98. The most complete survey of early Christianity in Greece during this era remains M. Le Quien, *Oriens Christianus,* 2 vols. (Paris, 1740). See also, H. von Sachen Max, *Das Christliche Hellas* (Leipzig, 1918); and Weiss, *Earliest Christianity.*

99. *Acta Sanctorum,* March, vol. 2, p. 4. Other martyrs at Corinth include Heliconis (*Acta Sanctorum,* May, vol. 6, p. 728), Alexandros, and those killed with Leonides (n. 101). Palladius (*Historia Lausiaca* 65) has preserved an inspiring story about an anonymous martyr who rescued a Christian woman from a brothel, where she had been placed as punishment, and was executed himself.

100. For the Church, see Wiseman, *LAC,* 85–86. Eustathius is not to be identified with the famous fourth-century bishop of Antioch who died in Trajanopolis, or Eustathius of Sebaste. Nothing more is known about him, as far as I can determine.

101. *Acta Sanctorum,* April, vol. 2, pp. 399, 402.

102. For the basilica, see D. I. Pallas, "Anaskaphai Lechaiou," *Archaiologikon Deltion* 17, no. 2 (1961–62): 69–78; D. I. Pallas, "Anaskaphai ereunai en Lechaio," *Praktica* (1965): 137–66. There is an important letter of Athanasius to Bishop Epictetus of Corinth concerning the Christological problem, and a brief letter of John Chrysostum written to Bishop Alexander in 406. As far as I know, Corinth was first officially described as the Metropolitan Church of Greece at the Council of Ephesus in 431, under the city's bishop Perigenes.

103. These are the Cemetery Basilica, the Kranion church, the church on Acrocorinth; perhaps the Julian Basilica was converted to a church in the fourth century (Scranton, *Corinth* 16, 9–11); and perhaps the Asklepieion, as well (Scranton, *Corinth* 16, pp. 7, 9).

104. Libanius, *Orationes* 14.

105. *Homily on the First Epistle of Paul to the Corinthians,* Argument, 1–2.

## Summary

1. This statement will seem like a cliché to anyone reading it. Yet, when the passage was written in the late eighth century B.C., it was a radical and new idea. A comparative study of Near Eastern wisdom literature shows that, until this time, wealth, "goodness" (*aretē*), and "fame" (*kleos*) depended on a completely different set of criteria. Among these criteria, obedience to authority was paramount. The caste or social class into which one was born, and one's ability to master a complex writing system (which generally required abundant leisure and high social status) were also important. These attainments were a prerequisite for the understanding of divine laws (from which goodness came), and would enable the individual to gain admission to the high priesthood or state bureaucracy from which one's socioeconomic status was determined. The notion expressed in Hesiod, that wealth, goodness, and fame depend on physical labor and not one's knowledge of divine laws or

one's position in the state bureaucracy, has been the basis of most Western economic systems since his time.

2. *AE*, 95.

3. *Areopagiticus* 15–36.

4. *Pol.* 1286b (3.10.8): *epei de kai meizous einai sumbebeke tas poleis, isos oude rhadion eti gignesthai politeian heteran para demokratian.*

5. C. Clark and M. Haswell, *The Economics of Subsistence Agriculture* (London, 1970), 105–7. See also appendix 5.

6. France from 1650 to 1788 provides an example. Here, rents nearly quadrupled from 10 percent to 39 percent of gross production, even though the per-capita increase in the productivity of land labor only doubled at best during the era, and there were probably more, not fewer opportunities for nonagricultural work. It seems that the rent increases were yet another indication of the increasing oppressiveness of the social and political institutions of prerevolutionary France.

7. Interesting in this context is the observation of D. Crawford (*Kerkeosiris* [Cambridge, 1971], 129–30) that the chained slaves on Cato's estates received more food than the average Egyptian peasant.

8. C. Starr, *The Economic and Social Growth of Early Greece* (Oxford, 1977), 155–56; A. Jardé, *Les céréales dans l'antiquité grecque* (Paris, 1925), 48–50.

9. The most extreme example of all would be a state where 90 percent of the land was owned by landlords and the rent rate was 20 percent. To get about 10,000 landlords in our city, we would need a total population supported by agriculture of about 55,000. However, we remember that Athens, one of the largest city-states of the ancient world, containing approximately 1,000 square miles, could only support about 53,000 from its *chora*. Again, we must ask, where would such a state exist, and is it reasonable to assume it was normative?

10. As any history of, for example, Latin America, will show. Twenty thousand of twenty-five thousand citizens owned some land in Athens in the late fifth century (A. Burford Cooper, "The Family Farm in Greece," *Classical Journal* 73 [1977–78]: 171). M. I. Finley (*AE*, 97) seems to me to evade the implications of this fact. Aristotle knew that democracies promoted the widespread ownership of property and prevented the concentration of wealth in the hands of a few (*Pol.* 1319a).

11. "Taxes and Trade in the Roman Empire," *Journal of Roman Studies* 70 (1980), 101–25.

12. *Pol.* 1313b (5.9.4). In addition to Aristotle's statement, which follows in the text, we have Plato, *Rep.* 856e–857a; Suetonius, *Divus Vespasianus* 16, and *Divus Titus* 7; Tacitus, *Annales* 13.50, 15.45; Tacitus, *Historiae* 1.51, 2.5, 4.26; and Tacitus, *Agricola* 19. One could add many other examples to the same effect: high land taxes were seen, even by the literary elite, as morally wrong, while a reduction in taxes was a great benefit. Since the publication of Jones, *The Roman Economy*, and de Ste. Croix, *Class Struggle*, it is doubtful that many will now maintain that higher taxes enhance productivity. I am grateful to Sherrill Taylor for discussing these issues with me.

13. Cf. J. Hector St. John Crèvecoeur, *Letters from an American Farmer* (1782 ed.; repr. New York, 1904), 55: "The American ought to love this country much better than that wherein either he or his forefathers were born. Here, the rewards of his industry follow with equal steps the progress of his labor; his labor is founded

on the basis of nature, self-interest; can it want a stronger allurement? Wives and children, who before in vain demanded of him a morsel of bread, now, fat and frolicsome, gladly help their father to clear those fields whence exuberant crops are to arise to feed and clothe them all; without any part being claimed, either by a despotic prince, a rich abbot, or a mighty lord."

14. For the proportion of peasants in the population, see P. Garnsey and R. Saller, *The Roman Empire: Economy, Society, and Culture* (Berkeley, 1987), 111; and R. MacMullen, "Peasants during the Principate," *ANRW* 2, no. 1 (1974): 253. This view of a larger surplus available to the Greco-Roman peasant than is now currently believed seems to receive support from the recent analysis of P. Millar in "The World of the *Golden Ass*," *Journal of Roman Studies* 71 (1981): 72–74. Cf. R. MacMullen, *Roman Social Relations* (New Haven, 1974), 53–56; R. P. Duncan-Jones, *The Economy of the Roman Empire* (Cambridge, 1974), 259–60.

15. Of course, not all rural peasants needed to go to the town or participate in the urban economy to obtain iron. Some were fortunte enough to have iron meteorites land in their backyards: "A Man's fields may lie far from his town but five years this lump will last, neither shepherd nor ploughman need go up to town for want of iron, he'll be supplied at home" (*Iliad* bk. 23, lines 832–35). I am grateful to David Sahlin for pointing this passage out to me.

However, it seems probable that an iron meteorite landing in one's backyard or presented as a gift would be a rare occurrence, and most peasants would indeed have to go to a town to obtain their iron, which had to be imported from elsewhere by ship, or overland to the town. The ship or pack train would stop at the town where the demand for iron was high, rather than in the open countryside, where demand for iron was low, and settlements scattered. From the town, an itinerant smith may take some metal to local villages.

Libanius (*Orat.* 11.230) speaks of large villages near Antioch where peasants go to exchange their products with each other at fairs, seldom venturing to Antioch. However, these villages are functioning as markets and perhaps production centers, and probably should be called towns, analogous to Cenchreae, Tenea, and Crommyon in the Corinthia. It is also possible that by the late Empire, peasants no longer had sufficient surplus at their disposal to spend part of it in the *asty.*

16. For Roman Britain: I. R. Hodder and M. Hassall, "The non-random spacing of Romano-British walled towns," *Man* 6 (1971): 391–407; I. R. Hodder, "Locational models and the study of Romano-British settlement," pp. 887–909 in *Models in Archaeology*, ed. D. L. Clarke (London, 1972). For the northeastern Peloponnese, see appendix 1.

17. Adam Smith, *The Wealth of Nations* (New York, 1937), 356–57.

18. The best example of this relationship is perhaps the Soviet Union, where approximately 3 percent of the land whose surplus belongs to the producers, produces about 30 percent of all agricultural goods (M. Goldman, *The Soviet Economy: Myth and Reality* [Englewood Cliffs, N.J., 1968], 99–103).

19. Sparta was as well. But Sparta has been more accurately described as a barracks, not a city.

20. M. Rostovtzeff (*The Social and Economic History of the Roman Empire*, 2 vols. [Oxford, 1957], 346) even called the Empire "urbanized to excess." Finley

noted that there was a higher proportion of individuals living in cities during the Roman Empire than until the mid-nineteenth century in some industrialized western nations (Finley, *AC*, 305). Of course, the gross number of cities in the Roman Empire was not exceeded in Europe for a millennium after Rome's collapse.

21. The litany of abuses that peasants suffered at the hands of grasping officials is well known. See MacMullen, *Roman Social Relations* (New Haven, 1974), 1–53; R. MacMullen, *Corruption and the Decline of Rome* (New Haven, 1988); and de Ste. Croix, *Class Struggle* (nearly every other page). Even in the early Empire, abuses existed, although the example given by de Ste. Croix (p. 499) for Egypt during the first century A.D. probably should not be extrapolated to the rest of the Empire during that era. The fact is that Egyptian peasants were always liable to be killed and their relatives sold into slavery for nonpayment of taxes, as we learn from *Papyrus Lansing* 6, dating to the Twentieth Dynasty (P. British Museum 9994), translated by M. Lichtheim (*Early Egyptian Literature*, vol. 2 [Berkeley, 1976], 170–71): "One says (to him): 'Give grain.' 'There is none.' He is beaten savagely. He is bound, thrown in the well, submerged head down. His wife is bound in his presence. His children are in fetters. His neighbors . . . abandon them and flee." In the late Empire, Egyptian administrative principles and practices such as this became more attractive to the bureaucracy. Cf. T. G. H. James, *Pharaoh's People* (Chicago, 1984), 103–19.

22. See appendix 3. In contrast to classical cities, in which public buildings were predominant in size and number (although temples occupied positions of honor), Mesopotamian cities were dominated by ziggurats indicating the power of the priesthood and their role in the city. Renaissance Italian cities were dominated by the towers of wealthy houses, the town halls, and the churches. The towns of independent German city-states were dominated by guild halls, the town hall, and church-supported institutions such as hospitals. See C. Thomas and R. Griffeth, *The City-State in Five Cultures* (Santa Barbara, 1981).

23. An earlier version of this chapter was given as a talk at the University of Chicago in October 1982; at Rice University in March 1983; at the Massachusetts Institute of Technology in November 1983; at the University of Florida in March 1984; and at the April 1984 meeting of the New England Colloquium of Ancient Historians at Brown University. I am especially grateful to the organizer of the latter meeting, Gerald Toomer, and to the respondant, Kurt Raaflaub. It was last given at the University of Arkansas in March 1986.

## Conclusion

1. Cited by P. T. Bauer, *Equality, the Third World, and Economic Delusion* (Cambridge, Mass., 1981), p. 213.

2. Surveying the works available to me at present, I find that Finley has devoted two paragraphs to the consumer city in *AE*, three paragraphs in *AC*; Hopkins has devoted four paragraphs in "Economic Growth of Towns in Classical Antiquity"; J. Stambaugh, one paragraph (on Rome) in *The Ancient Roman City*; and P. Garnsey, and R. Saller two paragraphs in *The Roman Empire: Economy, Society, and Culture* (Berkeley, 1987) (with more devoted to primitivism). This is not intended as a

criticism of these individuals, but to show how important unexamined assumptions have been concerning this issue. It must be stressed at the outset that, regardless of the origins of the theory, it has to be judged entirely on its own merit.

3. Still the best analysis of this development is M. Rostovtzeff, *Social and Economic History of the Hellenistic World,* vol. 1 (Oxford, 1941), 472–524; see also G. E. M. de Ste. Croix, *The Class Struggle in the Ancient Greek World* (Ithaca, N.Y., 1981), 156–58.

4. The view of A. H. M. Jones, *The Greek City from Alexander to Justinian* (Oxford, 1940), 287–97; and A. H. M. Jones, *Cities of the Eastern Roman Provinces* (Oxford, 1971), 293–94; cf. de Ste. Croix, *Class Struggle,* 18–19. The problem with this type of evidence is the questionable extent to which we can infer the economic exploitation of the town by the country from differences in language or culture.

5. A. H. M. Jones, *Cities of the Eastern Roman Provinces,* 293–94; de Ste. Croix, *Class Struggle,* 9–19. Rostovtzeff saw commerce and manufactures as important for the early imperial city, and rents and taxes for the late Roman cities.

6. De Ste. Croix, *Class Struggle,* 14, citing a passage from Galen's *On Wholesome and Unwholesome Foods,* does not mention that it referred to a time of famine. See the judicious comments by P. Garnsey and R. Saller (*The Roman Empire: Economy, Society and Culture* [Berkeley, 1987], 97). See also P. Garnsey, *Famine and Food Supply in the Graeco-Roman World* (Cambridge, 1988).

7. Occasionally, a classical source will tell us something about the practical concerns of earning a livelihood. Hesiod is an example, and so is Aristotle. Plato also had important things to say. His picture of Oligarchic Man in the *Republic* (553c–554b) shows us economic values absent from other literary sources. This type of character amasses property through thrift and hard work. He uses reason to show him how to make more money from less, and considers the accumulation of wealth to be honorable, as did Hesiod. We may not like these values, but we cannot ignore their presence, and they do *not* show primitivist, non-market behavior, as in our other elite sources. Another welcome corrective is A. Burford, *Craftsmen in the Greek and Roman World* (Ithaca, N.Y., 1973).

8. H. Brodsky, "Anti-Urbanism in the Bible: A Critique," *Urbanism Past and Present* 9 (1984): 36–41.

9. Augustine, *City of God* 1.32–34, 14.12–15, 15.1–5. Augustine noted that Rome was founded in fratricide when Romulus killed Remus, and this archetypical crime embodied the evil of cities, just as the sin of Adam and Eve embodied the evil of all later generations.

10. *Jerome,* Letter 125, chaps. 8, 15, 17. He also notes the archetypical fratricide of Romulus and Remus.

11. Tertulian, *On Prescriptions against Heretics,* chap. 7: "What then has Athens to do with Jerusalem, the Academy with the Church, the heretic with the Christian? . . . We have no need of curiosity after Jesus Christ, or of research after the Gospel. When we believe, we desire to believe nothing more. For we believe this first, that there is nothing else that we should believe" (my translation).

Cf. Augustine, *Enchiridion* 3.9: "Nor need we be afraid lest the Christian should be rather ignorant of the force and number of the elements, the motion, order, and eclipses of the heavenly bodies, the form of the heavens, the kinds and natures of animals, shrubs and stones. . . . It is enough for the Christian to believe that the cause of all created things . . . is none other than the goodness of the creator." Therefore, ignorance of nature is goodness and innocence, and knowledge is evil. From the murder of the mathematician Hypatia of Alexandria in 412 to the burning of Giordano Bruno in 1600 and the rejection of reason by modern development economists, Dark-Age antirationalism and values towards man have played a powerful role in coloring our attitudes toward cities.

12. See two works by E. Pagels, "The Politics of Paradise," *New York Review of Books* (12 May 1988): 28–37; and *Adam, Eve, and the Serpent* (New York, 1988), 98–154.

13. For a recent, provocative analysis of the role of Rousseau in Western thought, see A. Bloom, *The Closing of the American Mind* (New York, 1987), 157–72.

14. On Weber's intellectual development, see A. Mitzman, *The Iron Cage: An Historical Interpretation of Max Weber* (New York, 1970), esp. 76–147.

15. K. Marx and F. Engels: *L'idéologie allemande,* vol. 1 (Paris, 1977), 45–46; and *Le Capital,* vol. 1 (Paris, 1976), 256. A. H. M. Jones: *The Greek City from Alexander to Justinian* (Oxford, 1940), 287–97; and *Cities of the Eastern Roman Provinces* (Oxford, 1971), 293–94. Cf. G. de Ste. Croix, *The Class Struggle in the Ancient Greek World* (Ithaca, N.Y., 1981), 18–19.

M. Rostovtzeff, *The Social and Economic History of the Roman Empire,* vol. 1 (Oxford, 1957), 379–80, 531–41. In the earlier part of his work (130–91), he gave more attention to the roles of commerce and industry in the economies of cities. He believed that by the late Empire cities had become parasitical, a view with which I am in broad agreement.

16. Finley, *AE,* 95–149; Finley, *AC.*

17. K. Hopkins, in "Development of Towns" (1978) and in the introduction to *Trade in the Ancient Economy,* ed. P. Garnsey, et al. (Berkeley, 1983), xii–xiii. See also, Garnsey and Saller, *The Roman Empire,* 43–63.

18. Karl Polanyi was instrumental in formulating the comparison between modern primitive and archaic economies such as the Greco-Roman. See M. I. Finley, *Economy and Society in Ancient Greece,* ed. B. D. Shaw and R. P. Saller (New York, 1983), xix. Many writing in ancient economic history make comparisons with the economies of developing countries; one can clearly see the influence of the ideas of development economics in their writing on the subject. I have previously suggested that there are pitfalls in making explicit or implicit comparisons between modern primitives and Greeks and Romans in demography. See D. Engels, "The Use of Historical Demography in Ancient History," *Classical Quarterly* 34 (1984): 386–93.

19. P. T. Bauer, *Dissent on Development* (Cambridge, Mass., 1972), 147–82; P. T. Bauer, *Equality, the Third World, and Economic Delusion* (Cambridge, Mass., 1981), 1–85; Khieu Samphan, *Cambodia's Economy and Industrial Development* (Ph.D. diss., University of Paris, 1959), trans. Laura Summers, Cornell University South East Asia Program, Department of Asian Studies (March 1979), 30–31. More will be said about this remarkable document below. See also, K. Polanyi, *The Great Transformation* (New York, 1944), 163–64.

20. Samphan, *Cambodia's Economy,* 33–37; C. Etcheson, *The Rise and Demise*

*of Democratic Kampuchea* (Boulder, Colo., 1984), 28; A. Coulson, *Tanzania* (Oxford, 1982), 103; A. Mascarenhas, "After Villagization—What?" p. 146 in *Towards Socialism in Tanzania* by B. U. Mwansasu and C. Pratt (Toronto, 1981); J. N. Karioki, *Tanzania's Human Revolution* (University Park, Penn., 1979), 32–55; Bauer, *Equality*, 193–203; Polanyi, *The Great Transformation*, 157–58, 290–93.

21. Coulson, *Tanzania*, 176; Samphan, *Cambodia's Economy*, 52–55, 63, 100.

22. This is the way many living in developing countries perceived their cities, and therefore the perception must have a basis in fact; see Samphan, *Cambodia's Economy*, 32–55; Coulson, *Tanzania*, 176. The horrific rent rates in C. Clark and M. Haswell, *The Economics of Subsistence Agriculture* (London, 1970), 105–7, tell their own story. Is it valid to extend the observations about a city such as Phnom Penh to classical Athens?

23. W. E. Peterson, "The Social Roots of Hunger and Overpopulation," *Public Interest* 68 (1982): 37–52; B. Yamey and P. T. Bauer, "Foreign Aid: What is at Stake?" *Public Interest* 68 (1982): 53–69; J. S. Henry, "Where the Money Went," *The New Republic* (14 April 1986): 20–23; P. T. Bauer, *Equality*. Henry notes that so much U.S. aid money is stolen by Third World military bureaucrats, that the United States is actually a net *debtor* to many of those countries. This is because the stolen money is deposited in U.S. banks, or is used to purchase stocks and bonds on which interest and dividends must be paid.

24. Henry, "Where the Money Went," 21–22.

25. Peterson, "The Social Roots of Hunger," 47–52.

26. These views seem naive and even humorous today, but their seriousness was all too deadly. Polanyi quotes approvingly from several anthropologists of the 1930s in *The Great Transformation*, 291–93; for example, Thrunwald arguing against the peace Europeans brought to the African continent: "peace over a vast area shatters clan life, patriarchal authority, the military training of youth. . . . War must have given a keenness to native life which is sadly lacking in these times of peace." For a critique of Margaret Mead in Samoa, see D. Freeman, *Margaret Mead and Samoa: The Making and Unmaking of an Anthropological Myth* (Cambridge, Mass., 1983). In reading Polanyi and Margaret Mead, one is reminded of the story of the Garden of Eden and the Fall of Man. See, now, the important work of A. Kuper, *The Invention of Primitive Society: Transformations of an Illusion* (New York, 1989). Marx himself spoke of the idiocy of rural life.

27. For an excellent view of the use of primitive economies as models for the modern world, see R. Heilbroner, *An Inquiry into the Human Prospect* (New York, 1974), 127–44. All of these trends were part of a much larger cultural movement of the sixties and seventies that stressed the "value" of the primitive and the evils of civilization. Its impact can be seen in such diverse aspects as the Cultural Revolution in China, the Sendero Luminoso in Peru, the Hippie movement, the American Indian movement, the growth of ethnic chauvanism of all types, and even some aspects of the women's movement. In the field of classical history, the influences can be seen in the history of science, literature on the status of women, and bizarre notions about the Fall of Rome. Here, Germanic racial theory combines with primitivism to give us a view somewhat at odds with Gibbon.

28. P. T. Bauer, *Dissent;* Bauer, *Equality.* Tanzania has recently stopped destroying its own people by compelling them to be primitive: see J. Davidson, *Wall Street Journal* (27 January 1988): 1, 4. Vietnam, which now controls Kampuchea, has recently initiated freemarket reforms, as has mainland China.

29. See n. 19.

30. Almost as important as the work itself is the translator's introduction. She constantly refers to Samphan as a "progressive" with a "radical commitment to national democracy." She is incredulous that the Cambodian government during the late sixties and early seventies tried to suppress him and the Khmer Rouge movement because it thought they were a threat to the Cambodian people; this in March of 1979, when reports of the genocide were widespread. An even more astonishing work is *The New Face of Kampuchea* (Chicago, 1979), by R. Brown and D. Kline, who were *actually present in Cambodia* in 1978 at the height of the slaughter. Yet the book contains little besides fulsome praise for the Khmer Rouge, and photographs of smiling peasants. "When reason sleeps the demons dance"—Francisco Goya.

31. Samphan, *Cambodia's Economy,* 33–55, 63, 100; Etcheson, *The Rise and Demise of Democratic Kampuchea,* 27–30, 212.

32. Etcheson, 148–49.

33. Nyerere's regime was notorious for having the lowest per capita food consumption and the highest per capita foreign aid assistance.

34. Finley, *AE,* 95–149; Garnsey and Saller, *The Roman Empire,* 43–63; P. Cartledge, "'Trade and Politics' Revisited: Archaic Greece," p. 1 in Garnsey, et al., *Trade in the Ancient Economy.*

35. H. W. Pearson in the editor's introduction to Karl Polanyi, *The Livelihood of Man* (New York, 1977), xviii. This is a work never cited in my field. Perhaps at the end of his life Polanyi began to understand the consequences of the ideas that had motivated his work.

36. Ibid., xxix.

37. Cartledge, "'Trade and Politics' Revisited," 5.

38. Of course, this is not the first time that academic myths have had a disastrous impact. Germanic racial theories and the subsequent genocidal policies can be traced back to various errors made by academics, many of them acting in good faith and unaware of the consequences. At one time, even in the field of ancient history, cultural, linguistic, material, and technological changes were sometimes associated with the introduction of "new" (usually Aryan) blood by a conquering race. Suitable skulls were produced from excavations, and their measurements "proved" the theory. Cultural decline (e.g., of the Roman Empire) was attributed to "race mixture." Ideas have consequences; this is a fact that cannot be changed.

I am grateful to Ernst Badian for reminding me of this earlier myth and its impact on the field of ancient history. Just as the victims of the earlier myth were initially ignored, so too are the Cambodians today. One Cambodian refugee poignantly expressed the problem this way: "How many of those who say they are unreservedly in support of the Khmer revolution would consent to endure one hundredth of the present sufferings of the Cambodian people. Even organizations whose sole aim is the defense of man . . . have never answered the cries of distress from the Khmers or their friends. On Christmas Day, 1975, one of my Khmer friends remarked to me with some bitterness: 'In France there are societies for the protection of animals and factories which manufacture special food for dogs and cats. The Cambodian people must be less than animals then, since nobody can be bothered to defend them'" (F. Ponchaud, *Cambodia: Year Zero* [New York, 1978], 193).

39. Polanyi, *The Livelihood of Man*, 145–46, 273–76. The "consumer city" and "primitivist" views of the ancient economy can scarcely be supported by any ancient evidence. The foregoing analysis of contemporary economic theories (or myths) has attempted to show why these views have such widespread support. It is by no means exhaustive. We need to examine thoroughly the concepts of development economics and its impact on our field and on economic anthropology. Nor am I alone in criticizing current orthodoxy: see the excellent articles by W. E. Thompson "An Athenian Commercial Case," *Revue d'Histoire du Droit* 48 (1980): 137–49, and "The Athenian Entrepreneur," *L'Antiquité Classique* 51 (1982): 53–85. For a criticism of Polanyi's views on the ancient Near Eastern economy, see M. Silver, *Economic Structures of the Ancient Near East* (New York, 1987). Chester Starr, *The Roman Empire, 27 B.C.-A.D. 476* (Oxford, 1982), 101–3, has also expressed reservations about the consumer-city model for the Principate.

40. No one understood this better than John Locke—the conceptual founder of Anglo-Saxon democracies. He spent considerable time and effort in his "Essay Concerning Human Understanding," refuting the view that mankind is evil from conception. The concept of original sin, in religious or secular form, has played a powerful role in the support of despotism throughout history (the concept actually originated in ancient Mesopotamia). In secularized form (e.g., in R. Heilbroner, *An Inquiry into the Human Prospect* [New York, 1974]), it has even supported authoritarian and coercive policies in modern democracies.

### Appendix One

1. The bibliography on central place studies is immense: for general theory, see W. Christaller, *Central Places in Southern Germany* (Englewood Cliffs, N.J., 1966); A. Lösch, *The Economics of Location* (New Haven, 1954); P. Haggett, et al., *Locational Analysis in Human Geography* (New York, 1977), esp. 139–190. For applications of the theory to ancient regions: G. A. Johnson, "A Test of the Utility of Central Place Theory in Archaeology," pp. 769–86 in *Man, Settlement, and Urbanism*, ed. P. Ucko (London, 1972); I. R. Hodder and M. Hassall, "The Non-Random Spacing of Romano-British Walled Towns," *Man* 6 (1971): 391–407; I. R. Hodder, "Locational Models and the Study of Romano-British Settlement" pp. 887–909 in *Models in Archaeology*, ed. D. L. Clarke (London, 1972); R. T. Marchese, "A History of Urban Organization in the Lower Maeander River Valley: Regional Settlement Patterns to the Second Century A.D." (Ph.D. diss., New York University, 1976); J. Marcus, "Territorial Organization of the Lowland Classic Maya," *Science* (1973): 911–15. For some important modern applications, see G. W. Skinner, "Marketing and Social Structure in Rural China," *Journal of Asian Studies* 24 (1964–65): 3–43, 195–228, 363–399; and S. Plattner, "Rural Market Networks," *Scientific American* 245 (May, 1975): 66–79.

2. The Heraeum seems to have been occupied only during festivals and did not constitute a town (Wiseman, *LAC*). The sanctuary at Nemea seems to have fallen on hard times during the Empire; Pausanias (2.15.2) notes that the temple of Zeus was ruined and deserted in his day. The sanctuary of Isthmia was large and flourishing during the Roman era, as Aristeides makes clear; but what sort of occupation was there when the festival was not being celebrated?

3. Crommyon: Wiseman, *LAC*, 19; Cenchreae: R. Scranton, et al., *Kenchreai* 3; Wiseman, *LAC*, 52; Tenea: Wiseman, *LAC*, 92; Cleonae: M. Sakellariou and N. Faraklas, *Corinthia-Cleonaea* (Athens, 1971), 158; Pausanias 2.15.1; Strabo 8.6.19; Ayios Charalambos: "The largest ancient town in the northwestern Corithia" (Wiseman, *LAC*, 100); and Asprokambos: "Clearly the ancient town of Asprokambos was a settlement of considerable size and importance" (Wiseman, *LAC*, 36).

4. Hodder, "Locational Models," 892; F. Braudel, *The Mediterranean and the Mediterranean World in the Age of Philip II* (New York, 1976), 1:25–53. For the methodologies of locational analysis, see P. Haggett, et al., *Locational Analysis in Human Geography* (New York, 1977), 414–46.

5. For an attempt to use Thiessen polygons to delimit the market regions of city-states in the Maeander Valley of Anatolia, see Marchese ("Urban Organization in the Lower Maeander Valley"), who has also used quadrant counts and nearest neighbor analyses for that region.

6. Cf. Hodder, "Locational Models," 892, 897; Hodder and Hassall, "Non-Random Spacing," 400. Part of the problem is that the method was originally developed for inland plains and not for mountainous regions or coastal areas. It is hoped that newer methodologies will reduce these problems.

7. Pausanias 2.25.9.

8. Pausanias 2.34.1.

9. R. A. Tomlinson, *Argos and the Argolid* (Ithaca, N.Y., 1972), 39; Pausanias 2.25.4–6.

10. Pausanias 1.36.3: "not even the emperor Hadrian could make the Megarians thrive; they were his only failure in Greece." For the best account of Megarian history during the classical era, see R. P. Legon, *Megara: The Political History of a Greek City-State to 336 B.C.* (Ithaca, N.Y., 1981).

11. Sakellariou and Faraklas, *Corinthia-Cleonaea*, 123.

## Appendix Two

1. For a previous attempt to measure a town's population from its water supply, see P. Grimal, *MEFR* 54 (1937): 117ff. Robert Bull has informed me that he may also attempt to estimate the population of Caesarea by using its water supply.

2. H. S. Robinson, "Excavations at Corinth," *Hesperia* 31 (1962): 96; chap. 3, n. 53.

3. The flow rates of some ancient fountains such as Glauke cannot be measured because their sources have either dried up or burst forth in other locations.

4. For the capacities of the reservoirs of the Asklepieion, Glauke, and Peirene, see C. Roebuck, *Corinth* 14, 106.

5. Frontinus, *De Aquaeductibus Urbis Romae* 78, shows that slightly more than 3 percent of Rome's water supply went for ornamental fountains, and slightly more than 16 percent went to public structures. However, because of the difficulties in measuring the flow rates of water, Frontinus' figures are only approximations; see K. D. White, *Greek and Roman Technology* (Ithaca, N.Y., 1984), 167.

6. M. Evenari, et al., *The Negev: The Challenge of a Desert* (Cambridge, 1971), 148–51.

7. Steam-driven pumps were first installed for the Paris water-supply system in 1778 (R. Furon, *The Problem of Water* [New York, 1967], 96), and for Philadelphia in 1801 by the great American architect Benjamin Latrobe (W. H. Pierson, Jr., *American Buildings and Their Architects* [New York, 1976], 357). Modern plumbing devices began to be used in the 1820s (T. Hamlin, *Greek Revival Architecture in America* [New York, 1944], 112).

8. Furon, *The Problem of Water*, 96–97; R. J. Forbes, *Studies in Ancient Technology*, vol. 1 (Leiden, 1964), 171.

9. If Corinth's total water supply was 315,360 cubic meters per year (twice the flow rate of Peirene); and 80 percent of it (252,288 cubic meters per year) went for domestic and industrial consumption, as was the case in Rome; then a per-capita rate of consumption of 1.5 cubic meters per year could support 168,192 people, and a yearly consumption rate of 4.5 cubic meters could support 56,064.

10. J. Bintliff, *Natural Environment and Human Settlement in Prehistoric Greece*, British Archaeological Reports, Suppl. ser. 28, vol. 1 (1977), 51–74.

## Appendix Three

1. S. Dyson, "New Methods and Models in the Study of Roman Town-Country Systems," *Ancient World* 2 (1982): 91–95; R. A. Raper, "The Analysis of the Urban Structure of Pompeii: A Sociological Examination of Land Use," pp. 189–221 in *Spatial Archaeology*, ed. D. L. Clarke (London, 1977).

2. L. F. Schnore, "The City as a Social Organism," pp. 32–39 in *Internal Structure of the City*, ed. L. S. Bourne (New York, 1971). This is an important and influential article. Unfortunately, the influence has had a negative impact on modern cities. Schnore goes too far in comparing cities to animals (communication systems are compared to nervous systems, transportation systems to circulatory systems, and so on). Where are the human beings in his analogy? They are much like cells and, "as in the organism, cells may come and go and the organism itself may survive" (p. 34). Migration and demographic change become, in this analogy, "cellular turnover." Do cells create the organisms in which they reside?

3. I hope to publish an article on the urban geography of ancient Rome in the future.

4. Chap. 2, n. 17.

5. Chap. 4, n. 63.

6. Chap. 4, n. 62.

7. For Rome: J. Lugli, *Fontes ad Topographiam Veteris Urbis Romae Pertinentes*, vol. 8 (Rome, 1962), 125–212. For Athens in both the Greek and Roman eras: H. A. Thompson and R. E. Wycherly, *The Athenian Agora*, vol. 14 (Princeton, 1972), 174–85. Cf. Thucydides 3.72 for Corcyra.

8. G. Sjoberg, *The Preindustrial City* (New York, 1965), 97–103. A much-maligned book, but what else is there?

9. J. Carcopino, *Daily Life in Ancient Rome* (New York, 1940), 46ff.

10. M. Gelzer, *The Roman Nobility* (Oxford, 1969), 54f., 104f.; J. P. V. D. Balsdon, *Life and Leisure in Ancient Rome* (London, 1969), 21–24; Carcopino, *Daily Life*, 171–73. The aristocracy of Roman Corinth was Italian, and would share the same Italian values and customs.

11. This pattern may also reflect (as in the city of Rome) land prices and rent structure; usually, the highest rents are found in the central area and lower rents in outlying regions.

12. Sjoberg, *The Preindustrial City*, 101.

13. In the city of Rome, jewelers and goldsmiths were located in the Sacra Via, which passes the Palatine and Veleia, where their services would be easily accessible to the urban elite who lived in those areas (S. B. Platner and T. Ashby, *A Topographical Dictionary of Ancient Rome* [Oxford, 1929], s.v. Sacra Via).

14. Corinth: Alciphron 3.24; Rome: Martial 7.61.

15. Mycenaean pottery has been found on the site of the sanctuary of Demeter and Kore, and this may indicate some survival of the cult from that era. In the city of Rome, as in other large cities, shrines of some divinities were located in neighborhoods where they were particularly important. For example, many Syrians, Jews, and Christians lived in the Trans-Tiber region of Rome, the location of the city's synagogues, temples of Syrian deities, and many early Christian cemeteries and churches. It may be also that the sanctuaries of Isis and Serapis, and Cybele (Mother of the Gods), located along the northern slope of Acrocorinth, were in an area of Corinth inhabited by many Easterners.

## Appendix Five

1. The poverty of research concerning rents has been noted by Hopkins in "Taxes and Trade in the Roman Empire," *Journal of Roman Studies* 70 (1980): 104 n. 14. So little has been done that even G. E. M. de Ste. Croix, in an otherwise excellent book, can claim that for share cropping "half and half was common, but the landlord's share . . . might be as much as two-thirds and was hardly ever less than one-third" (*The Class Struggle in the Ancient Greek World* [Ithaca, N.Y., 1981], 216). This statement is made, uncharacteristically, with no supporting evidence.

2. For the Delian rents, see J. A. O. Larsen, "Roman Greece," in *An Economic Survey of Ancient Rome*, vol. 4, ed. T. Frank (Baltimore, 1938), 402–7; based on *IG* 11.2, nos. 135, 144, 287. A great deal has been written about Attic leases, most recently by M. H. Jameson, "The Leasing of Land in Rhamnous," *Hesperia* Suppl. 19 (1982): 66–74; and M. B. Walbank, "Leases of Sacred Properties in Attica, Part 4," *Hesperia* 52 (1983): 207–31.

3. Aristotle, *Ath. Pol.* 2.2; Plutarch, *Solon* 13. Plutarch specifically states that the *hectemoroi* paid one-sixth.

4. Compare the rent rates in C. Clark and M. Haswell, *The Economics of Subsistence Agriculture* (London, 1970), 105–7. The comparative evidence shows that rent rates seldom reach 50 percent of gross production. T. W. Gallant has attempted

to show that the *hectemoroi received* one-sixth from lands they cultivated for the rich. The *hectemoroi* owned other lands from which they derived the bulk of their subsistence ("Agricultural Systems, Land Tenure and the Reforms of Solon," *Annual of the British School at Athens* 77 [1982]: 111–24). The problem here is that Aristotle clearly states (*Ath. Pol.* 2.2) that all the land of Attica was owned by the rich. This would leave little room for peasants to own their own land. He further states that the *hectemoroi* and *pelatai* were enslaved to the rich, not a condition suitable for peasant proprietors. Nor am I convinced by arguments concerning population growth based on counting the number of village sites. In Arkansas, there were more rural villages fifty years ago than now, yet the state's population has grown. Numbers of settlements mean little unless we also know their size. I do agree, however, that Athens' population grew during the sixth century B.C., partially through natural increase, and partially through emmigration especially to the *asty*.

5. For the Egyptian peasant's rent payment during the Ptolemaic era, see C. Préaux, *L'Economie royal des Lagides* (Brussels, 1939), 133; A. H. M. Jones, *The Roman Economy*, ed. P. A. Brunt (Oxford, 1974), 179, 184; *Papyrus Cologne* 54. His rent payment included the taxes his landlord would have to pay to the state.

6. D. Crawford, *Kerkeosiris* (Cambridge, 1971), 129–30.

7. W. G. Forrest, *The Emergence of Greek Democracy* (New York, 1975), 168–69.

8. The situation in France before and after the Revolution is of interest. Here, rents had risen to 39 percent on average by 1788. After the Revolution and Napoleonic Wars, when ownership of land was more widespread, rent rates declined to an average of 26 percent by 1845 and to 18 percent in 1885; even though France's population had increased by 70 percent during that period (Clark and Haswell, *Subsistence Agriculture*, 107).

9. *Areopagiticus* 15–36.

10. A. Jardé, *Les céréales dans l'antiquité grecque* (Paris, 1925), 96 n. 2, 116 n. 2. It would seem possible to estimate rents from the rates of return in M. B. Walbank, "Leases." The annual rates of return were frequently 10 percent to 12.5 percent of the full value of the property. Let us take, for example, one acre, worth 200 drachmas, at 50 drachmas per plethron (A. Burford-Cooper, "The Family Farm in Greece," *Classical Journal* 73 (1977–78): 169). If the gross average yield is twenty bushels of grain per acre, and grain sells for 3.3 drachmas per bushel (5 drachmas per *medimnos*), this will give a gross yield of 66 drachmas a year per acre. If the rent was 10 percent of the value of the property, the rent would be 20 drachmas per year, and would give a rent rate, expressed in terms of gross yield, of 33 percent. However, there are too many unknowns about the lands in question for them to yield meaningful rent rates. We do not know the productivity of the lands, or the types of crops they produced. Many rental properties also included a dwelling, and this would be a substantial rental cost in itself; see M. B. Walbank, "Leases," 208, no. 28; 218, no. 78. Cf. Larsen, "Roman Greece," 403.

There are similar problems with the Delian rents. Here, the value of the properties is unknown, but the properties themselves are described, often in great detail; they usually include a house and other buildings. Unfortunately, the details do not appear adequate enough at present to provide good rent rates.

11. Jameson, "The Leasing of Land in Rhamnous," 74 n. 35.
12. Ibid., 73.
13. M. B. Walbank, "Leases," 225.
14. Jameson, "The Leasing of Land in Rhamnous," 73.
15. Burford-Cooper, "The Family Farm in Greece," 171.
16. Appian, *Bellum Civile* 1.1.7.
17. *CIL* 8, 25902. Other related documents are from the same volume: nos. 25943, 26416, and 10570. See R. M. Haywood, "Roman Africa," in *An Economic Survey of Ancient Rome*, vol. 4, ed. T. Frank (1938), 102.
18. P. Garnsey, *Famine and Food Supply in the Graeco-Roman World* (Cambridge, 1988), 249; P. A. Brunt in Jones, *The Roman Economy*, 184.
19. Jones, *The Decline of the Ancient World* (New York, 1978), 156.
20. Jones, *The Roman Economy*, 83; A. H. M. Jones, *The Later Roman Empire*, 2 (Oxford, 1964), 2:821; from *Papyrus Italicus* 2. For labor rents, see *CIL*, 8, 25902; *P. Ital.* 3, for the church lands in Ravenna under Justinian.
21. That a 6 percent return was normal was stated by Pliny, *Epistulae* 7.18; Columella, *De Re Rustica* 3.3.9–10, and also in inscriptions concerning loans made to Italian farmers which bore an interest rate of 5 percent to 6 percent (*ILS* 3546, 3775, 6271, 6328a, 6663, 6664, 8370). For a valiant attempt to show that the return on investments from a vineyard may have been 7 percent to 10 percent, see R. P. Duncan-Jones, *The Economy of the Roman Empire* (Cambridge, 1974), 33–59.

Attempts have been made to find the rate of return from Phaenippus' estate in Demosthenes 42, but it seems impossible. If de Ste. Croix has calculated the dimensions of the estate accurately at 500 plethra (cited in Burford-Cooper, "The Family Farm in Greece," 170), then the return would have been about 365 drachmas per acre, just for the return on wine and barley, an impossibly high figure. Either Phaenippus' estate was larger than is supposed, or Demosthenes has exaggerated its size, so his client can escape the performance of a liturgy through an *antidosis*.

22. Larsen, "Roman Greece," 406; Finley, *AE*, 114–15; Jameson, "The Leasing of Land in Rhamnous," 73.
23. In general, see Jones, *The Roman Economy*, 82–89, 151–85 (with addenda by P. A. Brunt); Jones, *The Later Roman Empire*, 2:819–23; L. Neesen, *Untersuchungen zu den Direkten Staatsabgaben der römischen Kaiserzeit* (Bonn, 1980); P. A. Brunt, "The Revenues of Rome," *Journal of Roman Studies* 71 (1981): 161–72.
24. C. B. Welles, *Royal Correspondence in the Hellenistic Age* (New Haven, 1934), nos. 41, 47, 51; Appian, *Bellum Civile* 5.4. In general, see Jones, *The Roman Economy*, 160–79; M. Rostovtzeff, *The Social and Economic History of the Hellenistic World* (1941), 1:354, 465–66, 562; 2:813–814.
25. Sicily: Cicero, *In Verrem* 3.5.11–6.15; Egypt: Préaux, *L'Economie royale*, 117–37; Rostovtzeff, *Social and Economic History of the Hellenistic World*, 1:354.
26. Judaea: Rostovtzeff, *Social and Economic History of the Hellenistic World*, 2:1000; Syria: Appian, *Syr.* 50.
27. Jones, *The Roman Economy*, 178–79. This is probably not equivalent to a 20 percent income tax, as Brunt (p. 184) and Garnsey (*Famine and Food Supply*, 245) suggest. They believe that the 1 percent tax on the value of property should be seen

as a proportion of the return on investment from agriculture, which was about 5 percent. However, an income tax is a tax on gross income, not a tax levied solely on profits; that is, what remains after all expenses have been deducted. If an income tax only taxed us on what we had remaining after we deducted our own maintenance, we would all be very well off indeed. A 1 percent annual tax on the value of property would be a tenth of the rents levied annually in Attica.

28. Suetonius, *Vesp.* 16.

29. *Orat.* 38.26.

30. Lactantius, *De Mortibus Persecutorum* 7.3; Aurelius Victor, *De Caesaribus* 39.32; Themistius, *Orat.* 8.113c; Valentinian, *Novellae* 15, pr. Procopius, *Historia Arcana* 23.20. All these sources cannot be wrong, and the admission by the Emperor Valentinian is especially damning. In general, see Jones, *The Later Roman Empire*, 2:819–23; Jones, *The Roman Economy*, 84–89.

31. See de Ste. Croix, *Class Struggle*, 207, 474–503.

32. Jones, *The Later Roman Empire*, 2:820, from *P. Cairo* 67057.

33. Jones, *The Later Roman Empire*, 2:821; Jones, *The Roman Economy*, 83.

34. 1 Maccabees 10:29. The taxes were repealed in 142 B.C. by the Seleucids, but apparently continued under the Maccabees.

35. Rostovtzeff, *Social and Economic History of the Hellenistic World*, 2:1000.

# Bibliography

Translations of the major literary sources concerning Roman Corinth—the New Testament, Pausanias, Strabo, Apuleius, and Pliny the Elder—are readily available. Only those works from which I have quoted are included below.

Abbot, F. F., and A. C. Johnson. 1926. *Municipal Administration in the Roman Empire*. Princeton.

Abrams, P., and E. A. Wrigley, eds. 1978. *Towns in Societies*. Cambridge.

Adams, R. M. 1981. *The Heartland of Cities: Surveys of Ancient Settlement and Land Use on the Central Flood Plain of the Euphrates*. Chicago.

———. 1965. *The Land Behind Baghdad*. Chicago.

Adkins, A. W. H. 1960. *Merit and Responsibility*. Oxford.

*Anthologia Graeca*, trans. W. R. Paton. New York, 1919.

*Apuleius, The Golden Ass*, trans. J. Lindsay. Bloomington, Ind., 1971.

*Aristotle, The Politics*, trans. T. A. Sinclair. New York, 1979.

Alonso, W. 1971. "A Theory of the Urban Land Market." Pp. 154–59 in *Internal Structure of the City*, ed. L. S. Bourne. New York.

Badian, E. 1958. *Foreign Clientelae*. Oxford.

Bagdikian, A. 1953. "The Civic Officials of Roman Corinth." M. A. thesis, University of Vermont.

Balsdon, J. P. V. D. 1969. *Life and Leisure in Ancient Rome*. London.

Barrett, C. K. 1968. *A Commentary on the First Epistle to the Corinthians*. New York.

Bauer, P. T. 1981. *Equality, The Third World, and Economic Delusion*. Cambridge, Mass.

———. 1972. *Dissent on Development*. Cambridge, Mass.

Beaton, A. E., and P. Clement. 1976. "The Date of the Destruction of the Sanctuary of Poseidon on the Isthmus of Corinth." *Hesperia* 45:267–79.

Bell, C. 1928. *The People of Tibet*. Oxford.

Beloch, J. 1886. *Die Bevölkerung der griechisch-römischen Welt* Leipzig.

Benevolo, L. 1980. *the History of the City*. Cambridge, Mass.

Benjamin, B. 1964. "The Urban Background to Public Health Changes in England and Wales, 1900–1950." *Population Studies* 17:225–48.

Biers, W. R. 1978. "Water from Stymphalos." *Hesperia* 47:171–84.

Biers, W. R., and D. J. Geagan. 1970. "A New List of Victors in the Caesarea at Isthmia." *Hesperia* 39:79–93.

Bintliff, J. 1977. *Natural Environment and Human Settlement in Prehistoric Greece*. British Archaeological Reports, Suppl. ser. 28, vol. 1. Oxford.

Bloom, A. 1987. *The Closing of the American Mind*. New York.

Boak, A. E. R. 1955. *Manpower Shortage and the Fall of the Roman Empire in the West*. New York.

Bolchazy, L. J. 1977. *Hospitality in Early Rome: Livy's Concept of its Humanizing Force*. Chicago.

Bookidis, N., and J. E. Fisher. 1972. "The Sanctuary of Demeter and Kore on Acrocorinth, Preliminary Report IV." *Hesperia* 41:283–331.

Bookidis, N. and R. S. Stroud. 1987. *Demeter and Persephone in Ancient Corinth*. *Corinth Notes* 2. Princeton, N.J.

Boon, G. C. 1974. "Counterfeiting in Roman Britain." *Scientific American* 246:121–30.

Borza, E. N. 1973. "Alexander's Communications." *Ancient Macedonia* 2:295–303.

Bourne, L. S., ed. 1971. *Internal Structure of the City*. New York.

Bowersock, G. W. 1969. *Greek Sophists in the Roman Empire*. Oxford.

Boyd, R. 1972. "Urbanism, Morbidity, and Mortality." Pp. 345–52 in *Man, Settlement, and Urbanism*, ed. P. Ucko. London.

Bradford, J. 1956. "Fieldwork on Aerial Discoveries in Attica and Rhodes," *Antiquaries Journal* 36:57–69, 172–80.

Braudel, F. 1976. *The Mediterranean and the Mediterranean World in the Age of Philip II*. 2 vols. New York.

Brodsky, H. 1984. "Anti-Urbanism in the Bible: A Critique." *Urbanism Past and Present* 9:36–41.

Broneer, O. 1962. "The Apostle Paul and the Isthmian Games." *Biblical Archaeology* 25:2–31.

———. 1947. "Investigations at Corinth, 1946–74." *Hesperia* 16.

———. 1941. "Colonia Laus Iulia Corinthiensis." *Hesperia* 10:388–90.

Brothwell, D. 1972. "Community Health as a Factor in Urban Cultural Evolution." Pp. 353–62 in *Man, Settlement, and Urbanism*, ed. P. Ucko. London.

Brown, R., and D. Kline. 1979. *The New Face of Kampuchea*. Chicago.

Bruneau, P. 1977. "Lampes corinthiennes, II." *Bulletin de Correspondance Hellénique* 101:249–95.

———. 1971. "Lampes corinthiennes." *Bulletin de Correspondance Hellénique* 95:437–501.

Brunt, P. A. 1981. "The Revenues of Rome." *Journal of Roman Studies* 71:161–72.

Burford, A. 1973. *Craftsmen in Greek and Roman Society*. Ithaca, N.Y.

———. 1969. *The Greek Temple Builders at Epidauros*. Toronto.

———. 1960. "Heavy Transport in Classical Antiquity." *Economic History Review* 13:1–18.

Burford-Cooper, A. 1977–78. "The Family Farm in Greece." *Classical Journal* 73:162–75.

Burgess, E. W. 1929. "Urban Areas." Pp. 114–23 in *Chicago: An Experiment in Social Science Research*, ed. T. V. Smith and L. D. White. Chicago.

Burns, A. 1974. "Ancient Greek Water Supply and City Planning." *Technology and Culture* 15:389–412.

Caley, E. R. 1941. "The Corroded Bronze of Corinth." *Proceedings of the American Philosophical Society* 84:689–761.

Capps, E. Jr. 1938. "Pergamene Influence at Corinth." *Hesperia* 7:539–56.

Carcopino, J. 1940. *Daily Life in Ancient Rome*. New York.

Carpenter, R. 1960. *Greek Sculpture*. Chicago.

Cartledge, P. 1983. " 'Trade and Politics' Revisited: Archaic Greece." Pp. 1–15 in *Trade in the Ancient Economy*, ed. P. Garnsey, et al. Berkeley.

Casson, L. 1961. *The Ancient Mariners*. New York.

Chevallier, R. 1958. "Pour une interprétation archéologique de la couverture aérienne grecque: Note sur les centuriations romaines de Grece." *Bulletin de Correspondance Hellénique* 82:635–36.

Chisholm, M. 1962. *Rural Settlement and Land Use: An Essay in Location*. London. Rev. ed. 1968.

Christaller, W. 1966. *Central Places in Southern Germany*. Englewood Cliffs, N.J.

Cicero. *On the Commonwealth*, trans. G. H. Sabine and S. B. Smith. Columbus, Ohio, 1929.

——. *De Republica, De Legibus*, trans. C. W. Keyes. New York, 1928.

——. *Tusculan Disputations*, trans. J. E. King. New York, 1927.

Cizek, E. 1972. *L'Epoque de Neron et ses controverses idéologiques*. Leiden.

Clark, C., and M. Haswell. 1970. *The Economics of Subsistence Agriculture*. London.

Clarke, D. L. 1977. *Spatial Archaeology*. London.

——, ed. 1972. *Models in Archaeology*. London.

Coale, A. J., and P. Demeny. 1966. *Regional Model Life Tables and Stable Populations*. Princeton.

Cockburn, T. A. 1971. "Infectious Diseases in Ancient Populations." *Current Anthropology* 12:45–62.

Colin, J. 1965. "Apulee en Thessalie: Fiction ou vérité?" *Latomus* 24:330–45.

Collart, P. 1937. *Philippes, ville de Macedone*. Paris.

Cook, R. M. 1979. "Archaic Greek Trade: Three Conjectures." *Journal of Hellenic Studies* 99:152–55.

Cooke, R. U., and J. H. Johnson. 1969. *Trends in Geography*. Oxford.

Crawford, D. 1971. *Kerkeosiris*. Cambridge.

Crook, J. 1967. *Law and Life of Rome*. Ithaca, N.Y.

Coulson, A. 1982. *Tanzania*. Oxford.

Cummer, W. W. 1971. "A Roman Tomb at Corinthian Cenchreae." *Hesperia* 40:205–32.

Daley, A., and B. Benjamin. 1964. "London as a Case Study." *Population Studies* 17:249–62.

Darrow, F. S. 1906. "The History of Corinth from Mummius to Herodes Atticus." Ph.D. diss., Harvard University.

Darwin, C. 1903. *More Letters of Charles Darwin*, ed. F. Darwin and A. C. Seward. London.

Davis, J. L., and J. F. Cherry. 1981. *Papers in Cycladic Prehistory*. Los Angeles.

Davis, K. 1974. "The Migrations of Human Populations." *Scientific American* 246:93–105.

———, ed. 1973. *Cities: Their Origin, Growth, and Human Impact.* San Francisco.

Day, J. 1942. *An Economic History of Athens under Roman Domination.* New York.

DeGrazia, C. E. 1973. "Excavations of the American School of Classical Studies at Corinth: The Roman Portrait Sculpture." Ph.D. diss., Columbia University.

Dengate, J. 1981. "Coin Hoards from the Gymnasium Area at Corinth." *Hesperia* 50:147–88.

De Roche, C. D. 1983. "Population Estimates from Settlement Areas and Number of Residences." *Journal of Field Archaeology* 10:187–92.

De Ste. Croix, G. E. M. 1981. *The Class Struggle in the Ancient Greek World.* Ithaca, N.Y.

———. 1956. "Greek and Roman Accounting." Pp. 14–74 in *Studies in the History of Accounting,* ed. A. C. Littleton and B. S. Yamey. London.

De Weale, F. J. 1961. *Corinthe et Saint Paul.* Paris.

Dill, S. 1957. *Roman Society from Nero to Marcus Aurelius.* New York.

Donaldson. T. L. 1965. *Architectura Numismatica.* Chicago.

Doxiades, C. A. 1968. *Ekistics: An Introduction to the Science of Human Settlement.* New York.

Duff, A. M. 1928. *Freedmen in the Early Roman Empire.* Oxford.

Duncan-Jones, R. P. 1974. *The Economy of the Roman Empire.* Cambridge.

———. 1965. "An Epigraphic Survey of Costs in Roman Italy." *Papers of the British School at Rome* 33:189–306.

Dyson, S. 1982. "New Methods and Models in the Study of Roman Town-Country Systems." *Ancient World* 2:91–95.

Earl, D. 1976. *The Moral and Political Tradition of Rome.* Ithaca, N.Y.

Ellis, S. P. 1988. "The End of the Roman House." *American Journal of Archaeology* 92:565–76.

Ellison, A., and J. Harriss. 1972. "Settlement and Land Use in the Prehistory and Early History of Southern England, a Study Based on Locational Models." Pp. 911–62 in *Man, Settlement, and Urbanism,* ed. P. Ucko. London.

Elvin, M. 1978. "Chinese Cities since the Sung Dynasty." In *Towns in Societies,* ed. P. Abrams and E. A. Wrigley. Cambridge.

Edwards, K. M. 1937. "Report on the Coins Found in the Excavations at Corinth during the Years 1930–1935." *Hesperia* 6:241–56.

Engels, D. 1984. "The Use of Historical Demography in Ancient History." *Classical Quarterly* 34:386–93.

Etcheson, C. 1984. *The Rise and Demise of Democratic Kampuchea.* Boulder, Colo.

Evans, J. K. 1981. "Wheat Production and its Social Consequences in the Roman World." *Classical Quarterly* 31:428–42.

Evenari, M., et al. 1971. *The Negev: The Challenge of a Desert.* Cambridge.

Finley, M. I. 1983. *Economy and Society of Ancient Greece,* ed. B. D. Shaw and R. P. Saller. New York.

———. 1978. *The World of Odysseus.* New York.

Fisher, J. E. 1984. "Coins: Corinth Excavations, 1977, Forum Southwest." *Hesperia* 53:217–50.

———. 1980. "Coins: Corinth Excavations, 1976, Forum Southwest." *Hesperia* 49:1–29.

Forbes, R. J. 1964. *Studies in Ancient Technology,* vol. 1. Leiden.

Forrest, W. G. 1975. *The Emergence of Greek Democracy.* New York.

Foxhall, L., and H. A. Forbes. 1982. "*Sitometreia*." *Chiron* 12:41–90.

Francis, R. G., ed. 1958. *The Population Ahead.* Minneapolis.

Frank, T. 1938. *An Economic Survey of Ancient Rome,* vol. 4. Baltimore.

Freeman,D. 1983. *Margaret Mead and Samoa: The Making and Unmaking of an Anthropological Myth.* Cambridge, Mass.

French, A. 1964. *The Growth of the Athenian Economy.* New York.

Friedl, E. 1963. *Vasilika: A Village in Modern Greece.* New York.

Friedländer, L. 1968. *Roman Life and Manners Under the Early Empire,* vol. 1, trans. L. A. Magnus. New York.

Fuks, A. 1970. "The Bellum Achaicum and Its Social Aspect." *Journal of Hellenic Studies* 90:78–89.

Furon, R. 1967. *The Problem of Water.* New York.

Gallant, T. W. 1982. "Agricultural Systems, Land Tenure, and the Reforms of Solon." *Annual of the British School at Athens* 77:111–24.

Garnet, K. S. 1975. "Late Roman Corinthian Lamps from the Fountain of the Lamps." *Hesperia* 44:173–206.

Garnsey, P. 1988. *Famine and Food Supply in the Graeco-Roman World.* Cambridge.

Garnsey, P., K. Hopkins, and C. R. Whittaker, eds. 1983. *Trade in the Ancient Economy.* Berkeley.

Garnsey, P., and R. Saller. 1987. *The Roman Empire: Economy, Society and Culture,* Berkeley.

Geagan, D. J. 1979. "Roman Athens: Some Aspects of Its Life and Culture, I: 86 B.C. to A.D. 267." *Aufstieg und Niedergang der römischen Welt* 7(1):371–437.

———. 1968. "Notes on the Agonistic Institutions of Roman Corinth." *Greek, Roman and Byzantine Studies* 9:69–80.

Gelzer, M. 1968. *The Roman Nobility.* Oxford.

Gerster, B. 1884. "L'Isthme de Corinthe: Tentatives de percenant dans l'antiquité." *Bulletin de Correspondance Hellénique* 8:224–32.

Glass, D. V. 1964. "Some Indicators of Differences between Urban and Rural Mortality in England and Wales and Scotland." *Population Studies* 17:263–67.

Goldman, M. 1968. *The Soviet Economy: Myth and Reality.* Englewood Cliffs, N.J.

Goodspeed, E. 1961. *Paul.* New York.

Graindor, P. 1930. *Un Milliadaire antique: Herode Atticus et sa famille.* Cairo.

Grant, M. 1971. *Cities of Vesuvius: Pompeii and Herculanium.* New York.

Grimal, P. 1937. *Mélanges d'Archéologie et d'Histoire d'Ecole Française de Rome* 54:117ff.

Gruen, E. 1984. *The Hellenistic World and the Coming of Rome.* 2 vols. Berkeley.

———. 1976. "The Origins of the Achaean War." *Journal of Hellenic Studies* 96:46–69.

Guthrie, W. K. C. 1955. *The Greeks and Their Gods*. Boston.

Haggett, P., et al. 1977. *Locational Analysis in Human Geography*. New York.

Hamlin, T. 1944. *Greek Revival Architecture in America*. New York.

Hammond, N. G. L., and F. Walbank. 1988. *A History of Macedonia*. Vol. 3: 336–167 B.C. Oxford.

Harris, J. 1941. "Coins Found at Corinth." *Hesperia* 10:143–62.

Harris, W. V. 1980. "Roman Terracotta Lamps: The Organisation of an Industry." *Journal of Roman Studies* 70:126–45.

Harrison, A. R. W. 1968. *The Law of Athens*. Oxford.

Haywood, R. M. 1938. "Roman Africa." Pp. 3–119 in *An Economic Survey of Ancient Rome*, vol. 4, ed. T. Frank. Baltimore.

Head, B. V. 1963. *Catalogue of Greek Coins in the British Museum: Corinth, Colonies of Corinth, etc.* Bologna.

Heilbroner, R. 1974. *An Inquiry into the Human Prospect*. New York.

Henrichs. A. 1987. "Between Country and City: Cultic Dimensions of Dionysos in Athens and Attica." *American Philological Association Abstracts*, 1987 Annual Meeting.

Henry, J. S. 1986. "Where the Money Went." *The New Republic*, April 14, pp. 20–23.

Heyob, S. K. 1975. *The Cult of Isis Among Women in the Graeco-Roman World*. Leiden.

Hodder, I.R. 1972. "Locational Models and the Study of Romano-British Settlement." Pp. 887–909 in *Models in Archaeology*, ed. D. L. Clarke. London.

Hodder, I. R., and M. Hassall. 1971. "The Non-Random Spacing of Romano-British Walled Towns." *Man* 6:391–407.

Hodder, I. R., and R. Reece. 1977. "A Model for the Distribution of Coins in the Western Roman Empire." *Journal of Archaeological Science* 4:1–18.

Hogan, J. 1988. "Cosmic Complex." *Scientific American* 259:20–21.

Hombert, M., and C. Préaux. 1952. "Recherches sur le recensement dans l'Egypte romaine." *Papyrologica Lugduno-Batavia*, vol. 5.

Homer. *The Iliad of Homer*, trans. R. Lattimore. Chicago, 1961.

Hopkins, K. 1983. "Introduction." Pp. ix-xxv in *Trade in the Ancient Economy*, ed. Peter Garnsey, et al. Berkeley.

———. 1980. "Taxes and Trade in the Roman Empire (200 B.C. to A.D. 400)." *Journal of Roman Studies* 70:101–25.

———. 1978a. *Conquerors and Slaves*. Cambridge.

———. 1978b. "Economic Growth and Towns in Classical Antiquity." Pp. 35–77 in *Towns in Societies*, ed. P. Abrams and E. A. Wrigley. Cambridge.

———. 1966. "On the Probable Age Structure of the Roman Population." *Population Studies* 19:245–64.

———. 1965. "The Age of Roman Girls at Marriage." *Population Studies* 18:309–27.

Hoyt, H. 1939. *The Structure and Growth of Residential Neighborhoods in American Cities*. Washington, D.C.

Imhoof-Blumer, F., and P. Gardner. 1964. *Ancient Coins Illustrating Lost Masterpieces of Greek Art: A Numismatic Commentary on Pausanias*. Chicago.

Isard, W. 1956. *Location and Space Economy*. Cambridge, Mass.

Jacobs, J. 1970. *The Economy of Cities*. New York.

Jameson, M. H. 1982. "The Leasing of Land in Rhamnous." *Hesperia Suppl.* 19:66–74.

———. 1977–78. "Agriculture and Slavery in Classical Athens." *Classical Journal* 73:122–41.

Jardé, A. 1925. *Les céréales dans l'antiquité grecque*, Paris.

Johnson, G. A. 1972. "A Test of the Utility of Central Place Theory in Archaeology." Pp. 769–86 in *Man, Settlement, and Urbanism*, ed. P. Ucko. London.

Jones, A. H. M. 1978. *The Decline of the Ancient World*. New York.

———. 1974. *The Roman Economy*, ed. P. A. Brunt. Oxford.

———. 1971. *Cities of the Eastern Roman Provinces*. Oxford.

———. 1964. *The Later Roman Empire*. 2 vols. Oxford.

———. 1940. *The Greek City from Alexander to Justinian*. Oxford.

Karioki, J. N. 1979. *Tanzania's Human Revolution*. University Park, Penn.

Kayser, B., and K. Thompson. 1964. *Economic and Social Atlas of Greece*. Athens.

Kee, H. C., et al. 1965. *Understanding the New Testament*. Englewood Cliffs, N.J.

Keys, A. 1958. "Minimum Subsistence." Pp. 27–39 in *The Population Ahead*, ed. R. G. Francis. Minneapolis.

Kuper, A. 1989. *The Invention of Primitive Society: Transformation of an Illusion*. New York.

Lane Fox, R. 1987. *Pagans and Christians*. New York.

Larsen, J. A. O. 1968. *Greek Federal States: Their Institutions and History*. Oxford.

———. 1938. "Roman Greece." Pp. 259–499 in *An Economic Survey of Ancient Rome*, vol. 4, ed. T. Frank. Baltimore.

Lee, R. B. 1969. "!Kung Bushmen Subsistence: An Input-Output analysis." Pp. 46–79 in *Environment and Cultural Behavior*, ed. A. P. Vayda. New York.

Legon, R. P. 1981. *Megara: The Political History of a Greek City-State to 336 B.C.* Ithaca, N.Y.

Le Quien, M. 1740. *Oriens Christianus*. 2 vols. Paris.

Lewis, N., and M. Reinhold. 1966. *Roman Civilization*. 2 vols. New York.

Lichtheim, M. 1976. *Ancient Egyptian Literature*. 3 vols. Berkeley.

Lisle, R. 1955. "The Cults of Corinth." Ph.D. diss., Johns Hopkins University.

Littleton, A. C., and B. S. Yamey. 1956. *Studies in the History of Accounting*. London.

Lösch, A. 1954. *The Economics of Location*. New Haven.

Lugli, J. 1962. *Fontes ad Topographiam Veteris Urbis Romae Pertinentes*, vol. 8. Rome.

MacDonald, B. R. 1986. "The Diolkos." *Journal of Hellenic Studies* 106:191–95.

MacDonald, D. J. 1974. "Aphrodisias and Currency in the East, A.D. 259–305." *American Journal of Archaeology* 78:279–86.

McDonald, W. A., ed. 1972. *The Minnesota Messenia Expedition*. Minneapolis.

McDonald, W. L. 1965. *Architecture of the Roman Empire*. New Haven.

McKeown, T., and R. G. Record. 1962. "The Reasons for the Decline of Mortality in England and Wales during the Nineteenth Century." *Population Studies* 16:94–122.

MacMullen, R. 1988. *Corruption and the Decline of Rome*. New Haven.

———. 1981. *Paganism in the Roman Empire*. New Haven.

———. 1974a. "Peasants during the Principate." *Aufstieg und Niedergang der römischen Welt* 2(1):253–61.

———. 1974b. *Roman Social Relations*. New Haven.

Marchese, R. T. 1976. "A History of Urban Organization in the Lower Maeander River Valley: Regional Settlement Patterns to the Second Century A.D." Ph.D. diss., New York University.

Marcus, J. 1973. "Territorial Organization of the Lowland Classic Maya." *Science* 180:911–15.

Marx, K., and F. Engels. 1977. *L'Idéologie allemande*, vol. 1. Paris.

———. 1976. *Le Capital*, vol. 1. Paris.

Mascarhenas, A. 1981. "After Villagization—What?" Pp. 145–65 in *Towards Socialism in Tanzania*, ed. B. U. Mwansasu and C. Pratt. Toronto.

Mason, H. J. 1971. "Lucius at Corinth." *Phoenix* 25:160–65.

Mattusch, C. C. 1977. "Corinthian Metalworking in the Forum Area." *Hesperia* 46:380–89.

Meeks, W. 1983. *The First Urban Christians: The Social World of the Apostle Paul*. New Haven.

Meiggs, R. 1960. *Roman Ostia*. Oxford.

Merino. C. G. 1975. *Poblacion y Poblamiento en Hispania romana, el Conventus Cluniensis*. Valladolid.

Mette, H. J., ed. 1949. *Nachtrag zum Supplementum Aeschyleum*. Berlin.

Mickwitz, G. 1937. "Economic Rationalism in Graeco-Roman Agriculture." *English Historical Review* 52:577–89.

Millar, F. 1981. "The World of the *Golden Ass*." *Journal of Roman Studies* 71:63–75.

Mitzman, A. 1970. *The Iron Cage: An Historical Interpretation of Max Weber*. New York.

Mols, R. 1955. *Introduction à la démographie historique des villes d'Europe du XIV au XVIII siècle*, vol. 2. Louvain.

Morrison, P. 1987. "The Ring of Truth." Public Broadcasting Service television program, 24 November 1987.

Moule, C. F. D. 1962. *The Birth of the New Testament*. New York.

Muller, K. 1882. *Geographi Graeci Minores*. Paris.

Murphy-O'Connor, J. 1983. *Saint Paul's Corinth: Texts and Archaeology*. Wilmington, Del.

Mwansasu, B. U., and C. Pratt, eds. 1981. *Towards Socialism in Tanzania*. Toronto.

Neesen, L. 1980. *Untersuchungen zu den Direkten Staatsabgaben der römischen Kaiserzeit*. Bonn.

O'Neill, J. G. 1930. *Ancient Corinth with a Topological Sketch of the Corinthia*. Baltimore.

Packer, J. E. 1967. "Housing and Population in Imperial Ostia and Rome," *Journal of Roman Studies* 57:80–95.

Pagels, E. 1988a. "The Politics of Paradise." *New York Review of Books* (12 May): 28–37.

———. 1988b. *Adam, Eve and the Serpent.* New York.

Pallas, D. I. 1965. "Anaskaphai ereunai en Lechaio." *Praktika,* 137–66.

———. 1961–62. "Anaskaphai Lechaiou." *Archaiologikon Deltion* 17(2):69–78.

Paris, J. 1915. "Contributions à l'étude des ports antiques du monde grec, I: Notes sur Lechaion." *Bulletin de Correspondance Hellénique* 39:5–16.

Park, R. E., and E. W. Burgess. 1925. *The City.* Chicago.

Patterson, C. B. 1978. *Pericles' Citizenship Law.* Chicago.

Pemberton, E. G. 1981. "The Attribution of Corinthian Bronze." *Hesperia* 50:101–11.

Perlzweig, J. 1961. *The Athenian Agora, 7: Lamps of the Roman Period.* Princeton.

Peterson, W. E. 1982. "The Social Roots of Hunger and Overpopulation." *Public Interest* 68:37–52.

Philippson, A. 1959. *Griechische Landschaften.* Bd. 3, t. 1. Berlin.

———. 1892. *Der Peloponnes.* Berlin.

Pierson, W. H., Jr. 1976. *American Buildings and Their Architects.* New York.

Platner, S. B., and T. Ashby. 1929. *A Topographical Dictionary of Ancient Rome.* Oxford.

Plattner, S. 1975. "Rural Market Networks." *Scientific American* 234:66–79.

Plutarch. *Moralia,* vol. 8, trans. P. A. Clement and H. B. Hoffleit. Cambridge, Mass., 1969.

Polanyi, K. 1977. *The Livelihood of Man.* New York.

———. 1944. *The Great Transformation.* New York.

Ponchaud, F. 1978. *Cambodia: Year Zero.* New York.

Préaux, C. 1939. *L'Economie royale des Lagides.* Brussels.

Price, M. J., and B. Trell. 1977. *Coins and Their Cities.* Detroit.

Raper, R. A. 1977. "The Analysis of the Urban Structure of Pompeii: A Sociological Examination of Land Use." Pp. 189–221 in *Spatial Archaeology,* ed. D. L. Clarke. London.

Reece, R. 1973. "Roman Coinage in the Western Empire." *Britannia* 4:227–51.

Renfrew, C. 1984. *Approaches to Social Archaeology.* Cambridge, Mass.

———. 1972. *The Emergence of Civilization: The Cyclades and the Aegean in the Third Millennium B.C.* London.

Rich, N. 1977. *The Age of Nationalism and Reform: 1850–1890.* New York.

Ridgeway, B. S. 1981. "Sculpture from Corinth." *Hesperia* 50:422–48.

Ringel, J. 1975. *Césarée de Palestine.* Paris.

Robert, L. 1940. *Les gladiateurs dans l'Orient grec.* Paris.

Robinson, H. S. 1962. "Excavations at Corinth." *Hesperia* 31 (1962): 96–130.

———. 1959. *the Athenian Agora, 5: The Roman Pottery.* Princeton.

Roebuck, C. 1972. "Some Aspects of Urbanization in Corinth." *Hesperia* 41:96–127.

Rostoker, W., and E. R. Gebhard. 1980. "The Sanctuary of Poseidon at Isthmia: Techniques of Metal Manufacture." *Hesperia* 49:347–63.

Rostovtzeff, M. 1957. *The Social and Economic History of the Roman Empire.* 2 vols. Oxford.

———. 1941. *The Social and Economic History of the Hellenistic World.* 3 vols. Oxford.

Russell, J. P. 1958. "Late Ancient and Medieval Population." *Transactions of the American Philosophical Society* 48, no. 3.

St. John Crèvecoeur, J. H. 1904. *Letters from an American Farmer.* New York.

Sakellariou, M., and N. Faraklas. 1971. *Corinthia-Cleonaea.* Athens.

Salmon, J. 1984. *Wealthy Corinth: A History of the City to 338 B.C.* Oxford.

Samuel, A. E., et al. 1971. *Death and Taxes.* American Studies in Papyrology, vol. 10. Toronto.

Samphan, K. 1979. *Cambodia's Economy and Industrial Development,* trans. L. Summers. Cornell University South East Asia Program, Department of Asian Studies.

Sandler, L. F., ed. 1964. *Essays in Honor of Karl Lehmann.* New York.

Schmithals. W. 1971. *Gnosticism in Corinth.* Nashville.

Schnore, L. F. 1971. "The City as a Social Organism." Pp. 32–39 in *Internal Structure of the City,* L. S. Bourne, ed. New York.

Shear, T. L. 1931. "The Excavation of Roman Chamber Tombs at Corinth in 1931." *American Journal of Archaeology* 35:424–41.

———. 1930. "A Hoard of Coins Found in Corinth in 1930." *American Journal of Archaeology* 25:139–51.

Shoe, L. 1964. "The Roman Ionic Base at Corinth." Pp. 300–304 in *Essays in Honor of Karl Lehmann,* ed. L. F. Sandler. New York.

Siestieri, P. C. 1957. "Greek Elea—Roman Velia." *Archaeology* 10:2–10.

Silver, M. 1987. *Economic Structures of the Ancient Near East.* New York.

Sjoberg, G. 1965. *The Preindustrial City.* New York.

Skinner, G. W. 1964–65. "Marketing and Social Structure in Rural China." *Journal of Asian Studies* 24:3–43, 195–228, 363–99.

Smith, A. 1937. *The Wealth of Nations.* New York.

Smith, T. V., and L. D. White, eds. 1929. *Chicago: An Experiment in Social Science Research.* Chicago.

Spawforth, A. J., and S. Walker. 1986. "the World of the Panhellenion, II: The Dorian Cities." *Journal of Roman Studies* 76:88–105.

———. 1985. "The World of the Panhellenion, I: Athens and Eleusis." *Journal of Roman Studies* 75:78–104.

Sperber, D. 1970. "Costs of Living in Roman Palestine, IV." *Journal of the Economic and Social History of the Orient* 13:1–15.

Spitzer, D. C. 1942. "Roman Relief Bowls from Corinth." *Hesperia* 11:162–92.

Stambaugh, J. 1988. *The Ancient Roman City.* Baltimore.

Starr, C. 1977. *The Economic and Social Growth of Early Greece.* Oxford.

Stevenson, H. 1939. *Roman Provincial Administration.* Oxford.

Stillwell, R., et al. 1976. *The Princeton Encyclopaedia of Classical Sites.* Princeton.

Strabo. *The Geography of Strabo,* trans. H. L. Jones. New York, 1932.

Stroud, R. S. 1968. "The Sanctuary of Demeter and Kore on Acrocorinth, Preliminary Report II, 1964–65." *Hesperia* 37:299–330.

Sullivan, W. 1981. "Testing of Relics Results in Surprises." *The New York Times,* 24 May, 39.

Sutherland, C. H. V. 1974. *Roman Coins.* New York.

Swift, E. H. 1921. "A Group of Imperial Portraits at Corinth." *American Journal of Archaeology* 25:142–363.

Syme, R. 1958. *Colonial Elites: Rome, Spain and the Americas.* Oxford.

Tarn, W. W. 1934. "The War Against the West." *Cambridge Ancient History,* vol. 10, 66–111. Cambridge: Cambridge University Press.

Thomas, C., and R. Griffeth. 1981. *The City-State in Five Cultures.* Santa Barbara.

Thompson, A., and R. E. Wycherly. 1972. *The Athenian Agora, 14: The Agora of Athens.* Princeton.

Thompson, K. 1963. *Farm Fragmentation in Greece.* Athens.

Thompson, M. 1954. *The Athenian Agora, 2: Coins from the Roman through the Venetian Period.* Princeton.

Thompson, W. E. 1982. "The Athenian Entrepreneur." *L'Antiquité classique* 51:53–85.

———. 1980. "An Athenian Commercial Case." *Revue d'Histoire du Droit* 48:137–49.

Thucydides. *The Peloponnesian War,* trans. Rex Warner. Baltimore, 1974.

Tomlinson, R. A. 1972. *Argos and the Argolid.* Ithaca, N.Y.

Treggiari, S. 1969. *Roman Freedmen during the Late Republic.* Oxford.

Ucko, P., ed. 1972. *Man, Settlement, and Urbanism.* London.

Vayda, A. P., ed. 1969. *Environment and Cultural Behavior.* New York.

Veblen, T. 1953. *The Theory of the Leisure Class.* New York.

Verdelis, N. M. 1956. "Der Diolkos am Isthmus von Korinth." *Ath. Mitt.* 71:51–59.

Vidman, L. 1969. *Sylloge inscriptionum religionis Isiacae et Serapiacae.* Berlin.

Vita-Finzi, C. 1969. "Early Man and the Environment." Pp. 102–9 in *Trends in Geography,* ed. R. U. Cooke and J. H. Johnson. Oxford.

Vita-Finzi, C., and E. S. Higgs. 1970. "Prehistoric Economy in the Mount Carmel Area of Palestine: Site Catchment Analysis." *Proceedings of the Prehist. Society* 36:1–37.

Von Freyberg, B. 1973. *Geologie des Isthmus von Korinth.* Erlanger Geologische Abhandlungen 95.

Von Sachsen Max, H. 1918. *Das Christliche Hellas.* Leipzig.

Von Thünen, J. H. 1826. *Der isolierte Staat in Beziehung auf Landwirtschaft und Nationalökonomie.* Hamburg.

Wagstaff, J. M. 1976. *Aspects of Land Use in Melos.* Southampton.

Walbank, F. W. 1969. *The Awful Revolution: The Decline of the Roman Empire in the West.* Toronto.

———. 1957. *A Historical Commentary on Polybius,* vol. 1. Oxford.

———. 1940. *Philip V of Macedon.* Cambridge.

Walbank, M. B. 1983. "Leases of Sacred Properties in Attica, Part 4." *Hesperia* 52:207–31.

Weiss, J. 1959. *Earliest Christianity.* 2 vols. New York.

Weitz, R. 1973. *Urbanization in the Developing Countries.* New York.

Welles, C. B. 1934. *Royal Correspondence in the Hellenistic Age.* New Haven.

West, L. C. 1941. *Gold and Silver Standards in the Roman Empire, Numismatic Notes* 94.

White, K. D. 1984. *Greek and Roman Technology.* Ithaca, N.Y.

———. 1970. *Roman Farming.* Ithaca, N.Y.

Wilken, R. 1984. *The Christians as the Romans Saw Them.* New Haven.

Will, E. 1955. *Korinthiaka: Recherches sur l'histoire et la civilization de Corinthe des origines aux guerres mediques.* Paris.

Williams, C. K., II. 1963. "Excavations at Corinth." *Archaiologikon Deltion* 18:79.

Williams, C. K., II, and J. E. Fisher. 1975. "Corinth, 1974: Forum Southwest." *Hesperia* 44:1–50.

———. 1973. "Corinth, 1972: The Forum Area." *Hesperia* 42:1–44.

———. 1972. "Corinth, 1971: Forum Area." *Hesperia* 41:143–84.

———. 1971. "Corinth, 1970: Forum Area." *Hesperia* 40:1–51.

Williams, C. K., II, et al. 1974. "Excavations at Corinth, 1973." *Hesperia* 43:1–76.

Williams, C. K., II, and H. O. Zervos. 1989. "Corinth 1988: East of the Theater." *Hesperia* 58:2, fig. 2.

———. 1986. "Corinth, 1985: East of the Theater." *Hesperia* 55:129–75.

———. 1985. "Corinth, 1984: East of the Theater." *Hesperia* 54:55–96.

———. 1982. "Corinth, 1981: East of the Theater." *Hesperia* 51:115–63.

Wills, G. 1984. *Cincinnatus: George Washington and the Enlightenment.* Garden City, N.Y.

Wiseman, J. 1972. "The Gymnasium Area at Corinth." *Hesperia* 41:1–42.

Witt, R. E. 1971. *Isis in the Graeco-Roman World.* Ithaca, N.Y.

Wolf, E. R. 1966. *Peasants.* Englewood Cliffs, N.J.

Wright, K. S. 1977. "Early Roman Terra Sigillata and its Local Imitations from the Post-War Excavations at Corinth." Ph.D. diss., Bryn Mawr College.

Wrigley, E. A. 1976. *Population and History.* New York.

Wycherly, R. E. 1957. *The Athenian Agora, 3: Literary and Epigraphical Testimonia.* Princeton.

Yamey, B., and P. T. Bauer. 1982. "Foreign Aid: What is at Stake." *Public Interest* 68:53–69.

Zervos, O. H. 1986. "Coins Excavated at Corinth, 1978–1980." *Hesperia* 55:183–205.

# Index

197 n.26, 217 n.5; on Peirene, 100; on religions, 43, 93, 94, 209 n.2, 215 n.73,
225 nn. 3, 5, 6, 8, 226 nn. 15, 22, 24,
227 n.33, 228 n.37
Peasants, Athenian, 189; collection of taxes
from, 41, 66, 84, 122, 132; in developing world, 140; distances to fields, 28–
29, 121; economic demand of, 49; Egyptian, 233 n.7; exploitation of, 133; Khmer
Rouge theory of, 139; oppression of,
190, 235 n.21; participation of in urban
markets, 115, 125, 128, 234 n.15; proprietors, 30, 131, 244 n.4; rights of, 122,
126, 129; services for, 125; subsistence,
24, 41; surplus of, 1, 2, 24, 39–42, 48,
63, 124, 125, 126, 127, 128, 129, 132,
133, 191, 192, 208 nn. 92, 94, 234 nn.
14, 15. See also Agriculture; Tenants
Pegasus and Bellerophon, 52, 99–100, 104,
106, 209 n.3, 227 nn. 27, 28
Peirene, Fountain of, 10, 13, 36, 37, 77,
98, 99, 179, 180, 216 n.85, 220 nn. 52,
53, 227 n.28, 241 n.4
Perachora, 9
Peter, Saint (Cephas), 110, 111
Phlius (Phlious), 176, 209 n.2
Phnom Penh, 142, 238 n.22
Phoebe, deacon of Cenchreae, 71, 109
Physicians, doctors, 47, 101, 105
Plato, 5, 85; on human geography, 22, 186,
195 nn. 11, 200 n.3, 224 n.85; on the effects of high taxes, 233 n.12
Plutarch, 1, 45, 51, 61, 69, 197 n.26,
199 n.80, 201 n.16, 206 nn. 59, 60,
210 nn. 7, 12, 13, 211 n.42, 214 nn. 65,
66, 216 n.89, 217 n.1, 226 n.21, 243 n.3
Polanyi, Karl, 136, 140–41, 237 n.18,
238 n.26, 239 n.35, 240 n.39
Pompeii, 39, 79, 81, 82, 90, 111, 133,
182, 185, 221 n.58, 222 n.68
Population, birth rates (fertility), 66, 74–
76; death rates (mortality), 49, 66, 74–
76, 77, 220 n.50; decline of, 63, 64; densities of, 81–82, 221 n.58, 223 n.68; European pattern of, 42; growth of, 63, 67,
200 n.9; migration of, 66, 68, 73, 76, 78,
106, 113, 200 n.9, 230 n.57; size of Corinth's, 28, 33, 66, 79–84, 179–81,
204 n.32, 223 n.80; surplus of rural over
urban, 49, 74
Poseidon, 52, 57, 60, 93, 94, 95, 96–97,

99, 102, 106, 119, 225 n.1; Fountain of,
at Corinth, 97; sanctuary at Lechaion,
12, 97; temple at Cenchreae, 97, 105;
temple at Isthmia, 96–98, 214 n.70
Primitivism, theory of, 1, 3, 4, 26, 27,
133, 135–42, 235 n.2, 236 n.7, 238 n.27,
239 n.28, 240 n.39
Priscilla (Prisca) and Aquilla, 32, 71, 107,
109
Public baths. See Baths, public
Public health, 22, 66, 74–78; Black Death,
221 n.56; disease, spread of, 74–76, 78,
88, 220 n.51; food supply, 75–78, 88, 89,
133; latrines and, 77, 220 n.53, 221 n.56;
in Middle Ages, 221 n.56; policies, 128;
public physicians and, 88. See also
Baths; Cats; Rats; Water

Quinctius Flamininus, Titus, 14, 20

Rats, and public health, 74, 88, 221 n.56
Reason, rejection of, 91, 135, 237 n.11; in
Stoicism, 5–6, 113
Rents, 5, 22, 25, 28, 29, 30, 31, 32, 33,
39–41, 48, 49, 66, 84, 88, 121, 124,
126, 128, 129, 133, 187, 205 n.41,
208 nn. 89, 92; increases of 133; labor,
191, 245 n.20; rates of Athenian, 189–
90, 244 n.10; rates of Egyptian, 189,
244 n.5; rates of French, 244 n.8; rates of
general, 30, 32, 40–41, 122, 131, 133,
233 n.9; rates of Greek, 189; rates of,
near city of Rome, 201 n.20; rates of, in
Ravenna under Justinian, 245 n.20; rates
of Roman, 190–91
Rome, city of, 1, 21, 24, 45, 54, 67, 75,
81, 92, 126, 180, 182, 184, 185,
201 nn. 16, 20, 221 n.58; urban geography of, 242 n.7, 243 nn. 11, 13, 14
Rome, state, 5, 6, 14, 15, 16, 17, 67, 141,
196 n.15
Rostovtzeff, Michael, 136, 217 n.98,
234 n.20, 236 nn. 5, 15, 237 n.15,
245 nn. 24, 25, 246 n.35

Sandstone, Corinthian (poros), 10, 12, 62,
80, 196 n.4
Senate, senators (decurio, decurions), Corinthian, 17, 18, 67, 68, 70, 198 nn. 30,
31; Roman, 119, 229 n.49